1

Connected ✻ Mathematics™

UNIT	STRAND
Prime Time *Factors and Multiples*	**Number and Operations**
Data About Us *Statistics*	**Data Analysis and Probability**
Shapes and Designs *Two-Dimensional Geometry*	**Geometry**
Bits and Pieces I *Understanding Rational Numbers*	**Number and Operations**
Covering and Surrounding *Two-Dimensional Measurement*	**Measurement**
How Likely Is It? *Probability*	**Data Analysis and Probability**
Bits and Pieces II *Using Rational Numbers*	**Number and Operations**
Ruins of Montarek *Spatial Visualization*	**Geometry**

Glenda Lappan   James T. Fey
William M. Fitzgerald   Susan N. Friel
Elizabeth Difanis Phillips

Prentice
Hall

Glenview, Illinois
Needham, Massachusetts
Upper Saddle River, New Jersey

Connected Mathematics™ was developed at Michigan State University with the support of National Science Foundation Grant No. MDR 9150217.

This project was supported, in part,
by the
National Science Foundation
Opinions expressed are those of the authors
and not necessarily those of the Foundation

The Michigan State University authors and administration have agreed that all MSU royalties arising from this publication will be devoted to purposes supported by the Department of Mathematics and the MSU Mathematics Education Enrichment Fund.

Prentice
Hall

ISBN 0-13-067734-5
1 2 3 4 5 6 7 8 9 10   05 04 03 02 01

The Connected Mathematics Project Staff

Project Directors

James T. Fey
University of Maryland

William M. Fitzgerald
Michigan State University

Susan N. Friel
University of North Carolina at Chapel Hill

Glenda Lappan
Michigan State University

Elizabeth Difanis Phillips
Michigan State University

Project Manager

Kathy Burgis
Michigan State University

Technical Coordinator

Judith Martus Miller
Michigan State University

Curriculum Development Consultants

David Ben-Chaim
Weizmann Institute

Alex Friedlander
Weizmann Institute

Eleanor Geiger
University of Maryland

Jane Mitchell
University of North Carolina at Chapel Hill

Anthony D. Rickard
Alma College

Collaborating Teachers/Writers

Mary K. Bouck
Portland, Michigan

Jacqueline Stewart
Okemos, Michigan

Graduate Assistants

Scott J. Baldridge
Michigan State University

Angie S. Eshelman
Michigan State University

M. Faaiz Gierdien
Michigan State University

Jane M. Keiser
Indiana University

Angela S. Krebs
Michigan State University

James M. Larson
Michigan State University

Ronald Preston
Indiana University

Tat Ming Sze
Michigan State University

Sarah Theule-Lubienski
Michigan State University

Jeffrey J. Wanko
Michigan State University

Evaluation Team

Mark Hoover
Michigan State University

Diane V. Lambdin
Indiana University

Sandra K. Wilcox
Michigan State University

Judith S. Zawojewski
National-Louis University

Teacher/Assessment Team

Kathy Booth
Waverly, Michigan

Anita Clark
Marshall, Michigan

Theodore Gardella
Bloomfield Hills, Michigan

Yvonne Grant
Portland, Michigan

Linda R. Lobue
Vista, California

Suzanne McGrath
Chula Vista, California

Nancy McIntyre
Troy, Michigan

Linda Walker
Tallahassee, Florida

Software Developer

Richard Burgis
East Lansing, Michigan

Development Center Directors

Nicholas Branca
San Diego State University

Dianne Briars
Pittsburgh Public Schools

Frances R. Curcio
New York University

Perry Lanier
Michigan State University

J. Michael Shaughnessy
Portland State University

Charles Vonder Embse
Central Michigan University

Special thanks to the students and teachers at these pilot schools!

Baker Demonstration School
Evanston, Illinois

Bertha Vos Elementary School
Traverse City, Michigan

Blair Elementary School
Traverse City, Michigan

Bloomfield Hills Middle School
Bloomfield Hills, Michigan

Brownell Elementary School
Flint, Michigan

Catlin Gabel School
Portland, Oregon

Cherry Knoll Elementary School
Traverse City, Michigan

Cobb Middle School
Tallahassee, Florida

Courtade Elementary School
Traverse City, Michigan

Duke School for Children
Durham, North Carolina

DeVeaux Junior High School
Toledo, Ohio

East Junior High School
Traverse City, Michigan

Eastern Elementary School
Traverse City, Michigan

Eastlake Elementary School
Chula Vista, California

Eastwood Elementary School
Sturgis, Michigan

Elizabeth City Middle School
Elizabeth City, North Carolina

Franklinton Elementary School
Franklinton, North Carolina

Frick International Studies Academy
Pittsburgh, Pennsylvania

Gundry Elementary School
Flint, Michigan

Hawkins Elementary School
Toledo, Ohio

Hilltop Middle School
Chula Vista, California

Holmes Middle School
Flint, Michigan

Interlochen Elementary School
Traverse City, Michigan

Los Altos Elementary School
San Diego, California

Louis Armstrong Middle School
East Elmhurst, New York

McTigue Junior High School
Toledo, Ohio

National City Middle School
National City, California

Norris Elementary School
Traverse City, Michigan

Northeast Middle School
Minneapolis, Minnesota

Oak Park Elementary School
Traverse City, Michigan

Old Mission Elementary School
Traverse City, Michigan

Old Orchard Elementary School
Toledo, Ohio

Portland Middle School
Portland, Michigan

Reizenstein Middle School
Pittsburgh, Pennsylvania

Sabin Elementary School
Traverse City, Michigan

Shepherd Middle School
Shepherd, Michigan

Sturgis Middle School
Sturgis, Michigan

Terrell Lane Middle School
Louisburg, North Carolina

Tierra del Sol Middle School
Lakeside, California

Traverse Heights Elementary School
Traverse City, Michigan

University Preparatory Academy
Seattle, Washington

Washington Middle School
Vista, California

Waverly East Intermediate School
Lansing, Michigan

Waverly Middle School
Lansing, Michigan

West Junior High School
Traverse City, Michigan

Willow Hill Elementary School
Traverse City, Michigan

Prime Time
Factors and Multiples

Mathematical Highlights	4
The Unit Project: My Special Number	5
Investigation 1: The Factor Game	6
1.1 Playing the Factor Game	6
1.2 Playing to Win the Factor Game	10
Applications—Connections—Extensions	12
Mathematical Reflections	16
Investigation 2: The Product Game	17
2.1 Playing the Product Game	17
2.2 Making Your Own Product Game	19
2.3 Classifying Numbers	20
Applications—Connections—Extensions	22
Mathematical Reflections	25
Investigation 3: Factor Pairs	26
3.1 Arranging Space	26
3.2 Finding Patterns	27
3.3 Reasoning with Odd and Even Numbers	28
Applications—Connections—Extensions	30
Mathematical Reflections	35
Investigation 4: Common Factors and Multiples	36
4.1 Riding Ferris Wheels	36
4.2 Looking at Locust Cycles	38
4.3 Planning a Picnic	39
Applications—Connections—Extensions	40
Mathematical Reflections	45
Investigation 5: Factorizations	46
5.1 Searching for Factor Strings	46
5.2 Finding the Longest Factor String	48
5.3 Using Prime Factorizations	50
Applications—Connections—Extensions	52
Mathematical Reflections	57
Investigation 6: The Locker Problem	58
6.1 Unraveling the Locker Problem	58
Applications—Connections—Extensions	61
Mathematical Reflections	64
The Unit Project: My Special Number	65
Looking Back and Looking Ahead: Unit Reflections	66
Glossary	68
Index	71

Data About Us

Statistics

Mathematical Highlights	4
The Unit Project: Is Anyone Typical?	5
Investigation 1: Looking at Data	6
1.1 Organizing Your Data	6
1.2 Interpreting Graphs	7
1.3 Identifying the Mode and Range	9
1.4 Identifying the Median	11
1.5 Experimenting with the Median	13
Applications—Connections—Extensions	15
Mathematical Reflections	21
Investigation 2: Types of Data	22
2.1 Category and Number Questions	22
2.2 Counting Pets	23
Applications—Connections—Extensions	26
Mathematical Reflections	29
Investigation 3: Using Graphs to Group Data	30
3.1 Traveling to School	30
3.2 Jumping Rope	34
Applications—Connections—Extensions	37
Mathematical Reflections	41
Investigation 4: Coordinate Graphs	42
4.1 Relating Height to Arm Span	42
4.2 Relating Travel Time to Distance	45
Applications—Connections—Extensions	47
Mathematical Reflections	52
Investigation 5: What Do We Mean by *Mean?*	53
5.1 Evening Things Out	54
5.2 Finding the Mean	57
5.3 Data with the Same Mean	58
5.4 Using Your Class's Data	59
5.5 Watching Movies	60
Applications—Connections—Extensions	62
Mathematical Reflections	67
The Unit Project: Is Anyone Typical?	68
Looking Back and Looking Ahead: Unit Reflections	69
Glossary	71
Index	76

Shapes and Designs
Two-Dimensional Geometry

Mathematical Highlights 6

The Unit Project: What I Know About Shapes and Designs 7

Investigation 1: Bees and Polygons 8
    1.1 Tiling a Beehive 9
    Applications—Connections—Extensions 11
    Mathematical Reflections 14

Investigation 2: Building Polygons 15
    2.1 Building Triangles 16
    2.2 Building Quadrilaterals 17
    2.3 Building Parallelograms 18
    Applications—Connections—Extensions 19
    Mathematical Reflections 21

Investigation 3: Polygons and Angles 22
    3.1 Follow the Dancing Bee 22
    3.2 Estimating Angle Measures 25
    3.3 Developing More Angle Benchmarks 27
    3.4 Playing Four in a Row 29
    3.5 Using an Angle Ruler 30
    3.6 Analyzing Measuring Errors 32
    Applications—Connections—Extensions 35
    Mathematical Reflections 41

Investigation 4: Polygon Properties and Tiling 42
    4.1 Relating Sides to Angles 42
    4.2 Measuring Irregular Polygons 44
    4.3 Back to the Bees! 46
    Applications—Connections—Extensions 47
    Mathematical Reflections 50

Investigation 5: Side-Angle-Shape Connections 51
    5.1 Flipping and Turning Triangles 52
    5.2 Flipping and Turning Quadrilaterals 54
    Applications—Connections—Extensions 57
    Mathematical Reflections 63

Investigation 6: Turtle Tracks 64
    6.1 Drawing with Logo 66
    6.2 Debugging Computer Programs 67
    6.3 Making Polygons 68
    Applications—Connections—Extensions 69
    Mathematical Reflections 75

The Unit Project: What I Know About Shapes and Designs 76

Looking Back and Looking Ahead: Unit Reflections 77

Glossary 79

Index 84

vii

Bits and Pieces I
Understanding Rational Numbers

Mathematical Highlights	4
Investigation 1: Fund-Raising Fractions	5
1.1 Reporting Our Progress	5
1.2 Using Fraction Strips	6
1.3 Comparing Classes	8
1.4 Exceeding the Goal	10
1.5 Using Symbolic Form	12
Applications—Connections—Extensions	14
Mathematical Reflections	18
Investigation 2: Comparing Fractions	19
2.1 Comparing Fractions	19
2.2 Finding Equivalent Fractions	20
2.3 Making a Number Line	22
2.4 Comparing Fractions to Benchmarks	23
2.5 Fractions Greater Than One	24
Applications—Connections—Extensions	26
Mathematical Reflections	30
Investigation 3: Cooking with Fractions	31
3.1 Area Models for Fractions	31
3.2 Baking Brownies	32
Applications—Connections—Extensions	34
Mathematical Reflections	38
Investigation 4: From Fractions to Decimals	39
4.1 Designing a Garden	39
4.2 Making Smaller Parts	41
4.3 Using Decimal Benchmarks	43
4.4 Playing Distinguishing Digits	44
Applications—Connections—Extensions	46
Mathematical Reflections	52
Investigation 5: Moving Between Fractions and Decimals	53
5.1 Choosing the Best	53
5.2 Writing Fractions as Decimals	54
5.3 Moving from Fractions to Decimals	57
Applications—Connections—Extensions	58
Mathematical Reflections	66
Investigation 6: Out of One Hundred	67
6.1 It's Raining Cats	68
6.2 Dealing with Discounts	73
6.3 Changing Forms	75
6.4 It's Raining Cats and Dogs	76
Applications—Connections—Extensions	77
Mathematical Reflections	83
Looking Back and Looking Ahead: Unit Reflections	84
Glossary	87
Index	91

Covering and Surrounding
Two-Dimensional Measurement

Mathematical Highlights	4
The Unit Project: Plan a Park	5
Investigation 1: Measuring Perimeter and Area	6
1.1 Designing Bumper-Car Rides	6
1.2 Decoding Designs	8
1.3 Computing Costs	10
1.4 Getting Your Money's Worth	12
Applications—Connections—Extensions	13
Mathematical Reflections	18
Investigation 2: Measuring Odd Shapes	19
2.1 Making the Shoe Fit	19
Applications—Connections—Extensions	21
Mathematical Reflections	28
Investigation 3: Constant Area, Changing Perimeter	29
3.1 Building Storm Shelters	29
3.2 Stretching the Perimeter	30
Applications—Connections—Extensions	32
Mathematical Reflections	34
Investigation 4: Constant Perimeter, Changing Area	35
4.1 Fencing in Spaces	35
4.2 Adding Tiles to Pentominos	36
Applications—Connections—Extensions	38
Mathematical Reflections	45
Investigation 5: Measuring Parallelograms	46
5.1 Finding Measures of Parallelograms	46
5.2 Designing Parallelograms Under Constraints	48
5.3 Rearranging Parallelograms	50
Applications—Connections—Extensions	51
Mathematical Reflections	55
Investigation 6: Measuring Triangles	56
6.1 Finding Measures of Triangles	56
6.2 Designing Triangles Under Constraints	58
6.3 Making Parallelograms from Triangles	59
Applications—Connections—Extensions	60
Mathematical Reflections	68
Investigation 7: Going Around in Circles	69
7.1 Pricing Pizza	70
7.2 Surrounding a Circle	71
7.3 Covering a Circle	72
7.4 "Squaring" a Circle	73
7.5 Replacing Trees	75
Applications—Connections—Extensions	76
Mathematical Reflections	81
The Unit Project: Plan a Park	82
Looking Back and Looking Ahead: Unit Reflections	84
Glossary	87
Index	90

How Likely Is It?

Probability

Mathematical Highlights	4
Investigation 1: A First Look at Chance	5
1.1 Flipping for Breakfast	5
1.2 Analyzing Events	7
Applications—Connections—Extensions	9
Mathematical Reflections	13
Investigation 2: More Experiments with Chance	14
2.1 Tossing Marshmallows	14
2.2 Pondering Possible and Probable	16
Applications—Connections—Extensions	17
Mathematical Reflections	21
Investigation 3: Using Spinners to Predict Chances	22
3.1 Bargaining for a Better Bedtime	22
Applications—Connections—Extensions	24
Mathematical Reflections	28
Investigation 4: Theoretical Probabilities	29
4.1 Predicting to Win	29
4.2 Drawing More Blocks	32
4.3 Winning the Bonus Prize	33
Applications—Connections—Extensions	35
Mathematical Reflections	41
Investigation 5: Analyzing Games of Chance	42
5.1 Playing Roller Derby	42
Applications—Connections—Extensions	44
Mathematical Reflections	48
Investigation 6: More About Games of Chance	49
6.1 Scratching Spots	49
Applications—Connections—Extensions	51
Mathematical Reflections	56
Investigation 7: Probability and Genetics	57
7.1 Curling Your Tongue	57
7.2 Tracing Traits	58
Applications—Connections—Extensions	61
Mathematical Reflections	64
Looking Back and Looking Ahead: Unit Reflections	65
Glossary	68
Index	70

Bits and Pieces II

Using Rational Numbers

Mathematical Highlights		4
Investigation 1:	1.1 Taxing Tapes	5
	1.2 Computing Tips	7
	1.3 Finding Bargains	9
	1.4 Spending Money	10
	Applications—Connections—Extensions	12
	Mathematical Reflections	17
Investigation 2:	2.1 Finding Percents	18
	2.2 Finding a General Strategy	19
	2.3 Clipping Coupons	20
	2.4 Making Circle Graphs	21
	Applications—Connections—Extensions	24
	Mathematical Reflections	30
Investigation 3:	3.1 Getting Close	31
	3.2 Getting Even Closer	33
	Applications—Connections—Extensions	35
	Mathematical Reflections	42
Investigation 4:	4.1 Dividing Land	43
	4.2 Redrawing the Map	44
	4.3 Pirating Pizza	46
	4.4 Designing Algorithms	48
	Applications—Connections—Extensions	49
	Mathematical Reflections	53
Investigation 5:	5.1 Selling Brownies	54
	5.2 Discounting Brownies	56
	5.3 Buying the Biggest Lot	58
	5.4 Designing a Multiplication Algorithm	59
	Applications—Connections—Extensions	60
	Mathematical Reflections	63
Investigation 6:	6.1 Buying School Supplies	64
	6.2 Moving Decimal Points	66
	6.3 Multiplying Decimals	68
	6.4 Shifting Decimal Points	70
	6.5 Fencing a Yard	71
	Applications—Connections—Extensions	72
	Mathematical Reflections	76
Investigation 7:	7.1 Fractions in Fund-raising	77
	7.2 Share and Share Alike	80
	7.3 Summer Work	81
	Applications—Connections—Extensions	83
	Mathematical Reflections	87
Looking Back and Looking Ahead: Unit Reflections		88
Glossary		91
Index		95

Ruins of Montarek
Spatial Visualization

Mathematical Highlights   6

Investigation 1: Building Plans   7
    1.1 Building from Base Plans   8
    1.2 Reflecting Figures   10
    1.3 Making Drawings of Cube Models   13
    1.4 Unraveling Mysteries   14
    1.5 Matching a Building to Its Plans   15
    1.6 Which Building Is Which?   16
    Applications—Connections—Extensions   19
    Mathematical Reflections   25

Investigation 2: Making Buildings   26
    2.1 Reconstructing Ruins   26
    2.2 Constructing Buildings from Plans   28
    2.3 Building from Incomplete Plans   30
    Applications—Connections—Extensions   33
    Mathematical Reflections   39

Investigation 3: Describing Unique Buildings   40
    3.1 Finding All the Possibilities   40
    3.2 Finding Maximal and Minimal Buildings 41
    3.3 Unraveling an Ancient Mystery   43
    Applications—Connections—Extensions   45
    Mathematical Reflections   51

Investigation 4: Isometric Dot Paper Representations   52
    4.1 Drawing a Cube   53
    4.2 Drawing a Cube Model   54
    4.3 Drawing More Complex Buildings   56
    4.4 Creating Your Own Building   57
    Applications—Connections—Extensions   58
    Mathematical Reflections   61

Investigation 5: Ziggurats   62
    5.1 Building Ziggurats   62
    5.2 Representing Ziggurats   64
    Applications—Connections—Extensions   65
    Mathematical Reflections   71

Investigation 6: Seeing the Isometric View   72
    6.1 Viewing a Building   72
    6.2 Removing Cubes   74
    6.3 Adding Cubes   75
    6.4 Putting the Pieces Together   76
    Applications—Connections—Extensions   77
    Mathematical Reflections   81

The Unit Project: Design a Building   82

Looking Back and Looking Ahead: Unit Reflections   83

Glossary   85

Index   86

Connected Mathematics™

Factors and Multiples

Student Edition

Glenda Lappan
James T. Fey
William M. Fitzgerald
Susan N. Friel
Elizabeth Difanis Phillips

Prentice
Hall

Glenview, Illinois
Needham, Massachusetts
Upper Saddle River, New Jersey

The Connected Mathematics Project was developed at Michigan State University with the support of National Science Foundation Grant No. MDR 9150217.

This project was supported, in part,
by the
National Science Foundation
Opinions expressed are those of the authors
and not necessarily those of the Foundation

The Michigan State University authors and administration have agreed that all MSU royalties arising from this publication will be devoted to purposes supported by the Department of Mathematics and the MSU Mathematics Education Enrichment Fund.

Contents

Mathematical Highlights   4

The Unit Project: My Special Number   5

Investigation 1: The Factor Game   6
   1.1 Playing the Factor Game   6
   1.2 Playing to Win the Factor Game   10
   Applications—Connections—Extensions   12
   Mathematical Reflections   16

Investigation 2: The Product Game   17
   2.1 Playing the Product Game   17
   2.2 Making Your Own Product Game   19
   2.3 Classifying Numbers   20
   Applications—Connections—Extensions   22
   Mathematical Reflections   25

Investigation 3: Factor Pairs   26
   3.1 Arranging Space   26
   3.2 Finding Patterns   27
   3.3 Reasoning with Odd and Even Numbers   28
   Applications—Connections—Extensions   30
   Mathematical Reflections   35

Investigation 4: Common Factors and Multiples   36
   4.1 Riding Ferris Wheels   36
   4.2 Looking at Locust Cycles   38
   4.3 Planning a Picnic   39
   Applications—Connections—Extensions   40
   Mathematical Reflections   45

Investigation 5: Factorizations   46
   5.1 Searching for Factor Strings   46
   5.2 Finding the Longest Factor String   48
   5.3 Using Prime Factorizations   50
   Applications—Connections—Extensions   52
   Mathematical Reflections   57

Investigation 6: The Locker Problem   58
   6.1 Unraveling the Locker Problem   58
   Applications—Connections—Extensions   61
   Mathematical Reflections   64

The Unit Project: My Special Number   65

Looking Back and Looking Ahead: Unit Reflections   66

Glossary   68

Index   71

Prime Time

Why is time measured using 60 seconds in a minute (not 50 or 100), 60 minutes in an hour, and 24 hours in a day (not 23 or 25)?

Insects called cicadas spend most of their lives underground. Many come above ground only every 13 years or 17 years. In North America, many people call these cicadas 13-year locusts and 17-year locusts. Why are there no 12-year, 14-year, or 16-year locusts?

Why does your birthday fall on a different day of the week from one year to the next? Why is the same pattern also true for New Year's Day and the Fourth of July?

Everyone uses numbers. Think about the ways you can use them—for counting, for measuring, for making decisions. Numbers help you communicate, find information, use technology, and make purchases. Numbers also can help you think about situations like those on the opposite page.

Whole numbers have interesting properties and structures you may not have thought about before. Some numbers can be divided by many numbers, while others can be divided by only a few. In *Prime Time*, you will learn how to use these ideas about the structure of numbers to explain some curious patterns and to solve some interesting problems including the three on the opposite page.

Mathematical Highlights

In *Prime Time* you will explore important properties of whole numbers, especially those related to multiplication and division. The unit should help you to

● Understand relationships among factors, multiples, divisors, and products;

● Recognize and use properties of prime and composite numbers, even and odd numbers, and square numbers;

● Link area and dimensions of rectangles with products and factors;

● Develop strategies for finding factors and multiples, least common multiples, and greatest common factors;

● Recognize and use the fact that every whole number can be written in exactly one way as a product of primes;

● Use factors and multiples to solve problems and to explain some numerical facts of everyday life; and

● Develop a variety of strategies for solving problems—building models, making lists and tables, drawing diagrams, and solving simpler problems.

As you work on the problems of this unit, get in the habit of asking questions about situations that involve whole numbers and relationships: *What are the factors of given numbers and how can those factors be found? What common factors and common multiples do the numbers have? What do the factors and multiples of the numbers tell about the situations in which they occur?*

My Special Number

Many people have a number they find interesting. Choose a whole number between 10 and 100 that you especially like.

In your journal

- record your number
- explain why you chose that number
- list three or four mathematical things about your number
- list three or four connections you can make between your number and your world

As you work through the investigations in *Prime Time,* you will learn lots of things about numbers. Think about how these new ideas apply to your special number, and add any new information about your number to your journal. You may want to designate one or two "special number" pages in your journal, where you can record this information. At the end of the unit, your teacher will ask you to find an interesting way to report to the class about your special number.

The Factor Game

Today Jamie is 12 years old. Jamie has three younger cousins: Cam, Emilio, and Ester. They are 2, 3, and 8 years old respectively. The following mathematical sentences show that Jamie is

6 times as old as Cam,   4 times as old as Emilio,   and $1\frac{1}{2}$ times as old as Ester

$$12 = 6 \times 2$$ $$12 = 4 \times 3$$ $$12 = 1\frac{1}{2} \times 8$$

Notice that each of the whole numbers 2, 3, 4, and 6 can be multiplied by another whole number to get 12. We call 2, 3, 4, and 6 *whole number factors* or *whole number divisors* of 12. Although 8 is a whole number, it is not a whole number factor of 12, since we cannot multiply it by another whole number to get 12. To save time, we will simply use the word **factor** to refer to whole number factors.

1.1 Playing the Factor Game

The Factor Game is a two-person game in which players find factors of numbers on a game board. To play the game you will need Labsheet 1.1 and colored pens, pencils, or markers.

Problem 1.1

Play the Factor Game several times with a partner. Take turns making the first move. Look for moves that give the best scores. In your journal, record any strategies you find that help you to win.

■ Problem 1.1 Follow-Up

Talk with your partner about the games you played. Be prepared to tell the class about a good idea you discoved for playing the game well.

The Factor Game

1	2	3	4	5
6	7	8	9	10
11	12	13	14	15
16	17	18	19	20
21	22	23	24	25
26	27	28	29	30

Factor Game Rules

1. Player A chooses a number on the game board and circles it.
2. Using a different color, Player B circles all the proper factors of Player A's number. The **proper factors** of a number are all the factors of that number, except the number itself. For example, the proper factors of 12 are 1, 2, 3, 4, and 6. Although 12 is a factor of itself, it is not a proper factor.
3. Player B circles a new number, and Player A circles all the factors of the number that are not already circled.
4. The players take turns choosing numbers and circling factors.
5. If a player circles a number that has no factors left that have not been circled, that player loses a turn and does not get the points for the number circled.
6. The game ends when there are no numbers remaining with uncircled factors.
7. Each player adds the numbers that are circled with his or her color. The player with the greater total is the winner.

A sample game is shown on the following pages.

Sample Game

The first column describes the moves the players make. The other columns show the game board and score after each move.

Moves	Game Board	Cathy	Keiko
Cathy circles 24. Keiko circles 1, 2, 3, 4, 6, 8, and 12—the proper factors of 24.	The Factor Game ① ② ③ ④ 5 ⑥ 7 ⑧ 9 10 11 ⑫ 13 14 15 16 17 18 19 20 21 22 23 ㉔ 25 26 27 28 29 30	24	36
Keiko circles 28. Cathy circles 7 and 14—the factors of 28 that are not already circled.	The Factor Game ① ② ③ ④ 5 ⑥ ⑦ ⑧ 9 10 11 ⑫ 13 ⑭ 15 16 17 18 19 20 21 22 23 ㉔ 25 26 27 ㉘ 29 30	24 21	36 28
Cathy circles 27. Keiko circles 9—the only factor of 27 that is not already circled.	The Factor Game ① ② ③ ④ 5 ⑥ ⑦ ⑧ ⑨ 10 11 ⑫ 13 ⑭ 15 16 17 18 19 20 21 22 23 ㉔ 25 26 ㉗ ㉘ 29 30	24 21 27	36 28 9
Keiko circles 30. Cathy circles 5, 10, and 15—the factors of 30 that are not already circled.	The Factor Game ① ② ③ ④ ⑤ ⑥ ⑦ ⑧ ⑨ ⑩ 11 ⑫ 13 ⑭ ⑮ 16 17 18 19 20 21 22 23 ㉔ 25 26 ㉗ ㉘ 29 ㉚	24 21 27 30	36 28 9 30
Cathy circles 25. All the factors of 25 are circled. Cathy loses a turn and does not receive any points for this turn.	The Factor Game ① ② ③ ④ ⑤ ⑥ ⑦ ⑧ ⑨ ⑩ 11 ⑫ 13 ⑭ ⑮ 16 17 18 19 20 21 22 23 ㉔ ㉕ 26 ㉗ ㉘ 29 ㉚	24 21 27 30	36 28 9 30

		Cathy	Keiko
Keiko circles 26. Cathy circles 13—the only factor of 26 that is not circled.		24 21 27 30 13	36 28 9 30 26
Keiko circles 22. Cathy circles 11—the only factor of 22 that is not circled.		24 21 27 30 13 11	36 28 9 30 26 22
No numbers remain with uncircled factors. Keiko wins the game.		24 21 27 30 13 11	36 28 9 30 26 22
	Total	**126**	**151**

1.2 Playing to Win the Factor Game

Did you find that some numbers are better than others to pick for the first move in the Factor Game? For example, if you pick 22, you get 22 points and your opponent gets only $1 + 2 + 11 = 14$ points. However, if you pick 18, you get 18 points, and your opponent gets $1 + 2 + 3 + 6 + 9 = 21$ points!

Make a table of all the possible first moves (numbers from 1 to 30) you could make. For each move, list the proper factors, and record the scores you and your opponent would receive. Your table might start like this:

First move	Proper factors	My score	Opponent's score
1	none	lose a turn	0
2	1	2	1
3	1	3	1
4	1, 2	4	3

Problem 1.2

Use your list to figure out the best and worst first moves.

A. What is the best first move? Why?

B. What is the worst first move? Why?

C. Look for other patterns in your list. Describe an interesting pattern that you find.

■ Problem 1.2 Follow-Up

1. List all the first moves that allow your opponent to score only one point. These kinds of numbers have a special name. They are called **prime numbers.**

2. Are all prime numbers good first moves? (A number is a good first move if the player picking the number scores more points than his or her opponent.) Explain your answer.

3. List all the first moves that allow your opponent to score more than one point. These kinds of numbers also have a special name. They are called **composite numbers.**

4. Are composite numbers good first moves? Explain your answer.

5. Which first move would make you lose a turn? Why?

Did you know?

The search for prime numbers has fascinated mathematicians for a very long time. We know that there are an infinite number of primes, but we have no way to predict which numbers are prime. We must test each number to see if it has exactly two factors—1 and itself. For very large numbers, this testing takes a long time, even with the help of a supercomputer that can perform 16 billion calculations per second!

In 1994, David Slowinski, a computer scientist at Cray Research, found a prime number with 258,716 digits. The previous record holder had 227,832 digits. Large prime numbers are of special importance in coding systems for transmitting secret information. The difficulty of breaking these codes depends on the difficulty of factoring a composite number with 100 or more digits into prime factors with at least 50 digits. Computer programmers think that such a problem would require over a billion years on the largest imaginable supercomputer.

Adapted from Phillips et al., *Addenda Series, Grades 5–8: Patterns and Functions* (Reston, Va.: National Council of Teachers of Mathematics, 1991), p. 21, and information provided by Cray Research, Inc.

As you work on these ACE questions, use your calculator whenever you need it.

Applications

1. Your opponent in the Factor Game claims that 6 is a factor of 24. How can you check to see whether this is correct?

2. What factor is paired with 6 to give 24?

3. What factor is paired with 5 to give 45?

4. What factor is paired with 3 to give 24?

5. What factor is paired with 6 to give 45?

6. What factor is paired with 6 to give 48?

7. What factor is paired with 11 to give 121?

8. What factor is paired with 12 to give 48?

9. What factor is paired with 11 to give 111?

10. The Factor Game can be played on a 49-board, which contains whole numbers from 1 to 49.

The Factor Game

1	2	3	4	5	6	7
8	9	10	11	12	13	14
15	16	17	18	19	20	21
22	23	24	25	26	27	28
29	30	31	32	33	34	35
36	37	38	39	40	41	42
43	44	45	46	47	48	49

a. Extend your table for analyzing first moves on a 30-factor game board to include all the numbers on a 49-board.

b. What new primes do you find?

11. Suppose your opponent has the first move on the 49-board and chooses 49.

    a. How many points does your opponent score for this round?

    b. How many points do you score for this round?

12. What is the best first move on a 49-board? Why?

13. What is the worst first move on a 49-board? Why?

14.   **a.** What do you get when you use your calculator to divide 84 by 14? What does this tell you about 14 and 84?

    b. What do you get when you use your calculator to divide 84 by 15? What does this tell you about 15 and 84?

15. Use the ideas from this investigation to list at least five facts about the number 30.

16. What is my number?

    Clue 1 My number has two digits, and both digits are even.

    Clue 2 The sum of my number's digits is 10.

    Clue 3 My number has 4 as a factor.

    Clue 4 The difference between the two digits of my number is 6.

Connections

17. A class of 30 students is to be divided into equal-size groups. What group sizes are possible?

18. Long ago, people observed the sun rising and setting over and over at about equal intervals. They decided to use the amount of time between two sunrises as the length of a day. They divided the day into 24 hours. Use what you know about factors to answer these questions:

    a. Why is 24 a more convenient choice than 23 or 25?

    b. If you were to select a number different from 24 to represent the hours in a day, what number would you choose? Why?

Extensions

19. Suppose you and a friend decide to use a 100-board to play the Factor Game.
  a. What would your score be if your friend chose 100 as the first move?
  b. What would your score be if your friend chose 99 as the first move?
  c. What is the best first move?

20. The sum of the proper factors of a number may be greater than, less than, or equal to the number. Ancient mathematicians used this idea to classify numbers as **abundant, deficient,** and **perfect.** Each whole number greater than 1 falls into one of these three categories.
  a. Draw and label three circles as shown below. The numbers 12, 15, and 6 have been placed in the appropriate circles. Use your factor list to figure out what each label means. Then, write each whole number from 2 to 30 in the correct circle.

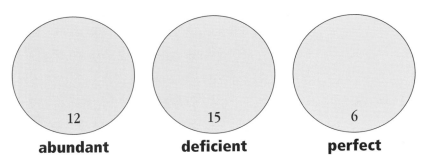

       12   15   6

   abundant   **deficient**   **perfect**

  b. Do the labels seem appropriate? Why or why not?
  c. In which circle would 36 belong?
  d. In which circle would 55 belong?

21. a. If you choose 16 as a first move in the Factor Game, how many points does your opponent get? How does your opponent's score for this turn compare to yours?
  b. If you choose 4 as a first move, how many points does your opponent get? How does your opponent's score for this turn compare to yours?
  c. Find some other numbers that have the same pattern of scoring as 4 and 16. These numbers could be called **near-perfect numbers.** Why do you think this name fits?

Did you know?

Is there a largest perfect number? Mathematicians have been trying for hundreds of years to find the answer to this question. You might like to know that the next largest perfect number, after 6 and 28, is 496!

Mathematical Reflections

In Investigation 1, you played and analyzed the Factor Game. These questions will help you summarize what you have learned:

1. Which numbers are good first moves? What makes these numbers good moves?

2. Which numbers are bad first moves? What makes these numbers bad moves?

3. What did your analysis of the factor game tell you about prime numbers?

Think about your answers to these questions, discuss your ideas with other students and your teacher, and then write a summary of your findings in your journal.

Have you remembered to write about your special number?

The Product Game

In the Factor Game, you start with a number and find its factors. In the Product Game, you start with factors and find their product. The diagram shows the relationship between factors and their product.

2.1 Playing the Product Game

The Product Game board consists of a list of factors and a grid of products. Two players compete to get four squares in a row—up and down, across, or diagonally. To play the Product Game, you will need Labsheet 2.1, two paper clips, and colored markers or game chips. The rules for the Product Game are given on the next page.

The Product Game

1	2	3	4	5	6
7	8	9	10	12	14
15	16	18	20	21	24
25	27	28	30	32	35
36	40	42	45	**48**	49
54	56	63	64	72	81

Factors:

1 2 3 4 5 6 7 8 9

Problem 2.1

Play the Product Game several times with a partner. Look for interesting patterns and winning strategies. Make notes of your observations.

Product Game Rules

1. Player A puts a paper clip on a number in the factor list. Player A does not mark a square on the product grid because only one factor has been marked; it takes two factors to make a product.

2. Player B puts the other paper clip on any number in the factor list (including the same number marked by Player A) and then shades or covers the product of the two factors on the product grid.

3. Player A moves *either one* of the paper clips to another number and then shades or covers the new product.

4. Each player, in turn, moves a paper clip and marks a product. If a product is already marked, the player does not get a mark for that turn. The winner is the first player to mark four squares in a row—up and down, across, or diagonally.

▪ Problem 2.1 Follow-Up

1. Suppose one of the paper clips is on 5. What products can you make by moving the other paper clip?

The products you listed in question 1 are multiples of 5. A **multiple** of a number is the product of that number and another whole number.

If a number is a multiple of 5, then 5 is a factor of that number. These four sentences are all ways of expressing $5 \times 3 = 15$:

5 is a factor of 15.
3 is a factor of 15.
15 is a multiple of 5.
15 is a multiple of 3.

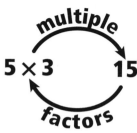

2. List five multiples of 5 that are not on the game board.

3. Suppose one of the paper clips is on 3. What products can you make by moving the other paper clip?

4. List five multiples of 3 that are not on the game board.

2.2 Making Your Own Product Game

Suppose you want to create a product game that takes less time to play or, perhaps, more time to play than the game with the 6 × 6 product grid. You would have to decide what numbers to include in the factor list and what products to include in the product grid.

Problem 2.2

Work with your partner to design a new game board for the Product Game.
*   Choose factors to include in your factor list.
*   Determine the products you need to include on the game board.
*   Find a game board that will accommodate all the products.
*   Decide how many squares a player must get in a row—up and down, across, or diagonally—to win.

Make the game board. Play your game against your partner; then make any changes you both agree would make your game better.

Switch game boards with another pair, and play their game. Give them some written suggestions about how they can improve their game. Read the suggestions for improving your game, then make any changes you and your partner think are necessary.

■ Problem 2.2 Follow-Up

Write a paragraph about why you think your game board is interesting to use for playing the Product Game. In the paragraph, describe any problems you ran into while making the board, and explain how you solved them.

2.3 Classifying Numbers

Now that you know how to find the factors and multiples of a number, you can explore how the factors and multiples of two or more numbers are related. Venn diagrams are useful tools for exploring these relationships. A **Venn diagram** uses circles to show things that belong together. For example, the Venn diagram below shows one way to group whole numbers.

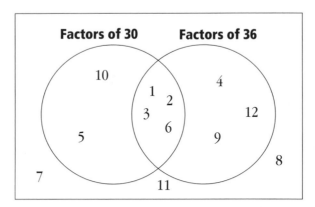

One circle represents all the whole numbers that are factors of 30. The other circle represents all the whole numbers that are factors of 36. The first 12 whole numbers have been placed in the correct regions of the diagram. Notice that the numbers that are not factors of 30 or 36 lie outside the circles. Why do the circles intersect (overlap)? What do the numbers in the intersection have in common?

Problem 2.3

Copy the Venn diagram below.

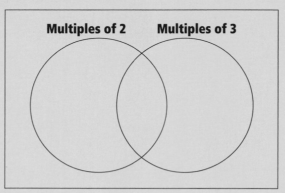

Find at least five numbers that belong in each region of the diagram. Think about what numbers belong in the intersection of the circles and what numbers belong outside of the circles.

Problem 2.3 Follow-Up

1. What factors do the numbers in the intersection of the circles have in common?
2. Add a new circle to the diagram with the label "Multiples of 5," as shown below. Replace your numbers in the correct regions, and make sure you have at least two numbers in each part of the diagram.

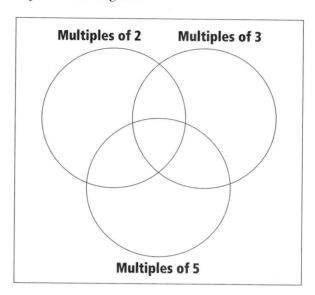

As you work on these ACE questions, use your calculator whenever you need it.

Applications

1. Marena just marked 18 on the 6×6 Product Game board. On which factors might the paper clips be? List all the possibilities.

2. Find two products on the board, other than 18, that can be made in more than one way. List all the factor pairs that give each product.

3. On the 6×6 Product Game board, 81 is a multiple of which factors?

4. On the 6×6 Product Game board, suppose your markers are on 16, 18, and 28, and your opponent's markers are on 14, 21, and 30. The paper clips are on 5 and 6. It is your turn to move a paper clip.

The Product Game

1	2	3	4	5	6
7	8	9	10	12	**14**
15	**16**	**18**	20	**21**	24
25	27	**28**	**30**	32	35
36	40	42	45	48	49
54	56	63	64	72	81

Factors:
1 2 3 4 5 6 7 8 9

a. List the possible moves you could make.

b. Which move(s) would give you three markers in a row?

c. Which move(s) would allow you to block your opponent?

d. Which move would you make? Explain your strategy.

In 5–8, find two numbers that can be multiplied to give each product. Do not use 1 as one of the numbers.

5. 84   **6.** 145   **7.** 250   **8.** 300

9. What factors were used to create this Product Game board?

4	6	14
9	21	49

Factors:

—— —— ——

10. What factors were used to create this Product Game board? What number is missing from the grid?

9	15	18	■
21	?	30	35
■	36	42	49

Factors:

—— —— —— —— ——

11. Draw and label a Venn diagram in which one circle represents multiples of 3 and another circle represents multiples of 5. Place the multiples of 3 and the multiples of 5 from 1 to 60 in the appropriate regions of the diagram. The numbers that are multiples of both 3 and 5 are the **common multiples** of 3 and 5. These numbers go in the intersection of the two circles.

12. Find at least five numbers that belong in each of the regions of this Venn diagram.

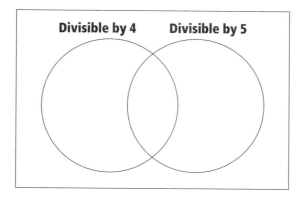

Connections

13. What numbers is 36 a multiple of?

14. Using the words *factor, divisor, multiple, product,* and *divisible by,* write as many statements as you can about the mathematical sentence $7 \times 9 = 63$.

15. Draw and label a Venn diagram in which one circle contains the **divisors** (factors) of 42 and the other contains the divisors of 60. The divisors of both 42 and 60 are the **common factors** of the two numbers. The common factors should go in the intersection of the two circles.

16. Find all the common multiples of 4 and 11 that are less than 100.

17. The cast of the school play had a party at the drama teacher's house. There were 20 cookies and 40 carrot sticks served as refreshments. Each cast member had the same number of whole cookies and the same number of whole carrot sticks, and nothing was left over. The drama teacher did not eat. How many cast members might have been at the party? Explain your answer.

18. A restaurant is open 24 hours a day. The manager wants to divide the day into workshifts of equal length. Show the different ways this can be done. The shifts should not overlap, and all shifts should be a whole number of hours long.

19   **a.** In developing ways to calculate time, astronomers divided an hour into 60 minutes. Why is 60 a good choice (better than 59 or 61)?

      b. If you were to select another number to represent the minutes in an hour, what would be a good choice? Why?

Extensions

20. What is my number?
     Clue 1   When you divide my number by 5, the remainder is 4.
     Clue 2   My number has two digits, and both digits are even.
     Clue 3   The sum of the digits is 10.

Mathematical Reflections

In this investigation, you played and analyzed the Product Game. These questions will help you summarize what you have learned:

1 In the Product Game, describe the relationship between the numbers in the factor list and the products in the grid.

2 What are the multiples of a number and how do you find them?

3 Using the words *factor, divisor, multiple,* and *divisible by,* write as many statements as you can about this mathematical sentence:

$$4 \times 7 = 28$$

Think about your answers to these questions, discuss your ideas with other students and your teacher, and then write a summary of your findings in your journal.

Write something new that you have learned about your special number now that you have played the Factor Game and the Product Game. Would your special number be a good first move in either game? Why or why not?

Factor Pairs

In the Factor Game and the Product Game, you found that factors come in pairs. Once you know one factor of a number, you can find another factor. For example, 3 is a factor of 12, and because $3 \times 4 = 12$, you know 4 is also a factor of 12. In this investigation, you will look at factor pairs in a different way.

3.1 Arranging Space

Every year, Meridian Park has an exhibit of arts and crafts. People who want to exhibit their work rent a space for $20 per square yard. All exhibit spaces must have a rectangular shape. The length and width of an exhibit space must be whole numbers of yards.

Problem 3.1

Terrapin Crafts wants to rent a space of 12 square yards.

A. Use 12 square tiles to represent the 12 square yards. Find all the possible ways the Terrapin Crafts owner can arrange the squares. Copy each rectangle you make onto grid paper, and label it with its dimensions (length and width).

B. How are the rectangles you found and the factors of 12 related?

Suppose Terrapin Crafts decided it wanted a space of 16 square yards.

C. Find all the possible ways the Terrapin Crafts owner can arrange the 16 square yards. Copy each rectangle you make onto grid paper, and label it with its dimensions.

D. How are these rectangles and the factors of 16 related?

■ **Problem 3.1 Follow-Up**

What factors do 12 and 16 have in common?

3.2 Finding Patterns

Will likes to find number patterns. He wonders if there are any interesting patterns in the rectangles that can be made for the numbers from 1 to 30.

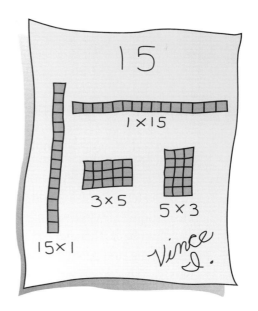

In this problem, your class will make rectangles for all the whole numbers from 1 through 30. When all the rectangles are displayed, you can look for interesting patterns.

Work with a partner or a small group so that you can check each other's work. With your teacher, decide which numbers your group will be responsible for.

Problem 3.2

Work with your group to decide how to divide up the work for the numbers you have been assigned.

Cut out a grid-paper model of each rectangle you can make for each of the numbers you have been assigned. You may want to use tiles to help you find the rectangles.

Write each number at the top of a sheet of paper, and tape all the rectangles for that number to the sheet. Display the sheets of rectangles in order from 1 to 30 around the room.

When all the numbers are displayed, look for patterns. Be prepared to discuss patterns you find with your classmates.

■ Problem 3.2 Follow-Up

1. Which numbers have the most rectangles? What kind of numbers are these?

2. Which numbers have the fewest rectangles? What kind of numbers are these?

3. Which numbers are **square numbers** (numbers whose tiles can be arranged to form a square)?

4. If you know the rectangles you can make for a number, how can you use this information to list the factors of the number? Use an example to show your thinking.

3.3 Reasoning with Odd and Even Numbers

An **even number** is a number that has 2 as a factor. An **odd number** is a number that does not have 2 as a factor. In this problem, you will study patterns involving odd and even numbers. First, you will learn a way of modeling odd and even numbers. Then, you will make conjectures about sums and products of odd and even numbers. A *conjecture* is your best guess about a relationship. You can use the models to justify, or prove, your conjectures.

"AN ODD NUMBER"

Will's friend, Jocelyn, makes models for whole numbers by arranging square tiles in a special pattern. Here are Jocelyn's tile models for the numbers from 1 to 7.

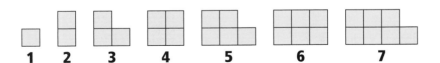

Discuss with your class how the models of even numbers are different from the models of odd numbers. Then describe the models for 50 and 99.

Problem 3.3

Make a conjecture about whether each result below will be even or odd. Then use tile models or some other method to justify your conjecture.

A. The sum of two even numbers

B. The sum of two odd numbers

C. The sum of an odd number and an even number

D. The product of two even numbers

E. The product of two odd numbers

F. The product of an odd number and an even number

■ Problem 3.3 Follow-Up

1. Is 0 an even number or an odd number? Explain your answer.

2. Without building a tile model, how can you tell whether a sum of numbers—such as 127 + 38—is even or odd?

As you work on these ACE questions, use your calculator whenever you need it.

Applications

In 1–6, give the dimensions of each rectangle that can be made from the given number of tiles. Then, use the dimensions of the rectangles to list all the factor pairs for each number.

1. 24   **2.** 32   **3.** 48

4. 45   **5.** 60   **6.** 72

In 7 and 8, write a description, with examples, of numbers that have the given factors.

7. exactly two factors   **8.** an odd number of factors

9. Lupe has chosen a mystery number. His number is larger than 12 and smaller than 40, and it has exactly three factors. What could his number be? Use the displays of rectangles for the numbers 1 to 30 to help you find Lupe's mystery number. You may need to think about what the displays for the numbers 31 to 40 would look like.

10. Without building a tile model, how can you tell whether a sum of numbers—such as 13 + 45 + 24 + 17 is even or odd?

In 11–14, make a conjecture about whether each result will be odd or even. Use tiles, a picture, or some other way to justify your conjectures.

11. An even number minus and even number

12. An odd number minus an odd number

13. An even number minus an odd number

14. An odd number minus an even number

15. How can you tell whether a number is even or odd? Explain or illustrate your answer in at least two ways.

Connections

16. a. List all the numbers less than or equal to 50 that are divisible by 5.

b. Describe a pattern you see in your list that you can use to determine whether a large number—such as 1,276,549—is divisible by 5.

c. Which numbers in your list are divisible by 2?

d. Which numbers in your list are divisible by 10?

e. How do the lists in parts c and d compare? Why does this result make sense?

17. A group of students designs card displays for football games. They use 100 square cards for each display. Each card contains part of a picture or message. At the game, 100 volunteers hold up the cards to form a complete picture. The students have found that the pictures are most effective if the volunteers sit in a rectangular arrangement. What seating arrangements are possible? Which would you choose? Why?

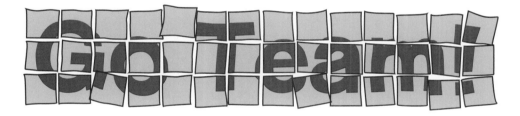

18. The school band has 64 members. The band marches in the form of a rectangle. What rectangles can the band director make by arranging the members of the band? Which of these arrangements is most appealing to you? Why?

19. How many rectangles can you build with a prime number of square tiles?

Extensions

20. Find three numbers you can multiply to get 300.

In 21–23, tell whether each number is a square number. Justify your answer.

21. 196   **22.** 225   **23.** 360

24. **a.** Find at least five numbers that belong in each region of the Venn diagram below.

   b. What do the numbers in the intersection have in common?

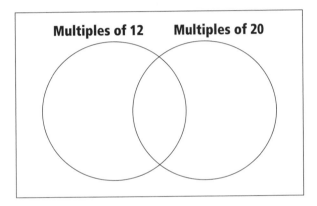

25. **a.** Below is the complete list of the proper factors of a certain number. What is the number?

   1, 2, 3, 4, 6, 7, 12, 14, 21, 28, 42, 49, 84, 98, 147, 196, 294

   b. List each of the factor pairs for the number.

   c. What rectangles could be made to show the number?

26. For any three consecutive numbers (whole numbers in a row), such as 31, 32, 33, or 52, 53, 54, what is true about odds and evens? Explain your thinking.

27. Ji Young conjectured that, in every three consecutive whole numbers, one number will be divisible by 3. Do you think Ji Young is correct? Explain.

28. How many consecutive numbers do you need to guarantee that one of the numbers is divisible by 5?

29. How many consecutive numbers do you need to guarantee that one of the numbers is divisible by 6?

30. Choose a nonprime number between 900 and 1000, and find all of the factors of the number. The chart on the next page will help you select an interesting number.

Factor Counts ∎ Each * Stands for a Factor

900	* *	951	* * * *
901	* * * *	952	* * * * * * * * * * * * * * * *
902	* * * * * * * *	953	* *
903	* * * * * * * *	954	* * * * * * * * * * * *
904	* * * * * * * *	955	* * * *
905	* * * *	956	* * * * * *
906	* * * * * * * *	957	* * * * * * * *
907	* *	958	* * * *
908	* * * * * *	959	* * * *
909	* * * * * *	960	* *
910	* * * * * * * * * * * * * * * *	961	* * *
911	* *	962	* * * * * * * *
912	* * * * * * * * * * * * * * * * * * * *	963	* * * * * *
913	* * * *	964	* * * * * *
914	* * * *	965	* * * *
915	* * * * * * * *	966	* * * * * * * * * * * * * * * *
916	* * * * * *	967	* *
917	* * * *	968	* * * * * * * * * * * *
918	* * * * * * * * * * * * * * * *	969	* * * * * * * *
919	* *	970	* * * * * * * *
920	* * * * * * * * * * * * * * * *	971	* *
921	* * * *	972	* * * * * * * * * * * * * * * * * *
922	* * * *	973	* * * *
923	* * * *	974	* * * *
924	* *	975	* * * * * * * * * * * *
925	* * * * * *	976	* * * * * * * * * *
926	* * * *	977	* *
927	* * * * * *	978	* * * * * * * *
928	* * * * * * * * * * * *	979	* * * *
929	* *	980	* * * * * * * * * * * * * * * * * *
930	* * * * * * * * * * * * * * * *	981	* * * * * *
931	* * * * * *	982	* * * *
932	* * * * * *	983	* *
933	* * * *	984	* * * * * * * * * * * * * * * *
934	* * * *	985	* * * *
935	* * * * * * * *	986	* * * * * * * *
936	* *	987	* * * * * * * *
937	* *	988	* * * * * * * * * * * *
938	* * * * * * * *	989	* * * *
939	* * * *	990	* *
940	* * * * * * * * * * * *	991	* *
941	* *	992	* * * * * * * * * * * *
942	* * * * * * * *	993	* * * *
943	* * * *	994	* * * * * * * *
944	* * * * * * * * * *	995	* * * *
945	* * * * * * * * * * * * * * * *	996	* * * * * * * * * * * *
946	* * * * * * * *	997	* *
947	* *	998	* * * *
948	* * * * * * * * * * * *	999	* * * * * * * *
949	* * * *	1000	* * * * * * * * * * * * * * * *
950	* * * * * * * * * * * *		

Mathematical Reflections

In this investigation, you analyzed factor pairs. You found that factor pairs for a number are related to the rectangles that can be made from that number of square tiles. You also investigated even and odd numbers. These questions will help you summarize what you have learned:

1 Explain how the rectangles you can make using 24 tiles are related to the factor pairs of the number 24.

2 Summarize what you know about the sums and products of odd and even numbers. Justify your statements.

3 How can you tell if a number is divisible by 2? By 5? By 10?

Think about your answers to these questions, discuss your ideas with other students and your teacher, and then write a summary of your findings in your journal.

Write about your special number! What can you say about your number now? Is it even? Is it odd? How many factor pairs does it have?

Common Factors and Multiples

There are many things in the world that happen over and over again in set cycles. Sometimes we want to know when two things with different cycles will happen at the same time. Knowing about factors and multiples can help you to solve such problems.

Let's start by comparing the multiples of 20 and 30.

- The multiples of 20 are 20, 40, 60, 80, 100, 120, . . .
- The multiples of 30 are 30, 60, 90, 120, 150, 180, . . .

The numbers 60, 120, 180, 240, . . . are multiples of both 20 and 30. We call these numbers **common multiples** of 20 and 30.

Now let's compare the factors of 12 and 30.

- The factors of 12 are 1, 2, 3, 4, 6, and 12.
- The factors of 30 are 1, 2, 3, 5, 6, 10, 15, and 30.

The numbers 1, 2, 3, and 6 are factors of both 12 and 30. We call these numbers **common factors** of 12 and 30.

4.1 Riding Ferris Wheels

One of the most popular rides at a carnival or amusement park is the Ferris wheel.

Did you know?

The largest Ferris Wheel was built for the World's Columbian Exposition in Chicago in 1893. The wheel could carry 2160 people in its 36 passenger cars. Can you figure out how many people could ride in each car?

Problem 4.1

You and your little sister go to a carnival that has both a large and a small Ferris wheel. You get on the large Ferris wheel at the same time your sister gets on the small Ferris wheel. The rides begin as soon as you are both buckled into your seats. Determine the number of seconds that will pass before you and your sister are both at the bottom again

A. if the large wheel makes one revolution in 60 seconds and the small wheel makes one revolution in 20 seconds.

B. if the large wheel makes one revolution in 50 seconds and the small wheel makes one revolution in 30 seconds.

C. if the large wheel makes one revolution in 10 seconds and the small wheel makes one revolution in 7 seconds.

■ Problem 4.1 Follow-Up

For parts A–C in Problem 4.1, determine the number of times each Ferris wheel goes around before you and your sister are both on the ground again.

4.2 Looking at Locust Cycles

Cicadas spend most of their lives underground. Some cicadas—commonly called 13-year locusts—come above ground every 13 years, while others—called 17-year locusts—come out every 17 years.

Problem 4.2

Stephan's grandfather told him about a terrible year when the cicadas were so numerous that they ate all the crops on his farm. Stephan conjectured that both 13-year and 17-year locusts came out that year. Assume Stephan's conjecture is correct.

A. How many years pass between the years when both 13-year and 17-year locusts are out at the same time? Explain how you got your answer.

B. Suppose there were 12-year, 14-year, and 16-year locusts, and they all came out this year. How many years will it be before they all come out together again? Explain how you got your answer.

■ **Problem 4.2 Follow-Up**

For parts A and B of Problem 4.2, tell whether the answer is less than, greater than, or equal to the product of the locust cycles.

"BELIEVE ME, THEY'RE NOT EXPECTING US. WE'RE 387-YEAR LOCUSTS."

©1991 by Sidney Harris. From *You Want Proof? I'll Give You Proof!* W.H. Freeman, New York.

Common factors and common multiples can be used to figure out how many people can share things equally.

Problem 4.3

Miriam's uncle donated 120 cans of juice and 90 packs of cheese crackers for the school picnic. Each student is to receive the same number of cans of juice and the same number of packs of crackers.

What is the largest number of students that can come to the picnic and share the food equally? How many cans of juice and how many packs of crackers will each student receive? Explain how you got your answers.

■ Problem 4.3 Follow-Up

If Miriam's uncle eats two packs of crackers before he sends the supplies to the school, what is the largest number of students that can come to the picnic and share the food equally? How many cans of juice and how many packs of crackers will each receive?

As you work on these ACE questions, use your calculator whenever you need it.

Applications

In 1–4, list the common multiples between 1 and 100 for each pair of numbers. Then find the least common multiple for each pair.

1. 8 and 12

2. 3 and 15

3. 7 and 11

4. 9 and 10

In 5–7, find two pairs of numbers with the given number as their least common multiple.

5. 10

6. 36

7. 60

In 8–10, list the common factors for each pair of numbers. Then find the greatest common factor for each pair.

8. 18 and 30

9. 9 and 25

10. 60 and 45

In 11–13, find two pairs of numbers with the given number as their greatest common factor.

11. 8

12. 1

13. 15

Connections

14. Mr. Vicario and his 23 students are planning to have hot dogs at their class picnic. Hot dogs come in packages of 12, and hot dog buns come in packages of 8.

    a. What is the smallest number of packages of hot dogs and the smallest number of packages of buns Mr. Vicario can buy so that everyone including him gets the same number of hot dogs and buns and there are no leftovers? How many hot dogs and buns does each person get?

    b. If the class invites the principal, the secretary, the bus driver, and three parents to help supervise, how many packages of hot dogs and buns will Mr. Vicario need to buy? How many hot dogs and buns will each person get if there are to be no leftovers?

15. The school cafeteria serves pizza every sixth school day and applesauce every eighth school day. If pizza and applesauce are both on today's menu, how many school days will it be before they are both on the menu again?

16. Two neon signs are turned on at the same time. Both signs blink as they are turned on. One sign blinks every 9 seconds. The other sign blinks every 15 seconds. In how many seconds will they blink together again?

Extensions

17. Stephan told his biology teacher his conjecture that the terrible year of the cicadas occurred because 13-year and 17-year locusts came out at the same time. The teacher thought Stephan's conjecture was probably incorrect, because cicadas in a particular area seem to be either all 13-year locusts or all 17-year locusts, but not both. Stephan read about cicadas and found out that they are eaten very quickly by lots of predators. However, the cicadas are only in danger if their cycle occurs at the same time as the cycles of their predators. Stephan suspects that the reason there are 13-year and 17-year locusts but not 12-year, 14-year, or 16-year locusts has to do with predator cycles.

    a. Suppose cicadas have predators with 2-year cycles. How often would 12-year locusts face their predators? Would life be better for 13-year locusts?

    b. Suppose 12-year and 13-year locusts have predators with both 2-year and 3-year cycles. Suppose both kinds of locusts and both kinds of predators came out this year. When would the 12-year locusts again have to face both kinds of predators at the same time? What about the 13-year locusts? Which type of locust do you think is better off?

18. Suppose that in some distant part of the universe there is a star with four orbiting planets. One planet makes a trip around the star in 6 earth years, the second planet takes 9 earth years, the third takes 15 earth years, and the fourth takes 18 earth years. Suppose that at some time the planets are lined up as pictured. This phenomenon is called *conjunction*. How many years will it take before the planets return to this position?

19. Examine the number pattern below. You can use the tiles to help you see a pattern.

1	= 1
1 + 3	= 4
1 + 3 + 5	= 9
1 + 3 + 5 + 7	= 16

1   **1 + 3**   **1 + 3 + 5**

a. Complete the next four rows in the number pattern.

b. What is the sum in row 20?

c. In what row will the sum be 576? What is the last number in the sum in this row? Explain how you got your answers.

20. Examine the pattern below. Using tiles may help you see a pattern.

2	= 2
2 + 4	= 6
2 + 4 + 6	= 12
2 + 4 + 6 + 8	= 20

a. Complete the next four rows in the pattern.

b. What is the sum in row 20?

c. In what row will the sum be 110? What is the last number in the sum in this row? Explain how you got your answers.

21. Ms. Soong has a lot of pens in her desk drawer. She says that if you divide the total number of pens by 2, 3, 4, 5, or 6, you get a remainder of 1. What is the smallest number of pens that could be in Ms. Soong's drawer?

22. What is the mystery number pair?
Clue 1 The greatest common factor of the mystery pair is 7.
Clue 2 The least common multiple of the mystery pair is 70.
Clue 3 Both of the numbers in the mystery pair have two digits.
Clue 4 One of the numbers in the mystery pair is odd and the other is even.

23. While Min Ji was reading through her old journals, she noticed that on March 31, 1993, she had written the date 3-31-93. It looked like a multiplication problem, $3 \times 31 = 93$. Find as many other such dates as you can.

Mathematical Reflections

In this investigation, you used the ideas of common factors and common multiples to help you solve problems. These questions will help you summarize what you have learned:

1 Look at the three problems in this investigation. For which problems was it helpful to find common multiples? For which problems was it helpful to find common factors?

2 Make up a word problem you can solve by finding common factors and a different problem you can solve by finding common multiples. Solve your problems, and explain how you know your answers are correct.

3 Describe how you can find the common factors for two numbers.

4 Describe how you can find the common multiples for two numbers.

Think about your answers to these questions, discuss your ideas with other students and your teacher, and then write a summary of your findings in your journal.

Don't forget to write about your special number!

Factorizations

Some numbers can be written as the product of several different pairs of factors. For example, 100 can be written as 1×100, 2×50, 4×25, 5×20, and 10×10. It is also possible to write 100 as the product of three factors, such as $2 \times 2 \times 25$ and $2 \times 5 \times 10$. Can you find a longer string of factors with a product of 100?

5.1 Searching for Factor Strings

The Product Puzzle on Labsheet 5.1 is a number-search puzzle. Your task is to find strings of numbers with a product of 840.

The Product Puzzle

30	×	14	×	8	×	7	×	210	×
×	2	×	4	×	3	×	2	×	2
105	×	2	×	5	×	84	×	56	×
×	21	×	2	×	7	×	8	×	3
40	×	20	×	4	×	7	×	5	×
×	4	×	28	×	5	×	3	×	2
6	×	8	×	21	×	2	×	105	×
×	2	×	10	×	2	×	5	×	2
32	×	3	×	14	×	60	×	56	×
×	5	×	8	×	15	×	7	×	3

Strings Found in the Product Puzzle

$105 \times 2 \times 4$

_____

_____

_____

_____

_____

_____

_____

_____

_____

_____

_____

Problem 5.1

In the Product Puzzle, find as many factor strings for 840 as you can. A string can go around corners as long as there is a multiplication sign, ×, between any two numbers. When you find a string, draw a loop around it. Keep a record of the strings you find.

■ Problem 5.1 Follow-Up

1. Name two strings with a product of 840 that are not in the puzzle.

2. What is the longest string you found?

3. If possible, name a string with a product of 840 that is longer than any string you found in the puzzle. Do not consider strings that contain 1.

4. How do you know when you have found the longest possible string of factors for a number?

5. How many distinct longest strings of factors are there for a given number? Strings are distinct if they are different in some way other than the order in which the factors are listed. Do not consider strings that contain 1.

Finding the Longest Factor String

The strings of factors for a number are called *factorizations* of the number. When you search for factorizations of large numbers, it helps to keep an orderly record of your steps. One way to do this is to make a *factor tree*.

To find the longest factorization for 100, for example, you might proceed as follows:

Find two factors with a product of 100. Write 100 and then draw two "branches," with the factors at the ends. Here we start three different factor trees using the pairs 2×50, 25×4, and 10×10.

Where possible, break down each of the factors into the product of two factors. Write these factors in a new row of your tree. Draw branches to show how these factors are related to the numbers in the row above. The 2 in the first tree below does not break down any further, so we draw a single branch and repeat the 2 in the next row.

The numbers in the bottom row of the last two trees do not break down any further. These trees are complete. The bottom row of the first tree contains 25, so we complete this tree by breaking 25 into 5×5.

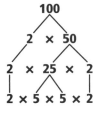

Notice that the bottom row of each tree contains the same factors, although the order of the factors is different. All three trees indicate that the longest factorization for 100 is $2 \times 2 \times 5 \times 5$. Think about why you cannot break this string down any further.

You can use a shortcut to write $2 \times 2 \times 5 \times 5$. In this shortcut notation, the string is written $2^2 \times 5^2$, which is read "2 squared times 5 squared." The small raised numbers are called exponents. An *exponent* tells us how many times the factor is repeated. For example, $2^2 \times 5^4$ means that the 2 is repeated twice and the 5 is repeated four times. So $2^2 \times 5^4$ is the same as $2 \times 2 \times 5 \times 5 \times 5 \times 5$.

Problem 5.2

Work with a partner to find the longest factorization for 600. You may make a factor tree or use another method. When you are finished, compare your results with the results of your classmates.

Did everyone produce the same results? If so, what was is the longest factorization for 600? If not, what differences occurred?

■ Problem 5.2 Follow-Up

1. Find the longest factorizations for 72 and 120.

2. What kinds of numbers are in the longest factor strings for the numbers you found?

3. How do you know that the factor strings you found cannot be broken down any further?

4. Rewrite the factor strings you found for 72, 120, and 600 using shortcut notation.

Using Prime Factorizations

In Investigation 4, you found common multiples and common factors of numbers by comparing lists of their multiples and factors. In this problem, you will explore a method for finding the *greatest common factor* and the *least common multiple* of two numbers by using their prime factorizations.

Heidi says she can find the greatest common factor and the least common multiple of a pair of numbers by using their prime factorizations. The **prime factorization** of a number is a string of factors made up only of primes. Below are the prime factorizations of 24 and 60.

$$24 = 2 \times 2 \times 2 \times 3 \qquad\qquad 60 = 2 \times 2 \times 3 \times 5$$

Heidi claims that the greatest common factor of two numbers is the product of the longest string of prime factors that the numbers have in common. For example, the longest string of factors that 24 and 60 have in common is $2 \times 2 \times 3$.

$$24 = 2 \times \underline{2 \times 2 \times 3} \qquad\qquad 60 = \underline{2 \times 2 \times 3} \times 5$$

According to Heidi's method, the greatest common factor of 24 and 60 is $2 \times 2 \times 3$, or 12.

Heidi claims that the least common multiple of two numbers is the product of the shortest string that contains the prime factorizations of both numbers. The shortest string that contains the prime factorizations of 24 *and* 60 is $2 \times 2 \times 2 \times 3 \times 5$.

Contains the prime factorization of 24   Contains the prime factorization of 60
$\underline{2 \times 2 \times 2 \times 3} \times 5$ $2 \times \underline{2 \times 2 \times 3 \times 5}$

According to Heidi's method, the least common multiple of 24 and 60 is $2 \times 2 \times 2 \times 3 \times 5$, or 120.

Problem 5.3

A. Try using Heidi's methods to find the greatest common factor and least common multiple of 48 and 72 and of 30 and 54.

B. Are Heidi's methods correct? Explain your thinking. If you think Heidi is wrong, revise her methods so they are correct.

Problem 5.3 Follow-Up

1. The greatest common factor of 25 and 12 is 1. Find two other pairs of numbers with a greatest common factor of 1. Such pairs of numbers are said to be **relatively prime.**

2. The least common multiple of 6 and 5 is 30. Find two other pairs of numbers for which the least common multiple is the product of the numbers.

3. Find two pairs of numbers for which the least common multiple is smaller than the product of the two numbers. For example, the product of 6 and 8 is 48; the least common multiple is 24.

4. How you can tell from the prime factorization whether the least common multiple of two numbers is the product of the two numbers or is less than the product of the two numbers? Explain your thinking.

As you work on these ACE questions, use your calculator whenever you need it.

Applications

In 1–6, find the prime factorization of each number.

1. 36   **2.** 180   **3.** 525

4. 165   **5.** 293   **6.** 840

7. Rewrite the prime factorizations you found in problems 1–6 using the shortcut notation described on page 49.

To solve a multiplication maze, you must find a path of numbers from the entrance to the exit so that the product of the numbers in the path equals the puzzle number. No diagonal moves are allowed. Below is the solution of a multiplication maze with puzzle number 840.

Multiplication Maze 840

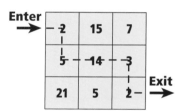

In 8 and 9, solve the multiplication maze. Hint: It may help to find the prime factorization of the puzzle number.

8.

Multiplication Maze 840

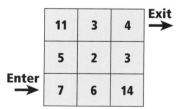

9.

Multiplication Maze 360

2	11	7
15	5	6
3	4	8

Enter →

Exit →

10. Make a multiplication maze with puzzle number 720. Be sure to record your solution.

11. Find all the numbers less than 100 that have only 2s and 5s in their prime factorization. What do your notice about these numbers?

12. Find all the numbers less than 100 that are the product of exactly three different prime numbers.

In 13–15, find the greatest common factor and least common multiple for each pair of numbers.

13. 36 and 45 **14.** 30 and 75 **15.** 78 and 104

Connections

16. The number 1 is not prime. Why do you think mathematicians decided not to call 1 a prime number?

I'M #1! I'M #1!

17. a. Find the multiples of 9 that are less than 100.

b. Find the multiples of 21 that are less than 100.

c. Find the common multiples of 9 and 21 that are less than 100.

d. What would the next common multiple of 9 and 21 be?

18. In a and b, use the year you or one of your family members was born as your number.

a. Find the prime factorization of your number.

b. Write a paragraph describing your number to a friend, giving your friend as much information as you can about the number. Here are some things to include: Is the number square, prime, even, or odd? How many factors does it have? Is it a multiple of some other number?

19. Rosa claims the longest string of factors for 30 is $2 \times 3 \times 5$. Lon claims there is a longer string, $1 \times 2 \times 1 \times 3 \times 1 \times 5$. Who is correct? Why?

20. Hiroshi and Sharlina work on weekends and holidays doing odd jobs at the grocery store. They are paid by the day, not the hour. They each earn the same whole number of dollars per day. Last month Hiroshi earned $184 and Sharlina earned $207. How many days did each person work? What is their daily pay?

21. What is my number?
Clue 1 My number is a multiple of 2 and 7.
Clue 2 My number is less than 100 but larger than 50.
Clue 3 My number is the product of three different primes.

22. What is my number?
Clue 1 My number is a perfect square.
Clue 2 The only prime number in its prime factorization is 2.
Clue 3 My number is a factor of 32.
Clue 4 The sum of its digits is odd.

Extensions

23. Every fourth year is divided into 366 days; these years are called *leap years*. All other years are divided into 365 days. A week has 7 days.

    a. How many weeks are in a year?

    b. January 1, 1992, fell on a Wednesday. On what dates did the next three Wednesdays of 1992 occur?

    c. The year 1992 was a leap year; it had 366 days. What day of the week was January 1, 1993?

    d. What is the pattern, over several years, for the days on which your birthday will fall?

Did you know?

If you were born on any day other than February 29, leap day, it takes at least 5 years for your birthday to come around to the same day of the week. It follows a pattern of 5 years, then 6 years, then 11 years, then 6 years (or some variation of that pattern) to fall on the same day of the week. If you were born on February 29, it takes 28 years for your birthday to fall on the same day of the week!

24. Mr. Barkley has a box of books. He says the number of books in the box is divisible by 2, 3, 4, 5, and 6. How many books could be in the box? Add a clue so that there is only one possible solution.

Mathematical Reflections

In this investigation, you found strings of factors for a number in the Product Puzzle. You learned to make a factor tree to find the prime factorization for a number. You also learned that the prime factorization of a number is the longest string of factors for the number (not including 1 as a factor). These questions will help you summarize what you have learned:

1 Why is finding the prime factorization of a number useful?

2 Describe how you would find the prime factorization of 125.

3 How can you use the prime factorization of two numbers to determine whether they are relatively prime?

4 How can you use the prime factorization of two numbers to find their common multiples?

Think about your answers to these questions, discuss your ideas with other students and your teacher, and then write a summary of your findings in your journal.

Don't forget your special number! What is its prime factorization?

The Locker Problem

You have learned a lot about whole numbers in the first five investigations. In this investigation, you will use what you have learned to solve the Locker Problem. As you explore the problem, look for interesting number patterns.

6.1 Unraveling the Locker Problem

There are 1000 lockers in the long hall of Westfalls High. In preparation for the beginning of school, the janitor cleans the lockers and paints fresh numbers on the locker doors. The lockers are numbered from 1 to 1000. When the 1000 Westfalls High students arrive from summer vacation, they decide to celebrate the beginning of school by working off some energy.

The first student, student 1, runs down the row of lockers and opens every door.

Student 2 closes the doors of lockers 2, 4, 6, 8, and so on to the end of the line.

Student 3 changes the state of the doors of lockers 3, 6, 9, 12, and so on to the end of the line. (The student opens the door if it is closed and closes the door if it is open.)

Student 4 changes the state of the doors of lockers 4, 8, 12, 16, and so on.

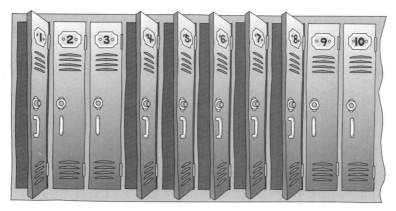

Student 5 changes the state of every fifth door, student 6 changes the state of every sixth door, and so on until all 1000 students have had a turn.

Problem 6.1

When the students are finished, which locker doors are open?

■ Problem 6.1 Follow-Up

1. Work through the problem for the first 50 students. What patterns do you see as the students put their plan into action?
2. Give the numbers of several lockers that were touched by exactly two students.
3. Give the numbers of several lockers that were touched by exactly three students.
4. Give the numbers of several lockers that were touched by exactly four students.
5. Which was the first locker touched by both student 6 and student 8?
6. Which of the students touched both locker 24 and locker 36?
7. Which students touched both locker 100 and locker 120?
8. Which was the first locker touched by both student 100 and student 120?

As you work on these ACE questions, use your calculator whenever you need it.

Applications

1. What is the first prime number greater than 50?

2. Ivan said that if a number ends in 0, both 2 and 5 are factors of the number. Is he correct? Why?

3. Prime numbers that differ by 2, such as 3 and 5, are called *twin primes*. Find five pairs of twin primes that are greater than 10.

4. What is my number?
   Clue 1 My number is a multiple of 5 and is less than 50.
   Clue 2 My number is between a pair of twin primes.
   Clue 3 My number has exactly 4 factors.

5. What is my number?
   Clue 1 My number is a multiple of 5, but it does not end in 5.
   Clue 2 The prime factorization of my number is a string of three numbers.
   Clue 3 Two of the numbers in the prime factorization are the same.
   Clue 4 My number is bigger than the seventh square number.

6. Now it's your turn! Make up a set of clues for a mystery number. You might want to use your special number as the mystery number. Include as many ideas from this unit as you can. Try out your mystery number on a classmate.

7. **a.** Find all the numbers between 1 and 1000 that have 2 as their only prime factor.

   b. What is the next number after 1000 that has 2 as its only prime factor?

8. The numbers 2 and 3 are prime, consecutive numbers. Are there other such pairs of *adjacent primes?* Why or why not?

Connections

In 9 and 10, describe the numbers that have both of the given numbers as factors.

9. 2 and 3   **10.** 3 and 5

11. If you find the factors of a number by starting with 1 and finding every factor pair, you will eventually find that the factors start to repeat. For example, if you used this method to find the factors of 12, you would find that, after checking 3, you get no new factors.

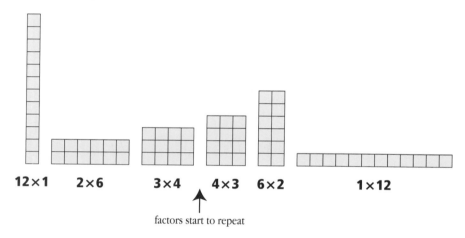

factors start to repeat

For a given number, how do you determine the largest number you need to check to make sure you have found all the factors?

Hint: It may help to first determine the answer for one or two small numbers. For example, you could look at 12 and 16. How would you know, without checking every number, that you will find no new factor pairs for 12 after checking 3? How would you know, without checking every number, that you will find no new factor pairs for 16 after checking 4? It may help to look at the rectangles you made for these numbers.

12. Which group of numbers—evens or odds—contains more prime numbers? Why?

13. Based on what you found out in the Locker Problem, make a conjecture about the number of factors for square numbers. Test this conjecture on all of the square numbers from 1 to 1000.

14. Goldbach's Conjecture is a famous conjecture that has never been proven true or false. The conjecture states that every even number, except 2, can be written as the sum of two prime numbers. For example, 16 can be written as 5 + 11, which are both prime numbers.

   a. Write the first six even numbers larger than 2 as the sum of two prime numbers.

   b. Write 100 as the sum of two primes.

   c. The number 2 is a prime number. Can an even number larger than 4 be written as the sum of two prime numbers if you use 2 as one of the primes? Why or why not?

Extensions

15. Can you find a number less than 200 that is divisible by four different prime numbers? Why or why not?

16. In question 3, you listed five pairs of twin primes. Starting with the twin primes 5 and 7, look carefully at the numbers between twin primes. What do they have in common? Why?

17. Adrianne had trouble finding all the factors of a number. If the number was small enough, such as 8, she had no problem. But with a larger number, such as 120, she was never sure she had found all the factors. Albert told Adrianne that he had discovered a method for finding all the factors of a number by using its prime factorization. Try to discover a method for finding all the factors of a number using its prime factorization. Use your method to find all the factors of 36 and 480.

18. If a number has 2 and 6 as factors, what other numbers must be factors of the number? What is the smallest this number can be? Explain your answers.

19. If a number is a multiple of 12, what other numbers is it a multiple of? Explain your answer.

20. If 10 and 6 are common factors of two numbers, what other factors must the numbers have in common? Explain your answer.

Mathematical Reflections

In this investigation, you solved a problem about open and closed lockers. Then you analyzed relationships among the lockers and the students who touched those lockers. These questions will help you summarize what you have learned:

1 Were lockers with prime numbers open or closed at the end? Explain your answer.

2 Which lockers were open at the end? Why were they open?

3 If factors come in pairs, how can a number have an odd number of factors?

4 Write a problem about students and lockers that can be solved by finding a common multiple.

Think about your answers to these questions, discuss your ideas with other students and your teacher, and then write a summary of your findings in your journal.

Don't forget your special number. What new things can you say about your number?

The Unit Project

My Special Number

At the beginning of this unit, you chose a special number and wrote several things about it in your journal. As you worked through the investigations, you used the concepts you learned to write new things about your number.

Now it is time for you to show off your special number. Write a story, compose a poem, create a poster, or find some other way to highlight your number. Your teacher will use your project to determine how well you understand the concepts in this unit, so be sure to include all the things you have learned while working through the investigations. You may want to start by looking back through your journal to find the things you wrote after each investigation. In your project, be sure you use all the vocabulary your teacher has asked you to record in your journal for *Prime Time*.

Looking Back and Looking Ahead

Unit Reflections

While working on the problems in this unit, you investigated some important properties of whole numbers. Finding *factors* and *multiples* of numbers and identifying *prime numbers* helped in answering questions about clocks and calendars, puzzles and games, and rectangular patterns of tiles. Factoring also focused attention on the properties of *even* and *odd* numbers, *square* numbers, *greatest common factors*, and *least common multiples*.

Using Your Understanding of Numbers— Test your understanding of factors, multiples, and prime numbers on these problems where number patterns are the keys to solutions.

1 *The Mystate University marching band consists of 60 members. The band director wants to arrange the band into a rectangular array for the half-time activities.*

    a. How many ways can she arrange the band? Make a sketch of each arrangement.

    b. How many rectangular arrangements are possible if the band adds one member and becomes a 61-member band?

2 *The Red Top Taxi company wants to keep its cars in good operating condition, so it has a schedule for regular maintenance checks on each car. Oil is to be changed once every 6 weeks, and brakes are to be inspected and repaired every 10 weeks.*

    a. When a new cab is put in service, is there ever a week when that cab is scheduled for both an oil change and a brake inspection? If so, what is the first such time?

    b. If the oil change time is extended to 8 weeks and the brake inspection to 12 weeks, is there ever a week when the cab is due for both oil change and brake inspection? If so, when will such a coincidence occur?

3 *The prime factorization of Meredith's special number is $2 \times 2 \times 3 \times 11$ and the prime factorization of Elizabeth's special number is $3 \times 3 \times 5 \times 5$.*

    a. What is the least common multiple of the two special numbers?

    b. What is the greatest common factor of the two special numbers?

c. List all the factors of Meredith's special number.

d. Is Meredith's special number even or odd? How about Elizabeth's special number?

e. Is Meredith's special number a square number? Elizabeth's?

4 *Andrea gave three clues for her secret number.*

> *Clue 1: My number is a factor of 90.*

Can you tell what Andrea's secret number is?

a. What is the smallest Andrea's number can be? What is the largest her number can be?

b. Brandon says the secret number must also be a factor of 180. Is he correct?

> *Clue 2: My number is prime.*

c. Now can you tell what the secret number is?

> *Clue 3. Twenty-one is a multiple of my secret number.*

d. Now can you tell what the secret number is?

Explaining Your Reasoning— To answer Problems 1–4 you had to use knowledge of factors and multiples of a number.

1. What strategies can be used to find

    a. all the factors of a number?   **b.** the least common multiple of two numbers?

    c. the greatest common factor of two numbers?

2. How you can you decide whether a number is a(n)

    a. prime number?   **b.** square number?

    c. even number?   **d.** odd number?

3. Which of the following statements are *always true*, which are *never true*, and which are *sometimes true*. Explain your reasoning.

    a. If a number is greater than a second number, then the first number has more factors than the second number.

    b. The sum of two odd numbers is even.

    c. The product of an even number and an odd number is odd.

    d. The least common multiple of two different prime numbers is their product.

    e. The greatest common factor of two numbers is less than either of those numbers.

You will use ideas about factors, multiples, and primes in many future units, especially those that deal with properties of other numbers like fractions and decimals.

Glossary

abundant number A number with proper factors that add to more than the number. For example, 24 is an abundant number because its proper factors, 1, 2, 3, 4, 6, 8, and 12, add to 36.

common factor A factor that two or more numbers share. For example, 7 is a common factor of 14 and 35 because 7 is a factor of 14 ($14 = 7 \times 2$) and 7 is a factor of 35 ($35 = 7 \times 5$).

common multiple A multiple that two or more numbers share. For example, the first few multiples of 5 are 5, 10, 15, 20, 25, 30, 35, 40, 45, 50, 55, 60, 65, and 70. The first few multiples of 7 are 7, 14, 21, 28, 35, 42, 49, 56, 63, 70, 77, 84, and 91. From these lists we can see that two common multiples of 5 and 7 are 35 and 70.

composite number A whole number with factors other than itself and 1 (i.e., a whole number that is not prime). Some composite numbers are 6, 12, 20, and 1001.

deficient number A number with proper factors that add to less than the number. For example, 14 is a deficient number because its proper factors, 1, 2, and 7, add to 10. All prime numbers are deficient.

dimensions The dimensions of a rectangle are its length and its width. For example, the rectangle below has width 3 and length 5. We can refer to this rectangle as a 3×5 rectangle.

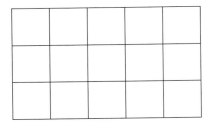

divisor A factor. For example, 5 is a factor of 20 because $5 \times 4 = 20$. And 5 is a divisor of 20 because the division $20 \div 5$ does not have a remainder. Any number that is a factor is also a divisor.

even number A multiple of 2. When you divide and even number by 2, the remainder is zero. Examples of even numbers are 2, 4, 6, 8, and 10.

factor One of two or more numbers that are multiplied to get a product. For example, 13 and 4 are both factors of 52 because $13 \times 4 = 52$.

Fundamental Theorem of Arithmetic The theory stating that, except for the order of the factors, a whole number can be factored into prime factors in only one way.

multiple The product of a given whole number and another whole number. For example, the first four multiples of 3 are 3, which is 3×1; 6, which is 3×2; 9, which is 3×3; and 12, which is 3×4. Note that if a number is a multiple of 3, then 3 is a factor of the number. For example, 12 is a multiple of 3, and 3 is a factor of 12.

near-perfect number A number with proper factors that add to 1 less than the number. All powers of 2 are near-perfect number. For example, 32 is a near-perfect number because its proper factors, 1, 2, 4, 8, and 16, add to 31.

odd number A whole number that is not a multiple of 2. When an odd number is divided by 2, the remainder is 1. Examples of odd numbers are 1, 3, 5, 7, and 9.

perfect number A number with proper factors that add to exactly the number. For example, 6 is a perfect number because its proper factors, 1, 2, and 3, add to 6.

prime factorization The longest factor string for a number, composed entirely of prime numbers. For example, the prime factorization of 1001 is $7 \times 11 \times 13$. The prime factorization of a number is unique except for the order of the factors.

prime number A number with only two factors, 1 and the number itself. Examples of primes are 11, 17, 53, and 101.

proper factors All the factors of a number, except the number itself. For example, the proper factors of 16 are 1, 2, 4, and 8.

relatively prime numbers Numbers with no common factors except for 1. For example, 20 and 33 are relatively prime because the factors of 20 are 1, 2, 4, 5, and 10, and 20, while the factors of 33 are 1, 3, 11, and 33. Notice that neither 20 nor 33 is itself a prime number.

square number The product of a number with itself. Examples of a square numbers are 9, 25, and 81. A square number of square tiles can be arranged to form a square.

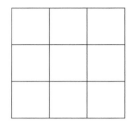

Venn diagram A diagram in which overlapping circles are used to show relationships among sets of objects that have certain attributes.

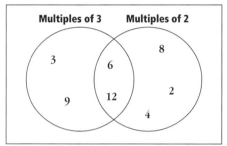
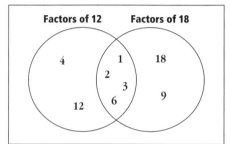

Index

Abundant number, 14
Adjacent primes, 61
Algebra, Fundamental Theorem of, 56
Arithmetic, Fundamental Theorem of, 56

Calculus, Fundamental Theorem of, 56
Classifying numbers, 20–21
Common factor, 24, 36–39
   ACE, 40–44, 63
Common multiple, 23, 36–39
   ACE, 40–44
Composite number, 4, 10
Conjecture, 28–29
Consecutive numbers, 32–33
Cray Research, 11
Cycle, 36–38

Deficient number, 14
Divisibility, 20–21
   ACE, 22–24, 31–33
Divisor, 6, 24

Even number, 4, 28–29
   ACE, 30–33
Exponent, 49
Exponential notation, 49

Factor, 4, 6, 17, 18, 20–21
   ACE, 12–14, 22–24, 30–33, 40–44,
   61–63
   common, 24, 36–39
   greatest common, 36–39
   pairs, 26–29
   patterns, 27–28
   proper, 7

   square number, 4, 28
   string, 4, 46–51
Factor Game, 4
   ACE, 12–14
   playing, 6
   rules, 7
   sample game, 8–9
   strategy, 10
Factorization, 46–51
   ACE, 52–55
   exponents and, 49
   factor tree and, 48–49
   prime, 50–51
Factor string, 4, 46–51
Factor tree, 48–49
Fundamental theorem, 56
Fundamental Theorem of Algebra, 56
Fundamental Theorem of Arithmetic, 56
Fundamental Theorem of Calculus, 56

Goldbach's Conjecture, 63
Greatest common factor (GCF), 4,
   36–39, 50–51
   ACE, 40–43

Investigations
   Common Factors and Multiples, 36–45
   Factorizations, 46–57
   Factor Pairs, 26–35
   The Factor Game, 6–16
   The Locker Problem, 58–64
   The Product Game, 17–25

Journal, 5, 16, 25, 35, 45, 57, 64, 65

Least common multiple (LCM), 4,
  36–39, 50–51
  ACE, 40–43
Looking Back and Looking Ahead:
  Unit Reflections, 66–67

Mathematical Highlights, 4
Mathematical Reflections, 16, 25, 35, 45,
  57, 64
Multiple, 4, 18, 20–21, 36–39
  ACE, 22–24, 32, 40–44
  common, 23, 36–39
  least common, 36–39, 50–51

Near–perfect number, 14
Number
  abundant, 14
  classifying, 20–21
  composite, 4, 10
  consecutive, 32–33
  deficient, 14
  even, 4, 28–29
  near-perfect, 14
  odd, 4, 28–29
  perfect, 14, 15
  prime, 4, 10, 48–49, 61
  rectangular, 26–29
  relatively prime, 51
  square, 4, 28

Odd number, 4, 28–29
  ACE, 30–33

Patterns, factor, 27–28
Perfect number, 14, 15
Prime factorization, 50–51
Prime number, 4, 10

ACE, 12–14, 61–63
  adjacent primes, 61
  factor tree, 48–49
  large, 11
  relatively prime, 51
  twin primes, 61
Product Game, 4
  ACE, 22–24
  designing, 19
  playing, 17–18
  rules, 18
Product Puzzle, 4, 46–47
Proper factor, 7

Rectangular numbers, 26–29
  ACE, 30–33
Relatively prime numbers, 51

Slowinski, David, 11
Square number, 4, 28

Time, 2–3
  day, 13
  hour, 24
  leap year, 55
  year, 55
Tree diagram, 48–49
Twin primes, 61
  ACE, 63

Unit Project, 5, 65

Venn diagram, 20–21
  ACE, 23

Whole number divisor, 6
Whole number factor, 6

Connected Mathematics™

Data About Us

Statistics

Student Edition

Glenda Lappan
James T. Fey
William M. Fitzgerald
Susan N. Friel
Elizabeth Difanis Phillips

Prentice
Hall

Glenview, Illinois
Needham, Massachusetts
Upper Saddle River, New Jersey

The Connected Mathematics Project was developed at Michigan State University with the support of National Science Foundation Grant No. MDR 9150217.

This project was supported, in part,
by the
National Science Foundation
Opinions expressed are those of the authors
and not necessarily those of the Foundation

The Michigan State University authors and administration have agreed that all MSU royalties arising from this publication will be devoted to purposes supported by the Department of Mathematics and the MSU Mathematics Education Enrichment Fund.

Contents

Mathematical Highlights 4

The Unit Project: Is Anyone Typical? 5

Investigation 1: Looking at Data 6
  1.1 Organizing Your Data 6
  1.2 Interpreting Graphs 7
  1.3 Identifying the Mode and Range 9
  1.4 Identifying the Median 11
  1.5 Experimenting with the Median 13
  Applications—Connections—Extensions 15
  Mathematical Reflections 21

Investigation 2: Types of Data 22
  2.1 Category and Number Questions 22
  2.2 Counting Pets 23
  Applications—Connections—Extensions 26
  Mathematical Reflections 29

Investigation 3: Using Graphs to Group Data 30
  3.1 Traveling to School 30
  3.2 Jumping Rope 34
  Applications—Connections—Extensions 37
  Mathematical Reflections 41

Investigation 4: Coordinate Graphs 42
  4.1 Relating Height to Arm Span 42
  4.2 Relating Travel Time to Distance 45
  Applications—Connections—Extensions 47
  Mathematical Reflections 52

Investigation 5: What Do We Mean by *Mean?* 53
  5.1 Evening Things Out 54
  5.2 Finding the Mean 57
  5.3 Data with the Same Mean 58
  5.4 Using Your Class's Data 59
  5.5 Watching Movies 60
  Applications—Connections—Extensions 62
  Mathematical Reflections 67

The Unit Project: Is Anyone Typical? 68

Looking Back and Looking Ahead: Unit Reflections 69

Glossary 71

Index 76

Data About Us

What kinds of information would you like to know about students in your class?

What do we mean when we talk about a "typical" student at your grade level or in your school?

What things could you find out by comparing information about your class with information about other groups of students?

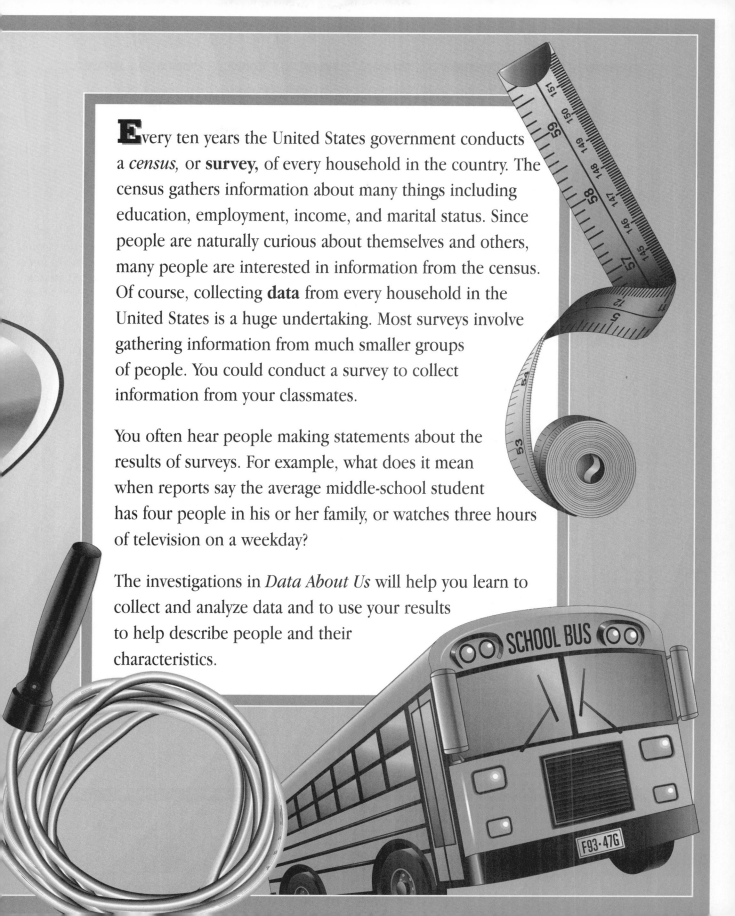

Every ten years the United States government conducts a *census,* or **survey,** of every household in the country. The census gathers information about many things including education, employment, income, and marital status. Since people are naturally curious about themselves and others, many people are interested in information from the census. Of course, collecting **data** from every household in the United States is a huge undertaking. Most surveys involve gathering information from much smaller groups of people. You could conduct a survey to collect information from your classmates.

You often hear people making statements about the results of surveys. For example, what does it mean when reports say the average middle-school student has four people in his or her family, or watches three hours of television on a weekday?

The investigations in *Data About Us* will help you learn to collect and analyze data and to use your results to help describe people and their characteristics.

Mathematical Highlights

In *Data About Us*, you will explore ways of collecting and analyzing data. This unit will help you to

● Understand and use the process of data investigation by posing questions, collecting data, analyzing data, and making interpretations to answer your questions;

● Represent data using line plots, bar graphs, stem-and-leaf plots, and coordinate graphs;

● Compute the mean, median, or mode and the range of a data set;

● Understand the distinctions between categorical data and numerical data and identify which graphs and statistics may be used to represent each kind of data;

● Make informed choices about which graph or graphs and which of the averages (mean, median, mode) and range may be used to describe a data set; and

● Develop strategies for comparing data sets.

As you work on the problems in this unit, ask questions about situations that involve data analysis: *What is the question being asked? How do I want to organize the data set? Which representation is best to use to analyze the data? Do I want to determine an average or the range of the data? If so, which average do I want to use and what will it tell me about the data set? How can I use graphs and statistics to describe a data set or to compare two data sets in order to answer my original question?*

Is Anyone Typical?

What are the characteristics of a typical middle-school student? Who would be interested in knowing these characteristics? Does a typical middle-school student really exist? As you proceed through this unit, you will identify some "typical" facts about your classmates, such as these:

- The typical number of letters in a student's full name
- The typical number of people in a student's household
- The typical height of a student

When you have completed the investigations in *Data About Us,* you will carry out a statistical investigation to answer this question: What are some of the characteristics of a typical middle-school student? These characteristics may include

- physical characteristics (for example, age, height, or eye color)
- family and home characteristics (for example, number of brothers and sisters or number of television sets)
- miscellaneous behaviors (for example, hobbies or number of hours spent watching television)
- preferences, opinions, or attitudes (for example, favorite musical group, or opinions about who should be elected class president)

Keep in mind that a statistical investigation involves posing questions, collecting data, analyzing data, and interpreting the results of the analysis. As you work through each investigation, think about how you might use what you are learning to help you with your project.

Looking at Data

The problems in this investigation involve people's names. Names are filled with symbolism and history. Because family traditions are often involved when a child is named, a person's name may reveal information about his or her ancestors.

Many people have interesting stories about how they were named. Here is one student's story of how her name was chosen: "I'm a twin, and my mom and dad didn't know they were going to have twins. My sister was born first, and she was named Susan. I was a surprise. My mom named me after the woman in the next hospital bed, whose name was Barbara."

Compare stories with your classmates about how you, or someone you know, were named.

1.1 Organizing Your Data

Most parents spend little time worrying about the number of letters in the names they choose for their children. Yet there are times that name length matters. For example, there is sometimes a limit to the number of letters that will fit on a friendship bracelet or a library card.

Did you know?

The longest name appearing on a birth certificate is Rhoshandiatellyneshiaunneveshenk Koyaanfsquatsiuty Williams.

Shortly after Rhoshandiatellyneshiaunneveshenk was born, her father filed an amendment that expanded her first name to 1019 letters and her middle name to 36 letters. Can you think of a good nickname for her?

Source: *Guinness Book of World Records*

What do you think is the typical number of letters in the full names (first and last names) of students in your class?

Problem 1.1

Gather data about the total number of letters in the first and last names of students in your class.

A. Find a way to organize the data so you can determine the typical name length.

B. Write some statements about your class data. Note any patterns you see.

C. What would you say is the typical name length for a student in your class?

D. If a new student joined your class today, what would you predict about the length of that student's name?

■ **Problem 1.1 Follow-Up**

Do you think the length of your name is typical for a student in your class? Explain why or why not.

1.2 Interpreting Graphs

A group of students in Ms. Jeckle's class made a **line plot** to display their class's name-length data.

Name Lengths of Ms. Jeckle's Students

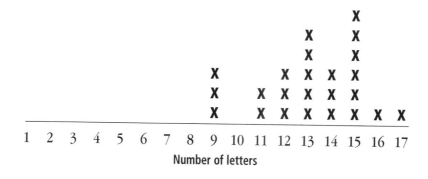

Another group displayed the same data in a bar graph.

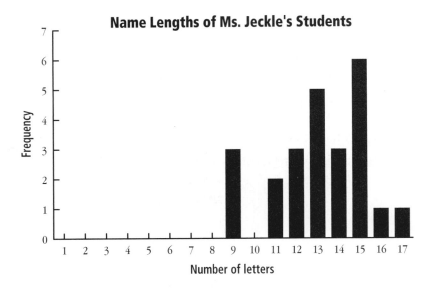

Name Lengths of Ms. Jeckle's Students

Problem 1.2

Examine the line plot and the **bar graph**.

A. Write some statements about the name lengths for students in Ms. Jeckle's class. Describe any interesting patterns you see in the data.

B. In what ways are the two graphs alike? In what ways are they different?

C. How does the data from Ms. Jeckle's class compare with the data from your class?

■ **Problem 1.2 Follow-Up**

1. How can you use each graph to determine the total number of letters in all the names?

2. Fahimeh Ghomizadeh said, "I have the most letters in my name, but the bar that indicates the number of letters in my name is one of the shortest. Why?" How would you answer this question?

3. Suppose a new student named Nicole Martin joined Ms. Jeckle's class. How could you change the graphs to include data for Nicole?

1.3 Identifying the Mode and Range

One way to describe what is typical, or average, about a set of data is to give the value that occurs most frequently. For example, in the data for Ms. Jeckle's class, the name length 15 occurs most frequently. Six students have 15 letters in their names. Notice that 15 has the highest stack of X's in the line plot and the tallest bar in the bar graph. We call the value that occurs most frequently the **mode** of the data set.

When describing a data set, it is also helpful to give the lowest value and the highest value that occur. The spread of data values from the lowest value to the highest value is called the **range** of the data. In Ms. Jeckle's class, the range of name lengths is from 9 letters to 17 letters.

Think about this!

What are the mode and range of the name-length data for your class? How do the mode and range for your class compare with the mode and range for Ms. Jeckle's class?

Problem 1.3

There are 15 students in a class. The mode of the name lengths for the class is 12 letters, and the range is from 8 letters to 16 letters.

A. Determine a set of name lengths that has this range and mode.

B. Make a line plot to display your data.

C. Use your line plot to help you describe the shape of your data. For example, your data may be bell-shaped, spread out in two or more clusters, or grouped together at one end of the graph.

■ Problem 1.3 Follow-Up

Compare your graph with the graphs some of your classmates drew. How are the graphs alike? How are they different?

Did you know?

Here are some interesting facts about family names.

• It wasn't until the 1800s that countries in eastern Europe and Scandinavia insisted that people adopt permanent family names.

• The most common family name in the world is Chang. An estimated 100 million Chinese people have this name.

• The most common name in the United States, Canada, and the United Kingdom is Smith. There are approximately 2.3 million Smiths in the United States alone.

• There are over 1.6 million different family names in the United States.

Identifying the Median

You have learned that one way to describe what is typical about a set of data is to give the value that occurs most frequently (the mode). Another way to describe what is typical is to give the middle value of the data set.

The table and line plot below show name-length data for a middle-school class in Michigan. Notice that these data have two modes, 11 and 12. The range of the data is from 8 letters to 19 letters.

Name	Letters
Jeffrey Piersonjones	19
Thomas Petes	11
Clarence Surless	15
Michelle Hughes	14
Shoshana White	13
Deborah Locke	12
Terry Van Bourgondien	19
Maxi Swanson	11
Tonya Stewart	12
Jorge Bastante	13
Richard Mudd	11
Joachim Caruso	13
Roberta Northcott	16
Tony Tung	8
Joshua Klein	11
Janice Vick	10
Bobby King	9
Jacquelyn McCallum	17
Kathleen Boylan	14
Peter Juliano	12
Linora Haynes	12

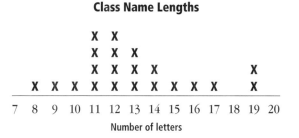

Problem 1.4

Cut a strip of 21 squares from a sheet of grid paper. Write the Michigan class's name lengths in order from smallest to largest on the grid paper as shown here.

Now, put the ends together and fold the strip in half.

A. Where does the crease land? How many numbers are to the left of the crease? How many numbers are to the right of the crease?

Suppose a new student, Suzanne Mannerstrale, joins the Michigan class. The class now has 22 students. On a strip of 22 squares, list the name lengths, including Suzanne's, in order from smallest to largest. Fold this strip in half.

B. Where is the crease? How many numbers are to the left of the crease? How many numbers are to the right of the crease?

■ Problem 1.4 Follow-Up

The first strip of paper had 21 data values. When you folded the strip, the crease was on the number 12. There were ten values to the left of 12 and ten values to the right of 12. We say that 12 is the *median* of the data set. The **median** of a data set is the value that divides the data in half—half of the values are below the median, and half the values are above the median.

The second strip you made had 22 values. When you folded this strip, the crease landed between 12 and 13. There were eleven values to the left of the crease and eleven values to the right of the crease. When a data set has an even number of values, the median is the value halfway between the two middle values. For this data set, the median is $12\frac{1}{2}$, the number halfway between 12 and 13.

Giving the median of a set of data is one way to describe what is typical about the data. Like the mode, the median is a type of *average*. The median and the mode are sometimes referred to as *measures of center*. You can see that this is a very appropriate description for the median, since it *is* the center of the data.

1. Find the median name length for your class.
2. Use the median, mode, and range to describe what is typical about your class's data.
3. Suppose a student named Chamique Holdsclaw joins your class. Add Chamique's name to your class data, and find the new median. How does the median change?

1.5 Experimenting with the Median

What happens to the median when you add values to or remove values from a set of data? Does adding a value that is much larger or much smaller than the rest of the data values have a greater effect on the median than adding a value that is closer to the other values?

Write each of the names listed below on an index card. On the back of each card, write the number of letters in the name.

Name	Letters
Thomas Petes	11
Michelle Hughes	14
Shoshana White	13
Deborah Locke	12
Tonya Stewart	12
Richard Mudd	11
Tony Tung	8
Janice Vick	10
Bobby King	9
Kathleen Boylan	14

front

back

Order the cards from shortest name to longest name, and find the median of the data.

Experiment with your cards to see if you can perform each task described below. Keep a record of the things you try and the discoveries you make.

A. Remove two names without changing the median.

B. Remove two names so the median increases.

C. Remove two names so the median decreases.

D. Add two new names so the median increases.

E. Add two new names so the median decreases.

F. Add two new names without changing the median.

■ Problem 1.5 Follow-Up

1. If a name with 16 letters were added to the data, what would the new median be?

2. If a name with 1019 letters were added to the data, what would the new median be?

Did you know?

Names from many parts of the world have special origins. European family names were often based on the father's first name. For example, Ian Robertson was the son of Robert, and Janos Ivanovich was the son (vich) of Ivan. Sometimes, the father's first name was used "as is" or with an "s" added to the end. For example, John Peters was the son of Peter, and Henry James was the son of James. Surnames were also created from words that told where a person lived, what a person did, or described personal characteristics. This resulted in names like William Hill, Geoffrey Marsh, Sean Forest, Gilbert Baker, James Tailor, and Kyle Butcher.

Surnames in China and Vietnam often have a long history and are almost always one-syllable words related to names of ruling families. Chang—a name mentioned earlier—is one such example.

Jewish names are sometimes made up of abbreviations that combine a number of words: Katz comes from *kohen tzedek* (righteous priest), and Schatz from *shalian tzibur* (representative of the congregation).

You can read more about names in books such as *Names from Africa* by O. Chuks-orji and *Do People Grow on Family Trees?* by Ira Wolfman.

As you work on these ACE questions, use your calculator whenever you need it.

Applications

For 1 and 2, use the names listed below.

Ben Carter
Ava Baker
Sarah Edwards
Juan Norinda
Ron Weaver
Bryan Wong
Toby Vanhook
Katrina Roberson
Rosita Ramirez
Kimberly Pace
Paula Wheeler
Darnell Cox
Jessica Otto
Erin Froyeh
Corey Buysse
Tijuana Degraffenreid

1. Make a table showing the length of each name. Then make both a line plot and a bar graph of the name lengths.

2. What is the typical name length for this class of students? Use the mode, median, and range to help you answer this question.

In 3–6, use the bar graph below.

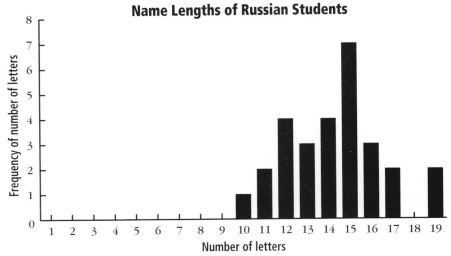

Name Lengths of Russian Students

3. Which value (name length) occurs most frequently? What do we call this value?

4. How many students are in this class? Explain how you got your answer.

5. What is the range of name lengths for this class?

6. What is the median name length? Explain how you got your answer.

For 7–10, make a line plot or bar graph of a set of data that fits the description.

7. 24 names, with a range from 8 letters to 20 letters

8. 7 names, with a median length of 14 letters

9. 13 names, with a range from 8 letters to 17 letters and a median of 13 letters

10. 16 names, with a median of $14\frac{1}{2}$ letters and a range from 11 letters to 20 letters

Connections

In 11–14, use the bar graphs on page 17, which show information about a class of middle-school students.

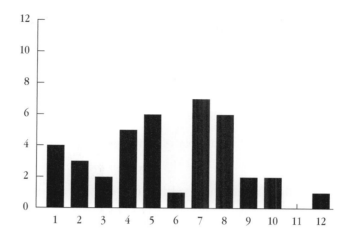

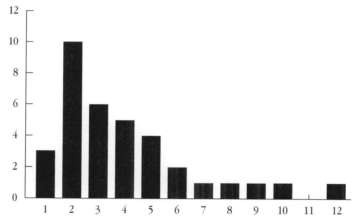

Graph C

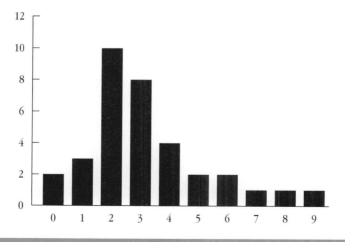

11. Which graph might show the number of children in the students' families? Explain your choice.

12. Which graph might show the birth months of the students? (Hint: Months are often written using numbers instead of names. For example, 1 means January, 2 means February, and 3 means March.) Explain your choice.

13. Which graph might show the number of toppings students like on their pizzas? Explain your choice.

14. Give a possible title, a label for the vertical axis, and a label for the horizontal axis for each graph based on your answers to 11–13.

Extensions

In 15–21, use the table and bar graphs below. A greeting card store sells stickers and street signs with first names on them. The store ordered 12 packages of stickers and 12 street signs for each name. The four bar graphs show the numbers of sticker packages and street signs that remain for the names that begin with the letter A.

Name	Stickers remaining	Street signs remaining
Aaron	1	9
Adam	2	7
Alice	7	4
Allison	2	3
Amanda	0	11
Amber	2	3
Amy	3	3
Andrea	2	4
Andrew	8	6
Andy	3	5
Angela	8	4
Ann	10	7

Graph A:
Stickers Remaining

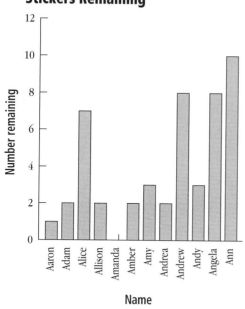

Graph B:
Street Signs Remaining

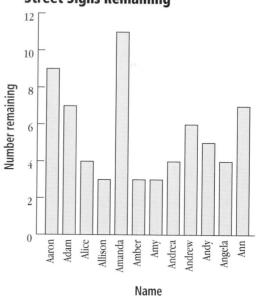

Graph C:
Stickers and Street Signs Remaining

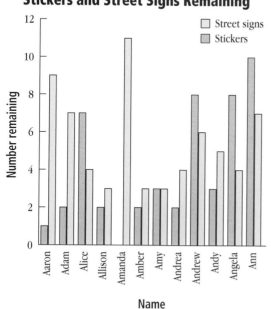

Graph D:
Stickers and Street Signs Remaining

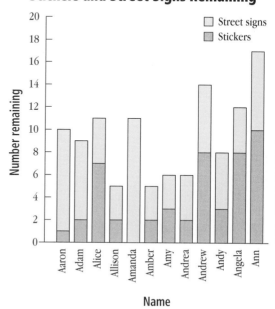

15. In "Graph A" locate the bar that shows the number of stickers left for the name Alice. Explain how you can determine how many stickers are left by reading the graph. Explain how you can determine how many stickers have been sold.

16. In "Graph B" locate the bar that shows the number of street signs left for the name Alice. Explain how you can determine how many street signs are left by reading the graph. Explain how you can determine how many street signs have been sold.

17. Are the stickers more popular than the street signs? Explain your answer.

18. If each package of stickers costs $1.50, how much money has the store made from selling name stickers for names beginning with A?

19. For which name have the most stickers been sold? For which name have the fewest stickers been sold?

20. "Graph C" is a *double bar graph*. Use this graph to determine the name(s) for which the number of street signs sold and the number of sticker packages sold are the same.

21. "Graph D" is a *stacked bar graph*. Use this graph to determine whether some names are more popular than others. Justify your answer.

Mathematical Reflections

In this investigation, you learned some ways to describe what is typical about a set of data. The following questions will help you summarize what you have learned:

1 How are a table of data, a line plot, and a bar graph alike? How are they different?

2 What does the mode tell you about a set of data?

3 What does the median tell you about a set of data?

4 Can the mode and the median for a data set be the same? Can they be different? Explain your answers.

5 Why is it helpful to give the range when you describe a set of data?

6 What does it mean to describe the shape of the data?

7 How can you describe what is typical about a set of data?

Think about your answers to these questions, discuss your ideas with other students and your teacher, and then write a summary of your findings in your journal.

At the end of this unit, you will be developing a survey to gather information about middle-school students. Think of a question or two you might ask. How would you display the information you might gather about each of these questions? Write your thoughts in your journal.

Types of Data

When we are interested in finding out more about something, we start asking questions about it. Some questions have answers that are words or categories, for example, What is your favorite sport? Other questions have answers that are numbers, for example, How many inches tall are you?

Read each of the questions below. Which questions have words or categories as answers? Which questions have numbers as answers?

- In what month were you born?
- What kinds of pets do you have?
- How many pets do you have?
- Who is your favorite author?
- How much time do you spend watching television in a day?
- What's your highest score in the game Yahtzee?
- What color are your eyes?
- How many movies have you watched in the last week?
- How do you get to school?

2.1 Category and Number Questions

The data you collect in response to a question you ask may be numbers or words.

Data that are words or categories are called **categorical data.** Categorical data are usually not numbers. If you asked people in which month they were born or what kinds of pets they have, their answers would be categorical data.

Data that are numbers are called **numerical data.** If you asked people how tall they are or how many pets they have, their responses would be numerical data.

Problem 2.1

Think of some things you would like to know more about. Then, develop some questions you could ask to gather information about those things.

A. Write two questions that have categorical data as answers.

B. Write two questions that have numerical data as answers.

■ **Problem 2.1 Follow-Up**

Is it possible to find the mode of a set of categorical data? Explain your answer.

2.2 Counting Pets

The pets people have often depend on where they live. People who live in cities often have small pets, while people who live on farms often have large pets. People who live in apartments are sometimes not permitted to have pets at all.

It is fun to find out what kinds of pets people have. One middle-school class gathered data about their pets by tallying students' responses to these questions:

What is your favorite kind of pet?

How many pets do you have?

The students' questions produced two kinds of data. When students told what their favorite pets were, their responses were categorical data. When students told how many pets they had, their responses were numerical data.

The students made tables to show the tallies or frequencies, and then made bar graphs to display the data.

Favorite Kinds of Pets

Pet	Frequency
cat	4
dog	7
fish	2
bird	2
horse	3
goat	1
cow	2
rabbit	3
duck	1
pig	1

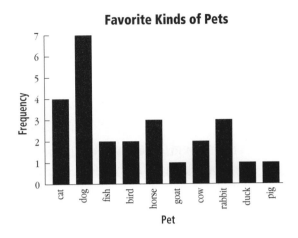

Numbers of Pets

Number of pets	Frequency
0	2
1	2
2	5
3	4
4	1
5	2
6	3
7	0
8	1
9	1
10	0
11	0
12	1
13	0
14	1
15	0
16	0
17	1
18	0
19	1
20	0
21	1

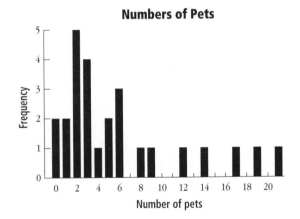

Problem 2.2

Decide whether each question below can be answered by using data from the graphs the students created. If a question can be answered, give the answer and explain how you got it. If a question cannot be answered, explain why not and tell what additional information you would need to answer the question.

A. Which graph shows categorical data, and which graph shows numerical data?

B. What is the total number of pets the students have?

C. What is the greatest number of pets that any student in the class has?

D. How many students are in the class?

E. How many students chose cats as their favorite kind of pet?

F. How many cats do students have as pets?

G. What is the mode for the favorite kind of pet?

H. What is the median number of pets students have?

I. What is the range of the numbers of pets students have?

J. Tomas is a student in this class. How many pets does he have?

K. Do the girls have more pets than the boys?

■ Problem 2.2 Follow-Up

Do you think the students surveyed live in a city, the suburbs, or the country? Explain your answer.

As you work on these ACE questions, use your calculator whenever you need it.

Applications

In 1–8, tell whether the answers to the question are numerical or categorical data.

1. What is your height in centimeters?

2. What is your favorite musical group?

3. On a scale of 1 to 7, with 7 being outstanding and 1 being poor, how would you rate the food served in the school cafeteria?

4. What would you like to do when you graduate from high school?

5. Are students in Mr. P's class older in months than students in Ms. J's class?

6. How many of your own feet tall are you?

7. What kind(s) of transportation do you use to get to school?

8. How much time do you spend doing homework?

Connections

9. Alicia has a rat that is three years old. She wonders if her rat is old compared to other rats. At the pet store, she finds out that the median age for a rat is $2\frac{1}{2}$ years.

a. What does the median tell Alicia about the life span for a rat?

b. What additional information would help Alicia predict the life span of her rat?

In 10–13, use the graph below, which shows the numbers of sodas consumed by 100 middle-school students in one day.

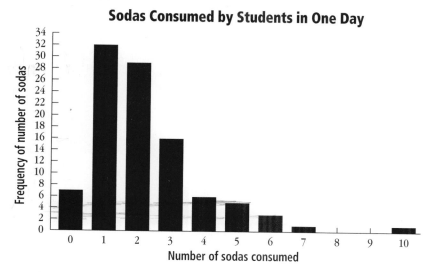

Sodas Consumed by Students in One Day

10. Are these data numerical or categorical? Explain your answer.

11. A student used this graph to estimate that the median number of sodas drunk by these students in a day was 5. Is this student correct? Explain your answer.

12. Another student estimated that the median number of sodas drunk in a day was 1. Is this student correct? Explain your answer.

13. What is the total number of sodas drunk by the 100 students in one day? Describe how you determined your answer.

14. Suppose these students were asked, What kinds of soda do you like to drink?

    a. Give three possible responses to this question.

    b. Describe how you would make a bar graph to show the data that would be collected to answer this question. What would the label for the horizontal axis be? What would the label for the vertical axis be? What would the title of the graph be? What would each bar on the graph show?

Extensions

In 15–17, use the data below. These data were collected from a large number of middle-school students and show the kinds of pets the students have. Of a total of 841 pets, the table shows that 61 are birds and 184 are cats. From this data we cannot tell how many students were surveyed. We only know that when the survey was completed, a total of 841 pets had been counted.

Kinds of Pets Students Have

Kind of pet	Frequency of kind of pet
bird	61
cat	184
dog	180
fish	303
gerbil	17
guinea pig	12
hamster	32
horse	28
rabbit	2
snake	9
turtle	13
Total	**841**

15. Make a bar graph to display this data. Think about how you will design and label the horizontal and vertical axes.

16. Use the information displayed in your graph to write a paragraph about the pets these students have.

17. What might be a good estimate of how many students were surveyed? Explain your reasoning.

Mathematical Reflections

In this investigation, you explored different kinds of data. These questions will help you summarize what you have learned:

1 How would you explain what categorical and numerical data are to a classmate who missed this investigation?

2 You have learned to use the mode and median to describe what is typical about a set of data. Can the mode or median be used to describe categorical data? Can the mode or median be used to describe numerical data?

3 The range is used to help describe how spread out a set of data are. Can you use the range to describe categorical data? Can you use the range to describe numerical data?

Think about your answers to these questions, discuss your ideas with other students and your teacher, and then write a summary of your findings in your journal.

To carry out a research project about characteristics of the typical middle-school student, you will need to pose questions. What questions might you ask that would have categorical data as answers? What questions might you ask that have numerical data as answers?

Using Graphs to Group Data

The data you have seen so far have had small ranges. For example, the name lengths in Problem 1.2 ranged from 9 to 17 letters, and the numbers of pets in Problem 2.2 ranged from 0 to 21 pets. You could see the shape of these data by examining a bar graph or a line plot. For data with a large range, a bar graph or a line plot, with a bar or stack of Xs for every value, often does not give a good idea of the shape of the data. In this investigation, you will learn about a type of graph that groups data values into intervals, making it easier to see the shape of the data.

3.1 Traveling to School

While investigating the times they got up in the morning, a middle-school class in Wisconsin was surprised to find that two students got up almost an hour earlier than their classmates. These students said they got up early because it took them so long to get to school. The class then wondered how much time it took each student to travel to school in the morning. The data they collected are on the next page.

Notice that the data about distances are recorded in decimal form: 4.50 miles means the same thing as $4\frac{1}{2}$ miles. What fractions would you write for 0.75 miles and 2.25 miles?

Think about this!

Look at the table of data and the labels for the columns, and consider these questions.
• What three questions did the students ask?
• How might the students have collected the data to answer these questions?
• Would a line plot be a good way to show the travel-time data? Why or why not?

Student's initials	Time (minutes)	Distance (miles)	Mode of travel
DB	60	4.50	bus
DD	15	2.00	bus
CC	30	2.00	bus
SE	15	0.75	car
AE	15	1.00	bus
FH	35	2.50	bus
CL	15	1.00	bus
LM	22	2.00	bus
QN	25	1.50	bus
MP	20	1.50	bus
AP	25	1.25	bus
AP	19	2.25	bus
HCP	15	1.50	bus
KR	8	0.25	walking
NS	8	1.25	car
LS	5	0.50	bus
AT	20	2.75	bus
JW	15	1.50	bus
DW	17	2.50	bus
SW	15	2.00	car
NW	10	0.50	walking
JW	20	0.50	walking
CW	15	2.25	bus
BA	30	3.00	bus
JB	20	2.50	bus
AB	50	4.00	bus
BB	30	4.75	bus
MB	20	2.00	bus
RC	10	1.25	bus
CD	5	0.25	walking
ME	5	0.50	bus
CF	20	1.75	bus
KG	15	1.75	bus
TH	11	1.50	bus
EL	6	1.00	car
KLD	35	0.75	bus
MN	17	4.50	bus
JO	10	3.00	car
RP	21	1.50	bus
ER	10	1.00	bus

The students decided to make a *stem-and-leaf plot* of the travel times.

Making a Stem-and-Leaf Plot

A **stem-and-leaf plot** looks something like a stem with leaves. It is sometimes simply called a *stem plot.*

To make a stem plot, begin by looking at the data values. Ignore the ones digits and look at the remaining digits of the numbers. These digits will make up the "stem." For these data, the stem will be made up of the tens digits. Since the travel times range from 5 minutes to 60 minutes, the stem will be made up of the digits 0, 1, 2, 3, 4, 5, and 6. Make a vertical list of the tens digits in order from smallest to largest, and draw a line to the right of the digits to separate the stem from the "leaves."

```
0 |
1 |
2 |
3 |
4 |
5 |
6 |
```

The "leaves" are the ones digits. For each data value, you add a leaf next to the appropriate tens digit on the stem. For example, the first data value is 60 minutes. You show this by writing a 0 next to the stem value of 6. The next value is 15 minutes. Indicate this by writing a 5 next to the stem value of 1.

```
0 |
1 | 5
2 |
3 |
4 |
5 |
6 | 0
```

The next few travel times are 30 minutes, 15 minutes, 15 minutes, 35 minutes, 15 minutes, 22 minutes, 25 minutes, and 20 minutes. Can you figure out how these data were added as leaves to the stem plot?

```
0 |
1 | 5 5 5 5
2 | 2 5 0
3 | 0 5
4 |
5 |
6 | 0
```

Copy and complete the stem plot, and compare it to the one below.

```
0 | 8 8 5 5 5 6
1 | 5 5 5 5 9 5 5 7 5 0 5 0 5 1 7 0 0
2 | 2 5 0 5 0 0 0 0 0 1
3 | 0 5 0 0 5
4 |
5 | 0
6 | 0
```

After you have added leaves for all the data values, redraw the plot, listing the ones digits in order from smallest to largest. Then, add a key showing how to read the plot and give the plot a title. Compare your new stem plot to the one below.

Travel Times to School (minutes)

```
0 | 5 5 5 6 8 8
1 | 0 0 0 0 1 5 5 5 5 5 5 5 5 5 7 7 9
2 | 0 0 0 0 0 0 1 2 5 5
3 | 0 0 0 5 5
4 |
5 | 0                        Key
6 | 0              2 | 5  means 25 minutes.
```

Problem 3.1

Read "Making a Stem-and-Leaf Plot" to explore how to make a stem-and-leaf plot of the travel-time data. After you have completed your stem plot of the data, answer these questions.

A. Which students probably get to sleep the latest in the morning? Why do you think this?

B. Which students probably get up earliest? Why do you think this?

C. What is the typical time it takes for these students to travel to school?

■ Problem 3.1 Follow-Up

Consider this question: What is the typical time it takes for a student in your class to travel to school?

1. Decide what data you need to collect to answer this question. Then, with your classmates, gather the appropriate data.

2. Find a way to organize and display your data.

3. After looking at your data, what would you say is the typical time it takes for a student in your class to travel to school?

3.2 Jumping Rope

While doing a jump-rope activity in gym class, a student in Ms. Rich's class wondered what was the typical number of jumps a middle-school student could make without stopping. The class decided to explore this question by collecting and analyzing data. After a practice turn, each student jumped as many times as possible, while a partner counted the jumps and recorded the total. When Mr. Kocik's class found out about the activity, they wanted to join in too.

The classes made a *back-to-back stem plot* (shown on the next page) to display their data. Look at this plot carefully, and try to figure out how to read it.

When the two classes compared their results, they disagreed about which class did better. Mr. Kocik's class pointed out that the range of their data was much greater. Ms. Rich's class said this was only because they had one person who jumped many more times than anybody else. They claimed that most of the students in their class jumped more times than most of the students in Mr. Kocik's class. Mr. Kocik's class disagreed, saying that, even if they did not count the person with 300 jumps, they still did better.

Numbers of Jumps

Ms. R's class		Mr. K's class
8 7 7 7 5 1 1	0	1 1 2 3 4 5 8 8
6 1 1	1	0 7
9 7 6 3 0 0	2	3 7 8
5 3	3	0 3 5
5 0	4	2 7 8
	5	0 2 3
2	6	0 8
	7	
9 8 0	8	
6 3 1	9	
	10	2 4
3	11	
	12	
	13	
	14	
	15	1
	16	0 0
	17	
	18	
	19	
	20	
	21	
	22	
	23	
	24	
	25	
	26	
	27	
	28	
	29	
	30	0

Key

7 | 3 | 0   means 37 jumps for
Ms. R's class and
30 jumps for Mr. K's class.

Which class did better overall in the jump-rope activity? Use what you know about statistics to help you justify your answer.

■ Problem 3.2 Follow-Up

In Mr. Kocik's class, there are some very large numbers of jumps. For example, one student jumped 151 times, and another student jumped 300 times. We call these data *outliers.* **Outliers** are values that stand out in a set of data.

1. Find two other outliers in the data for Mr. Kocik's class.

Statisticians question outliers and try to figure out why they might have occurred. An outlier may be a value that was recorded incorrectly, or it may be a signal that something special is happening that you may want to understand.

2. All the values recorded for Mr. Kocik's class are correct. What do you think might account for the few students who were able to jump many more times than their classmates?

In 3–5, use the data you collected in Problem 3.1 Follow-Up about the time it takes for you and your classmates to travel to school.

3. Make a back-to-back stem plot showing your class data and the data from the Wisconsin class that was used in Problem 3.1.

4. How do your data and the Wisconsin data compare?

5. Are there any outliers in either of the two data sets? Explain.

As you work on these ACE questions, use your calculator whenever you need it.

Applications

In 1–4, use this stem-and-leaf plot, which shows the number of minutes it took a class of students to travel to school.

Travel Times to School (minutes)

```
0 | 3  3  5  7  8  9
1 | 0  2  3  5  6  6  8  9
2 | 0  1  3  3  3  5  5  8  8
3 | 0  5
4 | 5                        Key
           2 | 5  means 25 minutes.
```

1. How many students spent 10 minutes traveling to school?

2. Can you use this plot to determine how many students spent 15 minutes or more traveling to school? Explain why or why not.

3. How many students are there in this class? Describe how you determined your answer.

4. What is the typical time it took for these students to travel to school? Describe how you determined your answer.

In 5–8, use the table below. This table shows the ages, heights, and foot lengths for a group of students.

Students Ages, Heights, and Foot Lengths

Age (months)	Height (cm)	Foot length (cm)
76	126	24
73	117	24
68	112	17
78	123	22
81	117	20
82	122	23
80	130	22
90	127	21
101	127	21
99	124	21
103	130	20
101	134	21
145	172	32
146	163	27
144	158	25
148	164	26
140	152	22
114	135	20
108	135	22
105	147	22
113	138	22
120	141	20
120	146	24
132	147	23
132	155	21
129	141	22
138	161	28
152	156	30
149	157	27
132	150	25

5. Make a stem-and-leaf plot that shows the ages in months of the students, starting with the stem shown here. Notice that the first value in the stem is 6, since there are no values less than 60 months.

```
 6 |
 7 |
 8 |
 9 |
10 |
11 |
12 |
13 |
14 |
15 |
```

6. What ages, in years, does the interval of 80–89 months represent? Explain your answer.

7. What is the median age of these students? Explain how you determined this age.

Connections

8. **a.** Make a stem plot that shows the heights in centimeters of the students.

b. Make a line plot of the heights in centimeters of the students.

c. Which of these plots seems the most appropriate for the data? Why?

d. Would a bar graph be a good way to show this data? Why or why not?

Extensions

In 9 and 10, use the jump-rope data from Ms. Rich's and Mr. Kocik's classes, which are shown on the next page.

Number of Jumps

Mrs. R's Class Data		Mr. K's Class Data	
boy	5	boy	1
boy	35	boy	30
girl	91	boy	28
boy	62	boy	10
girl	96	girl	27
girl	23	girl	102
boy	16	boy	47
boy	1	boy	8
boy	8	girl	160
boy	11	girl	23
girl	93	boy	17
girl	27	boy	2
girl	88	girl	68
boy	26	boy	50
boy	7	girl	151
boy	7	boy	60
boy	1	boy	5
boy	40	girl	52
boy	7	girl	4
boy	20	girl	35
girl	20	boy	160
girl	89	boy	1
boy	29	boy	3
boy	11	boy	8
boy	113	girl	48
boy	33	boy	42
girl	45	boy	33
girl	80	girl	300
		girl	104
		girl	53

9. Make a back-to-back stem-and-leaf plot that compares the girls in Ms. Rich's class with the girls in Mr. Kocik's class *or* the boys in Ms. Rich's class with the boys in Mr. Kocik's class. Did one class of girls (or boys) do better than the other class of girls (or boys)? Explain your reasoning.

10. Make a back-to-back stem-and-leaf plot that compares the girls in both classes with the boys in both classes. Did the girls do better in this activity than the boys? Explain your reasoning.

Mathematical Reflections

In this investigation, you learned how to make stem-and-leaf plots as a way to group a set of data so you can inspect its shape. You looked at two different situations: how long it takes for students to travel to school and how many times students can jump rope. These questions will help you summarize what you have learned:

1 Describe how to locate the median and range using a stem plot.

2 Numerical data can be displayed using more than one kind of graph. How do you decide when to use a line plot, a bar graph, or a stem-and-leaf plot?

3 Some data you gather will be categorical data. Can categorical data be displayed using line plots, bar graphs, or stem-and-leaf plots? Explain your reasoning.

Think about your answers to these questions, discuss your ideas with other students and your teacher, and then write a summary of your findings in your journal.

Think about the survey you will be developing to gather information about middle-school students. What kinds of questions can you ask that might involve using a stem-and-leaf plot to display the data?

Coordinate Graphs

In the first three investigations, you worked with one measure at a time. For example, you looked at the number of letters in students' names, the number of times students jumped rope, or the numbers of pets students had. Although you can find out some interesting things about one set of data, it is often interesting to look at how two sets of data are related to each other.

4.1 Relating Height to Arm Span

If you look around at your classmates, you might guess that taller people have wider arm spans. But is there *really* any relationship between a person's height and his or her arm span? The best way to find out more about this question is to collect some data.

Here are data on height and arm span (measured from fingertip to fingertip) that one class collected.

Height and Arm Span Measurements

Initials	Height (inches)	Arm span (inches)
NY	63	60
JJ	69	67
CM	73	75
PL	77	77
BP	64	65
AS	67	64
KR	72	72

One way to show data about two different measures (such as height and arm span) at the same time is to make a **coordinate graph.** Each point on a coordinate graph represents two measures for one person or thing. On a coordinate graph, the horizontal axis, or *x*-**axis,** represents one measure. The vertical axis, or *y*-**axis,** represents a second measure. For example, the graph below shows data for height along the *x*-axis and data for arm span along the *y*-axis. Each point on this graph indicates both the height and the arm span for one student.

Height and Arm Span Measurements

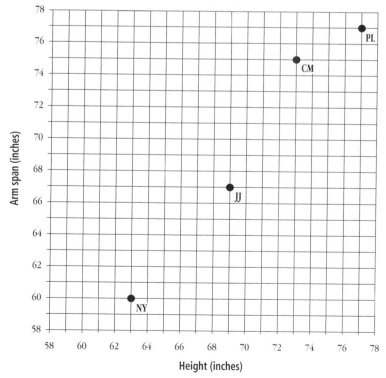

Study the table of data and the coordinate graph. Four points have already been plotted and labeled with the students' initials. We write the location for each point like this:

- NY is located at point (63, 60)
- JJ is located at point (69, 67)
- CM is located at point (73, 75)
- PL is located at point (77, 77)

Working with a partner, determine how to locate points on this graph. Where would you place the points and initials for the remaining three people? Why do the axes start at (58, 58)? What would the graph look like if the axes started at (0, 0)?

Problem 4.1

Think about this question: If you know the measure of a person's arm span, do you know anything about his or her height?

To help you answer this question, you will need to collect some data. With your class, collect the height and arm span of each person in your class. Make a coordinate graph of your data. Then, use your graph to answer the question above.

■ Problem 4.1 Follow-Up

Draw a diagonal line through the points on the graph where the measures for arm span and height are the same.

1. How many of your classmates' data are on this line? What is true about arm span compared to height for the points on this line?

2. What is true about arm span compared to height for the points *below* the line you drew?

3. What is true about arm span compared to height for the points *above* the line you drew?

4.2 Relating Travel Time to Distance

In Investigation 3, you made stem plots to show data about travel times to school. Using a coordinate graph, you can show both travel time and distance from home to school. For example, we can show the travel time and distance to school for the students in Problem 3.1 on a coordinate graph:

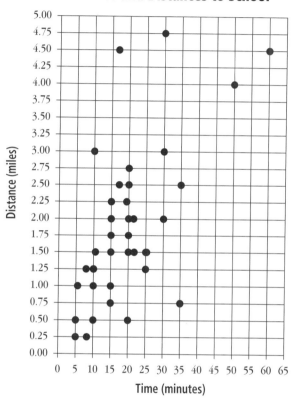

Times and Distances to School

Problem 4.2

Study the graph above, which was made using the data from Problem 3.1.

A. Look back at the data on page 31. On Labsheet 4.2, locate and label with initials the points for the first five students in the table.

B. If you know how long it takes a particular student to travel to school, can you know anything about that student's distance from school? Use the graph to help you answer this question. Write a justification for your answer.

1. Locate the points at (17, 4.50) and (60, 4.50) on the coordinate graph on Labsheet 4.2. What can you tell about the students these points represent?

2. Locate the points (30, 2.00), (30, 3.00), and (30, 4.75). What can you tell about the students these points represent?

3. What would the graph look like if the same scale were used for both axes?

As you work on these ACE questions, use your calculator whenever you need it.

Applications

In 1 and 2, use this table of data, which shows the ages, heights, and foot lengths for 30 students.

Student Age, Height, and Foot Length

Age (months)	Height (cm)	Foot length (cm)
76	126	24
73	117	24
68	112	17
78	123	22
81	117	20
82	122	23
80	130	22
90	127	21
101	127	21
99	124	21
103	130	20
101	134	21
145	172	32
146	163	27
144	158	25
148	164	26
140	152	22
114	135	20
108	135	22
105	147	22
113	138	22
120	141	20
120	146	24
132	147	23
132	155	21
129	141	22
138	161	28
152	156	30
149	157	27
132	150	25

1. **a.** Make a stem-and-leaf plot showing the heights of these students.

   b. Can you determine from your stem plot whether the youngest student is also the shortest? Can you determine this from the table? Explain why or why not.

2. **a.** On a piece of grid paper, make a coordinate graph showing each person's age (in months) on the horizontal axis and height (in centimeters) on the vertical axis. To help you choose a scale for each axis, look at the range of values you have to locate on the graph. What are the smallest and largest age values? What are the smallest and largest height values?

   b. Can you determine from your coordinate graph whether the youngest student is also the shortest student? Explain your reasoning.

   c. Using information from your coordinate graph, describe what happens to students' heights as students get older.

   d. We know people eventually stop growing. When does this happen? How would this affect the graph?

3. The coordinate graph on the next page displays height and foot length for 29 students. Notice that the x-axis is scaled in intervals of 5 centimeters and the y-axis is scaled in intervals of 1 centimeter.

   a. One student said that if you know a person's foot length, you can tell what that person's height is. Do you think she is right? Explain your reasoning.

   b. Determine the median height and the median foot length. Compare the median height with the median foot length. The median height is about how many times as large as the median foot length?

   c. Measure the length of your foot and your height in centimeters. Your height is about how many times as large as your foot length?

   d. Look at your responses to b and c. How can you use this information to decide whether the student's comment in a is correct?

   e. What would the graph look like if each axis started at 0?

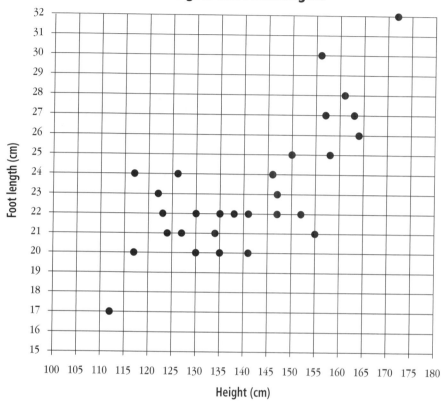

Heights and Foot Lengths

Connections

4. Make a coordinate graph that shows the numbers from 1 to 20 on the horizontal axis and the number of factors of each of these numbers on the vertical axis. What patterns do you see in your graph? Explain each pattern.

Extensions

5. A group of students challenged each other to see who could come the closest to guessing the number of seeds in his or her pumpkin. In October, they guessed the number of seeds in each of their pumpkins. In November, they opened their pumpkins and counted the seeds. They compared  their guesses with their actual counts by displaying their data on a coordinate graph. The data and graph are shown on the next page.

a. Describe what you notice about how spread out the actual counts are. What are the median and the range of the actual counts?

b. Describe what you notice about how spread out the guesses are. What are the median and the range of the guesses?

c. On Labsheet 4.ACE, draw a diagonal line on the graph to connect the points (0, 0), (250, 250), (500, 500), all the way to (2250, 2250).

d. What is true about the guesses compared to the actual counts for points on or near the line you drew?

e. What is true about the guesses compared to the actual counts for points above the line?

f. What is true about the guesses compared to the actual counts for points below the line?

g. In general, did the students make good guesses about the numbers of seeds in their pumpkins? Use what you know about the median and range of the actual counts and the guesses as well as other information from the graph to explain your reasoning.

h. The scales on the axes are the same, but the data are very bunched together. How would you change the scale to better show the data points?

Numbers of Seeds
in Pumpkins

Guess	Actual
630	309
621	446
801	381
720	505
1900	387
1423	336
621	325
1200	365
622	410
1000	492
1200	607
1458	498
350	523
621	467
759	423
900	479
500	512
521	606
564	494
655	441
722	455
202	553
621	367
300	442
200	507
556	462
604	384
2000	545
1200	354
766	568
624	506
680	486
605	408
1100	387

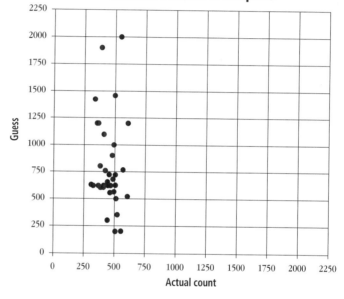

Numbers of Seeds in Pumpkins

Mathematical Reflections

In this investigation, you have learned how to make and read coordinate graphs. Coordinate graphs let you examine two sets of data at once so you can look for relationships between pairs of data. You looked at two different situations: how arm span relates to height, and how travel time relates to distance traveled. These questions will help you summarize what you have learned:

1 When you make a coordinate graph of data pairs, what do you consider when deciding what scale to use on each axis?

2 How do you locate a point on a coordinate graph?

3 If you make a coordinate graph of variables such as arm span and height, where the values of one measure get larger as the values of the other measure get larger, what will the pattern of points on the graph look like?

4 How are a coordinate graph and a line plot alike? How are they different?

Think about your answers to these questions, discuss your ideas with other students and your teacher, and then write a summary of your findings in your journal.

Think about how what you have learned about coordinate graphs might help you with your project. What kinds of questions can you ask to help you answer the question, "Is anyone typical?" that might involve using a coordinate graph to display the data?

What Do We Mean by *Mean?*

Since the first United States census was conducted in 1790, its primary use has been to find out how many people live in the United States. These data, organized by state, are used to determine how many representatives each state will have in the House of Representatives in the United States Congress.

Many people are interested in the census because it provides useful information about a number of other things, including household size. The term *household*, as used by the United States census, means all the people who occupy a "housing unit" (a house, an apartment or other group of rooms, or a single room like a room in a boarding house).

Remember that an *average* is a value used to describe what is typical about a set of data. An average can be thought of as a "measure of center." The mode and the median are two types of averages you have used quite a bit. The *mode* is the value that occurs most frequently in a set of data. The *median* is the value that divides a set of ordered data in half. This investigation explores a third kind of average, which is called the *mean*.

5.1 Evening Things Out

Six students in a middle-school class determined the number of people in their households using the United States census guidelines. Each student then made a cube tower to show the number of people in his or her household.

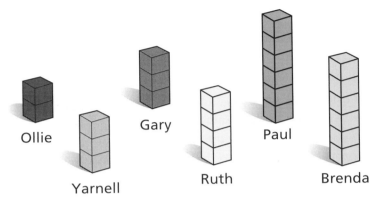

Ollie

Yarnell

Gary

Ruth

Paul

Brenda

You can easily see from the cube towers that the six households vary in size. The students wondered what the average number of people is in their households. Their teacher asked them what they might do, using their cube towers, to find the answer to their question.

Problem 5.1

What are some ways to determine the average number of people in these six households?

■ Problem 5.1 Follow-Up

The students had an idea for finding the average number of people in the households. They decided to rearrange the cubes to try to "even out" the number of cubes in each tower. Try this on your own and see what you find for the average number of people in the households, and then read on to see what the students did.

First, the students put the towers in order.

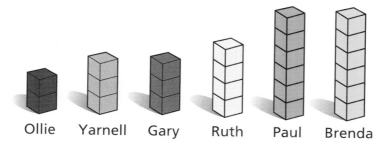

The students then moved cubes from one tower to another, making some households bigger than they actually were and making other households smaller than they actually were. When they were finished moving cubes, their towers looked like this:

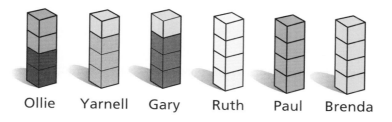

Each tower now had four cubes. Notice that the total number of cubes did not change.

Before	
Ollie	2 people
Yarnell	3 people
Gary	3 people
Ruth	4 people
Paul	6 people
Brenda	6 people
Total	24 people

After	
Ollie	4 people
Yarnell	4 people
Gary	4 people
Ruth	4 people
Paul	4 people
Brenda	4 people
Total	24 people

The students determined that the average number of people in a household was 4. The teacher explained that the average the students had found is called the **mean.** The mean number of people in the six households is 4.

The students decided to look at the data in another way. They used stick-on notes to make a line plot of the data. They used an arrow to show the mean on their line plot.

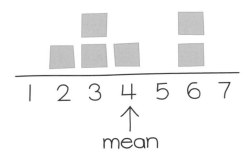

Notice that in the 6 households there is a total of 24 people: $2 + 3 + 3 + 4 + 6 + 6 = 24$. You can see that the mean is not the middle of the distribution since there are 2 households above the mean and 3 households below the mean.

One student said, "When you even out the cubes, it's like moving all the stick-on notes to the same place on the line plot." The students showed this on their line plot.

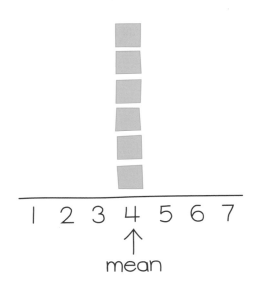

Notice that the total number of people in the households is still 24: $4 + 4 + 4 + 4 + 4 + 4 = 24$.

The mean is a kind of balance point in the distribution. You can see that the sizes of some households are less than the mean and the sizes of some households are more than the mean. However, there are enough people in the households above the mean that can be moved to the households below the mean so that the households can be "evened out" with 4 people in each.

5.2 Finding the Mean

The following data show the number of people in the households of six different students.

Name	Number of people in household
Geoffrey	6
Betty	4
Brendan	3
Oprah	4
Reilly	3
Tonisha	4

Problem 5.2

A. Make a set of cube towers to show the size of each household.

B. Make a line plot of the data.

C. How many people are there in the six households altogether? Describe how you determined your answer.

D. What is the mean number of people in the six households? Describe how you determined your answer.

■ Problem 5.2 Follow-Up

1. How does the mean for this set of six students compare to the mean for the six students in Problem 5.1?

2. How does the median for this set of six students compare to the median for the six students in Problem 5.1?

5.3 Data with the Same Mean

The line plots below show the data from Problem 5.1 and Problem 5.2. The data for the two situations look different, but the mean is the same.

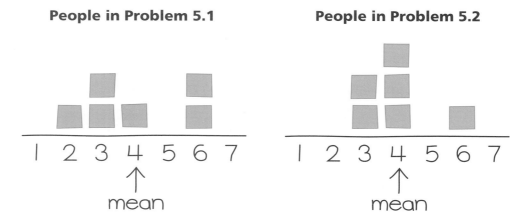

People in Problem 5.1   **People in Problem 5.2**

Think about these questions:
- How many households are there in each situation?
- How many total people are there in each situation?
- How are these facts related to the mean of 4 in each case?

Problem 5.3

A. Try to find two more sets of six households with a mean of 4 people. Use cubes to show each set, and then make line plots that show the information from the cubes.

B. Try to find two different sets of seven households with a mean of 4 people. Use cubes to show each set, and then make line plots to show the information from the cubes.

■ Problem 5.3 Follow-Up

1. A group of seven students has a mean number of 3 people in their households. Make a line plot showing a data set that fits this description.

2. A group of six students has a mean number of $3\frac{1}{2}$ people in their households. Make a line plot showing a data set that fits this description.

3. How can the mean be $3\frac{1}{2}$ people when "half" people do not exist?

5.4 Using Your Class's Data

Recall that the term *household* as used by the United States census refers to all people who occupy a "housing unit" (a house, an apartment or other group of rooms, or a single room like a room in a boarding house).

Problem 5.4

A. Using the definition from the United States census, how many people are in your household?

B. Collect household data from everyone in your class, and make a display to show the information.

C. What is the mean number of people in your class's households? Describe how you determined your answer.

■ Problem 5.4 Follow-Up

One student wrote, "In Problem 5.2, there are 6 households with a total of 24 people. There is a range of 3 to 6 people in the 6 households. The mean number of people in each household is 4. This is the number that tells me how many people each household would have if each household had the same number of people." Write a similar description for your class data about people in your households.

Watching Movies

A group of middle-school students was asked this question: How many movies did you watch last month? Here are a table and stem plot of the data:

Student	Number of movies
Joel	15
Tonya	16
Rachel	5
Lawrence	18
Meela	3
Leah	6
Beth	7
Mickey	6
Bhavana	3
Josh	11

Movies Watched

```
0 | 3 3 5 6 6 7
1 | 1 5 6 8
2 |
```

Key

1 | 5   means 15 movies.

Problem 5.5

A. Look at the table above and complete these statements.

The total number of students is _____.

The total number of movies watched is _____.

The mean number of movies watched is _____.

B. A new value is added for Lucia, who watched 42 movies last month. This value is an outlier. How does the stem plot change when this value is added? What is the new mean? Compare the mean from part A to the mean after this value is added. What do you notice?

C. A new value is added for Tamara, who was home last month with a broken leg. She watched 96 movies. What is the mean of the data now? Compare the means you found in parts A and B with this new mean. What do you notice? Why?

D. Data for eight more students are added:

Tommy	5	Robbie	4
Alexandra	5	Ana	4
Kesh	5	Alisha	2
Kirsten	5	Brian	2

These data are not outliers, but now there are several students who watched only a few movies in one month. What is the mean of the data now? Compare the means you found in parts A, B, and C with this new mean. What do you notice? Why?

Problem 5.5 Follow-Up

1. What happens to the mean when you add one or more values that are much larger than the values in the original data set? Why does this happen?

2. What happens to the mean when you add a number of values that are clumped with the smaller values in the original data set? Why does this happen?

As you work on these ACE questions, use your calculator whenever you need it.

Applications

In 1 and 2, use the line plot below, which shows information about the number of children found in 16 households.

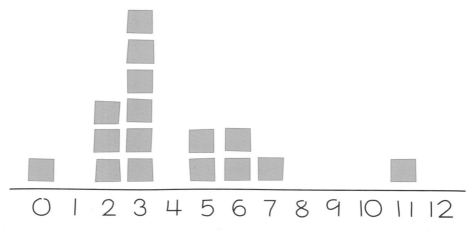

1. **a.** What is the median number of children in the 16 households? Explain how you found the median and what it tells you.

    b. Do any of the 16 households have the median number of children? Explain why this is possible.

2. **a.** What is the mean number of children in the 16 households? Explain how you found the mean and what it tells you.

    b. Do any of the 16 households have the mean number of children? Explain why this is possible.

3. The mean number of people in eight households is 6.

    a. What is the total number of people in the eight households?

    b. Make a line plot showing one possible arrangement for the numbers of people in the eight households.

c. Make a line plot showing a different possible arrangement for the numbers of people in the eight households.

d. Are the medians the same for the two arrangements you made?

4. A group of nine students has a mean of $3\frac{1}{2}$ people in their households. Make a line plot showing an example of this data set.

5. A group of nine students has a mean of 5 people in their households, and the largest household in the group has 10 people. Make a line plot of a data set fitting this description.

Connections

6. Jon has a pet rabbit that is 5 years old. He wonders if his rabbit is old compared to other rabbits. At the pet store, he finds out that the mean age for a rabbit is 7 years.

a. What does the mean tell Jon about the life span for a rabbit?

b. What additional information would help Jon to predict the life span of his rabbit?

7. A store carries nine different brands of granola bars. What are possible prices for each of the nine brands of granola bars if the mean price is $1.33? Explain how you determined the values for each of the nine brands. You may use pictures to help you.

8. Three candidates are running for the mayor of Slugville. Each has determined the typical income for the people in Slugville and is using this information to help in the campaign.

Mayor Phibbs is running for re-election. He says, "Slugville is doing great! The average income for each person is $2000 per week!"

Challenging candidate Louisa Louis says, "Slugville is nice, but it needs my help! The average income is only $100 per week."

Radical Ronnie Radford says, "No way! We must burn down the town—it's awful. The average income is $0 per week."

None of the candidates is lying. Slugville has only 16 residents, and their weekly incomes are $0, $0, $0, $0, $0, $0, $0, $0, $200, $200, $200, $200, $200, $200, $200, and $30,600.

a. Explain how each of the candidates determined what the "average" income was for the town. Check the computations to see whether you agree with the three candidates.

b. Does any person in Slugville have the mean income? Explain.

c. Does any person in Slugville have the median income? Explain.

d. Does any person in Slugville have the mode income? Explain.

e. What do you consider to be the typical income for a resident of Slugville? Explain.

f. If four more people moved to Slugville, each with a weekly income of $200, how would the mean, median, and mode change?

9. A recent survey asked 25 middle-school students how many movies they watch in one month. The data are shown on the next page. Notice that the data are quite spread out; the range is from 1 to 30 movies.

a. Make a stem-and-leaf plot to show these data. Describe the shape of the data.

b. Find the mean number of movies watched by the students for the month.

c. Describe how you found the mean number of movies.

d. What do the mean and the range tell you about the typical number of movies watched for this group of students?

e. Find the median number of movies watched. Are the mean and the median the same? Why do you think this is so?

Movies Watched by Students

Student	Movies per month
Wes	2
Sanford	15
Carla	13
Su Chin	1
Michael	9
Mara	30
Alan	20
Brent	1
Tanisha	25
Susan	4
Darlene	3
Eddie	2
Lonnie	3
Gerald	10
Kristina	15
Paul	12
Henry	5
Julian	2
Greta	4
TJ	1
Rebecca	4
Ramish	11
Art	8
Raymond	8
Angelica	17

Extensions

In 10 and 11, consider this newspaper headline:

10. Which average—median or mean—do you think is being used in this headline? Explain why you think this.

11. About how many hours per day does the average third grader watch television if he or she watches 1170 hours in a year?

12. Review the jump-rope data for Problem 3.2 on page 35.

    a. Compute the median and the mean for each class's data. How do the median and the mean for each compare?

    b. Which statistic—the median or the mean—would Mr. Kocik's class want to use to compare their performance with Ms. Rich's class? Why?

    c. What happens to the median of Mr. Kocik's class's data if you leave out the data for the student who jumped rope 300 times? Why does this happen?

    d. What happens to the mean of Mr. Kocik's class's data if you leave out the data for the student who jumped rope 300 times? Why does this happen?

    e. Can Ms. Rich's class claim to be better if the data of 300 jumps is left out of Mr. Kocik's class's data? Explain why or why not.

Mathematical Reflections

In this investigation, you explored a type of average called the mean. You used cubes to help you see what it means to "even out" data to locate the mean, and you created different data sets with the same mean. Then you developed a way to find the mean without using cubes. Finally, you looked at what happens to the mean when the data include very high or very low values. These questions will help you summarize what you have learned:

1 Describe a method that requires using only numbers for finding the mean. Explain why this method works.

2 You have used three measures of center: the mode, the median, and the mean.

   a. Why do you suppose these are called "measures of center"? What does each tell you about a set of data?

   b. Why might people prefer to use the median instead of the mean?

3 You have used one measure of spread: the range.

   a. Why do you suppose the range is called a "measure of spread"?

   b. Why might people prefer to describe a data set using both a measure of center and a measure of spread rather than just one or the other?

4 Once you collect data to answer questions, you will want to decide what measures of center and spread can be used to describe your data.

   a. One student said she could use only the mode to describe categorical data, but that she could use the mode, median, and mean to describe numerical data. Is she right? Explain why or why not.

   b. Can you determine a measure of spread for categorical data? Explain.

Think about your answers to these questions, discuss your ideas with other students and your teacher, and then write a summary of your findings in your journal.

You will soon be developing your own survey to gather information about middle-school students. What measures of center and spread can you use to describe the data you might collect for each question in your survey?

Is Anyone Typical?

You can use what you have learned in *Data About Us* to conduct a statistical investigation to answer the question, "What are some characteristics of a typical middle-school student?" When you have completed your investigation, make a poster, write a report, or find some other way to communicate your results.

Your statistical investigation should consist of four parts:

Posing questions
You will want to gather both numerical data and categorical data. Your data may include physical characteristics, family characteristics, miscellaneous behavior (such as hobbies), and preferences or opinions. Once you have decided what you want to know, you need to write appropriate questions. Make sure that your questions are clear so that everyone who takes your survey will interpret them in the same way.

Collecting the data
You may want to collect data from just your class or from a larger group of students. You also need to decide how to distribute and collect the survey.

Analyzing the data
Once you have collected your data, you need to organize, display, and analyze them. Be sure to think about what kinds of displays and which measures of center are most appropriate for each set of data values you collect.

Interpreting the results
Use the results of your analysis to describe some characteristics of the typical middle-school student. Is there a student that fits all the "typical" characteristics you found? If not, explain why.

Unit Reflections

Working on the problems in this unit, you explored some of the big ideas involved in conducting statistical investigations. You learned how to represent data using *bar graphs*, *line plots*, *stem-and-leaf plots*, and *coordinate graphs*. You explored ways of using statistics such as the *mean*, the *median*, and the *range* to answer questions about data such as "What's typical?" Finally, you developed a variety of ways to compare data sets.

Using Your Statistical Reasoning—Statistical reasoning is often used by naturalists in studies of wild animal population. For example, data in the following table show the lengths (in inches) and weights (in pounds) of 25 alligators captured in central Florida. Aerial photographs give data about the numbers and locations of other wild alligators. It is possible to estimate alligator length from photographs; it is harder to estimate weight.

1 *Consider the lengths of the alligators in the sample.*

a. Make a graph of the lengths of the 25 alligators and write a sentence describing the distribution of lengths shown in the graph.

Lengths and Weights of Captured Alligators

Gator Number	Length (inches)	Weight (pounds)		Gator Number	Length (inches)	Weight (pounds)
1	74	54		14	88	70
2	94	110		15	58	28
3	85	84		16	90	102
4	61	44		17	94	130
5	128	366		18	68	39
6	72	61		19	78	57
7	89	84		20	86	80
8	90	106		21	72	38
9	63	33		22	74	51
10	82	80		23	147	640
11	114	197		24	76	42
12	69	36		25	86	90
13	86	83				

b. What are the mean and median lengths? **c.** What is the range of the lengths?

2 *Consider the weights of alligators in the sample.*

    a. Make a graph of the weights of the 25 alligators and write a sentence describing the distribution of weights shown in the graph.

    b. What are the mean and median weights?

    c. What is the range of the weights?

3 *Explore the relationship between the length and weight of Florida alligators.*

    a. Make a coordinate graph of the (length, weight) data.

    b. What relationship do you notice between length and weight of alligators that are

        i. 61 and 63 inches long? **ii.** 82, 85, and 86 inches long?

        iii. 90, 94, and 114 inches long?

    c. What weight would you predict for an alligator that is

        i. 70 inches long? **ii.** 100 inches long? **iii.** 130 inches long?

    d. Based on your study of the alligator length and weight data, do you believe it is possible to make a good estimate for the weight of an alligator if you know its length?

Explaining Your Reasoning—When you describe a collection of data, you look for the shape of the distribution of the data. You can often visualize data patterns using graphs.

1. How do the *mean* and the *median* help in describing the numbers in a data set?

2. How does the *range* help in describing the numbers in a data set?

3. What kinds of numerical data are best displayed with

    a. line plots? **b.** stem-and-leaf plots? **c.** coordinate graphs?

4. What does it mean to say that a person's armspan *is related to* his or her height, or that the time it takes to travel to school *is related to* the distance traveled, or that the weight of an alligator *is related to* its length?

The ideas about numerical and graphic data analysis that you have learned in this unit will be used and extended in a variety of future *Connected Mathematics* units, especially Samples and Populations where you will collect, organize, and display numerical information. You'll also find that various statistical plots and data summaries appear in everyday news reports and in the technical work of science, business, and government.

axis, axes The number lines that are used to make a graph. There are usually two axes perpendicular to each other (see *bar graphs* or *coordinate graphs* for examples). The vertical axis is called the *y*-axis and the horizontal axis is called the *x*-axis.

bar graph (bar chart) A graphical representation of a table of data in which the height of each bar indicates its value. The bars are separated from each other to highlight that the data are discrete or "counted" data. The horizontal axis shows the values or categories and the vertical axis shows the frequency or tally for each of the values or categories on the horizontal axis.

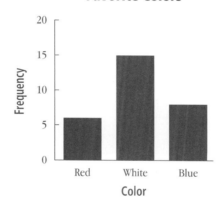

Favorite Colors

categorical data Values that are "words" that represent possible responses within a given category. Frequency counts can be made of the values for a given category. See the examples that follow.

- Months of the year in which people have birthdays (values may be January, February, March, and so on)
- Favorite color to wear for a t-shirt (values may be magenta, Carolina blue, yellow, and so on)
- Kinds of pets people have (values may be cats, dogs, fish, horses, boa constrictors, and so on)

coordinate graph A graphical representation of pairs of related numerical values. One axis shows one value of each pair (for example, height on the horizontal axis) and the other axis shows the other value of each pair (for example, arm span on the vertical axis). The graph below shows a coordinate graph of the data in the table.

Measures (inches)

Initials	Height	Arm Span
JJ	69	67
NY	63	60
CM	73	75
PL	77	77

Height and Arm Span Measurements

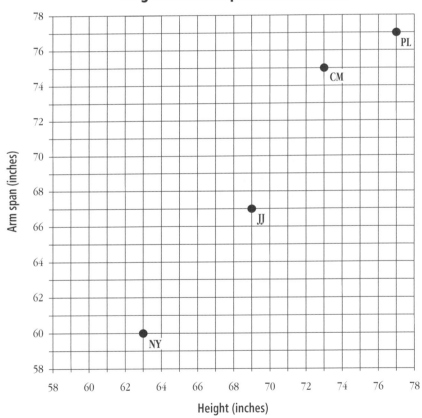

data Values such as counts, ratings, measurements, or opinions that are gathered to answer questions. The data in this table show mean temperatures in three cities.

Daily Mean Temperatures

City	Mean Temperature
Mobile, AL	67.5 °F
Boston, MA	51.3 °F
Spokane, WA	47.3 °F

line plot A quick, simple way to organize data along a number line where the Xs (or other symbols) above a number represent how often each value is mentioned.

Numbers of Siblings Students Have

```
            X
  X     X  X       X
  X  X  X  X  X  X
  X  X  X  X  X  X  X        X
  ─────────────────────────────
  0  1  2  3  4  5  6  7  8
        Number of siblings
```

mean A value that represents a middle value or typical value in a set of data. If all the data had the same value, the mean would be that value. For example, the total number of siblings for the above data is 56 siblings. If all 19 students had the same number of siblings, they would each have about 3 siblings.

median The numerical value that marks the middle of an ordered set of data. Half the data occur above the median, and half the data occur below the median. The median of the distribution of siblings is 3 because the tenth (middle) value in the ordered set of 19 values (0, 0, 0, 1, 1, 2, 2, 2, 2, 3, 3, 3, 4, 4, 5, 5, 5, 6, 8) is 3 siblings.

mode Of a distribution, the category or numerical value that occurs most often. For example, the mode of the distribution of the number of siblings is 2. It is possible for a set of data to have more than one mode.

numerical data Values that are numbers such as counts, measurements, and ratings. As an example, see *data* and the examples that follow.

- Numbers of children in families
- Pulse rates indicating how many heart beats occur in a minute
- Height
- How much time people spend reading in one day
- How much people value something, such as: On a scale of 1 to 5 with 1 as "low interest," how would you rate your interest in participating in the school's field day?

outlier One or more values that lie "outside" of a distribution of the data. An outlier is a value that may be questioned because it is unusual or because there may have been an error in recording or reporting the data.

range The range of a distribution is computed by stating the lowest and highest values. For example, the range of the number of siblings is from 0 to 8 people.

scale The size of the units on an axis of a graph or number line. For instance, each mark on the vertical axis might represent 10 units.

stem-and-leaf plot (stem plot) A quick way to picture the shape of a distribution while including the actual numerical values in the graph. For a number like 25, the stem 2 is written at the left of the vertical line, and the leaf, 5, is at the right.

Numbers of Movies Seen Over the Summer

```
0 |
1 | 5  5  5  5
2 | 2  5  0
3 | 0  5
4 |
5 |
6 | 0
```

Back-to-back stem plots may be used to compare two sets of the same kind of data. The units for one set of data are placed on one side of the stem, and the units for the other set are placed on the other side.

survey A method for collecting data that uses interviews. Surveys ask questions to find out information such as facts, opinions, or beliefs.

Favorite Colors

Color	Number of Students
Red	6
White	15
Blue	9

table A tool for organizing information in rows and columns. Tables let you list categories or values and then tally the occurrences. For an example, see *data*.

Index

Average, 4, 9, 12, 53   *See also* **Mean**;
   Median; **Mode**
Axis (axes), coordinate, 43

Back-to-back stem plot, 34–36
   ACE, 40
Bar graph, 4, 8
   ACE, 15–20, 24, 27–28
   double, 18–20
   stacked, 18–20

Categorical data, 4, 22–25
   ACE, 26–28
Census, 3, 53, 59
Chuks-orji, O., 14
Coordinate axes, 43
Coordinate graph, 4, 42–46
   ACE, 47–51

Data
   analyzing, 4, 7–14, 53–61
   categorical, 4, 22–25
   collecting, 3, 4
   grouping, 30–36
   interpreting, 4, 7–14, 45–46
   numerical, 4, 22–25
   organizing, 4, 6–7, 22–25, 30–36,
   42–44
   outliers and, 4, 36, 60–61
   patterns in, 7, 8, 49
   prediction with, 7
   shape of, 10

   types of, 22–23
Do People Grow on Family Trees?, 14
Double bar graph, 18–20

Estimation, ACE, 28

Family names, 10

Graph *See also* **Plots**
   bar, 4, 7–8, 15–20, 24, 27–28
   coordinate, 4, 42–52
   double bar, 18–20
   stacked bar, 18–20

Horizontal axis, 43

Interval
   ACE, 37–40
   stem-and-leaf plot, 30–36
Investigations
   Coordinate Graphs, 42–52
   Looking at Data, 6–21
   Types of Data, 22–29
   Using Graphs to Group Data, 30–41
   What Do We Mean by *Mean*?, 53–67

Line plot, 4, 7, 8
   ACE, 15–20, 39, 62–63
   mean and, 56–59
Looking Back and Looking Ahead:
   Unit Reflections, 69–70

Mathematical Highlights, 4
Mathematical Reflections, 21, 29, 41, 52, 67
Mean, 4, 53–61
   ACE, 62–66
   line plot and, 56–59
   outliers and, 4, 60–61
   stem-and-leaf plot and, 60–61
Measures of center, 12, 53 *See also*
   Average; **Mean**; **Median**; **Mode**
Median, 4, 11–14
   ACE, 15–20, 26–27, 39, 48, 50, 62–66
   as an average, 12, 53
Mode, 4, 9–10
   ACE, 15–20, 64
   as an average, 9, 53

Name meanings, 9
Name origins, 6, 14
Names from Africa, 14
Numerical data, 4, 22–25
   ACE, 26–28

Outliers, 4, 36
   mean and, 60–61

Patterns, in data, 7, 8, 49
Plot
   line, 4, 7, 8, 56–59
   stem-and-leaf, 4, 32–36, 60–61

Prediction
   using average, 63
   using data, 7

Range, 4, 9–10
   ACE, 15–20, 50, 65
   intervals, 30–36

Stacked bar graph, 18–20
Statistical investigation, 5, 68
Stem-and-leaf plot, 4, 32–36
   ACE, 37–40, 64
   back-to-back, 34–36
   mean and, 60–61
Survey, 3

Unit project, 5, 68

Vertical axis, 43

Wolfman, Ira, 14

x–**axis**, 43

y–**axis**, 43

Connected Mathematics™

Shapes and Designs

Two-Dimensional Geometry

Student Edition

Glenda Lappan
James T. Fey
William M. Fitzgerald
Susan N. Friel
Elizabeth Difanis Phillips

Prentice
Hall

Glenview, Illinois
Needham, Massachusetts
Upper Saddle River, New Jersey

The Connected Mathematics Project was developed at Michigan State University with the support of National Science Foundation Grant No. MDR 9150217.

 This project was supported, in part, by the
National Science Foundation
Opinions expressed are those of the authors and not necessarily those of the Foundation

The Michigan State University authors and administration have agreed that all MSU royalties arising from this publication will be devoted to purposes supported by the Department of Mathematics and the MSU Mathematics Education Enrichment Fund.

Contents

Mathematical Highlights   6

The Unit Project: What I Know About Shapes and Designs   7

Investigation 1: Bees and Polygons   8
    1.1 Tiling a Beehive   9
    Applications—Connections—Extensions   11
    Mathematical Reflections   14

Investigation 2: Building Polygons   15
    2.1 Building Triangles   16
    2.2 Building Quadrilaterals   17
    2.3 Building Parallelograms   18
    Applications—Connections—Extensions   19
    Mathematical Reflections   21

Investigation 3: Polygons and Angles   22
    3.1 Follow the Dancing Bee   22
    3.2 Estimating Angle Measures   25
    3.3 Developing More Angle Benchmarks   27
    3.4 Playing Four in a Row   29
    3.5 Using an Angle Ruler   30
    3.6 Analyzing Measuring Errors   32
    Applications—Connections—Extensions   35
    Mathematical Reflections   41

Investigation 4: Polygon Properties and Tiling   42
    4.1 Relating Sides to Angles   42
    4.2 Measuring Irregular Polygons   44
    4.3 Back to the Bees!   46
    Applications—Connections—Extensions   47
    Mathematical Reflections   50

Investigation 5: Side-Angle-Shape Connections   51
    5.1 Flipping and Turning Triangles   52
    5.2 Flipping and Turning Quadrilaterals   54
    Applications—Connections—Extensions   57
    Mathematical Reflections   63

Investigation 6: Turtle Tracks   64
    6.1 Drawing with Logo   66
    6.2 Debugging Computer Programs   67
    6.3 Making Polygons   68
    Applications—Connections—Extensions   69
    Mathematical Reflections   75

The Unit Project: What I Know About Shapes and Designs   76

Looking Back and Looking Ahead: Unit Reflections   77

Glossary   79

Index   84

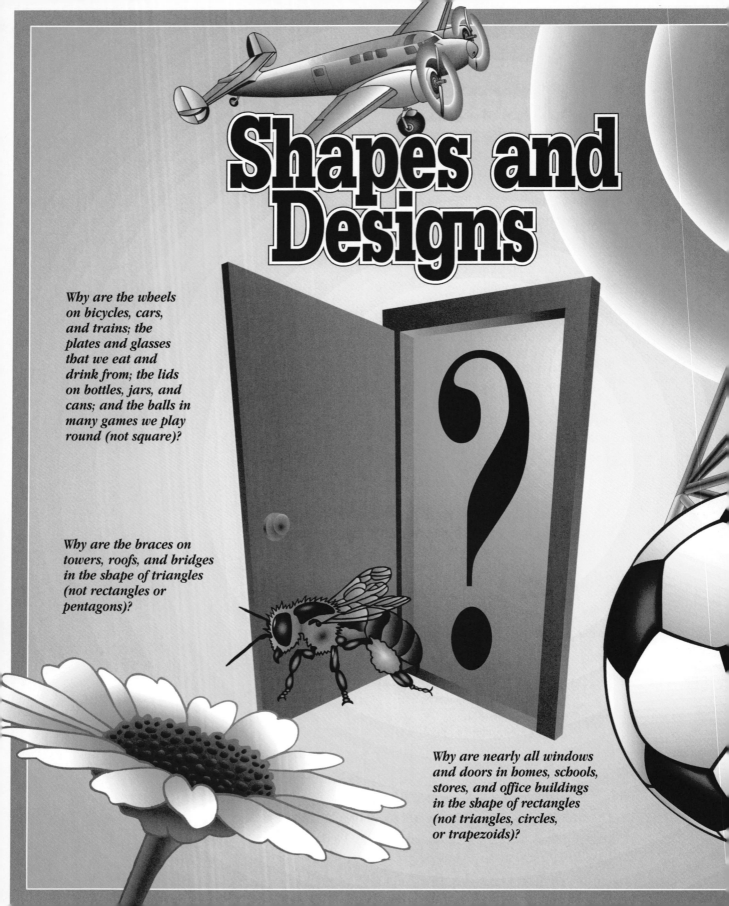

Shapes and Designs

Why are the wheels on bicycles, cars, and trains; the plates and glasses that we eat and drink from; the lids on bottles, jars, and cans; and the balls in many games we play round (not square)?

Why are the braces on towers, roofs, and bridges in the shape of triangles (not rectangles or pentagons)?

Why are nearly all windows and doors in homes, schools, stores, and office buildings in the shape of rectangles (not triangles, circles, or trapezoids)?

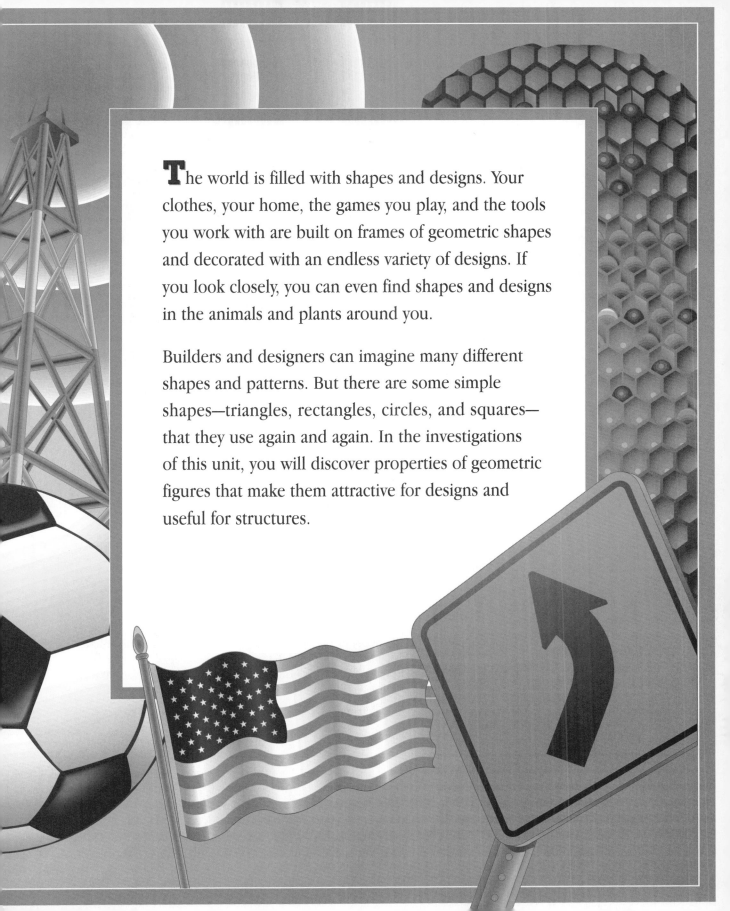

The world is filled with shapes and designs. Your clothes, your home, the games you play, and the tools you work with are built on frames of geometric shapes and decorated with an endless variety of designs. If you look closely, you can even find shapes and designs in the animals and plants around you.

Builders and designers can imagine many different shapes and patterns. But there are some simple shapes—triangles, rectangles, circles, and squares— that they use again and again. In the investigations of this unit, you will discover properties of geometric figures that make them attractive for designs and useful for structures.

What familiar geometric figures can you see in these designs from African, Asian, and American arts and crafts? Are the figures regular? Are the designs symmetric?

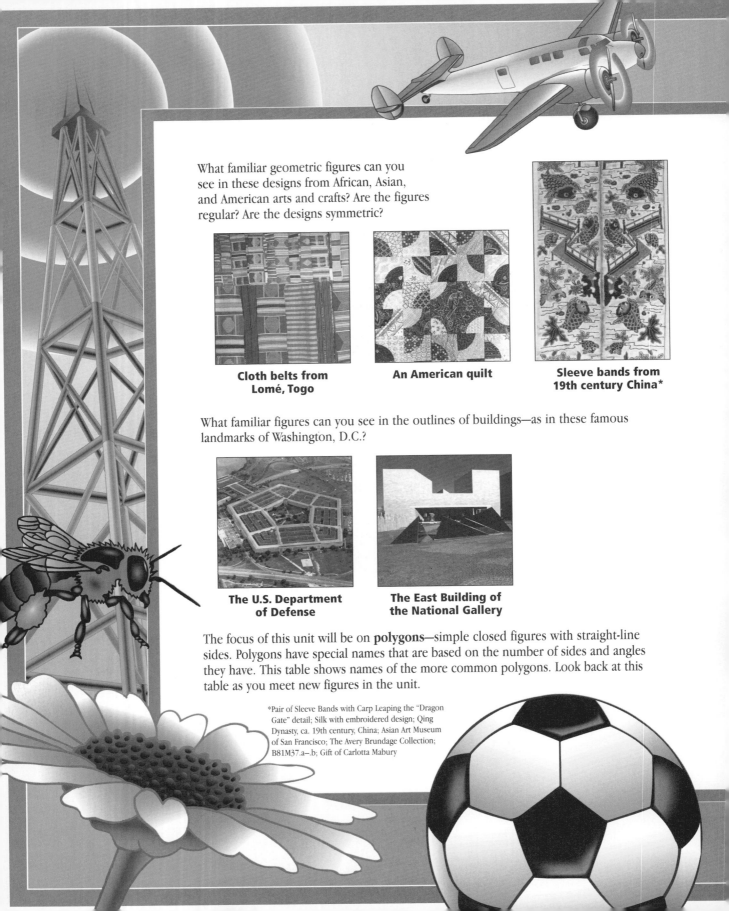

Cloth belts from Lomé, Togo

An American quilt

Sleeve bands from 19th century China*

What familiar figures can you see in the outlines of buildings—as in these famous landmarks of Washington, D.C.?

The U.S. Department of Defense

The East Building of the National Gallery

The focus of this unit will be on **polygons**—simple closed figures with straight-line sides. Polygons have special names that are based on the number of sides and angles they have. This table shows names of the more common polygons. Look back at this table as you meet new figures in the unit.

*Pair of Sleeve Bands with Carp Leaping the "Dragon Gate" detail; Silk with embroidered design; Qing Dynasty, ca. 19th century, China; Asian Art Museum of San Francisco; The Avery Brundage Collection; B81M37.a–.b; Gift of Carlotta Mabury

Number of Sides and Angles	Polygon Name
3	Triangle
4	Quadrilateral
5	Pentagon
6	Hexagon
8	Octagon
10	Decagon

As you study the properties of polygons, look for the ways that different combinations of sides and angles give different shapes. In particular, keep your eyes open for shapes that have attractive **symmetries,** such as *line symmetry* and *turn symmetry.* Line symmetry is also called *mirror symmetry,* since the half of the figure on one side of the line looks like it is being reflected in a mirror. Turn symmetry is also called *rotational symmetry,* because you have to rotate the figure around the centerpoint to find the places where it looks the same again.

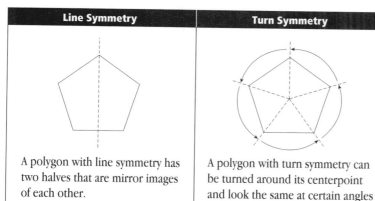

Line Symmetry	Turn Symmetry
A polygon with line symmetry has two halves that are mirror images of each other.	A polygon with turn symmetry can be turned around its centerpoint and look the same at certain angles of rotation.

Think about this!

Which common polygons and which kinds of symmetry appear
- in the designs, buildings, and other objects shown on the page before?
- in your classroom, your school, or places outside of your school?

In *Shapes and Designs,* you will explore important properties of polygons. The unit should help you to

● Recognize polygonal shapes and understand important properties of and relationships among polygons and angles of polygons;

● Investigate which polygons fit together to cover a flat surface and why;

● Explain why triangles are a useful structure in building structures;

● Investigate which side and angle relationships make rectangles useful for designs and for structures and why;

● Understand what the measure of an angle represents and how to estimate the size of any angle using reference to a right angle and other benchmark angles;

● Use tools for making more accurate angle measurements; and

● Reason about and solve problems involving shapes.

As you work on the problems of this unit, ask questions about situations that involve shapes such as: *Which shapes are involved? What properties of shapes are helpful? Is it important to find an exact angle measure? Is an estimate appropriate?*

What I Know About Shapes and Designs

As you work in this unit, you will be asked to think about the characteristics of different shapes and how unusual a shape can be and still be a triangle, quadrilateral, pentagon, or hexagon. You will also be asked to think about the relationships among these shapes. It is these characteristics of shapes and the relationships among them that affect the designs you see in your world.

One of the ways you will be asked to demonstrate what sense you are making of the mathematics in this unit is through a final project. At the end of this unit, you will use everything you have learned to create a project, such as a book, a poster, a report, a mobile, a movie, or a slide show.

You can start preparing for your project now. Create a special "shapes section" in your notebook, where you can collect information about:

- The characteristics of the following shapes: triangles, squares, rectangles, parallelograms, quadrilaterals, pentagons, hexagons, octagons
- The relationships among the shapes listed above
- Examples of places where these shapes can be found in your world.

After each investigation, record all the new information you have learned about shapes. Try to use as many of the new vocabulary words as you can. As you work through this unit, keep your eyes open for examples of the shapes listed above being used in many ways. Cut out examples from magazines and newspapers, and draw pictures of shapes you see used in the world around you. You may want to use an envelope for collecting and storing your examples.

At the end of the unit, you should have enough information to make a creative, interesting final project that shows all you have learned about shapes and designs.

Bees and Polygons

Honeybees live in colonies. In the wild, bee colonies build nests. Beekeepers provide wooden boxes called *hives* for the colonies they keep. About 60,000 residents are packed into a hive. Bees are fairly small insects, but packing a hive with 60,000 bees and their honey is tricky. Bees store their honey in a honeycomb, which is filled with tubes. An interesting pattern of polygons appears on the face of a honeycomb: it is covered with a design of identical hexagons that fit together like tiles on a floor.

Why do you think honeycombs are covered with hexagons instead of some other shape?

Did you know?

Each honeybee colony has a single queen and thousands of female *worker bees.* The worker bees find flowers to get nectar for making honey. They build the honeycomb, keep the beehive clean, take care of baby bees, feed and groom the queen bee, and guard the hive against intruders. Every hive also has several male bees, called *drones,* who have only one job: to fly around looking for a queen from another colony to mate with. Once a drone bee has mated, it dies.

1.1 Tiling a Beehive

The shapes pictured below are examples of **regular polygons.** The word *regular* means that all sides and angles of the polygon are the same size. (The *edges* of a figure are sometimes called the *sides* of a figure. Both words are correct.)

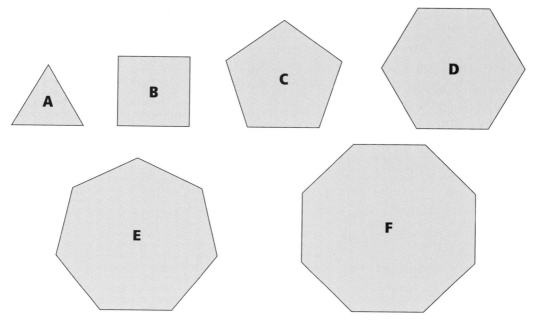

The honeycomb demonstrates that regular hexagons fit together to cover, or *tile*, a surface. Are there other shapes that have this same property?

Problem 1.1

Tiling means covering a flat surface with shapes that fit together without any gaps. Which of the regular polygons shown above will tile a flat surface?

Use shapes A–F from your Shapes Set or cutouts of the shapes shown above to explore this question. As you work, try to figure out why some shapes cover a space, while others do not. Consider two types of tilings:

A. Patterns in which all the tiles are the same

B. Patterns that combine two or more different tiles

As you experiment, make sketches to share with your classmates. Keep a record of shapes and combinations of shapes that cover a surface and those that do not.

■ Problem 1.1 Follow-Up

Look back at each tiling you made. Find a point on the tiling where the corners of the polygons fit together. This point is called a *vertex* of the tiling. For each tiling, describe exactly which polygons fit around a vertex and in what order they fit together.

Did you know?

Tilings are also called *tessellations*. Artists, designers, and mathematicians have been interested in tessellations for centuries. The Greek mathematician and inventor Archimedes (c. 287–212 B.C.) studied the properties of regular polygons that tiled the plane. From 700–1500 B.C., Moorish artists—forbidden by their religion to paint people, animals, and other real-world objects—used tessellating patterns extensively in their work. The Dutch artist M. C. Escher (1898–1972), inspired by Moorish designs, spent his life creating tessellations. He altered geometric tessellating shapes to make birds, reptiles, fish, and people.

As you work on these ACE questions, use your calculator whenever you need it.

Applications

1. Choose a rectangle from your Shapes Set, or draw your own. Find several ways that copies of your rectangle can be used to cover, or tile, a surface. Make sketches of the patterns you discover.

2. The shapes shown below are *parallelograms.* Choose a parallelogram from your Shapes Set or draw your own. Find several ways that copies of your parallelogram can be used to cover, or tile, a surface. Make sketches of the patterns you discover.

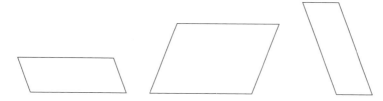

3. Choose a triangle from your Shapes Set, or draw your own. Find several ways that copies of your triangle can be used to cover, or tile, a surface. Make sketches of the patterns you discover.

Connections

4. Name the polygon that appears in each of these street signs. If you need help, refer to the table of polygon names on page 5.

In 5–8, find the dimensions of all the possible rectangles that can be made with the given number of square tiles. For example, the rectangle at right is made with 2 rows of 3 tiles each. We say that the *dimensions* of this rectangle are 2×3.

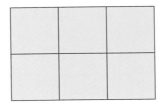

5. 30 square tiles

6. 24 square tiles

7. 36 square tiles

8. 17 square tiles

Extensions

9. Find pictures of American state flags and flags of other countries in a dictionary or encyclopedia. Sketch several flags that you think show interesting uses of geometric shapes in their design. Explain what you find interesting about the flags. Then draw a design that you would use as a flag of your own.

State flag of Maryland

In 10 and 11, create tiling patterns that use copies of both of the shapes in each pair. Use these shapes from your Shapes Set or cutouts of the shapes to help you find patterns. Make sketches of the patterns you discover.

10.

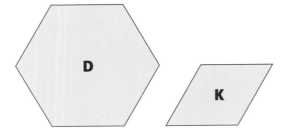

11.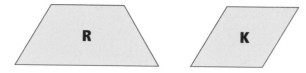

12. Below is a large square tiled with identical, smaller squares. Which other regular polygons can be tiled with identical, smaller copies of themselves? Sketch any patterns you think will work.

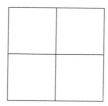

13. An *irregular polygon,* such as the one shown below, is a polygon in which the sides are not all the same length. Choose an irregular quadrilateral from your Shapes Set, or draw your own. Cut out several copies of your figure and see whether you can use them to tile a surface. Sketch your findings. Test other irregular quadrilaterals to see if they can be used to tile a surface. Summarize what you find about using quadrilaterals to tile a surface.

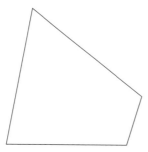

14. Can you make a tiling pattern with circles? Why or why not?

15. Does a circle have any turn symmetries? If so, explain and show some examples.

Mathematical Reflections

In this investigation, you found that some shapes can tile a surface, while others cannot. These questions will help you summarize what you have learned:

1 Which shapes seem to work as tiles and which do not?

2 Which polygons can tile alone and which need to be combined with other polygons to fill a space?

Think about your answers to these questions, discuss your ideas with other students and your teacher, and then write a summary of your findings in your journal.

Are you keeping your eyes open? What shapes and designs are you noticing in the world around you? Remember to write what you have discovered about triangles, squares, rectangles, parallelograms, quadrilaterals, pentagons, hexagons, and octagons from this investigation.

Building Polygons

Polygons come in many shapes and sizes. You can use polystrips and fasteners like these:

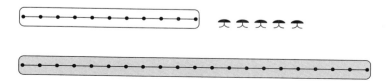

to build polygons and study their properties.

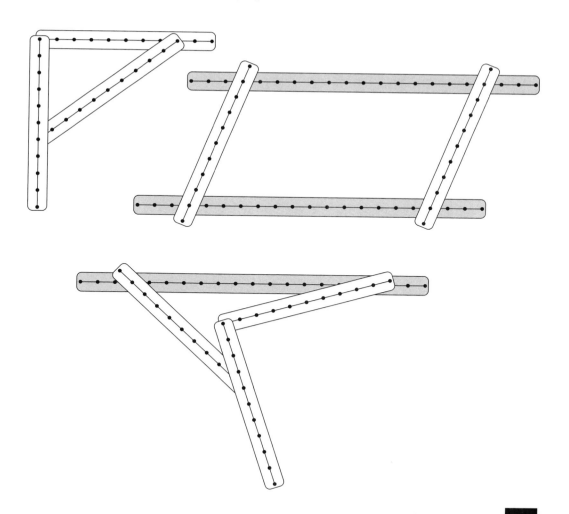

2.1 Building Triangles

Triangles are the simplest polygons. Although they have only three sides and three angles, triangles come in many different shapes with very useful properties. You can use polystrips to experiment with building triangles and to discover some important properties and characteristics about them. Problem 2.1 asks you to explore questions about the side lengths of triangles: If you are given three side lengths, can you always make a triangle? With three side lengths, can you make more than one triangle?

Problem 2.1

Suppose you are given three numbers to be lengths of sides in a triangle.

A. Will it always be possible to make a triangle with those side lengths?

B. Can you make two or more different triangles from the same side lengths?

Explore these questions by first selecting three numbers between 1 and 20 and then using polystrips to try to make a triangle with the numbers as side lengths. Repeat this several times with many different sets of three numbers. Sketch and label your results so you can share them with the class.

A good way to select numbers is to use number cubes. Toss three cubes, and use their sum as the length of one side. Toss the cubes two more times to get lengths for the other two sides.

■ Problem 2.1 Follow-Up

When you have completed the problem, look back over your examples, and use polystrips to explore these questions.

1. What combinations of side lengths give triangles like those you see often in designs and buildings?

2. What combinations of side lengths give triangles with strange shapes?

3. What combinations of side lengths give triangles that have symmetry?

When you make an interesting triangle, trace it on a large sheet of paper so you can share it with the class. On the paper, explain why you think the triangle is interesting. Be sure to focus on the *mathematical* properties that make the shape interesting.

2.2 Building Quadrilaterals

A polygon with four sides is called a **quadrilateral**. Many different kinds of quadrilaterals appear in the structures and designs all around us. In the last problem, you explored triangles and discovered some important properties about them. In this problem, you will explore quadrilaterals. As you work with quadrilaterals, think about ways quadrilaterals and triangles are similar and ways they are different.

Problem 2.2

Suppose you are given four numbers to be lengths of sides in a quadrilateral.

A. Will it always be possible to make a quadrilateral with those side lengths?

B. Can you make two or more different quadrilaterals from the same side lengths?

Explore these questions by first selecting four numbers between 1 and 20 and then using polystrips to try to make a quadrilateral with the numbers as side lengths. Repeat this several times with many different sets of four numbers. Sketch and label your results so you can share them with the class.

A good way to select numbers is to use number cubes. Toss three cubes, and use their sum as the length of one side. Toss the cubes three more times to get lengths for the other three sides.

Problem 2.2 Follow-Up

When you have completed the problem, look back over your examples, and use polystrips to explore these questions.

1. What combinations of side lengths give quadrilaterals like those you see often in designs and buildings?

2. What combinations of side lengths give quadrilaterals with strange shapes?

3. What combinations of side lengths give quadrilaterals that have symmetry?

When you make an interesting quadrilateral, trace it on a large sheet of paper so you can share it with the class. On the paper, explain why you think the quadrilateral is interesting. Be sure to focus on the *mathematical* properties that make the shape interesting.

2.3 Building Parallelograms

Rectangles may be the most common quadrilaterals. You can find them in buildings and designs everywhere. Here are five examples of rectangles:

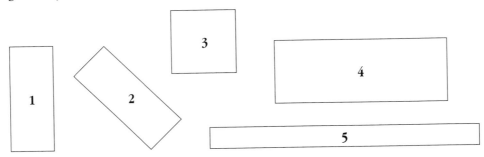

In your work with polystrips, you probably discovered that if you build a rectangle and then push on one of its corners, it easily changes into different shapes, such as these:

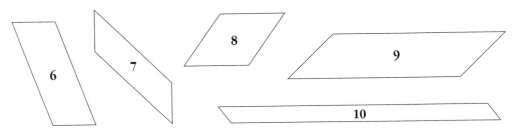

Problem 2.3

The ten quadrilaterals shown above are examples of **parallelograms.** The name *parallelogram* is based on the word *parallel.* Parallel lines are straight lines that never meet, no matter how far they are extended.

A. What do these ten quadrilaterals have in common that makes the name *parallelogram* sensible?

B. How do rectangles 1–5 differ from shapes 6–10 (which were formed by pressing on the corners of 1–5)?

C. How are the lengths of the sides of a parallelogram related?

Explore these questions by making a variety of parallelograms with polystrips. Sketch the results so you can share them with the class.

■ Problem 2.3 Follow-Up

Describe what happens to the four angles in the rectangle as you slowly push on a corner of the polystrip model.

As you work on these ACE questions, use your calculator whenever you need it.

Applications

In 1–8, sketch examples of shapes that can be made with the given set of side lengths. Be prepared to explain your strategy for finding examples and to discuss whether your examples are all that are possible.

1. Side lengths of 5, 5, and 3

2. Side lengths of 8, 8, and 8

3. Side lengths of 5, 5, 8, and 8

4. Side lengths of 5, 5, 6, and 14

5. Side lengths of 5, 8, and 15

6. Side lengths of 8, 8, 8, and 8

7. Side lengths of 5, 6, and 10

8. Side lengths of 4, 3, 5, and 14

In 9–12, determine which set or sets of side lengths from 1–8 above can make the following shapes.

9. A triangle with all angles the same size

10. A quadrilateral with all angles the same size

11. A parallelogram

12. A quadrilateral that is not a parallelogram

Connections

13. **a.** In what ways are all three quadrilaterals below alike?

b. In what ways does each quadrilateral differ from the others?

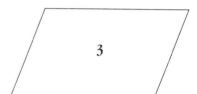

14. Based on your polystrip work with triangles and quadrilaterals, what explanations can you now give for the common appearance of triangular shapes in figures like radio and TV towers and in bridges?

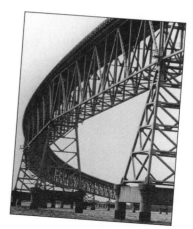

Extensions

15. A polygon with five sides is called a **pentagon**. In a–c, explore some pentagon shapes by using polystrips or making sketches.

    a. What combinations of side lengths give pentagons that you think are especially good for use in designs?

    b. Is it always possible to make a pentagon with any given five numbers as side lengths? Explain.

    c. Can you make two or more different pentagons from the same side lengths? Explain.

16. The shapes below are *not* polygons, although they are similar to polygons in some ways. In a–c, explain how the shape is different from the polygons pictured earlier in this unit.

    a.    **b.**    **c.**

17. What symmetries do each of the figures in question 16 have? Show and explain your answers.

Mathematical Reflections

In this investigation, you experimented with building polygons by choosing lengths for the sides, and then connecting those sides to make a simple closed figure. These questions will help you summarize what you have learned:

1. How many different triangles can you make from a set of three side lengths?

2. How can you tell by looking at the lengths of three line segments whether they can be used to form a triangle?

3. How many different quadrilaterals can you make from a set of four side lengths?

4. What combinations of side lengths will always give a parallelogram? A rectangle? A square?

Think about your answers to these questions, discuss your ideas with other students and your teacher, and then write a summary of your findings in your journal.

Remember to collect pictures and make drawings of how the shapes you are learning about are used in the world around you! In the project section of your journal, record what you have discovered about triangles and quadrilaterals.

Polygons and Angles

If you experiment with making polygons, you will quickly see that there is more to a shape than the lengths of its sides. For example, with ten line segments of equal length, you can build a regular decagon or a five-point star. How are these two polygons different? *It's all in the angles!*

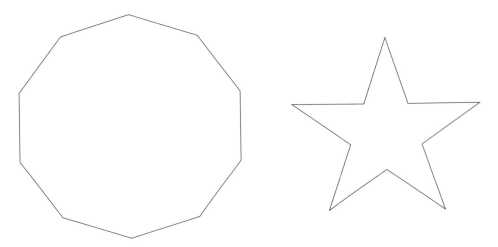

To describe polygons accurately, you must measure the **angles** formed where the sides of the polygon meet.

3.1 Follow the Dancing Bee

The workers in a honeybee hive fly great distances to find flowers with the nectar they need to make honey. When a bee finds a good patch of flowers, she returns to the hive and communicates the location of the flowers to the other bees. Scientific observation has shown that honeybees have an amazing method for giving directions from the hive to the flowers: they perform a lively dance!

During the direction dance, a honeybee moves in a combination of squiggly lines and half circles.

The squiggly lines in the dance indicate the direction of the flowers. If the flowers are in the direction of the sun, the bee dances in a line that is straight up and down.

Bee Dance   **Direction of Flowers**

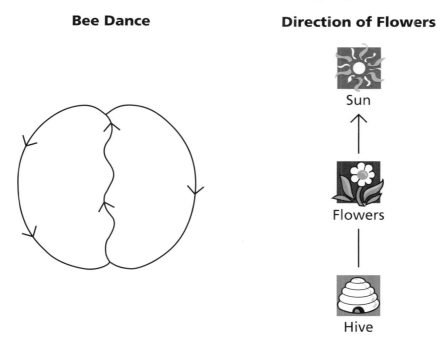

If the flowers are not in the direction of the sun, the bee dances in a tilted line. The angle of the tilt is the same as the angle formed by the sun, the hive, and the flowers.

Bee Dance   **Direction of Flowers**

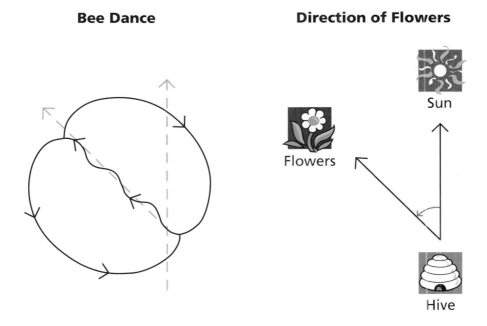

The bee dance illustrates one way that you can think about an angle—as a *turn*. When the honeybee dances along a tilted line, she is telling the other bees how far to *turn* from the sun to find the flowers.

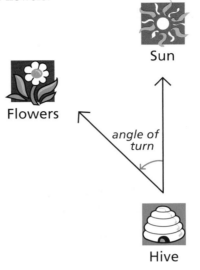

You can also think about an angle as a *wedge,* like a piece of pizza. Finally, you can think about an angle as *two sides* that meet at a point, like branches on a tree.

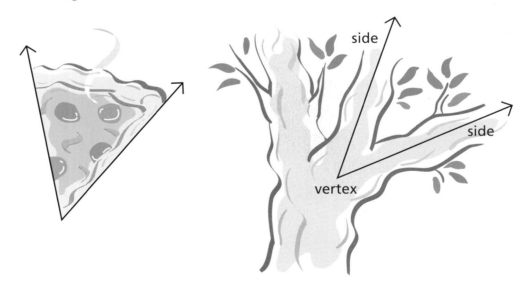

The point where the two sides touch is called the **vertex** of the angle. In the angle formed by the flowers, the hive, and the sun, the beehive is located at the vertex. The imaginary lines from the hive to the sun and from the hive to the flowers form the sides of the angle.

Problem 3.1

Look around your school, your home, and the other buildings and landscapes you see around you to find examples of angles. Find at least one example of each type of angle described.

A. An angle that occurs as the result of a *turning motion,* such as the opening of a door

B. An angle that occurs as a *wedge,* such as a piece of pizza

C. An angle that occurs as *two sides* with a *common vertex,* such as the branches on a tree

Explain where you found each angle, and make a sketch of the figure in which each angle appears. Be ready to share your findings with the class.

■ Problem 3.1 Follow-Up

Determine whether each angle you found is a **right angle**—with sides that meet to form a square corner—or whether it is bigger or smaller than a right angle.

3.2 Estimating Angle Measures

There are several ways to describe the size of an angle. The most common way is the **degree.** An angle of 1 degree (also written 1°) is a very small turn, or a very narrow wedge.

1°

The size of a degree was chosen so that a right angle has a measure of 90°. Here is a 90° angle. Imagine 90 copies of the 1° angle fitting into this angle.

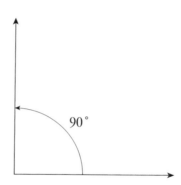

90°

Here is an angle formed by one half the turn of a right angle. It measures 45°.

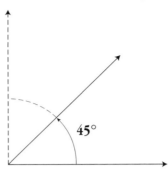

It is often useful to *estimate* the measures of angles and to sketch angles when a measurement is given.

Problem 3.2

Sketch and find the degree measures of the angles made by these turns. For each sketch, include an arrow indicating the angle of turn.

A. One third of a right-angle turn   **B.** Two thirds of a right-angle turn

C. One quarter of a right-angle turn   **D.** One and one half right-angle turns

E. Two right-angle turns   **F.** Three right-angle turns

The angle below has a measure of about 120°. In G–L, make sketches of angles with *approximately* the given measure. For each sketch, include an arrow indicating the angle of turn.

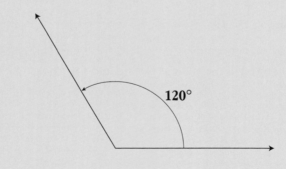

G. 20°   **H.** 70°

I. 150°   **J.** 180°

K. 270°   **L.** 360°

■ Problem 3.2 Follow-Up

When you measure an angle, it is important to keep in mind what is being measured. For example, the sides of the 1° angle shown on page 25 are very long, but a 1° angle is a very small angle. The sides of angles are *rays*, lines that continue in one direction forever. For a given angle, you can draw the sides as long or as short as you wish. The size of an angle is *the amount of turn* from one side to another.

Which of the angles below is the largest? Which is the smallest? Which is a right angle? Explain your reasoning.

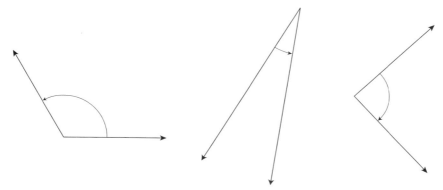

3.3 Developing More Angle Benchmarks

In Problem 3.2, you used a 90° angle as a *benchmark*, or reference, to help you sketch angles and estimate angle measures. The angles of some of the polygons in your Shapes Set can be other useful benchmarks.

Problem 3.3

Estimate and record the measure of each angle of shapes A, B, D, M, R, and V in your Shapes Set. Copy the shapes onto a sheet of paper, and label each angle with its measure.

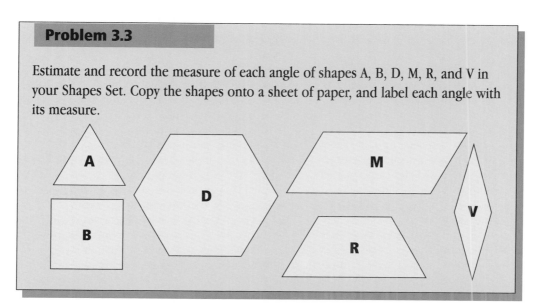

■ **Problem 3.3 Follow-Up**

Use what you have learned about the measures of the angles in your Shapes Set to estimate the measures of the angles below.

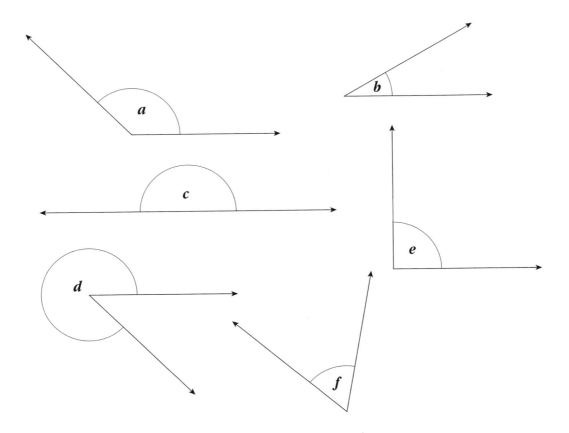

3.4 Playing Four in a Row

You know how to locate points on a grid by using ordered pairs of coordinates. To locate a point, you can think of starting at (0, 0), moving over the number of units given by the first coordinate, and then moving up the number of units given by the second coordinate. On the grid at right, point A has coordinates (1, 4), point B has coordinates (3, 2), and point C has coordinates (5, 6).

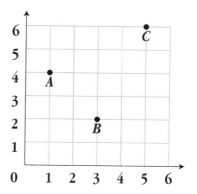

Mathematicians and scientists find it useful to locate points in other ways. One way to locate points is to use a circular grid. On this kind of grid, angle measures help describe the location of points.

Two examples of this kind of grid are shown below. They look very different from the grid shown above. The grid on the left has lines at 45° intervals. The grid on the right has lines at 30° intervals. The circles are numbered, moving out from the center at 0.

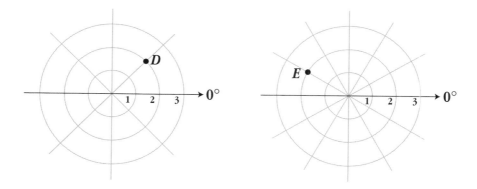

Points on these grids are described by giving a distance and an angle. For example, point D above has coordinates (2, 45°). To locate a point on one of these grids, start at the center of the grid and move over the number of units indicated by the first coordinate. Then, move along that circle the number of degrees given by the second coordinate. So to locate (2, 45°), move over to 2 on the 0° line and then move up to the 45° line. Can you find the coordinates of point E above?

In this problem, you will play a game called Four in a Row. The game can be played by two players or two teams.

Four in a Row Rules

Four in a Row is played on a circular grid. Players take turns saying the coordinates of a point aloud and then marking the point on the grid. One player uses X's, and the other uses O's. Marks can be placed only on points on the grid where circles and sides meet. The winner is the first player to get four in a row along a line or around a circle. While one player takes a turn, the other player should listen carefully. A player must give correct coordinates before he or she can mark a point on the grid.

Problem 3.4

Play Four in a Row several times. Play games with both the 30° grid and the 45° grid on Labsheet 3.4. Write down any winning strategies you discover.

■ Problem 3.4 Follow-Up

Work with your partner to make up new rules for playing the game or to create a different board on which to play the game.

3.5 Using an Angle Ruler

In many situations in which distance and angles are measured, estimates are good enough. But sometimes it is important to measure very precisely. If you were navigating an ocean liner, an airplane, or a rocket, you would not want to just estimate the angles needed to plot your course.

There are several tools that help with angle measurement. One of the easiest to use is the *angle ruler.* An angle ruler has two arms, like the sides of an angle. The arms are joined by a rivet that allows them to swing apart to form angles of various sizes. The rivet is at the center of a circular ruler whose edge is marked with numbers from 0° to 360°.

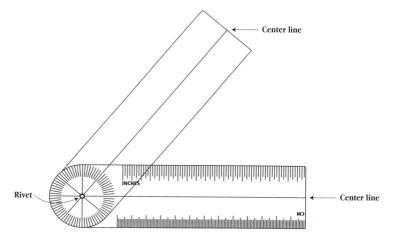

To measure an angle with an angle ruler, place the rivet over the vertex of the angle and set the center line of the arm passing through 0° on one side of the angle. Then swing the other arm around until its center line lies on the second side of the angle. The center line on the second arm will pass over a mark on the circular ruler, telling you the degree measure of the angle.

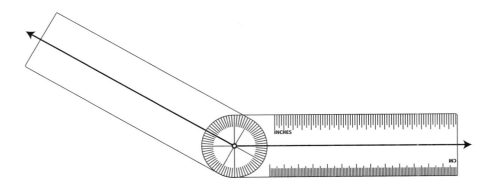

When you are measuring an angle on a wedge of some thickness, such as a block, you can place the object between the two arms of the angle ruler and read off the size of the angle, as shown here.

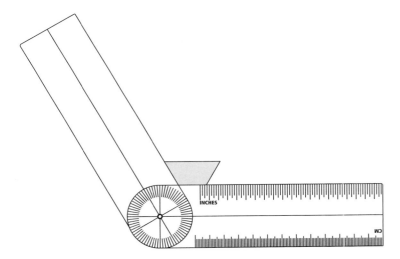

Problem 3.5

Measure each angle of shapes A, B, D, M, R, and V in your Shapes Set. Copy the shapes onto a sheet of paper, and label each angle with its measure. Use your results to answer the questions below.

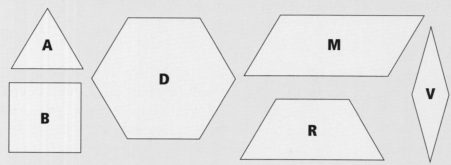

A. How do your measures with the angle ruler compare with your estimates from Problem 3.3?

B. Where do you find two or more angles of the same size in the same shape?

C. Where do you find two or more angles of the same size in different shapes?

D. What combinations of the six shapes pictured above will work together to make a tiling? What patterns do you see in the angles of these shapes?

■ Problem 3.5 Follow-Up

In each shape you measured, what kinds of symmetry do you find?

3.6 Analyzing Measuring Errors

In 1937, the famous aviator Amelia Earhart tried to become the first woman to fly around the world. She began her journey on June 1, when she took off from Miami, Florida. She reached Lae, New Guinea, and then headed east toward Howland Island in the Pacific Ocean. She never arrived at Howland Island.

In 1992, 55 years later, investigators found evidence that Earhart had crashed on the desert island of Nikumaroro, far off her intended course. Her navigator had apparently made errors in plotting the course. When flying long distances, even small errors can lead a flight far astray.

Did you know?

Amelia Earhart's tragic flight was not her first attempt to circle the globe. On March 17, 1937, she took off from Oakland, California, heading west around the world. Three days later, upon takeoff from Hawaii, her plane made a sharp, uncontrollable turn on the runway causing the landing gear to collapse and damaging the underside of her plane.

Every time we use a measurement tool, there is some error. No instrument gives absolutely precise measurements. Why is this?

The map on the following page shows Lae, New Guinea, Howland Island, and Nikumaroro Island. You can use the map and an angle ruler, to measure the angles involved in Earhart's flight.

Problem 3.6

How many degrees off course was Earhart's crash site from her intended destination?

■ Problem 3.6 Follow-Up

1. Use your angle ruler to measure the six angles in Problem 3.3 Follow-Up on page 28. (You have already estimated the angle measurements.)

2. Look at your measures and your estimates from Problem 3.3 Follow-Up. If there are differences, explain why.

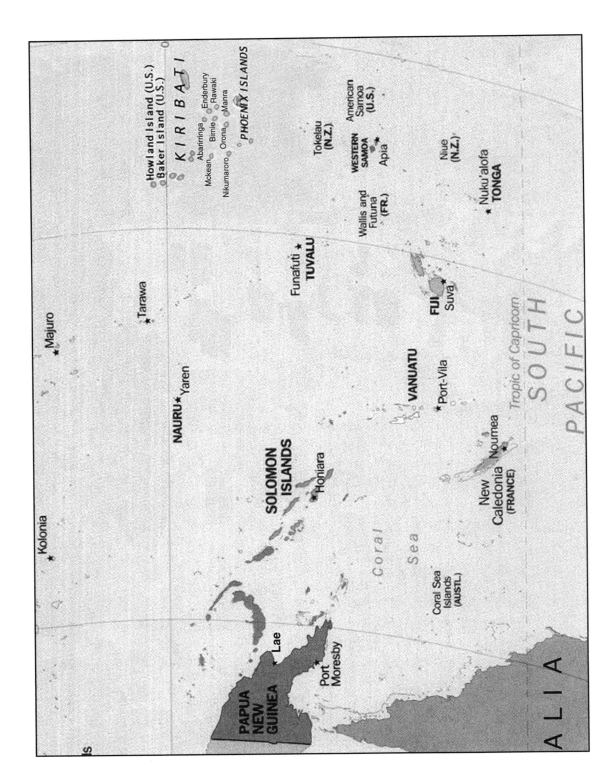

Adapted from *Small Blue Planet*. © Copyright 1993–1995 by Now What? Software, San Francisco. This map was created from original maps made by the Central Intelligence Agency and the Defense Mapping Agency.

As you work on these ACE questions, use your calculator whenever you need it.

Applications

In 1–4, estimate the measures of the angles of the following bee dances. Then check your estimates by using an angle ruler.

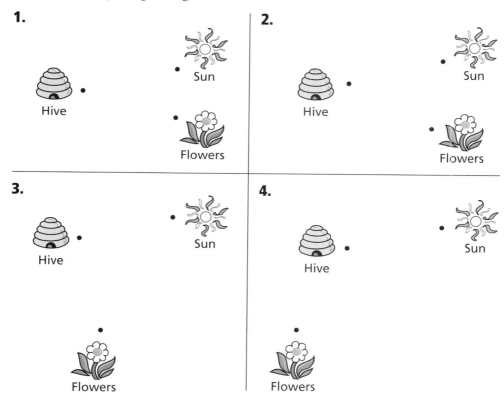

1.

2.

3.

4.

In 5–12, draw angles with the given measures.

5. 45°   **6.** 70°   **7.** 110°   **8.** 170°

9. 200°   **10.** 270°   **11.** 20°   **12.** 180°

In 13–18, give the degree measures of each turn.

13. One right-angle turn

14. Two right-angle turns

15. Three right-angle turns

16. One half of a right-angle turn

17. One third of a right-angle turn

18. Four right-angle turns

In 19–26, *without* using an angle ruler, determine the letter of the angle below with a measure closest to the measure given. Check your answers with an angle ruler.

19. 30°   **20.** 60°   **21.** 90°   **22.** 120°

23. 150°   **24.** 180°   **25.** 270°   **26.** 350°

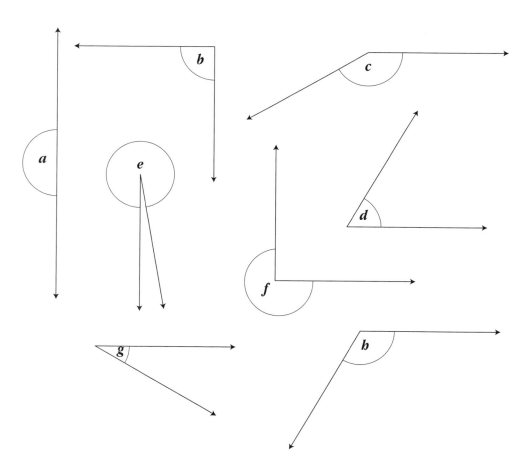

In 27–29, determine whether the angles are the same size. If they are not, tell which angle is larger.

27.

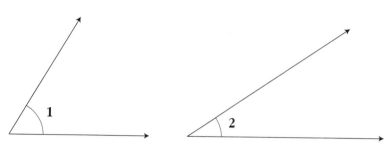

28.

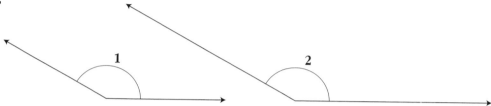

29.

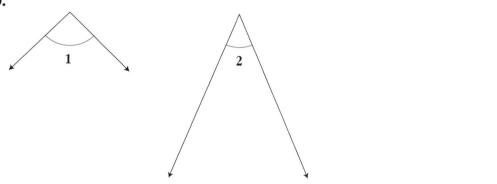

At the start of each hour, the minute hand of a clock points straight up, at the 12. In 30–35, determine the angle through which the minute hand passes as the given amount of time passes. Make a sketch to illustrate each situation.

30. 15 minutes   **31.** 30 minutes   **32.** 20 minutes

33. 1 hour   **34.** 5 minutes   **35.** $1\frac{1}{2}$ hours

Connections

36. Describe two situations in which angle measurements are used. Find one situation where very precise measurement is important and another situation where an estimate will be good enough.

37. Describe two situations in which length measurements are used. Find one situation where very precise measurement is important and another situation where an estimate will be good enough.

38. Here are the results ten students got when they measured the angles of the triangle below:

Angle *A:* 52°, 53°, 55°, 50°, 52°, 50°, 55°, 50°, 53°, 50°

Angle *B:* 37°, 35°, 35°, 35°, 40°, 40°, 37°, 35°, 35°, 38°

Angle *C:* 90°, 90°, 89°, 90°, 88°, 92°, 86°, 91°, 91°, 90°

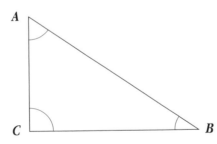

a. What method would you use to decide on the best measurement for each angle?

b. What degree measure will your method give for each angle?

c. Make line plots of the data for each angle, and explain how your choices of best measurements relate to the patterns in those plots.

39. This circle is divided into wedges formed by angles with vertices at the center of the circle. Such angles are called **central angles** of the circle. The central angles shown here each measure 90°.

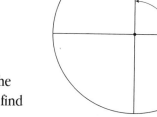

In a–c, sketch a circle divided into the given number of equal wedges, and find the measure of the central angles.

a. 8 equal pieces **b.** 6 equal pieces **c.** 3 equal pieces

d. What other ways could you cut a circle into equal wedges to give central angles with whole-number degree measurements? List the number of pieces and the measure of each central angle.

40. Measure each interior angle in the decagon and the star below. Look for patterns relating the angle measures in the two figures. Compare the lengths of the sides. What do you notice?

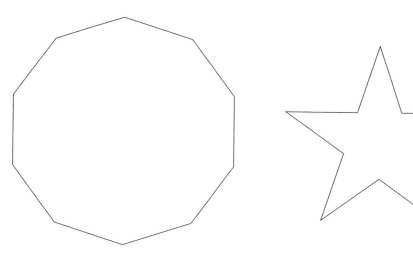

41. How do the perimeters (distance around) of the two figures in question 40 relate to each other?

Extensions

42. Below are two sets of parallel lines cut by another line.

    a. In each drawing, measure the angles formed where the single line cuts across each of the parallel lines.

    b. Describe any patterns you notice in the angle measurements.

    c. Look around your school and your home to find places where similar patterns are formed. Sketch and describe some of the patterns you discover.

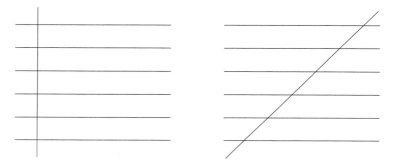

43. Design a new circular grid for playing Four in a Row. Play your game with a friend or a member of your family. Explain the ideas that led to your new design, and compare playing the game on the new grid to playing it on the grids you used in Problem 3.4.

44. Why are the wheels of bicycles, cars, and trains; the plates and glasses that we eat and drink from; the lids on bottles, jars, and cans; and the balls in many games we play round (not square or other polygon shapes)?

Mathematical Reflections

In this investigation, you thought about angles in several ways. You have become skilled at estimating measures of angles and using tools to make more precise measurements. These questions will help you summarize what you have learned:

1 Give examples of where angles occur as

    a. turns   **b.** wedges   **c.** sides with a common vertex

2 Explain what a *degree* is and how it is used to describe the size of an angle.

3 What is the importance of benchmark angles? How can they be used to make accurate estimates of angle measures?

4 Explain what an angle ruler is and how it can be used to measure the size of angles.

5 Name some situations in which angle measures must be precise. Name some other situations in which an estimate is all that is necessary.

Think about your answers to these questions, discuss your ideas with other students and your teacher, and then write a summary of your findings in your journal.

Don't forget to write about your new insights into angles! Are you remembering to collect examples of how shapes are used all around you?

Polygon Properties and Tiling

The shape of a polygon depends on the number of sides it has, the length of those sides, and the size of its angles. In order to see how sides and angles are related in polygons, you can gather some data from polygons, organize the data, and look for patterns. Patterns in the angle measures of regular polygons help to explain why hexagons show up in honeycombs.

4.1 Relating Sides to Angles

Below are six regular polygons that are already familiar to you. All of the sides in all of the polygons are the same length. The angles where the sides meet are clearly not the same in all the figures. What pattern do you see in the sizes of the interior angles as the number of sides increases?

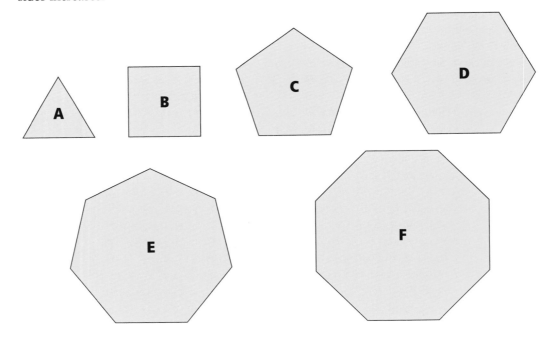

Problem 4.1

Count the sides of each of these six regular polygons. Measure the interior angles with your angle ruler.

A. Make a table that shows the name of each polygon, the number of sides it has, the measure of each of its angles, and the sum of the measures of all of its angles (this is called the *angle sum*).

B. In your table, look for patterns that relate the number of sides a polygon has to the measure of its angles and to its angle sum. Think about ways to complete these statements:

- If a regular polygon has _____ sides, the angle sum of the polygon is _____ degrees.

- If a regular polygon has _____ sides, each angle measures _____ degrees.

■ Problem 4.1 Follow-Up

The patterns you observed relating the number of sides of a regular polygon to the measures of its interior angles were based on measurements of one set of figures. Do you think the same patterns relating the number of sides and the sum of the angles will occur in larger or smaller regular polygons?

Below and on the next page are sets of regular polygons of different sizes. Measure the interior angles in each polygon to see whether the same side-angle patterns occur.

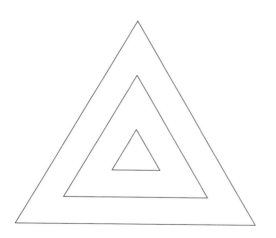 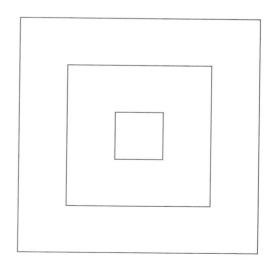

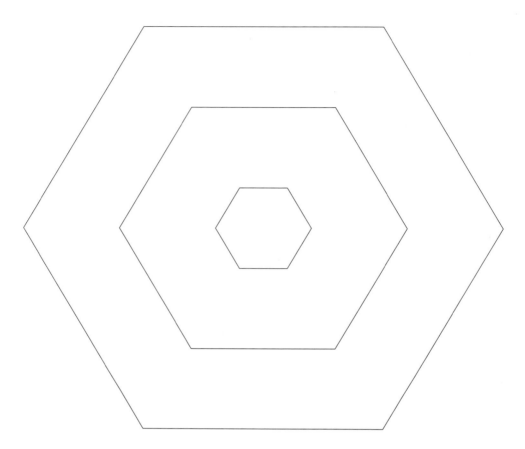

4.2 Measuring Irregular Polygons

In Problem 4.1, you discovered that the angle sum of any *regular* polygon can be predicted easily from the number of sides it has.

Regular polygon	Number of sides	Angle sum
Triangle	3	180°
Square	4	360°
Pentagon	5	540°
Hexagon	6	720°
Heptagon	7	900°
Octagon	8	1080°

In this problem, you will explore *irregular* polygons, like the ones shown below. An **irregular** polygon is a polygon in which the sides are not all the same length. Is there a relationship between the number of sides and the angle sum for irregular polygons?

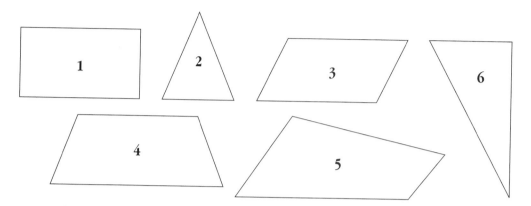

Problem 4.2

A. For each triangle and quadrilateral shown above, measure each interior angle and compute the angle sum.

B. How do the angle sums for these irregular polygons compare with the angle sums for the regular polygons?

C. Test the side-angle patterns you found by measuring the interior angles of some other triangles and quadrilaterals from your Shapes Set.

D. Use the information you have discovered about triangles and quadrilaterals to make a guess about the angle sums in irregular pentagons and hexagons. Test your guess by drawing and measuring some irregular pentagons and hexagons.

■ Problem 4.2 Follow-Up

Triangles with all sides equal are called **equilateral triangles**. Triangles with two sides equal, like shape 2 above, are called **isosceles triangles**. What can you say about the angles in an equilateral triangle? What can you say about the angles in an isosceles triangle?

4.3 Back to the Bees!

The surface of a honeycomb is covered with hexagons. It seems reasonable that a honeycomb is covered with a simple shape instead of several complex shapes, but we obviously can't ask bees why their honeycomb construction results in hexagons instead of pentagons or heptagons or some other shape. However, there are some mathematical properties of hexagons that may offer explanations.

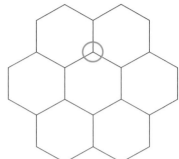

At right is a tiling of regular hexagons. Notice that three angles fit together exactly around each vertex point. Why do three regular hexagons fit together so neatly?

In Problem 1.1, you discovered which regular polygons fit together to cover a surface. In this problem, you will explore the properties of these shapes that allow them to fit together neatly around a vertex point.

Problem 4.3

Explore tilings made from a single type of regular polygon. Consider patterns with triangles only, squares only, pentagons only, hexagons only, heptagons only, and octagons only. Make sketches to show what you discover.

A. Which regular polygons fit around a vertex point exactly? What are the angle measures of these polygons?

B. Which regular polygons do not fit around a point exactly? What are the angle measures of these polygons?

C. What seems to be the key that tells which regular polygons will fit together in a tiling and which will not?

■ Problem 4.3 Follow-Up

Explore tilings made with parallelograms. Look for patterns in the angle measures of parallelograms that fit around a vertex point exactly. Make a record of your findings.

As you work on these ACE questions, use your calculator whenever you need it.

Applications

1. This figure is a regular decagon.

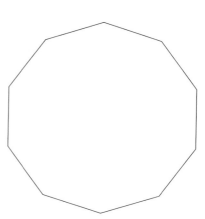

a. What angle sum do you expect for this polygon?

b. What measure do you expect for each interior angle of this polygon?

c. Can copies of this polygon be used to tile a surface? Explain your reasoning.

In 2–5, you are given measures of several angles. Find the measures of the other angles.

2.

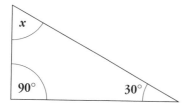

3.

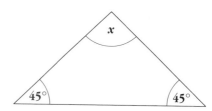

4.

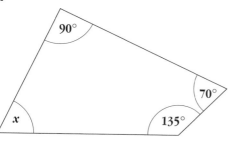

5.

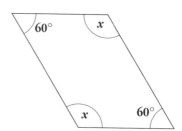

Connections

6. Shown below are a quadrilateral and a pentagon with *diagonals* drawn to form triangles. A **diagonal** of a polygon is a segment connecting two vertices that are not next to each other.

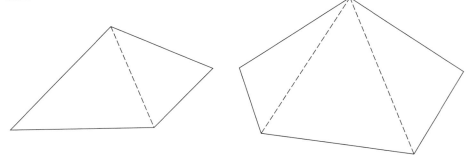

    a. How do these drawings show a connection between angle sums of triangles, quadrilaterals, and pentagons?

    b. What do the drawings show about ways to strengthen quadrilateral or pentagonal shapes in buildings?

7. In geometric figures, it is often useful to label points with letters. That way, you can describe any angle by using three letters. For example, the angle marked in the drawing below is angle DAC. In this notation, the middle letter is the vertex of the angle and the other two letters are points on each edge. To indicate that you are referring to an angle, you can write the word *angle* before the three letters (for example, angle DAC) or you can use an angle symbol (for example, ∠DAC).

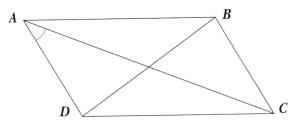

a. Find and measure ∠ABC, ∠ABD, ∠DBC, ∠BCA, ∠BCD, ∠ACD, ∠CDB, ∠CDA, ∠BDA, ∠DAC, ∠DAB, and ∠CAB. Record your answers.

b. What relationships do you see among the angles in this figure?

8. Choose a nonrectangular quadrilateral (such as shape U) from your Shapes Set, or draw your own. Try to fit copies of your quadrilateral exactly around a point. Sketch a picture to help you explain what you found.

9. Choose a nonregular triangle (such as shape I) from your Shapes Set, or draw your own. Try to fit copies of your triangle exactly around a point. Sketch a picture to help explain what you found.

Extensions

10. **a.** Measure the interior angles of the star below and compare your results to the angle measures for the regular decagon.

b. Draw other unusual polygons, and measure their interior angles to look for a pattern in the angle sums related to the number of sides.

11. Find all the line and turn symmetries for the star and the regular decagon above. How do the symmetries for the figures compare?

Mathematical Reflections

In this investigation, you have explored patterns in the angle sums of regular and irregular polygons. You have looked at the relationship between the number of sides in a regular polygon and the size of its interior angles. And you have discovered how the angle measures of a polygon determine whether copies of it will fit exactly around a vertex point. These questions will help you summarize what you have learned:

1 a. In regular polygons, what patterns relate the number of sides to the angle sum and the size of the interior angles?

b. In irregular polygons, what patterns relate the number of sides to the angle sum and the size of the interior angles?

2 How do these side-angle patterns explain why some polygons can tile the plane and others cannot?

Think about your answers to these questions, discuss your ideas with other students and your teacher, and then write a summary of your findings in your journal.

Are you noticing examples of tilings around you? Don't forget to write about them in your journal!

Side-Angle-Shape Connections

In your study of the sides, angles, and shapes of polygons, you have discovered some important facts of geometry. For example, if you want to build a rectangle, you know that you need to make opposite sides the same length and all angles 90°.

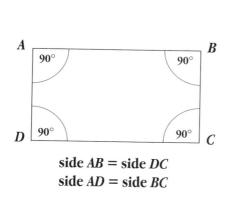

side AB = side DC
side AD = side BC

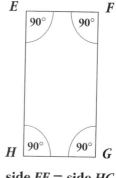

side EF = side HG
side EH = side FG

Knowing these properties of rectangles helps people to use rectangles to make designs and to construct buildings. Many other relationships among the sides and angles of polygons are useful properties.

Think about this!

What properties have you noticed about the sides and angles in triangles, quadrilaterals, pentagons, hexagons, and octagons? Consider relationships such as those found in the lengths of sides, measures of angles, or angle sums.

5.1 Flipping and Turning Triangles

The first pattern below is made with *equilateral triangles*. In an **equilateral triangle**, all three sides are the same length. The second pattern is made with *isosceles triangles*. In an **isosceles triangle**, two sides are the same length.

There is one piece missing from each pattern. To the left of each pattern is a triangle that will fit in the hole. The vertices of these triangles are numbered.

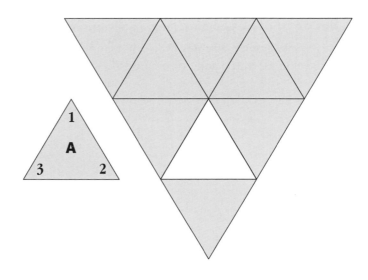

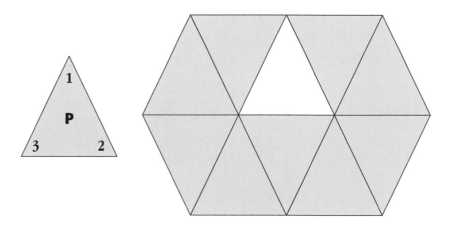

We can flip or turn the triangle so that it will fit into the space in the tiling. *Flipping* a shape means turning it over, like this:

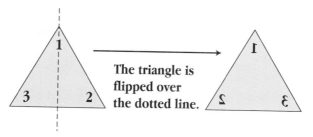

The triangle is flipped over the dotted line.

Turning a shape means rotating it, like this:

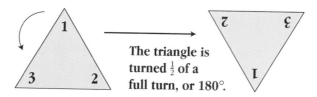

The triangle is turned $\frac{1}{2}$ of a full turn, or 180°.

There are many ways to flip and turn a shape.

Problem 5.1

A. In the tiling of equilateral triangles, describe all the different ways the shape can be placed in the hole. How many ways are there in all?

B. In the tiling of isosceles triangles, describe all the different ways the shape can be placed in the hole. Is the number of ways you can put the isosceles triangle in the hole less than, greater than, or equal to the number of ways you can put the equilateral triangle in the hole? Explain.

You may find it helpful to use your Shapes Set to investigate the different ways you can flip and turn the triangle. Use the numbers on the vertices of the triangles to help you describe how each triangle can be flipped and turned to position it in the hole in different ways.

■ Problem 5.1 Follow-Up

1. What do your answers indicate about relations between sides and angles in equilateral triangles?

2. What do your answers indicate about relations between sides and angles in isosceles triangles?

5.2 Flipping and Turning Quadrilaterals

The three tilings below and on the next two pages are made of squares, of rectangles, and of parallelograms. Again, one piece is missing from each pattern.

Problem 5.2

A. In the tiling of squares, describe all the different ways the shape can be placed in the hole. How many ways are there in all?

B. In the tiling of rectangles, describe all the different ways the shape can be placed in the hole. How many ways are there in all?

C. In the tiling of parallelograms, describe all the different ways the shape can be placed in the hole. How many ways are there in all?

You may find it helpful to use your Shapes Set to investigate the different ways you can flip and turn the shapes. Use the numbers on the vertices of the shapes to help you describe how each shape can be flipped and turned to position it in the hole in different ways.

◼ Problem 5.2 Follow-Up

1. What do your answers indicate about relations between sides and angles in squares?

2. What do your answers indicate about relations between sides and angles in rectangles?

3. What do your answers indicate about relations between sides and angles in parallelograms?

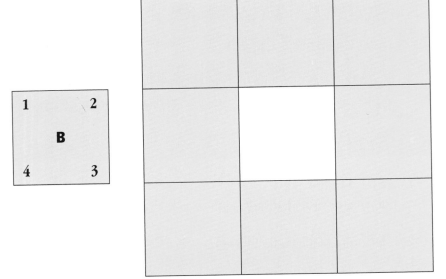

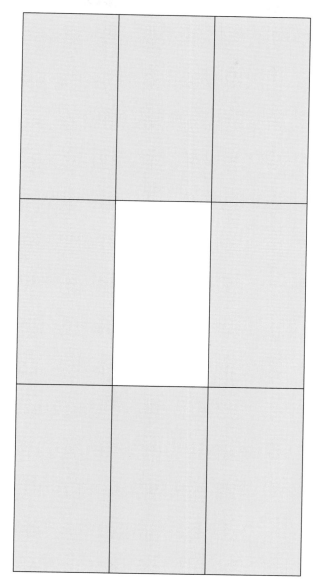

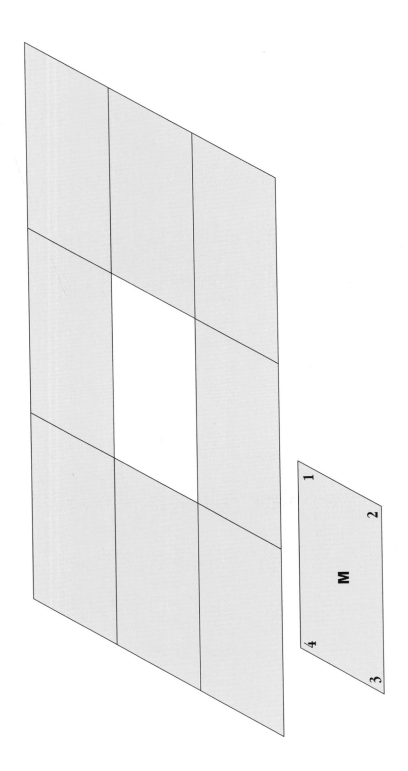

As you work on these ACE questions, use your calculator whenever you need it.

Applications

1. This map shows streets of Rectangle City, in which all city blocks are identical rectangles. Two side measurements are given.

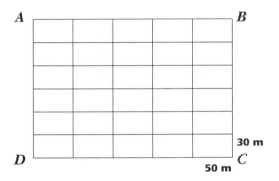

a. Find the shortest path from point *A* to point *C* along city streets. Explain how you know you have found the shortest path.

b. Find the shortest path from point *B* to point *D* along city streets. Explain how you know you have found the shortest path.

c. If you flew in a helicopter, you would not need to follow city blocks. Then which trip would be shorter—*A* to *C* or *B* to *D?*

2. This map shows streets of Parallelogram City, in which all city blocks are identical parallelograms. Two side measurements are given.

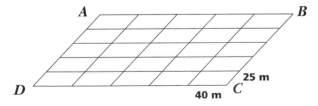

a. Find the shortest path from point *A* to point *C* along city streets. Explain how you know you have found the shortest path.

b. Find the shortest path from point *B* to point *D* along city streets. Explain how you know you have found the shortest path.

c. If you flew in a helicopter, you would not need to follow city blocks. Then which trip would be shorter—*A* to *C* or *B* to *D?*

3. Look at the angles formed by street corners in the map of Parallelogram City in question 2.

   a. Draw one of the blocks, and mark any angles that are the same size.

   b. Why do the sides of the blocks line up to give straight streets?

4. Below are the plans for a parking lot. The parking spaces are identical rectangles.

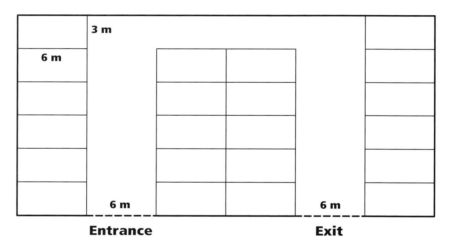

   a. What are the outside dimensions of the lot?

   b. How far would you have to walk to walk completely around the outside of the lot? Explain your reasoning.

Connections

5. Think back to the question posed at the start of this unit: Why are nearly all windows and doors in homes, schools, stores, and office buildings in the shape of rectangles (not triangles, circles, or trapezoids)? What have you learned in this unit that will help you to answer this question?

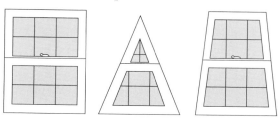

6. Below are three sets of identical quadrilaterals arranged around a point. What does the exact fit in each case show about the angle measures of the quadrilaterals?

7. **a.** The illustrations below show what happened when three copies of a paper triangle were put together with the three different vertices of the triangle touching a single point and the sides of the same length matched up. Repeat this process for two different triangles that you design. Tape your results together and onto your answer paper.

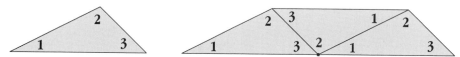

   b. What do your figures show about the sum of the measures of the angles in a triangle?

   c. What other figures do you see in the arrangement of your three triangles?

   d. What properties of angles do you see demonstrated in the arrangement of your three triangles?

At the Sleepy Hollow Pottery Shop, artists use square tiles to make tabletops with colorful designs. They arrange the tiles in a rectangular pattern and then bend a metal strip to form a border. One simple design is shown here.

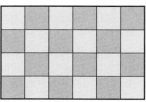

In 8–11, give the dimensions of every possible rectangle tabletop that could be made with the given number of tiles. For each possibility, find the length of the metal strip needed, and explain how it should be bent to make the border. You might find it helpful to use grid paper to draw and label the figures.

8. 128 tiles

9. 60 tiles

10. 35 tiles

11. 37 tiles

In 12–16, use a coordinate grid, like the one shown below.

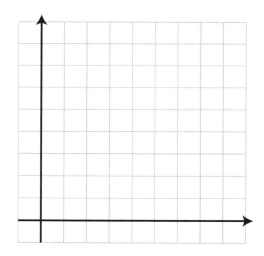

12. Give coordinates of four points that are vertices of a rectangle.

13. Give coordinates of four points that are vertices of a parallelogram that is *not* a rectangle.

14. If (0, 0) and (4, 6) are two vertices of a rectangle, what might be the coordinates of the other two vertices?

15. If (0, 0) and (1, 4) are two vertices of a parallelogram, what might be the coordinates of the other two vertices?

16. If (5, 0) and (6, 3) are two vertices of a parallelogram, what might be the coordinates of the other two vertices?

Extensions

17. Standard-size bricks are rectangular blocks that are approximately 5 cm by 10 cm by 20 cm. These bricks are often used like tiles to cover a sidewalk or the walls of a building.

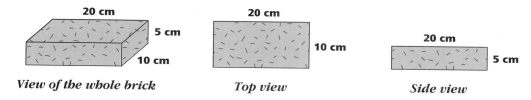

View of the whole brick   Top view   Side view

a. Draw several different patterns you could make with standard bricks.

b. If you look at the face of a brick wall, you usually see the pattern on the left below, not the simpler pattern on the right. Can you think of any reasons why bricklayers prefer the less simple pattern? (You might test your ideas by building a wall with blocks or dominoes.)

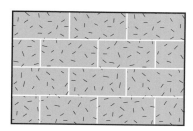   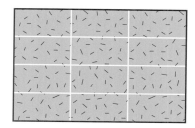

In 18 and 19, refer to this map of Rectangle City:

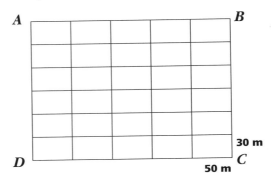

18. Find the longest possible path from point *A* to point *C*, walking along city streets but not covering any block side twice.

19. Find the longest possible path from point *A* to point *D*, walking along city streets but not covering any block side twice.

20. **a.** How could the parallelogram below be cut into two pieces and put back together to make a rectangle?

   b. What does your answer show about the relations among angles of a parallelogram?

Mathematical Reflections

In this investigation, you have explored side-angle relationships for triangles and quadrilaterals. These questions will help you summarize what you have learned:

1. What is true about the lengths of the sides and the measures of the angles in a triangle with three equal angles?

2. What is true about the lengths of the sides and the measures of the angles in a triangle with two equal angles?

3. What is true about the lengths of the sides and the measures of the angles in a square?

4. What is true about the lengths of the sides and the measures of the angles in a rectangle that is not a square?

5. What is true about the lengths of the sides and the measures of the angles in a parallelogram that is not a rectangle?

Think about your answers to these questions, discuss your ideas with other students and your teacher, and then write a summary of your findings in your journal.

What side-angle-shape connections have you noticed in the world around you? You may want to include drawings to help you communicate what you have discovered about side-angle-shape connections.

Turtle Tracks

For thousands of years, the designs on houses, clothing, dishes, and tools were painted, woven, molded, and carved by human hands.

Calendar from ancient Crete

Reed basket made by Seri Indians of Northern Mexico

Over the past 300 years, machines have been invented to help with these tasks. In the past 50 years, factories have been automated. Most machines are now run by electric motors and controlled by computers. But the machines are only as smart as the human beings who plan the operations and program the computers. The programs for computer-controlled machines are written in mathematical languages in which measures of length and angles are used to tell machines what to do and robot tools how to move.

You can use a computer language called *Logo* to write instructions for drawing lines on a computer screen. In Logo, you type commands that tell a "turtle" how to move around the screen. As it moves, the turtle's path is shown on the screen. You can create designs by telling the turtle how to move.

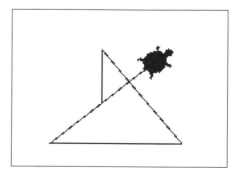

The turtle understands many different instructions, but you can make interesting designs by using just a few simple commands.

Greta wrote a set of Logo commands to draw her first initial. After typing each command, she pressed the **return** key to see the turtle move.

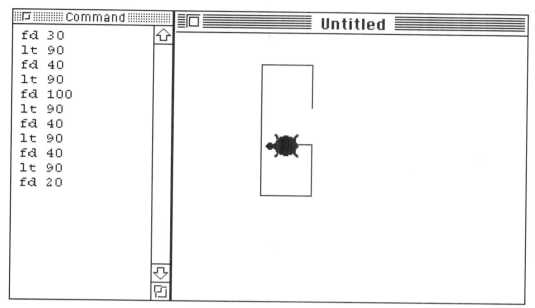

The commands that Greta used are from this list of common Logo commands. You can do all the problems in this investigation using only these eight commands. You can type the commands in capital letters or lowercase letters.

Common Logo Commands

fd   The *forward* command tells the turtle to move forward. The fd command must be followed by a space and a number telling the turtle how many steps to take. For example, fd 60 tells the turtle to move forward 60 steps.

bk   The *backward* command tells the turtle to move backward. The bk command must be followed by a space and a number telling the turtle how many steps to take. For example, bk 35 tells the turtle to move backward 35 steps.

lt The *left turn* command tells the turtle to turn to its left. The `lt` command must be followed by a space and a number telling the turtle how many degrees to turn. For example, `lt 30` tells the turtle to turn 30° to its left.

rt The *right turn* command tells the turtle to turn to its right. The `rt` command must be followed by a space and a number telling the turtle how many degrees to turn. For example, `rt 45` tells the turtle to turn 45° to its right.

st The *show turtle* command shows the turtle on the computer screen.

ht The *hide turtle* command hides the turtle. You will not see the turtle again until you type the `st` command.

pu The *pen up* command tells the turtle to lift its drawing pen, so you can move the turtle without making marks on the screen.

pd The *pen down* command tells the turtle to put its pen down, so you can begin drawing.

6.1 Drawing with Logo

In Problem 6.1, you use Logo to create some designs. If you don't have a computer to work on, you can do the problem using a pencil and paper. It might be easiest to work on grid paper. You could let each square represent 10 turtle steps.

Problem 6.1

Spend some time exploring the kinds of shapes and designs you can make with combinations of Logo commands. For example, you might try to draw letters or designs like those below. Try writing commands to draw the initials of your name.

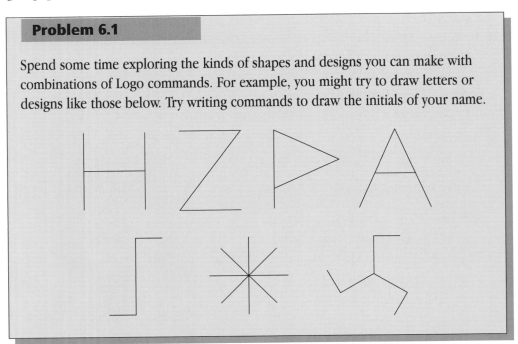

■ **Problem 6.1 Follow-Up**

The challenge of writing Logo commands to draw a desired design can be used to make a game for two players or two teams. One player could draw a design and challenge the other player to write Logo commands that will make that design. Or, one player could write some Logo commands and challenge the other player to sketch the design the commands will produce. Work with students in your group to make rules for a Turtle Challenge Game. Play the game you create, and modify the rules to improve the game.

6.2 Debugging Computer Programs

A set of computer commands that performs a task is called a *computer program.* In Problem 6.1, you wrote short computer programs to make some designs.

Computer programs usually won't run perfectly the first time you try them. Programs that don't run the way you expect them to are said to have "bugs" in them. You can "debug" your programs so that they run properly.

To debug a Logo program, use your computer mouse or the arrow keys to move to a command you want to change. Use the **delete** key to remove any words or numbers you want to change. Type in the new words or numbers, and then press the **return** key to see the turtle follow your new instructions.

Problem 6.2

In this problem, you will write a Logo computer program to draw a triangle. Follow these steps:

• On a piece of paper, write a Logo program that you think will draw a triangle.

• Type your Logo program into the computer.

• Debug your program. Keep making changes in your program until you have produced a triangle.

• Write down your new, debugged program for drawing a triangle.

■ **Problem 6.2 Follow-Up**

Were you surprised by anything as you wrote and debugged your triangle program?

6.3 Making Polygons

In earlier parts of this unit, you have seen that interesting designs often begin with simple shapes like triangles, squares, and rectangles. In this problem, you write Logo commands to make these basic shapes. If you don't have a computer, you can do this problem using a pencil and paper.

Problem 6.3

Write Logo programs to make each of the following shapes. Experiment at the computer to test and debug your programs. Each shape can be made in lots of different ways.

A. A square with sides of length 50

B. A rectangle with sides of length 50 and 100

C. A parallelogram—but not a rectangle—with sides of length 80 and 30

D. A parallelogram—but not a square—with all sides of length 70

■ Problem 6.3 Follow-Up

1. Explain how you used what you know about the measures of sides and angles of squares to help you write your programs.

2. Explain how you used what you know about the measures of sides and angles of rectangles to help you write your programs.

3. Explain how you used what you know about the measures of sides and angles of parallelograms to help you write your programs.

As you work on these ACE questions, use your calculator whenever you need it.

Applications

In 1–4, sketch the shape that each Logo program will produce. Use arrows to show the direction the turtle moves around the figure. If possible, check your answers on the computer.

1.
```
fd 50
rt 90
fd 100
rt 90
fd 50
rt 90
fd 100
```

2.
```
fd 100
lt 45
fd 70
lt 90
fd 70
lt 45
fd 100
lt 90
fd 100
```

3.
```
fd 100
lt 120
fd 40
lt 120
fd 40
```

4.
```
fd 100
rt 30
bk 50
lt 30
fd 25
rt 30
bk 10
```

In 5–8, write a Logo program that will produce the given shape.

5.

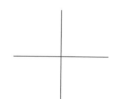

6.

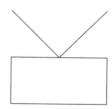

7.

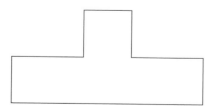

8.

Connections

In 9–11, a Logo program and the shape it created are given. Parts a and b show the same program, but with a bug (the bug is the command in bold print). Explain how the bug would affect the shape the program would draw.

9.

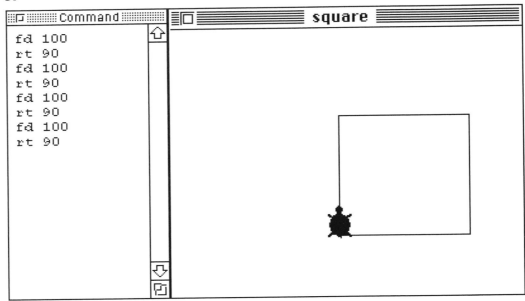

a.
```
fd 100
rt 80
fd 100
rt 90
fd 100
rt 90
fd 100
rt 90
```

b.
```
fd 120
rt 90
fd 100
rt 90
fd 100
rt 90
fd 100
rt 90
```

10.

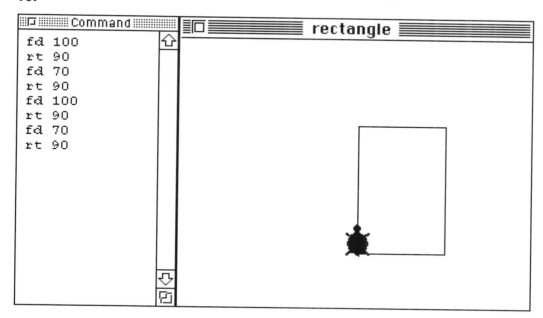

```
Command
fd 100
rt 90
fd 70
rt 90
fd 100
rt 90
fd 70
rt 90
```

```
rectangle
```

a.
```
fd 100
rt 90
fd 70
rt 90
fd 100
rt 90
fd 60
rt 90
```

b.
```
fd 100
rt 20
fd 70
rt 90
fd 100
rt 90
fd 70
rt 90
```

11.

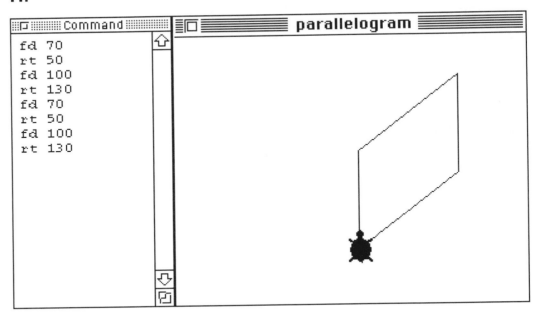

a.
```
fd 70
rt 50
fd 100
rt 110
fd 70
rt 50
fd 100
rt 130
```

b.
```
fd 70
rt 50
fd 100
rt 130
fd 40
rt 50
fd 100
rt 130
```

12. Suppose the turtle understood only the command for a 30° turn. What turns could you make by combining 30° turns?

13. Suppose the turtle understood only the command for a 45° turn. What turns could you make by combining 45° turns?

14. Suppose the turtle understood only the commands for 30° and 45° turns. What turns could you make by combining 30° and 45° turns?

15. Suppose the turtle understood only the command for a move of 10 steps. What moves could you make by combining 10-step moves?

16. Suppose the turtle understood only the command for a move of 15 steps. What moves could you make by combining 15-step moves?

17. Suppose the turtle understood only the commands for moves of 10 and 15 steps. What moves could you make by combining 10-step and 15-step moves?

Extensions

Questions 18–25 involve the `repeat` command. You use `repeat` to tell the turtle to follow a set of instructions a specified number of times. For example, the command `repeat 3 [rt 60 fd 40]` tells the turtle to follow the instructions `rt 60 fd 40` three times. Be sure to put spaces between the words and numbers and to put square brackets around the instructions to be repeated.

In 18–21, sketch the figure that the Logo commands would create.

18. `repeat 4 [fd 60 lt 90]`

19. `repeat 4 [fd 50 rt 90 fd 50 lt 90]`

20. `repeat 3 [fd 100 lt 120]`

21. `repeat 8 [fd 80 bk 80 rt 45]`

In 22–24, you are given Logo programs for drawing a square, a rectangle, and a parallelogram. Each of those programs can be shortened by using the `repeat` command.

22. **a.** Write a shortened program for drawing the square in question 9.

b. Explain how properties of squares make it possible to write a shorter program using `repeat`.

23. **a.** Write a shortened program for drawing the rectangle in question 10.

b. Explain how properties of rectangles make it possible to write a shorter program using `repeat`.

24. **a.** Write a shortened program for drawing the parallelogram in question 11.

b. Explain how properties of parallelograms make it possible to write a shorter program using `repeat`.

25. Write a Logo program that uses the `repeat` command to make a starburst design similar to the one below.

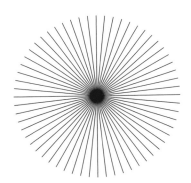

Mathematical Reflections

Use what you have learned in *Shapes and Designs* to write a geometric description of each object pictured below. Be sure to discuss

- the shapes, angles, and symmetry in the object
- possible reasons why the object has the shape that it does

A.

B.

C.

D.

Have you seen any new shapes and designs to add to your collection? Remember to write about all your discoveries in your journal!

The Unit Project

What I Know About Shapes and Designs

At the beginning of this unit, you were asked to think about the characteristics of different shapes and how unusual a shape can be and still be a triangle, quadrilateral, pentagon, or hexagon. You were also asked to think about the relationships among these shapes. It is now time to design your final project.

You can present your project in several different forms or combinations of forms. You may decide to present your information as a book, a poster or a set of posters, a story, a report, a mobile, a movie, a slide show, or any other appropriate form that you design. Whatever form you choose, remember that what you have to demonstrate and explain in your project are the following things:

- The characteristics of the following shapes: triangles, squares, rectangles, parallelograms, quadrilaterals, pentagons, hexagons, octagons
- The relationships among the shapes listed above
- Examples of places where these shapes can be found in your world.

Use the information you have collected, plus what you learned from your study of this unit, to prepare your final project. Be certain your project shows

- All the facts you know about the relations among the sides of polygons. Consider properties of all polygons and properties of special polygons, such as squares, rectangles, and other parallelograms.
- All the facts you know about the relations among angles of polygons. Again, consider properties of all polygons and properties of special polygons.

Looking Back and Looking Ahead

Unit Reflections

Working on problems in this unit, you explored properties of several geometric shapes. You learned how *side lengths* and *angle measures* determine the shapes of *triangles, rectangles, parallelograms,* and *regular polygons.* You found that some shapes fit together to form *tiling* patterns covering surfaces and others have important practical uses in the design of buildings, bee hives, road signs, and flight paths.

Using Your Knowledge of Shapes—Test your understanding of shapes on the following problems that show the range of applications for segments, angles, and polygons.

1. *The building below contains many angles. The vertices of some of the angles are labeled with letters. Making and using blueprints for such buildings requires angle sense—the ability to estimate and measure exactly the size of angles.*

    a. Which of the angles seem to measure 90°?

    b. Which of the angles seem to measure more than 90° and less than 180°?

    c. List the angles in order from smallest to largest, estimate the degree measure of each, and then use an angle ruler or protractor to measure each.

2. *Designers are always experimenting with new shapes for floor tiles. Explore the possibilities of tiles that are regular pentagons and regular hexagons.*

Interior angle

Interior angle

   a. What is the measure of each interior angle in a regular pentagon?

   b. Is it possible to cover a floor with many copies of such a regular pentagon?

   c. What is the measure of each angle in a regular hexagon?

d. Is it possible to cover a floor with many copies of such a regular hexagon?

3 *Parts a - e below give information about shapes. Answer these questions for each part.*

    i. *Is it possible to make a shape that meets the given conditions? If so, sketch it.*

    ii. *If it is possible to make a shape with the given properties, is it possible to make a different shape with the same properties? If so, sketch one or more such shapes.*

        a. a triangle with side lengths of 4, 6, and 9 cm

        b. a triangle with side lengths of 4, 7, and 2 cm

        c. a triangle whose angle measures are 60, 45, and 70 degrees

        d. a rectangle with a pair of opposite sides whose lengths are 8 cm

        e. a parallelogram whose side lengths are 8, 8, 6, and 6 cm

Explaining your reasoning—To answer questions about shapes you use several basic facts about the ways that angle measurement and side lengths determine the shapes of polygons.

1. In what different ways can one think about an angle? How can angle measures be estimated and how can angles be measured accurately?

2. Suppose you are asked to draw a triangle with three given side lengths.

    a. How can you tell if it is possible to draw a triangle with those side lengths?

    b. If you can draw one such triangle, are there others with the same side lengths?

    c. Why are triangles so useful in building structures?

3. Suppose that you are asked to draw a triangle given three angle measures.

    a. How can you tell if it is possible to draw a triangle with those angle measures?

    b. If you can draw one such triangle, are there different-shaped triangles with the same three angle measures?

4. When is it possible to draw a quadrilateral with four given side lengths or four given angle measures? If it is possible to draw one such quadrilateral, can you always draw others?

5. Why do hexagonal shapes appear on the surface of honeycombs and in the tilings of many flat surfaces? What properties of a shape determine whether it will make a tile that can be copied to cover a flat surface?

The properties of angles and polygons that you discovered in the investigations of this unit will be used in many future units, especially those that deal with measurement of perimeter, area, and volume of figures. As you've seen, the side and angle relationships in triangles and quadrilaterals are also applied in many construction and design tasks.

Glossary

angle The opening between two straight lines that meet at a vertex, measured in degrees or radians. The angle at point *A* on the triangle at right is identified as angle *BAC* or ∠*BAC*. The sides of an angle are rays that have the vertex as a starting point. Each of the three angles below is formed by the joining of two rays.

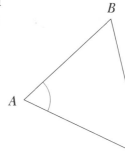

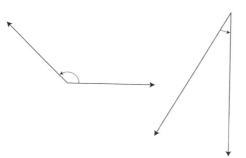

degree A unit of measure of angles equal to $\frac{1}{360}$ of a complete circle. The angle below measures about 1°; 360 of these would just fit around a point and fill in a complete circle; 90 of them make a right angle.

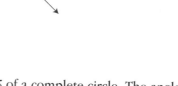

1°

diagonal A line segment connecting two non-adjacent vertices of a polygon. All quadrilaterals have two diagonals, as shown below. The two diagonals of a square are equal in length, and the two diagonals of a rectangle are equal in length. A pentagon has five diagonals, and a hexagon has 6 diagonals.

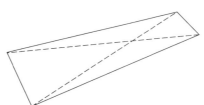

equilateral triangle A triangle with all three sides the same length.

isosceles triangle A triangle with two sides the same length.

parallel lines Lines that never meet no matter how long they are extended. The opposite sides of a regular hexagon are parallel. The polygons A and B below each have one pair of opposite sides parallel. In polygons C, D, and E, both pairs of opposite sides are parallel.

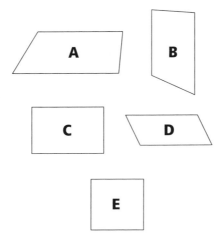

parallelogram A quadrilateral in which both pairs of opposite sides are equal and parallel. Both pairs of opposite angles are also equal. Figure D in the definition of parallel lines above, as well as rectangle C and square E, are all parallelograms.

polygon A closed, flat (two-dimensional) shape whose sides are formed by line segments. Below are examples of two polygons, a hexagon and a pentagon.

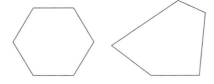

Special polygon names are derived from Greek prefixes that tell the number of sides or the number of angles in the polygon.

- *triangle*: A polygon with 3 sides and angles
- *quadrilateral*: A polygon with 4 sides and angles
- *pentagon*: A polygon with 5 sides and angles
- *hexagon*: A polygon with 6 sides and angles
- *heptagon*: A polygon with 7 sides and angles
- *octagon*: A polygon with 8 sides and angles
- *nonagon* (also called *enneagon*): A polygon with 9 sides and angles
- *decagon*: A polygon with 10 sides and angles
- *dodecagon*: A polygon with 12 sides and angles

properties of shapes Characteristics of shapes that are always valid. For example, you have learned that a property of parallelograms is that they have two pairs of parallel sides. The sum of the angles of a 6-sided polygon is $180° \times 4$ or $720°$. Triangles are stable figures, since their shape is completely determined by the lengths of their edges.

quadrilateral A polygon with four sides, as shown below.

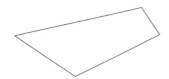

rectangle A parallelogram with all right angles, as shown below. Squares are a special type of rectangle.

regular polygon A polygon that has all of its sides equal and all of its angles equal. The hexagon below is regular, but the pentagon is not regular, because its sides and its angles are not equal.

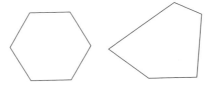

right angle An angle that measures 90°. All of the vertices in a rectangle, such as the one below, are right angles.

rhombus A quadrilateral that has all sides the same length.

square A rectangle with all sides equal. Thus squares have four right angles and four equal sides.

tiling Also called a tessellation. The filling of a plane surface with geometric shapes without gaps or overlaps. These shapes are usually regular polygons or other common polygons. The tiling below is made of triangles. You could remove some of the line segments to create a tiling of parallelograms, or remove still more to create a tiling of hexagons. In a tiling, a vertex is a point where the corners of the polygons fit together.

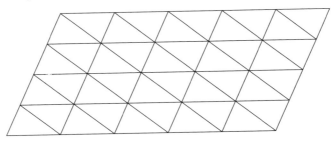

trapezoid A quadrilateral with one pair of opposite sides parallel. This definition means that parallelograms are trapezoids. The figures below are all trapezoids.

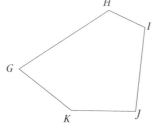

vertex The corners of a polygon. For example, *G, H, I, J,* and *K* are all vertices in the pentagon below. All angles have vertices; for example, in the hexagon below, angle *AFE* has a vertex at *F*.

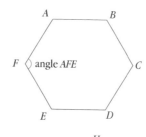

Index

Angle
ACE, 35–40
benchmarks, 25–28
central, 39
degree as measure of, 25
estimating the measure of, 25–27
interior, 39
labeling, 48
locating points on a circular grid with, 29–30
measuring, 6, 30–32
measuring errors, 32–34
of a polygon, 22–34, 42–44
of a ray, 27
right, 25
as a turn, 24–25
vertex of, 24
as a wedge, 24–25
Angle ruler, 30–32
Angle sum, 43
Archimedes, 10

Benchmarks, angle, 25–28

Central angle, 39
Circular grid, locating points on, 29–30
Computer program, 67–68
debugging, 67
Coordinate grid, 6
ACE, 60–61
locating points on, 29

Debugging
ACE, 70–72
Logo programs, 67–68
Degree, measure of an angle, 25
Diagonal, of a polygon, 48
Dimensions, of a rectangle, 12

Earhart, Amelia, 6, 32–34
Edge
of an angle, 24
of a polygon, 9
Equilateral triangle, 45, 52–53
Escher, M.C., 10
Estimation, of angle measure, 25–27

Flipping
quadrilaterals, 54–56
triangles, 53
Four in a Row Game, 29–30, 40

Heptagon
angle sum, 44
sides and angles, 42–44
Hexagon, 8–10
angle sum, 44
sides and angles, 42–44, 46

Interior angle, 39
Investigations
Bees and Polygons, 8–14
Building Polygons, 15–21
Polygon Properties and Tiling, 42–50

Polygons and Angles, 22–41
Side-Angle-Shape Connections, 51–63
Turtle Tracks, 64–75
Irregular polygon, 13, 44–45
Isosceles triangle, 45, 52–53

Journal, 14, 21, 41, 50, 63, 75

Line symmetry, 6
Logo, 64–68
ACE, 69–74
commands, 65–66
Looking Back and Looking Ahead:
Unit Reflections, 77–78

Mathematical Highlights, 6
Mathematical Reflections, 14, 21, 41, 50,
63, 75
Mirror symmetry, 6

Octagon
angle sum, 44
sides and angles, 42–44

Parallel lines, 18
ACE, 40
Parallelogram, 11
ACE, 19–20, 57–62
flipping and turning, 54, 56
Logo drawing of, 68
properties, 18
side-angle relationship, 54, 56
Pattern, sides and angles of regular
polygons, 42–44, 51–56

Pentagon, 20
angle sum, 44
diagonal of, 48
sides and angles, 42–44
Polygon, 5–6, 8–10
ACE, 11–13, 19–20, 35–40, 47–49,
57–62, 69–74
angles and, 22–34
building, 15–18
diagonal of, 48
edge, 9
hexagon, 8–10
irregular, 13, 44–45
labeling, 48
Logo drawings of, 66–68
properties, 15–18, 42–46
regular, 9, 10, 42–44
relating sides to angles, 42–44
side, 9
symmetry and, 6
table of, 5, 44
tiling, 9–10
vertex of, 10
Polystrips
parallelograms from, 18
quadrilaterals from, 17–18
triangles from, 16
Precision, in angle measurement, 32–34

Quadrilateral
ACE, 19–20
angle-side relationship, 6
diagonal of, 48
flipping and turning, 54–56

labeling, 48
properties, 17–18

Ray, of an angle, 27
Rectangle
ACE, 57–62
dimensions of, 12
flipping and turning, 54–55
Logo drawing of, 68
properties, 18, 51
side-angle relationship, 54–55
Regular polygon, 42–44
Right angle, 25
Rotational symmetry, 6

Side
of a parallelogram, 18
of a polygon, 9
of a quadrilateral, 17
of a rectangle, 51
of a triangle, 16
Square
angle sum, 44
flipping and turning, 54
Logo drawing of, 68
side-angle relationships, 54
sides and angles of, 42–44
Symmetry *See also* Turning
line, 6

mirror, 6
rotational, 6
turn, 6

Tessellation, 10
Tiling, 9–10, 46
ACE, 11–13, 49
Triangle
ACE, 19–20, 47–49
angle sum, 43–44, 59
equilateral, 45, 52–53
flipping and turning, 52–53
isosceles, 45, 52–53
Logo drawing of, 67
properties, 16
sides and angles, 6, 42–45
Turning
Logo command for, 66
quadrilaterals, 54–56
triangles, 53
Turn symmetry, 6

Unit project, 7, 76

Vertex
of an angle, 24
of a polygon, 10
tiling and, 46

Connected Mathematics™

Bits and Pieces I

Understanding Rational Numbers

Student Edition

Glenda Lappan
James T. Fey
William M. Fitzgerald
Susan N. Friel
Elizabeth Difanis Phillips

Prentice
Hall

Glenview, Illinois
Needham, Massachusetts
Upper Saddle River, New Jersey

The Connected Mathematics Project was developed at Michigan State University with the support of National Science Foundation Grant No. MDR 9150217.

This project was supported, in part,
by the
National Science Foundation
Opinions expressed are those of the authors
and not necessarily those of the Foundation

The Michigan State University authors and administration have agreed that all MSU royalties arising from this publication will be devoted to purposes supported by the Department of Mathematics and the MSU Mathematics Education Enrichment Fund.

Contents

Mathematical Highlights — 4

Investigation 1: Fund-Raising Fractions — 5
   1.1 Reporting Our Progress — 5
   1.2 Using Fraction Strips — 6
   1.3 Comparing Classes — 8
   1.4 Exceeding the Goal — 10
   1.5 Using Symbolic Form — 12
   Applications—Connections—Extensions — 14
   Mathematical Reflections — 18

Investigation 2: Comparing Fractions — 19
   2.1 Comparing Fractions — 19
   2.2 Finding Equivalent Fractions — 20
   2.3 Making a Number Line — 22
   2.4 Comparing Fractions to Benchmarks — 23
   2.5 Fractions Greater Than One — 24
   Applications—Connections—Extensions — 26
   Mathematical Reflections — 30

Investigation 3: Cooking with Fractions — 31
   3.1 Area Models for Fractions — 31
   3.2 Baking Brownies — 32
   Applications—Connections—Extensions — 34
   Mathematical Reflections — 38

Investigation 4: From Fractions to Decimals — 39
   4.1 Designing a Garden — 39
   4.2 Making Smaller Parts — 41
   4.3 Using Decimal Benchmarks — 43
   4.4 Playing Distinguishing Digits — 44
   Applications—Connections—Extensions — 46
   Mathematical Reflections — 52

Investigation 5: Moving Between Fractions and Decimals — 53
   5.1 Choosing the Best — 53
   5.2 Writing Fractions as Decimals — 54
   5.3 Moving from Fractions to Decimals — 57
   Applications—Connections—Extensions — 58
   Mathematical Reflections — 66

Investigation 6: Out of One Hundred — 67
   6.1 It's Raining Cats — 68
   6.2 Dealing with Discounts — 73
   6.3 Changing Forms — 75
   6.4 It's Raining Cats and Dogs — 76
   Applications—Connections—Extensions — 77
   Mathematical Reflections — 83

Looking Back and Looking Ahead: Unit Reflections — 84

Glossary — 87

Index — 91

Bits and Pieces I

In a survey of 200 cat owners, 59% said they fed their pet only pet food, not human food. How many people is this?

Samuel is getting a snack for himself and his little brother. There are two candy bars in the refrigerator. Samuel takes half of one candy bar for himself and half of the other candy bar for his little brother. His little brother complains that Samuel got more. Samuel says that he got half and his brother got half. What might be the problem?

Tisia made 19 out of 30 free throws; Clarise made 8 out of 13; and Dorothea made 14 out of 21. Who is the best free-throw shooter?

You often encounter situations in which a whole-number count or a whole-number label cannot communicate precise enough information. Sometimes you need to talk about parts of wholes: "What *fraction* of the students going on this trip are eighth graders?" "What *percent* of the students prefer a chicken sandwich?" You also need a way to discuss how to share or divide things: "What *part* of the pizza will we each get?" Fractions, decimals, and percents are all ways of expressing quantities that are not whole numbers.

People have been working on ways to talk about fractions and to do operations with them for a long, long time. As early as 1800 B.C., people were developing ways to communicate with each other about parts or pieces of things. A document called the Moscow Papyrus, written in 1850 B.C., contains the first record of humans working with fractions. The word **fraction** comes from the Latin word *fractio,* which means "a breaking."

The investigations in *Bits and Pieces I* involve settings in which knowledge of fractions, decimals, or percents can help you make sense of a situation. The opposite page gives three examples of the kinds of problems you will encounter in this unit.

Mathematical Highlights

In *Bits and Pieces I,* you will explore the meaning of rational numbers and the relationships among three forms of rational numbers—fractions, decimals, and percents. This unit will help you to

● Model situations involving fractions, decimals, and percents;

● Understand and use equivalent fractions to reason about situations;

● Compare and order fractions and decimals;

● Move flexibly among fraction, decimal, and percent representations;

● Use benchmarks, such as 0, $\frac{1}{2}$, 1, and $1\frac{1}{2}$, to help estimate the size of a number or sum;

● Develop and use benchmarks that relate different forms of representations of rational numbers (for example, 50% is the same as $\frac{1}{2}$ or 0.5); and

● Use context, physical models, drawings, patterns, or estimation to help reason about situations involving rational numbers.

As you work on the problems of this unit, make it a habit to ask questions about situations that involve rational numbers and relationships: *What models or diagrams might be helpful in understanding the situation and the relationships among quantities? Do I want to express the quantities in the situation as fractions, decimals, or percents? What techniques can I use to find equivalent forms of fractions, decimals, or percents, or to compare or order some set of fractions, decimals, and percents?*

Goal $300

Fund-Raising Fractions

Last year students at Thurgood Marshall School organized three fund-raising projects to raise money for sports and band equipment. The eighth-grade class held a calendar sale in October, the seventh-grade class sold popcorn in January, and the sixth-grade class sold art, music, and sports posters in March. The three grades competed to raise the most money.

1.1 Reporting Our Progress

The sixth-grade class set a goal of raising $300 during its ten-day poster sale. On each day of the sale, the class's progress was marked on a large "thermometer" near the school office.

The thermometer at right shows the progress of the sixth-grade fund-raiser after two days of sales. The goal of $300 is marked near the top of the thermometer. Every day during the fund-raising campaign, the sixth-grade class officers gave a public-address announcement reporting their progress.

Problem 1.1

Write a short—but clever and informative—announcement to report the progress of the sixth-grade poster sale after two days. Be sure to mention what part of the sales goal of $300 had been reached and what part remained to be raised.

■ Problem 1.1 Follow-Up

Describe the strategies you used to decide what part of the sales goal of $300 had been reached and what part remained to be raised.

Day 2

Sixth-Grade Poster Sale

Using Fraction Strips

The thermometers on the next page show the progress of the sixth-grade poster sale after two, four, six, eight, and ten days. One way to determine the progress of the fund-raiser is to use strips of paper the same length as the distance from the bottom of the thermometer to the goal. By folding the strips into fractional parts, you can determine what part of the goal has been reached.

Problem 1.2

Start with nine $8\frac{1}{2}$-inch strips. Fold the strips to show halves, thirds, fourths, fifths, sixths, eighths, ninths, tenths, and twelfths. Mark the folds in the strips with a pencil so you can see them more easily.

Use your strips to estimate the sixth-grade class's progress after two, four, six, eight, and ten days.

■ **Problem 1.2 Follow-Up**
1. Which fraction strips were easy to fold? Why?
2. Which fraction strips were difficult to fold? Why?

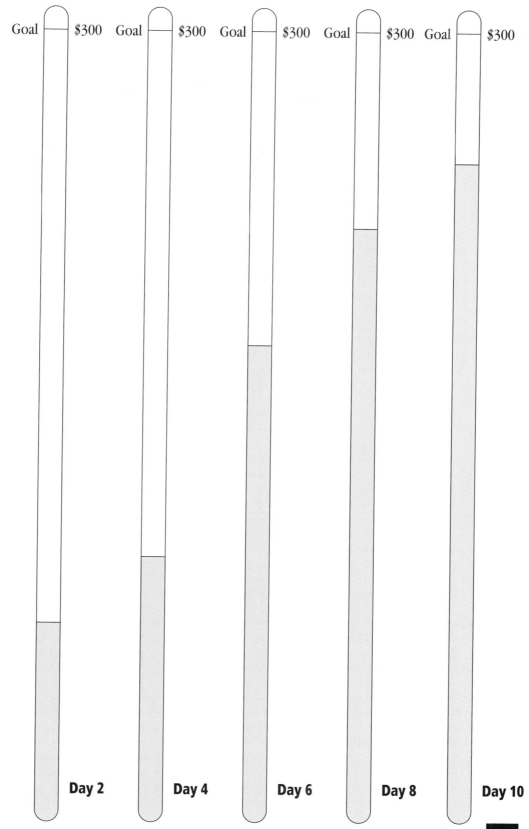

Goal — $300   Goal — $300   Goal — $300   Goal — $300   Goal — $300

Day 2   **Day 4**   **Day 6**   **Day 8**   **Day 10**

1.3 Comparing Classes

In Thurgood Marshall School, the seventh-grade class is larger than the sixth-grade class, and the eighth-grade class is smaller than the sixth-grade class. Because they are different sizes, each class set a different goal for its fund-raiser. The sixth grade set a goal of $300 for its poster sale, the seventh grade set a goal of $400 for its popcorn sale, and the eighth grade set a goal of $240 for its calendar sale.

The thermometers on the next page show the results of the sixth-grade, seventh-grade, and eighth-grade fund-raisers. Both the seventh graders and the eighth graders claimed to do better than the sixth graders.

Problem 1.3

Use the fraction strips you made in Problem 1.2 to investigate the seventh and eighth graders' claims.

A. How much money did each grade raise?

B. What fraction of the goal did each grade reach?

C. What argument could the eighth graders use to claim that their class did better than the sixth grade?

D. What argument could the seventh graders use to claim that their class did better than the sixth grade?

■ Problem 1.3 Follow-Up

Which of the three classes do you think did the best job? Explain your reasoning.

Goal — $300

Goal — $400

Goal — $240

Day 10

Sixth-Grade
Poster Sale

Day 10

Seventh-Grade
Popcorn Sale

Day 10

Eighth-Grade
Calendar Sale

1.4 Exceeding the Goal

In April, the Thurgood Marshall School needed money to put on the annual Year's End Festival. Since the students had worked hard on the earlier fund-raising campaigns, the teachers volunteered to raise the money. They decided to sell paperback books for summer reading, and they set a goal of $360.

The thermometers on the next page show the teachers' progress at the end of the second, sixth, and tenth days.

Problem 1.4

A. Notice that the teachers used a shorter thermometer than the students did to report their progress. Can you use your fraction strips to measure these thermometers? Explain.

B. What fraction of their goal did the teachers reach at the end of each of the days shown? Explain how you determined your answers.

C. How many dollars did the teachers raise by the end of each of these days?

■ Problem 1.4 Follow-Up
What school announcement might the teachers make at the end of the tenth day?

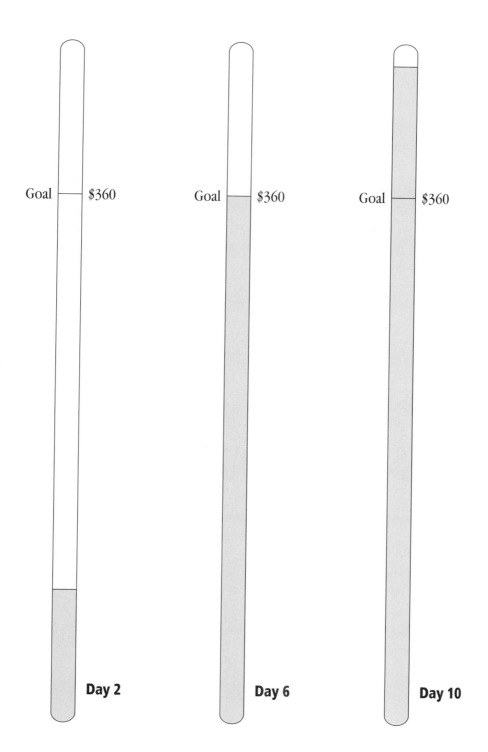

Goal	$360

Day 2

Goal	$360

Day 6

Goal	$360

Day 10

Teachers' Book Sale

1.5 Using Symbolic Form

Fractions can be written in *symbolic form,* using two whole numbers separated by a bar. For example, one half is written $\frac{1}{2}$ and two thirds is written $\frac{2}{3}$.

The number above the bar is called the **numerator,** and the number below the bar is called the **denominator.**

Think about this!

What do the numerator and the denominator tell you in the fractions $\frac{1}{2}$, $\frac{1}{3}$, $\frac{2}{3}$, and $\frac{4}{5}$?

Problem 1.5

The next page shows nine fraction strips of the same length. Each strip is divided into a different number of equal-length parts. On your copy of Labsheet 1.5, label each of the marks on the strips with fraction names in symbolic form. The label for a mark should represent the fraction of the strip to the left of the mark.

■ Problem 1.5 Follow-Up

Compare these fraction strips with the strips you made in Problem 1.2. Does $\frac{1}{4}$ represent the same length on both strips? Why or why not?

Save your labeled strips so you can use them for the ACE questions and for your work in the next investigation.

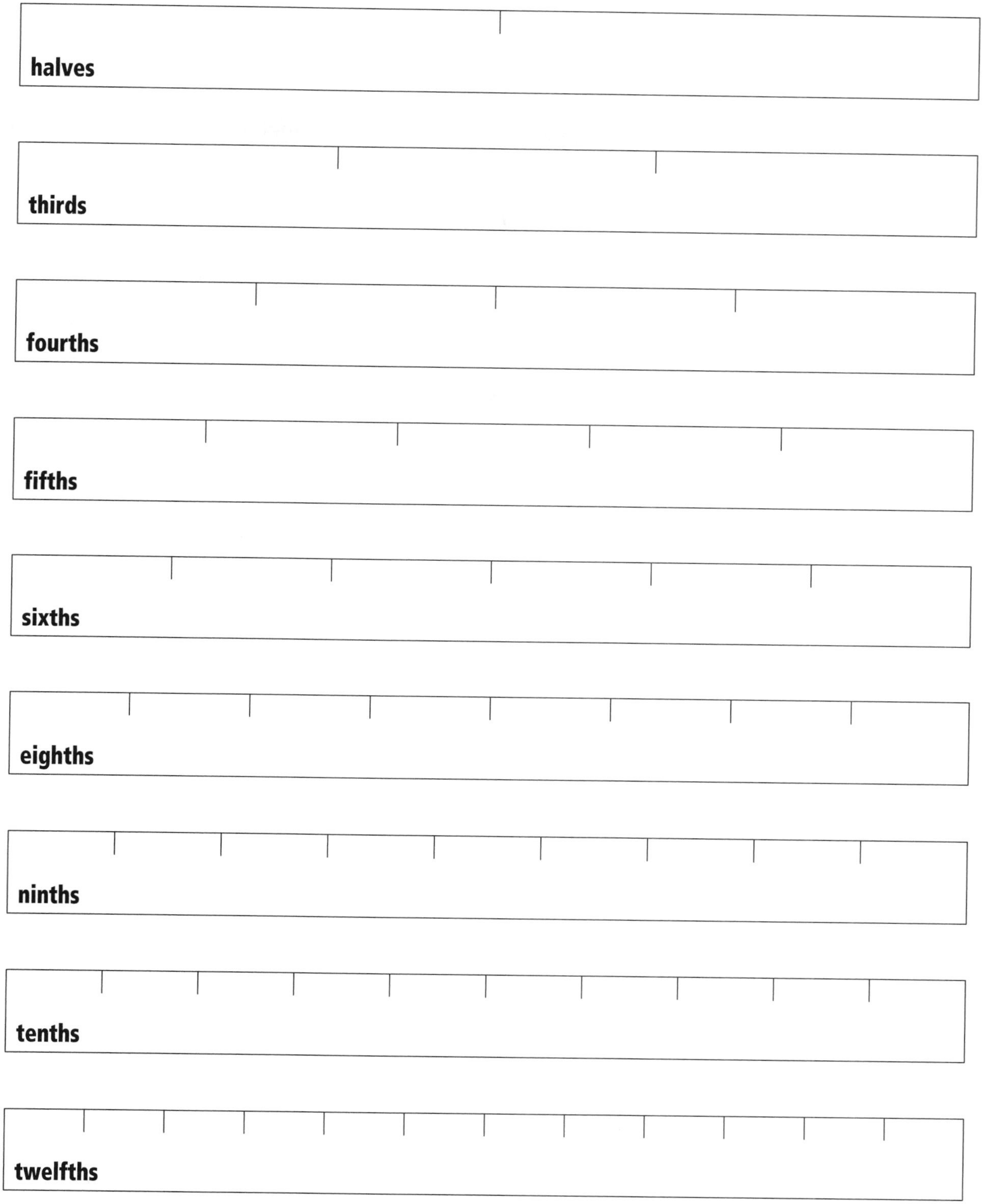

halves

thirds

fourths

fifths

sixths

eighths

ninths

tenths

twelfths

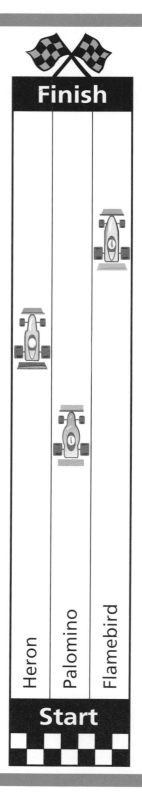

As you work on these ACE questions, use your calculator whenever you need it.

Applications

1. At right is a snapshot of three cars drag racing.

   a. For each car, measure from the front of the car to estimate the fraction of the race course completed and the fraction of the race course yet to be covered. You may want to use your fraction strips from Labsheet 1.5.

   b. The drag race course is 600 meters long. For each car, estimate the distance already covered and the distance yet to be covered.

In 2–5, use your fraction strips from Labsheet 1.5 to find something in your home with the given length. Record the name of each object.

2. half ($\frac{1}{2}$) the length of a fraction strip

3. two thirds ($\frac{2}{3}$) the length of a fraction strip

4. one and one half ($1\frac{1}{2}$) times the length of a fraction strip

5. twice the length of a fraction strip

6. Use your fraction strips from Labsheet 1.5 to measure three things in your home that are shorter than a fraction strip. Record the name of each object and its length in terms of a fraction strip.

7. Use your fraction strips from Labsheet 1.5 to measure three things in your home that are longer than a fraction strip. Record the name of each object and its length in terms of a fraction strip.

In 8–11, use this drawing of a restaurant drink container. The gauge on the side of the container shows how much of the liquid remains in the container.

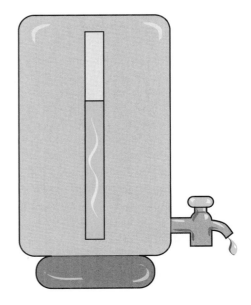

8. A full container holds 120 cups.

   a. About what fraction of the container is filled with liquid?

   b. About how many cups of liquid are in the container?

   c. About what fraction of the container is empty?

   d. About how many cups of liquid would it take to fill the container?

9. Tell whether each amount is closer to a full container, a half-full container, or an empty container.

   a. five sixths $(\frac{5}{6})$ of a full container

   b. three twelfths $(\frac{3}{12})$ of a full container

   c. five eighths $(\frac{5}{8})$ of a full container

10. About what fraction of the drink container is each of the following amounts?

    a. 37 cups

    b. 10 cups

    c. 55 cups

11. How many pitchers of liquid would it take to fill an empty drink container if a pitcher holds the given amount?

    a. one fourth $(\frac{1}{4})$ of a full container

    b. one third $(\frac{1}{3})$ of a full container

    c. two thirds $(\frac{2}{3})$ of a full container

12. Ricky found a beetle that was one fourth ($\frac{1}{4}$) the length of a fraction strip from Labsheet 1.5.

   a. How many beetles, placed end to end, would have a total length equal to the length of a fraction strip?

   b. How many beetles, placed end to end, would have a total length equal to three times the length of a fraction strip?

   c. Ricky lined up 13 paper beetles, end to end, each the same length as the one he found. How many times the length of a fraction strip is the length of Ricky's line of beetles?

Connections

In 13–21, tell what fraction of a foot (12 inches) the given length is.

13. 6 inches   **14.** 4 inches   **15.** 3 inches

16. 2 inches   **17.** 1 inch   **18.** 8 inches

19. 9 inches   **20.** 15 inches   **21.** 18 inches

In 22–25, estimate each length as a fraction of a foot.

22. the width of your hand

23. the length of your hand from wrist to fingertip

24. the distance from your wrist to your elbow

25. the distance from your fingertip to your elbow

Extensions

26. Look back at the thermometers on page 7, which show the sixth graders' progress toward their goal.

a. Make a coordinate graph that shows the sixth-grade fund-raising progress.

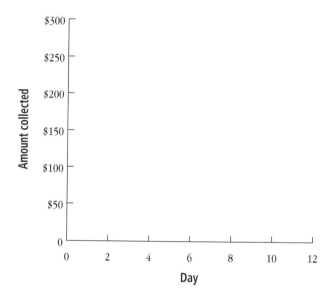

b. Predict from your graph when the sixth graders would reach their goal if the fund-raiser continued.

c. Describe the strategy you used to make your prediction.

Mathematical Reflections

In this investigation, you made fraction strips to help you identify fractional parts of a whole. These questions will help you summarize what you have learned:

1 What do the numerator and the denominator of a fraction tell you?

2 When you worked on Problem 1.4, did you make new fraction strips? Explain why or why not.

3 Both Ramón's class and Melissa's class reached $\frac{3}{5}$ of their fund-raising goals. Did the two classes raise the same amount of money? Explain your answer.

Think about your answers to these questions, discuss your ideas with other students and your teacher, and then write a summary of your findings in your journal.

INVESTIGATION 2

Comparing Fractions

In Investigation 1, you made fraction strips to help you determine what fraction of the fund-raising goal students had reached. You learned to interpret fractions as parts of a whole. In this investigation, you will look at situations in which you need to compare fractions. Your fraction strips will be a useful model to help you make comparisons.

Goal | $360

2.1 Comparing Notes

At the end of the fourth day of their fund-raising campaign, the teachers at Thurgood Marshall School had raised $270 of the $360 they needed to reach their goal. Three of the teachers got into a debate about how they would report their progress.

- Ms. Mendoza wanted to announce that the teachers had made it three-fourths of the way to their goal.

- Mr. Park said that six-eighths was a better description.

- Ms. Christos suggested that two-thirds was really the simplest way to describe the teachers' progress.

Problem 2.1

A. Which of the three teachers do you agree with? Why?

B. How could the teacher you agreed with in part A prove his or her case?

Day 4

Teachers' Book Sale

■ **Problem 2.1 Follow-Up**

Name another fraction that describes the teachers' progress.

2.2 Finding Equivalent Fractions

As you worked with your fraction strips, you found that some quantities can be described by several different fractions. In fact, *any* quantity can be described by an infinite number of different fractions!

Did you know?

Hieroglyphic inscriptions from more than 4000 years ago indicate that, with the exception of $\frac{2}{3}$, Egyptian mathematicians used only fractions with 1 in the numerator. Such fractions are known as *unit fractions.* Other fractions were expressed as sums of these unit fractions. The fraction $\frac{2}{7}$, for example, was expressed as $\frac{1}{4} + \frac{1}{28}$.

Two fractions that name the same quantity are called **equivalent fractions.** For example, you probably know several names for the quantity $\frac{1}{2}$. As long as the whole is the same, $\frac{1}{2}$ means the same as $\frac{2}{4}$, , $\frac{4}{8}$, $\frac{5}{10}$, and so on. You can show this with fraction strips.

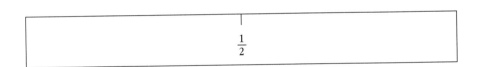

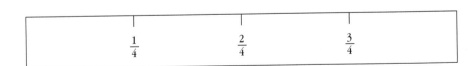

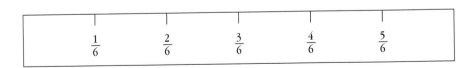

Problem 2.2

The fraction strips on the left below show $\frac{2}{3}$ and three fractions equivalent to $\frac{2}{3}$. The strips on the right show $\frac{3}{4}$ and three fractions equivalent to $\frac{3}{4}$. Study the two sets of strips. Look for patterns that will help you find other equivalent fractions.

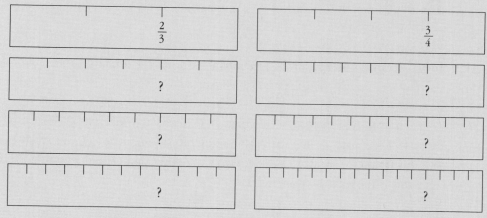

A. What are the three fractions shown that are equivalent to $\frac{2}{3}$? Name three more fractions that are equivalent to $\frac{2}{3}$.

B. What are the three fractions shown that are equivalent to $\frac{3}{4}$? Name three more fractions that are equivalent to $\frac{3}{4}$.

C. What pattern do you see that can help you find equivalent fractions?

■ Problem 2.2 Follow-Up

Test your ideas by naming at least five fractions equivalent to each given fraction.

1. $\frac{1}{8}$

2. $\frac{2}{5}$

3. $\frac{5}{6}$

2.3 Making a Number Line

It would be helpful to have one strip that shows all of the fractions in your set of fraction strips. That way, you could measure fractional lengths using only one strip.

To make this master strip, you can copy the fractions from all of your fraction strips onto a single number line. The result will be a number line from 0 to 1 with marks for $\frac{1}{4}$, $\frac{1}{3}$, $\frac{1}{2}$, $\frac{2}{4}$, $\frac{2}{3}$, $\frac{3}{4}$, and all the other fractions on your strips.

Here's one way to transfer all of the fractions from your fraction strips onto one number line.

1. Draw a line at the top of a sheet of paper. This will be your number line. Label the left end of the number line with the numeral 0. Line up one end of a fraction strip with this 0 point, and make a mark where the other end crosses the number line. Label this mark with the numeral 1.

2. Align the end of your halves fraction strip (from Labsheet 1.5) with the 0 mark. Make a mark where the $\frac{1}{2}$ mark crosses the number line. Label this mark with the fraction $\frac{1}{2}$.

3. Align the end of your thirds fraction strip with the 0 mark. Make and label marks where the $\frac{1}{3}$ and $\frac{2}{3}$ marks cross the number line.

4. Continue this process with the rest of your strips.

Problem 2.3

A. Make a number line as described above. When you find another name for a mark you have already labeled, record the new name below the first name.

B. Look for patterns in your finished number line. Record your findings.

■ Problem 2.3 Follow-Up

Mark and label three fractions on your number line that are not represented on your set of fraction strips.

2.4 Comparing Fractions to Benchmarks

When you solve problems involving fractions, you may find it useful to estimate the size of fractions quickly. One strategy is to compare each fraction to 0, $\frac{1}{2}$, and 1. These values serve as **benchmarks**—or reference points. First, you can decide whether a fraction is between 0 and $\frac{1}{2}$, between $\frac{1}{2}$ and 1, or greater than 1. Then you can decide whether the fraction is closest to 0, $\frac{1}{2}$, or 1.

Problem 2.4

A. Decide whether each fraction below is between 0 and $\frac{1}{2}$ or between $\frac{1}{2}$ and 1.

$\frac{1}{5}$ $\quad$ $\frac{2}{3}$ $\quad$ $\frac{8}{10}$ $\quad$ $\frac{3}{12}$ $\quad$ $\frac{3}{5}$ $\quad$ $\frac{5}{6}$ $\quad$ $\frac{5}{8}$ $\quad$ $\frac{4}{5}$ $\quad$ $\frac{3}{8}$ $\quad$ $\frac{3}{4}$ $\quad$ $\frac{2}{9}$ $\quad$ $\frac{7}{12}$ $\quad$ $\frac{1}{3}$

B. Decide whether each fraction from part A is closest to 0, $\frac{1}{2}$, or 1. Record your information in a table.

C. Explain your strategies for comparing fractions to 0, $\frac{1}{2}$, and 1.

D. Use benchmarks and other strategies to help you write the fractions from part A in order from smallest to largest.

■ Problem 2.4 Follow-Up

1. In a–d, decide which fraction is larger by using benchmarks or another strategy that makes sense to you. Then write each pair of fractions, inserting a less-than symbol (<), a greater-than symbol (>), or an equals symbol (=) between the fractions to make a true statement. Describe your reasoning.

a. $\frac{3}{12}$ $\qquad$ $\frac{7}{12}$ $\qquad$ **b.** $\frac{5}{6}$ $\qquad$ $\frac{5}{8}$

c. $\frac{2}{3}$ $\qquad$ $\frac{3}{9}$ $\qquad$ **d.** $\frac{13}{12}$ $\qquad$ $\frac{6}{5}$

2. In a–f, use your fraction strips or another method to compare the fractions in each pair. Then write each pair of fractions, inserting <, >, or = between the fractions to make a true statement. Describe your reasoning.

a. $\frac{4}{7}$ $\frac{6}{7}$ b. $\frac{7}{10}$ $\frac{8}{12}$

c. $\frac{5}{8}$ $\frac{6}{9}$ d. $\frac{10}{12}$ $\frac{5}{6}$

e. $\frac{2}{4}$ $\frac{5}{9}$ f. $\frac{3}{9}$ $\frac{3}{10}$

2.5   Fractions Greater Than One

The whole-number points on a number line follow one another in a simple, regular pattern. But, as you saw in Problem 2.3, between every pair of whole numbers are many other points that may be labeled with fractions.

The portion of the number line shown below has marks for halves, thirds, fourths, fifths, sixths, eighths, ninths, tenths, and twelfths. These marks are different from the marks you identified in Problem 2.3, because they indicate fractions that are between 1 and 2 instead of between of 0 and 1.

Problem 2.5

A. Use the fraction strips from Labsheet 1.5 to find as many labels as you can for each of the lettered points. For each point, record the letter and the fraction labels.

B. Copy the number line onto a sheet of paper. Mark and label a point fitting each description below. Do not use points that are already marked.

    1. a point close to, but larger than, 1

    2. a point close to, but smaller than, $1\frac{1}{2}$

    3. a point close to, but larger than, $1\frac{1}{2}$

    4. a point close to, but smaller than, 2

■ Problem 2.5 Follow-Up

Find an equivalent fraction, with a denominator greater than 12, for one of the lettered points. Explain how you arrived at your answer.

As you work on these ACE questions, use your calculator whenever you need it.

Applications

In 1–4, decide whether the statement is true or false. Explain your reasoning in words or by drawing pictures.

1. $\frac{1}{3} = \frac{4}{12}$ **2.** $\frac{4}{6} = \frac{2}{3}$ **3.** $\frac{2}{5} = \frac{1}{3}$ **4.** $\frac{2}{4} = \frac{5}{10}$

5. The drawing below shows the volume indicator on a stereo receiver. Use the fraction strips shown to find three fractions that describe the part of the maximum volume shown by the indicator.

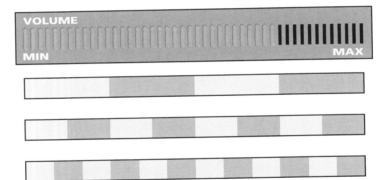

In 6 and 7, draw fraction strips to show that the two fractions are equivalent.

6. $\frac{2}{5}$ and $\frac{6}{15}$ **7.** $\frac{1}{9}$ and $\frac{2}{18}$

In 8–15, use benchmarks or another strategy that makes sense to you to decide which fraction is larger. Then write each pair of fractions, inserting a less-than symbol (<), a greater-than symbol (>), or an equals symbol (=) between the fractions to make a true statement. Describe your reasoning.

8. $\frac{8}{10}$ $\frac{3}{8}$ **9.** $\frac{2}{3}$ $\frac{4}{9}$

10. $\frac{3}{5}$ $\frac{5}{12}$ **11.** $\frac{1}{3}$ $\frac{2}{3}$

12. $\frac{3}{4}$ $\frac{3}{5}$ **13.** $\frac{3}{2}$ $\frac{7}{6}$

14. $\frac{8}{12}$ $\frac{6}{9}$ **15.** $\frac{9}{10}$ $\frac{10}{11}$

16. Describe, in writing or with pictures, how $\frac{7}{3}$ compares with $2\frac{1}{3}$.

17. Which is larger, $\frac{7}{6}$ or $\frac{13}{12}$? Explain your reasoning.

18. On the number line from 0 to 10, where is $\frac{13}{3}$ located? Explain your reasoning.

19. Write an explanation to a friend of how to find a fraction that is equivalent to $\frac{3}{5}$. You can use words and pictures to help explain.

Connections

In 20–25, copy each number line, and then estimate and mark where the numeral 1 would be.

20.

21.

22.

23.

24.

25.

In 26 and 27, write a fraction to describe the part of the length of an unsharpened pencil represented by the used pencil.

26.

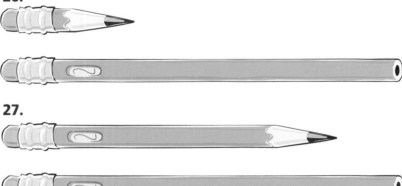

27.

In 28–36, compare each fraction to the benchmarks 0, $\frac{1}{2}$, 1, $1\frac{1}{2}$, and 2. Determine between which two benchmarks the fraction falls, and then determine to which benchmark the fraction is nearest. Organize your answers in a table. The columns of your table should be labeled as shown here:

Number	Lower benchmark	Upper benchmark	Nearest benchmark

28. $\frac{3}{5}$

29. $1\frac{2}{6}$

30. $\frac{12}{10}$

31. $\frac{2}{18}$

32. $1\frac{8}{10}$

33. $1\frac{1}{10}$

34. $\frac{12}{24}$

35. $\frac{9}{6}$

36. $1\frac{12}{15}$

37. These bars represent trips that Ms. Axler took in her job this week.

300 km

180 km

240 km

a. On a copy of each bar, shade in the distance Ms. Axler had traveled when she had gone one third of the total distance for the trip.

b. How many kilometers had Ms. Axler traveled when she was at the one-third point in each trip? Explain your reasoning.

Extensions

In 38–40, find every fraction with a denominator less than 50 that is equivalent to the given fraction.

38. $\frac{3}{15}$

39. $\frac{8}{3}$

40. $1\frac{4}{6}$

41. Find five fractions between $\frac{1}{4}$ and $\frac{1}{2}$.

42. Which of the fractions below represents the largest part of a whole? Explain your reasoning.

$$\frac{4}{5} \qquad \frac{17}{23} \qquad \frac{51}{68}$$

Mathematical Reflections

In this investigation, you explored equivalent fractions and compared fractions to benchmarks and other fractions. These questions will help you summarize what you have learned:

1 Find six fractions that are equivalent to $\frac{3}{5}$. Explain how you found the fractions.

2 How can you decide whether a given fraction is closest to 0, $\frac{1}{2}$, or 1?

3 How can you compare any two fractions to decide which is largest?

Think about your answers to these questions, discuss your ideas with other students and your teacher, and then write a summary of your findings in your journal.

Cooking with Fractions

You have made and used fraction strips to help you think about fractions as parts of wholes. You have used your strips to name fractional amounts, to compare fractions, to find equivalent fractions, and to make a number line showing fractions between whole numbers.

3.1 Area Models for Fractions

You can also think about fractions as parts of a region. For example, if a pizza is cut into eight slices of the same size, and you eat two of the slices, you have eaten two eighths of the pizza. If you eat five of the slices, you have eaten five eighths of the pizza.

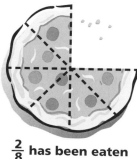

$\frac{2}{8}$ **has been eaten**

$\frac{5}{8}$ **has been eaten**

If you divide a square pan of brownies into equal-size brownies and then eat two brownies, what part of the batch have you eaten? To answer this question, you need to know the total number of brownies in the batch.

Problem 3.1

Use the squares on Labsheet 3.1 as models for pans of brownies. Show the cuts you would make to divide a pan of brownies into

A. 15 equal-size large brownies

B. 20 equal-size medium brownies

C. 30 equal-size small brownies

■ Problem 3.1 Follow-Up

1. What fraction of a whole pan is one small brownie? One medium brownie? One large brownie? Explain.

2. **a.** Is there more than one way to cut a pan of brownies into 15 equal-size large brownies? If so, show the other ways. If not, explain why it cannot be done.

   b. Is there more than one way to cut a pan of brownies into 20 equal-size medium brownies? If so, show the other ways. If not, explain why it cannot be done.

   c. Is there more than one way to cut a pan of brownies into 30 equal-size small brownies? If so, show the other ways. If not, explain why it cannot be done.

3.2 Baking Brownies

Next week, the eighth graders from Sturgis Middle School are attending school camp. Samantha, Romero, and Harold have the job of making brownies for an afternoon snack for the entire camp—all 240 people!

Chunky Brownies with a Crust

$1\frac{1}{4}$ cups flour
$\frac{1}{4}$ cup sugar
$\frac{1}{2}$ cup cold butter or margarine
1 14-ounce can sweetened condensed milk
$\frac{1}{4}$ cup unsweetened cocoa

1 egg
1 teaspoon vanilla
$\frac{1}{2}$ teaspoon baking powder
1 7-ounce bar milk chocolate, broken into small chunks
$\frac{3}{4}$ cup chopped nuts (optional)

Preheat the oven to 350 degrees. In a medium bowl, combine 1 cup of flour and the sugar. Cut in the margarine or butter until crumbly. Press the mixture firmly into the bottom of a 10-by-10-inch baking pan. Bake 15 minutes. Meanwhile, in a large mixing bowl, beat the sweetened condensed milk, the cocoa, the egg, the remaining flour, the vanilla, and the baking powder. Stir in the nuts and chocolate chunks. Spread over the prepared crust. Bake 20 minutes. Cool. Sprinkle with confectioner's sugar if desired. Store tightly covered at room temperature. Makes 15 large, 20 medium, or 30 small brownies.

Problem 3.2

A. Do you think Samantha, Romero, and Harold should make small, medium, or large brownies?

B. If they make brownies of the size you chose in part A, how much of each ingredient will they need to make enough to serve a brownie to each person at camp?

C. Describe the strategy you used to get your answer to part B.

■ Problem 3.2 Follow-Up

Compare your answers for part B to the answers of classmates who did calculations for the other two sizes.

Suppose you get to decide which size brownies will be served to the campers. Tell which size you would choose in each situation below. Explain your answer.

1. You are in charge of buying the ingredients, and you have a limited budget.
2. You have to help make the brownies.
3. You don't have to do any work, you just get to eat the brownies.

As you work on these ACE questions, use your calculator whenever you need it.

Applications

In 1–4, illustrate each fraction by drawing a square, subdividing it into equal-size regions, and shading the fractional part indicated.

1. $\frac{7}{20}$ **2.** $\frac{3}{15}$ **3.** $\frac{12}{18}$ **4.** $\frac{3}{7}$

In 5–8, illustrate each fraction by drawing a square and subdividing it in a different way than you did for questions 1–4.

5. $\frac{7}{20}$ **6.** $\frac{3}{15}$ **7.** $\frac{12}{18}$ **8.** $\frac{3}{7}$

9. Show $\frac{3}{12}$ in three different ways by subdividing and shading a square.

In 10–13, tell what fractional part of the whole figure is shaded.

10.
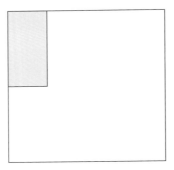

11.
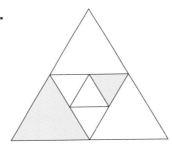

12.
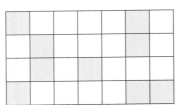

13.
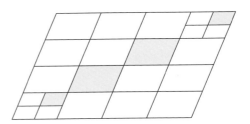

14. Gerhard wants to make Tahini Granola Cookies to bring on a hiking trip.

Tahini Granola Cookies

These cookies are an excellent high-energy snack
to take on camping trips or hikes.

$\frac{1}{2}$ cup tahini $\frac{1}{2}$ cup melted butter

$\frac{2}{3}$ cups honey   2 cups of your favorite granola

2 teaspoons vanilla $\frac{1}{4}$ cup chopped nuts

Preheat the oven to 350°. Blend the tahini and honey together. Add the vanilla
and butter and mix well. Add the granola and nuts and mix well. Drop by
tablespoon, $1\frac{1}{2}$ to 2 inches apart, on the cookie sheet and bake 10–15 minutes
or until golden brown. Transfer to a dry surface to cool. Makes about 3 dozen
cookies.

a. How much of each ingredient will Gerhard need to make five batches of
granola cookies?

b. Instead of dropping spoonfuls of dough onto the pans, Gerhard pressed the
dough evenly into square pans. When the granola cookie mix had baked, he
cut it into bars. Show several ways Gerhard can cut a pan of granola cookies
to get three dozen bars.

Connections

15. a. How many fourths are in $4\frac{1}{4}$? (A number like $4\frac{1}{4}$ is called a *mixed number*—i t
is a mix of a whole number and a fraction.)

b. Use your answer to part a to write $4\frac{1}{4}$ as a fraction with a denominator of 4.
(This is sometimes called changing the form of a number from a mixed
number to an *improper fraction*.)

16. **a.** How many fifths are in $1\frac{3}{5}$?

   b. Use your answer to part a to write $1\frac{3}{5}$ as a fraction with a denominator of 5.

17. **a.** How many sixths are in $3\frac{5}{6}$?

   b. Use your answer to part a to write $3\frac{5}{6}$ as a fraction with a denominator of 6.

In 18–23, draw, subdivide, and shade square regions to illustrate and complete each statement. For example, the statement $\frac{?}{10} = \frac{3}{5}$ can be illustrated like this:

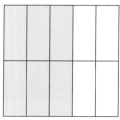 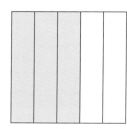

The illustration shows that $\frac{6}{10} = \frac{3}{5}$.

18. $\frac{3}{15} = \frac{?}{30}$ 19. $\frac{18}{30} = \frac{?}{15}$ 20. $\frac{1}{2} = \frac{?}{20}$

21. $\frac{?}{15} = \frac{3}{5}$ 22. $\frac{?}{20} = \frac{3}{5}$ 23. $\frac{9}{15} = \frac{?}{30}$

In 24 and 25, tell what fraction of each square is shaded.

24. 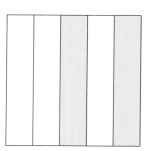   25.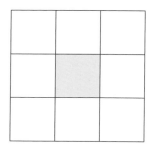

26. Draw a picture to illustrate a fraction with a denominator of 10 that is equivalent to the fraction shown in question 24.

27. Draw a picture to illustrate a fraction with a denominator of 27 that is equivalent to the fraction illustrated in question 25.

28. Order the following fractions from smallest to largest:

$$1\frac{7}{10} \qquad \frac{5}{3} \qquad 1\frac{12}{18} \qquad \frac{25}{15}$$

In 29–31, use this drawing of a portion of a ruler. The numbers indicate inches.

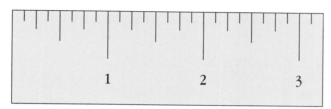

29. What fraction does each mark between the left end of the ruler and the 1-inch mark represent?

30. If the smallest sections of the ruler were each divided into two equal parts, how should the new parts between 0 and 1 be labeled?

31. What fractions do the marks between 1 inch and 2 inches represent?

Extensions

32. If a 13-by-9-inch brownie pan is divided into 20 equal-size brownies, what are the dimensions of one brownie?

Mathematical Reflections

In this investigation, you divided squares and rectangles into regions to help you model fractions. These questions will help you summarize what you have learned:

1. Describe your strategy for dividing a square to represent a fraction.

2. How can square models help you decide which of two fractions is larger?

3. How do you find the fraction name for a shaded part of a square? Use a specific example if it helps you to think about the process.

Think about your answers to these questions, discuss your ideas with other students and your teacher, and then write a summary of your findings in your journal.

From Fractions to Decimals

So far in this unit, you have expressed numbers as fractions. In the elementary grades, you studied another way to represent numbers—as *decimals*. Decimals are a convenient way to express fractions with denominators such as 10, 100, 1000, or 10,000. In this investigation, you will have a chance to review decimals and to connect the decimal representation of a number to the fraction representation of the same number.

4.1 Designing a Garden

In Dayton, Ohio, the town council and the Benjamin Wegerzyn Garden Center created the largest community garden in the world. A community garden is a garden that is shared by several people. The community garden in Dayton has 1173 square plots of land that can be used by that many individual people or families to make gardens. Each plot of land has an area of 100 square meters.

Justin's family has a plot in the community garden. His father wants Justin to design the vegetable garden for his family. Justin may decide how much of the land to allocate for each type of vegetable his family wants to grow, but he must satisfy a set of conditions they put on the garden. Justin has to present the plan to his family with a drawing of the garden that specifies what fraction of the plot will be planted with each kind of vegetable.

To help plan, Justin first draws a grid with 100 squares, each representing 1 square meter of the 100-square-meter plot.

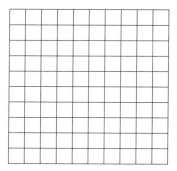

Problem 4.1

Here are the family's requirements for the garden.

- Justin's father wants to be sure potatoes, beans, corn, and tomatoes are planted. He wants twice as much of the garden to be planted in corn as potatoes. He wants three times as much land planted in potatoes as tomatoes.
- Justin's sister wants cucumbers in the garden.
- Justin's brother wants carrots in the garden.
- Justin's mother wants eggplant in the garden.
- Justin wants radishes in the garden.

Use Labsheet 4.1 to make a suitable plan for the garden. Write a description of the garden you plan. Name the fraction of the garden space that will be allotted to each kind of vegetable as part of your description. Explain how your garden will satisfy each member of Justin's family.

■ Problem 4.1 Follow-Up

1. Justin's father says that he will not plant less than a square meter of any vegetable. Design a garden with the largest possible amount of land planted in potatoes that fits the conditions of the problem and has at least one square meter allotted for each vegetable.

2. Design a garden with the smallest possible amount of land planted in potatoes that fits the conditions of the problem and has at least one square meter allotted for each vegetable.

Making Smaller Parts

Decimals give us a way to write special fractions that have denominators like 10, 100, 1000, and 10,000. A tenths grid can help you to understand decimals.

A *tenths grid* is divided into ten equal parts. It resembles the tenths fraction strip you have been using, only it is square.

$\frac{1}{10}$	$\frac{1}{10}$	$\frac{1}{10}$	$\frac{1}{10}$	$\frac{1}{10}$	$\frac{1}{10}$	$\frac{1}{10}$	$\frac{1}{10}$	$\frac{1}{10}$	$\frac{1}{10}$
0.1	0.1	0.1	0.1	0.1	0.1	0.1	0.1	0.1	0.1

Here are some examples of fractions represented on tenths grids. Fraction names and decimal names for the shaded part are given below each drawing.

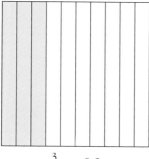

$\frac{3}{10}$ or 0.3

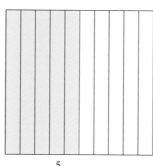

$\frac{5}{10}$ or 0.5

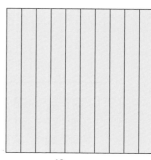

$\frac{10}{10}$ or 1.0

We can further divide a tenths grid by drawing horizontal lines to make ten rows. Now we have 100 parts. This *hundredths grid* is what Justin used to plan his garden.

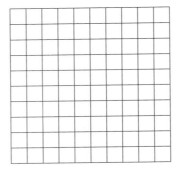

Fractions can also be represented on a hundredths grid. We can write fractional parts of 100 as decimal numbers.

Fraction	Decimal	Meaning	Representation on a hundredths grid
$\frac{7}{100}$	0.07	7 out of 100	
$\frac{27}{100}$	0.27	27 out of 100	
$\frac{51}{100}$	0.51	51 out of 100	

Look back at the original plan you drew for Justin's garden. Write each of the fractional parts for the vegetables in your plan as a decimal.

■ Problem 4.2 Follow-Up

1. a. What would a hundredths grid look like if each square of the grid were divided into ten equal parts? How many parts would the new grid have?

b. What is a fraction name for the smallest part of this new grid? A decimal name?

c. How would you shade an area of this new grid to show $\frac{1}{10}$?

d. What fraction or decimal names could you call this shaded area?

e. What would you call this new grid, which has every square of a hundredths grid divided into ten equal parts?

2. a. You can write $\frac{9}{100}$ as the decimal 0.09. How could you write $\frac{9}{1000}$ as a decimal?

b. How could you write $\frac{469}{1000}$ as a decimal?

3. a. What would you need to do to the new grid you discovered in question 1 to make a grid that shows *ten-thousandths?*

b. How could you write $\frac{9}{10,000}$ as a decimal?

c. How could you write $\frac{469}{10,000}$ as a decimal?

4.3 Using Decimal Benchmarks

In Investigation 2, we developed benchmarks to help us estimate fractions. Benchmarks can also help us estimate and compare decimals. You can use what you already know about fractions to make estimating and comparing decimals easier.

Did you know?

Throughout history mathematicians have used many different notations to represent decimal numbers. For example, in 1585, Simon Stevinus would have written 2.57 as either 2, 5' 7" or 2 ⓪ 5 ①7 ②. In 1617, John Napier would have written 2/57. Other commonly-used notations included an underscore, 2_57_, and a combination of a vertical line and an underscore, 2|_57_. Even today, the notation varies from country to country. For example, in England, 2.57 is written as 2•57, and, in Germany, it is written as 2,57.

Problem 4.3

A. Rename each of these fraction benchmarks as a decimal.

1. 0   **2.** $\frac{1}{4}$ **3.** $\frac{1}{2}$ **4.** $\frac{3}{4}$ **5.** 1

B. Now use the decimal benchmarks and other strategies that make sense to you to help you order each set of numbers from smallest to largest.

1. 0.23   0.28   0.25

2. 2.054   20.54   2.54

3. 0.78   0.708   0.078

C. For each of the three decimals in parts 1 and 3 of question B, give the name of the decimal in words, and tell which benchmark the number is nearest. Give the benchmark as a fraction and as a decimal. For each decimal benchmark chosen, explain your reasoning. Organize your work in a table like the one below.

Number	Name in words	Nearest decimal benchmark	Nearest fraction benchmark	Reasoning
0.23				
0.28				
0.25				
0.78				
0.708				
0.078				

▪ Problem 4.3 Follow-Up

1. Write, as a decimal, a fraction with a denominator of 10,000 that is near, but less than, $\frac{3}{4}$.

2. Write, as a decimal, a fraction with a denominator of 1000 that is near, but less than, 1.

Playing Distinguishing Digits

Distinguishing Digits is a collection of number puzzles. In each puzzle, you use clues to help find a Mystery Number.

For each puzzle, a Mystery Number Card is presented for everyone on the team to see. It shows blank spaces for the digits of a Mystery Number. Then the team inspects several Clue Cards for clues to help them decode the Mystery Number.

Look at the following example. As a class, decide what the Mystery Number must be.

Mystery Number

1 ___ . ___ ___ ___

Clue 1 The digit in the thousandths place is double the digit in the ones place.
Clue 2 The digit in the tenths place is odd, and it represents the sum of the digits in the tens place and the thousandths place.
Clue 3 There are exactly two odd digits in the Mystery Number.
Clue 4 The digit in the hundredths place is three times the digit in the ones place.

Problem 4.4

Play the Distinguishing Digits puzzles with your group. Record the strategies you use to solve the puzzles.

■ **Problem 4.4 Follow-Up**

With your group, create a new Distinguishing Digits puzzle. Try out the puzzle on another group. If the other group finds a problem with your puzzle, rework the clues until your puzzle works.

As you work on these ACE questions, use your calculator whenever you need it.

Applications

In 1–6, the hundredths grid is partially shaded. Write fraction and decimal names to describe the shaded part.

1.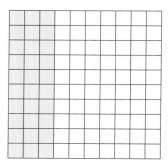

2.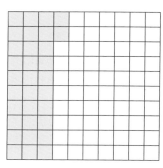

3.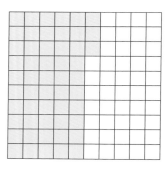

4.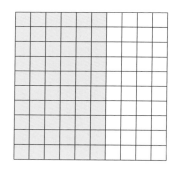

5.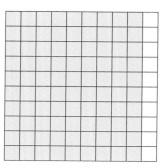

6.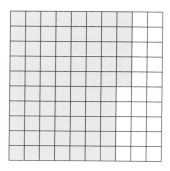

In 7–8, the whole is one hundredths grid. Write fraction and decimal names to describe the shaded part.

7.

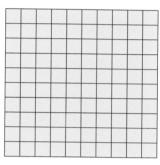

8.

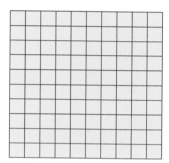

9. In a–f, use the blank hundredths grids on Labsheet 4.ACE to shade the given fractional part. Write the fraction as an equivalent decimal.

a. $\frac{1}{2}$ of the hundredths grid

b. $\frac{3}{4}$ of the hundredths grid

c. $\frac{99}{100}$ of the hundredths grid

d. $1\frac{3}{10}$ of the hundredths grids

e. $2\frac{7}{10}$ of the hundredths grids

f. $1\frac{3}{5}$ of the hundredths grids

In 10–13, rewrite each pair of numbers, inserting a less-than symbol (<), a greater-than symbol (>), or an equals symbol (=) between the numbers to make a true statement.

10. $\frac{3}{5}$ 0.3

11. 0.205   0.21

12. 0.1   0.1000

13. $\frac{37}{50}$ 0.74

In 14–16, rewrite the numbers in order from smallest to largest.

14. 0.33   0.12   0.127   0.2 $\frac{45}{10}$

15. $\frac{3}{100}$ 0.005 $\frac{3}{1000}$ 0.34

16. 0.827   1.23 $\frac{987}{100}$ $\frac{987}{1000}$

In 17–20, copy the part of the number line given. Then, find the "step" by determining the difference from one mark to another. Label the unlabeled marks with decimal numbers. The first step is given for you.

17. The step is 0.2.
0.2   0.8

18. The step is _____.
0.15   0.17

19. The step is _____.
0.028   0.029

20. The step is _____.
1.8   1.9

In 21–35, rewrite each pair of numbers, inserting a less-than symbol (<), a greater-than symbol (>), or an equals symbol (=) between the numbers to make a true statement.

21. 0.3   0.6

22. 0.4 $\frac{3}{5}$

23. 0.7 $\frac{1}{2}$

24. 0.34   0.23

25. 0.60   0.6

26. 0.52 $\frac{2}{4}$

27. 0.34   0.4

28. 0.08   0.8

29. 0.92   0.9

30. 2.45   2.3

31. 0.56   0.056

32. 0.037   0.029

33. 0.7   0.725

34. 0.41   0.405

35. 0.10   0.108

Connections

36. Su computed her free-throw average on her calculator and got 0.6019. Ahmed computed his free-throw average and got 0.602. Solange's free-throw average was 0.62. Who is the best free-throw shooter? Explain your answer.

37. Chad, Roman, and Kari wanted to know who was the best free-throw shooter among them. Chad's free-throw average was about 0.588. Roman's average was close to 0.611. Kari consistently made 6 out of 10. Who is the best free-throw shooter? Explain your answer.

In 38–40, show the fraction by drawing and shading squares. Then, write each improper fraction as an equivalent mixed number.

38. $\frac{7}{5}$ **39.** $\frac{7}{3}$ **40.** $\frac{11}{6}$

41. Determine what part of each figure is shaded.

a.

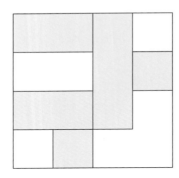

b.

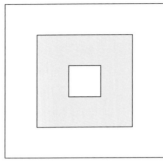

c.

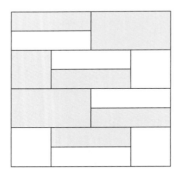

Extensions

Problems 42–43 involve the Dewey Decimal system, which is used in many libraries to catalog books. The Dewey Decimal system is based on the decimal number system.

42. Serita looked up *elephant* in the library's computer. She saw that there were several books about elephants, with these call numbers: 599.55, 599.504, 599.5, and 599.5044. The librarian showed Serita the guide numbers on the ends of the shelves and explained that the books were arranged in numerical order from smallest to largest and from left to right. In what order will the books about elephants be arranged on the shelf? Explain your reasoning.

43. Huang wanted to reshelve two books he had been reading about the history of rock and roll music. The books' call numbers were 782.42 and 781.66. Huang located the shelf where his book belonged, but the other books he found there were completely out of order: 781.5, 782.005, 781.053, 781.035, and 782.409. He rearranged the books already on the shelf and then placed his books among them. In what order did Huang put the books that were already on the shelf? Where did he put his books?

44. Microchips can process information in as little as one billionth of a second, which is called a *nanosecond*. Write the decimal representation of a nanosecond.

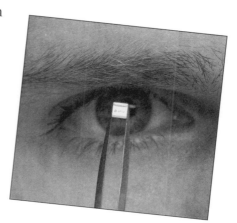

Mathematical Reflections

In this investigation, you used square grids to help you model decimals. You found that decimals are special kinds of fractions. These questions will help you summarize what you have learned:

1 Describe the process of dividing a square to represent tenths; to represent hundredths; to represent thousandths.

2 When comparing two decimals, how can you decide which decimal represents a larger number?

3 Decimals are an extension of the place-value system you studied for whole numbers in elementary school. Tell what each digit in 25,708.201 represents.

4 Express each of the following decimal numbers in words.

0.16   1.069   33.109   431.0115

Think about your answers to these questions, discuss your ideas with other students and your teacher, and then write a summary of your findings in your journal.

Moving Between Fractions and Decimals

In your daily life, you often need to choose among options. You might have to decide which option is the best buy, gives the best outcome, or yields the most money. In these situations, mathematics can help you make comparisons so you can make a good decision.

5.1 Choosing the Best

The Portland Middle School basketball team is playing the Coldwater Colts. The game is tied 58 to 58. In her excitement the Coldwater coach steps onto the court just as the buzzer sounds, and a technical foul is called.

The Portland coach has to choose one of her players to shoot the free throw. If the player makes the free throw, Portland will win.

Did you know?

Basketball was invented in 1891 by James Naismith, a physical education teacher who wanted to create a team sport that could be played indoors during the winter. The game was originally played with a soccer ball, and peach baskets were used as goals.

Problem 5.1

The coach has three players to choose from to shoot the free throw. In their pregame warm-ups:

- Angela made 17 out of 25 free throws
- Emily made 15 out of 20 free throws
- Carma made 7 out of 10 free throws

Which player should the Portland coach select to shoot the free throw? Explain your reasoning.

■ **Problem 5.1 Follow-Up**

Of the top four free-throw shooters on the Coldwater Colts:

- Naomi averages 19 out of 25 free throws
- Bobbie averages 8 out of 10 free throws
- Kate averages 36 out of 50 free throws
- Olympia averages 16 out of 20 free throws

If you were the coach of the Colts, which player would you choose to take the free-throw on a technical foul? Explain your reasoning.

5.2 Writing Fractions as Decimals

The Portland coach chose Emily to take the shot. Emily missed the free throw, but the team won in overtime.

The next day, the players asked their math teacher, Mr. Martinez, what he thought about the problem of whom to choose to take the free throw. He said he always tries to find a decimal name for fractions whose values he needs to compare.

Mr. Martinez explained, "Our fraction strips can help us find decimal names that are good approximations for some fractions. Decimals are ways to express fractions with denominators of 10 or 100. We can use our tenths strip to help us find decimal approximations. We could find even closer approximations if we had a fraction strip divided into hundredths."

Problem 5.2

On the next page are the fraction strips with which you are already familiar. Below these strips is a hundredths strip, which is a tenths strip that has each segment divided into ten parts. Work with your group to find a way to use the fraction strips to help you estimate each of the fractions represented on the halves, thirds, fourths, fifths, sixths, eighths, ninths, tenths, and twelfths fraction strips as decimals.

You might think about doing this by comparing the marks on each fraction strip to marks on the hundredths strip. For example, to find a decimal name for $\frac{5}{12}$, you can find the mark on the hundredths strip that is nearest to the length $\frac{5}{12}$, since hundredths can easily be written as decimals. Since the mark at $\frac{42}{100}$ on the hundredths strip is the closest mark to $\frac{5}{12}$ on the twelfths strip, $\frac{5}{12}$ is approximately equal to 0.42. Sometimes it is easier to look at the tenths strip. For example, $\frac{1}{2}$ on the fraction strip is at the same mark as $\frac{5}{10}$ on the tenths strip, so $\frac{1}{2}$ is equivalent to 0.5.

On Labsheet 5.2, label each mark on the halves, thirds, fourths, fifths, sixths, eighths, ninths, tenths, and twelfths fraction strips with an approximate decimal representation. Be prepared to explain your answers.

■ Problem 5.2 Follow-Up

1. Did you find any patterns that helped you to predict what some of the fractions would be as decimals?

2. How did your knowledge of equivalent fractions help you to find decimal names for some of your fractions?

3. In a–d, find an approximate fraction for the decimal.
   a. 0.17
   b. 0.29
   c. 0.609
   d. 0.92

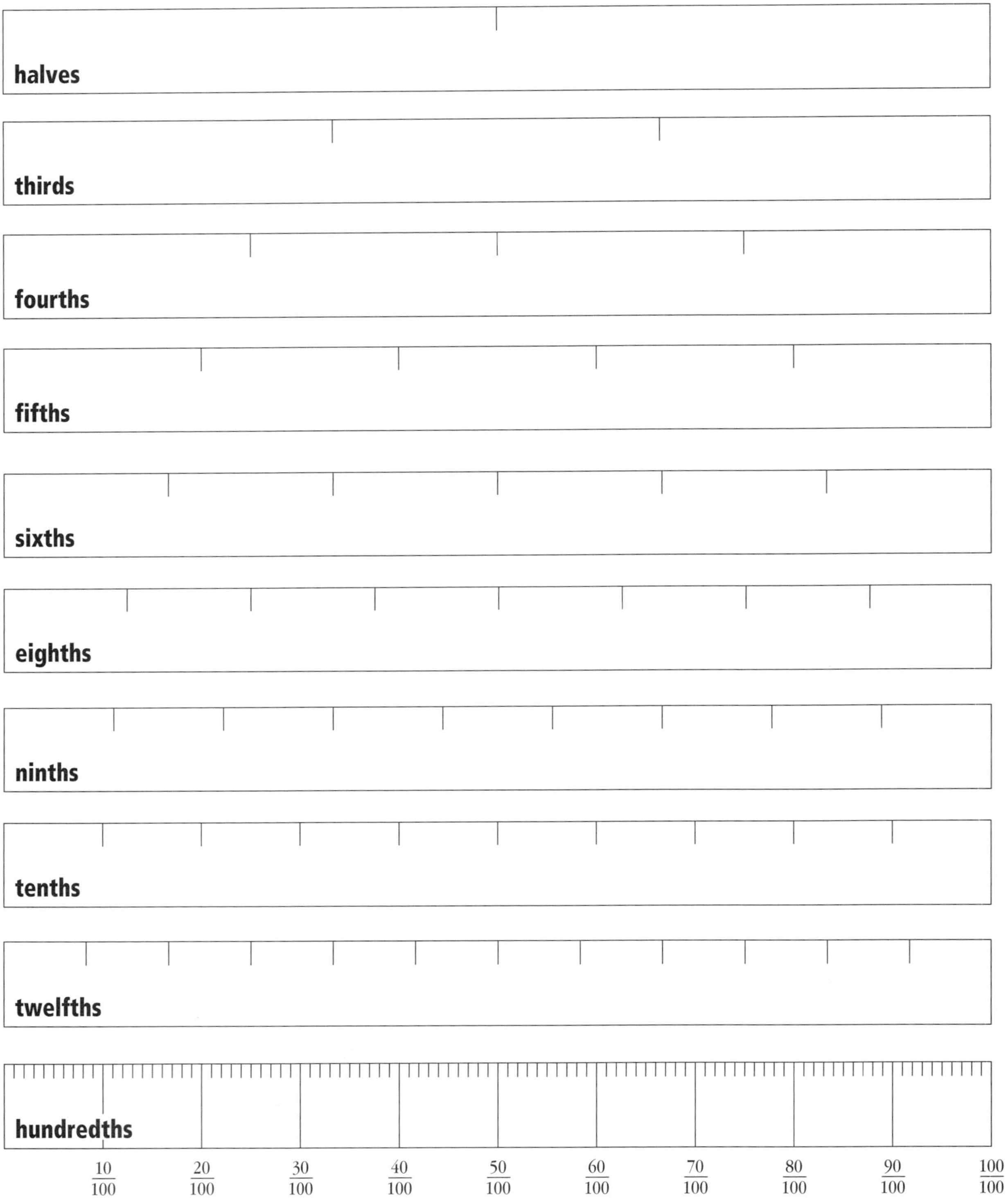

halves

thirds

fourths

fifths

sixths

eighths

ninths

tenths

twelfths

hundredths

$\frac{10}{100}$ $\frac{20}{100}$ $\frac{30}{100}$ $\frac{40}{100}$ $\frac{50}{100}$ $\frac{60}{100}$ $\frac{70}{100}$ $\frac{80}{100}$ $\frac{90}{100}$ $\frac{100}{100}$

Moving from Fractions to Decimals

In 1992, a hurricane swept through the Bahamas, Florida, and Louisiana, destroying many homes and causing lots of damage to land and buildings. The storm was named Hurricane Andrew. Many people lost everything, and had no place to live and very little clothing and food. In response to the disaster, people from all over collected clothing, household items, and food in a relief effort to send to the victims of the hurricane.

One group of students decided to collect food to distribute to some of the families whose homes were destroyed. They would pack what they collected in boxes to send it to the families. The students had to solve some problems while they were packing the boxes.

Problem 5.3

The students had 24 boxes for packing the food they collected. They wanted to share the supplies equally among the families who would receive the boxes. They had small bags and plastic containers to use to repack items for the individual boxes.

The students collected the following items:

48	tins of cocoa mix	6	pounds of Swiss cheese
72	boxes of powdered milk	3	pounds of hot pepper cheese
264	boxes of juice	7	pounds of peanuts
120	boxes of granola bars	5	pounds of popcorn kernels
36	pounds of wheat crackers	475	apples
18	pounds of peanut butter	195	oranges
12	pounds of cheddar cheese		

A. How much of each item should the students include in each box? Explain your reasoning.

B. What operation $(+, -, \times, \div)$ did you use to find your answers? Why did this operation work?

C. How can your calculator help you decide how to distribute the food items?

■ **Problem 5.3 Follow-Up**

One student calculated the amount of Swiss cheese to include in each box by entering 6 into her calculator and dividing by 24. Is this a good method? Why or why not?

As you work on these ACE questions, use your calculator whenever you need it.

Applications

1. Name three fractions whose decimal equivalent is 0.25. Explain your answer. Draw a picture if it helps explain your thinking.

2. Name two fractions whose decimal equivalent is 0.40. Explain your answer. Draw a picture if it helps explain your thinking.

In 3–6, give a good fraction estimate for the decimal.

3. 0.08   **4.** 0.4   **5.** 0.04   **6.** 0.84

7. Mr. Paul's class wants to send 18 identical food boxes to victims of a hurricane. The class has collected the following items:

63 pounds of pretzels	60 pounds of mozzarella cheese
72 melons	4 pounds of grated parmesan cheese
12 pounds of pecans	162 pizza crusts
24 pounds of peanut butter	108 cans of pizza sauce

How much of each kind of food will go into each box?

8. a. Sarah and Antonio went fishing in the Grand River, and each caught one fish. Sarah's fish was $\frac{5}{8}$ of a foot long and Antonio's was $\frac{2}{3}$ of a foot long. Which fish was longer? Explain.

     b. If Sarah and Antonio had measured their fish in decimals, would it have been easier for them to tell which fish was longer? Explain.

9. Each small square represents $\frac{1}{100}$. What decimal is represented by this set of grids?

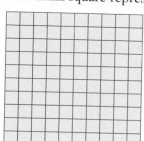 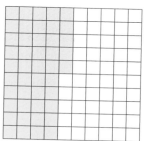

10. Each small square represents $\frac{1}{100}$. What decimal is represented by this set of grids?

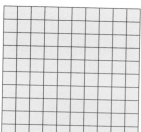 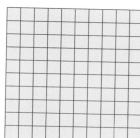 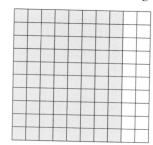

In 11–13, use the fraction strips on Labsheet 5.2 to help you estimate a good decimal equivalent for the fraction.

11. $\frac{3}{4}$ **12.** $\frac{2}{3}$ **13.** $\frac{5}{12}$

In 14–16, find a fraction with a denominator of 10 or less that is a good estimate for the decimal.

14. 0.6   **15.** 0.91   **16.** 0.33

In 17–20, compare the two numbers. Then rewrite the numbers, inserting <, >, or = between them to make a true statement.

17. $\frac{4}{6}$ $\frac{2}{3}$ **18.** 0.34   4

19. $\frac{2}{5}$ $\frac{1}{3}$ **20.** 0.08   0.3

21. Which are easier to compare, fractions or decimals? Why?

22. Which is greater, 0.45 or 0.9? Explain your reasoning. Draw a picture if it helps explain your thinking.

23. Which is greater, seventy-five hundredths or six tenths? Explain your reasoning. Draw a picture if it helps explain your thinking.

24. Which is greater, 0.6 or 0.60? Explain your reasoning. Draw a picture if it helps you explain.

25. James says a fraction is another way to represent a division problem. For example, he says $\frac{3}{8}$ means the same thing as $3 \div 8$. What do you get when you do this division on your calculator? Compare your decimal answer with your fraction strips to see if this is reasonable. Describe your findings.

In 26–31, use your calculator to find a decimal form for the fraction. Then use the hundredths strip or other fraction strips on Labsheet 5.2 to check whether your answer is reasonable.

26. $\frac{3}{4}$

27. $\frac{5}{8}$

28. $\frac{13}{25}$

29. $\frac{17}{25}$

30. $\frac{1}{20}$

31. $\frac{7}{10}$

32. Suppose a new student starts school today and your teacher asks you to teach her how to find decimal representations for fractions. What would you tell her? How would you convince the student that your method works?

Connections

33. Ten students went to a pizza parlor together. They ordered eight small pizzas.

  a. How much will each student receive if they share the pizzas equally? Express your answer as a fraction and as a decimal.

  b. Explain how you thought about the problem. Draw a picture that would convince someone that your answer is correct.

34. Zachary says division should be called a "sharing operation." Why might he say this?

35. If we look through a microscope that makes objects appear ten times larger, 1 centimeter on a metric ruler looks like this:

0   1 cm

   a. Copy this microscope's view of 1 centimeter. Subdivide the length for 1 centimeter into ten equal parts. What fraction of a centimeter does each of these parts represent?

   b. Now think of subdividing one of these smaller parts into ten equal parts. What part of a centimeter does each of the new segments represent?

   c. If you were to subdivide one of these new small parts into ten parts again, what part of a centimeter would each of the new small parts represent?

36. Here is what one of the fleas that live on the dog at Mr. Valicenti's fishing camp looks like through the microscope that makes objects appear ten times larger.

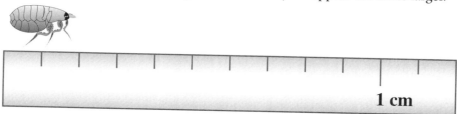

   a. About how long is the flea in centimeters?

   b. How long would a line of 10 fleas be?

   c. How many fleas would it take to equal 1 centimeter?

37. There are also ferocious flies at Mr. Valicenti's camp.

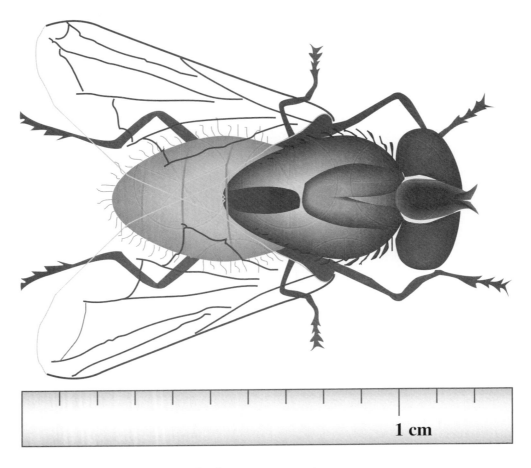

1 cm

a. About how long is the fly in centimeters?

b. If we line up ten of these flies end to end, how long would the line of flies be?

c. About how many fleas lined up end to end (see question 36) would equal the length of a line of ten flies?

38. a. Copy the number line below. Show 0.4 and 0.5 on your number line. Can you place five numbers between 0.4 and 0.5? If yes, place them on your number line with labels. If no, explain why not.

0   1

b. Now, enlarge the line segment from 0.4 to 0.5. Make your new line segment approximately the length of the original number line. Place 0.45 and 0.50 on your new number line. Can you find five numbers that belong between 0.45 and 0.50? If yes, place them on your number line with labels. If no, explain why not.

39. Using the fraction benchmarks 0, $\frac{1}{4}$, $\frac{1}{2}$, $\frac{3}{4}$, and 1 and the number line below, copy and complete the table to show what two fraction benchmarks each decimal is between. Also, tell which benchmark each decimal is nearest.

0          $\frac{1}{4}$ $\frac{1}{2}$ $\frac{3}{4}$ 1

Decimal	Lower benchmark	Upper benchmark	Nearest benchmark
0.17	0	$\frac{1}{4}$	$\frac{1}{4}$
0.034			
0.789			
0.092			
0.9			
0.491			
0.627			
0.36			

Extensions

In 40–44, copy the segment of the number line given. Then, find the "step" by determining the difference from one mark to another. Label the unlabeled marks with decimals. Here is an example:

The step is 0.01.

0.19   0.23

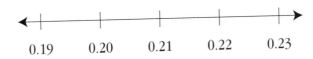

0.19   0.20   0.21   0.22   0.23

40.

The step is _____ .

0.003   0.403

41.

The step is _____ .

0.198   0.200   0.202

42.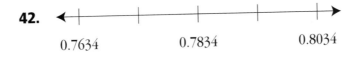

The step is _____ .

0.7634   0.7834   0.8034

43.

The step is _____ .

0.512   0.520

44.

The step is _____ .

0.3   0.4

In 45–50, find an estimate if you cannot find an exact answer. You may find that making a number line or a diagram is useful in solving the problem. Explain how you reasoned about each problem.

45. What is $\frac{1}{4}$ of 12?

46. What is $\frac{3}{4}$ of 8?

47. What is $\frac{2}{9}$ of 18?

48. What is $\frac{2}{9}$ of 3?

49. What is $\frac{1}{4}$ of 3?

50. What is $\frac{3}{4}$ of 3?

Mathematical Reflections

In this investigation, you developed ways to represent fractions as decimals. You used your fraction strips to find fractions and decimals that are close to each other. These questions will help you summarize what you have learned:

1. Describe how to find a decimal equivalent to a given fraction. How can you check your strategy to see that it works?

2. Describe how to find a fraction equivalent to a given decimal. Explain why your strategy works.

3. When comparing two decimals—such as 0.57 and 0.559—how can you decide which decimal represents the larger number?

Think about your answers to these questions, discuss your ideas with other students and your teacher, and then write a summary of your findings in your journal.

Out of One Hundred

Because fractions that have 100 as their denominator are so useful, there are many ways to represent them. Two ways you have already studied are with decimals and with hundredths grids.

Another useful way to express a fraction with a denominator of 100 is to use a special symbol: the percent symbol, %. **Percent** means "out of 100."

For example, suppose 78 out of 100 middle-school students say they like to swim. You already know how to represent the portion who like to swim with a fraction ($\frac{78}{100}$), a decimal (0.78), and a hundredths grid:

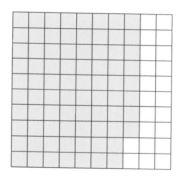

You can also write the fraction of students who like to swim as a percent: 78%.

Look at this grid. How can the shaded part be written as a fraction, a decimal, and a percent?

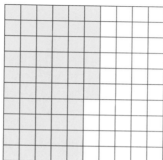

An advertisement in a local newspaper says that a clothing store is having a 30% off sale. This means that all prices have been reduced by $30 for every $100. If a jacket regularly costs $100, it will cost $70 during the sale. You can represent this situation with a hundredths grid:

$1	$1	$1	$1	$1	$1	$1	$1	$1	$
$1	$1	$1	$1	$1	$1	$1	$	$1	1
$1	$1	$1	$1	$1	$1	$1	$	$1	$1
$1	$1	$1	$1	$1	$1	$1	$1	$	$1
$1	$1	$1	$1	$1	$1	$1	$1		$1
$1	$1	$1	$1	$1	$1	$1	$1		$1
$1	$1	$1	$1	$1	$1	$1	$1		$1
$1	$1	$1	$1	$1	$1	$1	$1	$1	$1
$1	$1	$1	$1	$1	$1	$1	$	$1	1
$1	$1	$1	$1	$1	$1	$1	$	$1	$1

30% off

You can write the discount on the jacket in other ways as well.
- 30% of the $100 cost = $30 off
- $100 cost − $30 off = $70 sale price

Think about this!

Think of several situations where you have seen or heard percents used. How was percent used in each case?

6.1 It's Raining Cats

A middle-school class has assembled a database of 100 cats owned by students in the school. The database information about each cat is shown on the next three pages.

Cat Database

Cat	Gender	Age (yrs)	Weight (lbs)	Eye color	Pad color
Alex	m	18	11	green	black
Amanda	f	4.5	9.75	blue	gray
Augustus	m	2	10	yellow/green/blue	pink/black
Baguera	m	0.17	13	yellow	brown
Black Foot	m	0.33	1.5	yellow	gray
Blacky	f	1	5	yellow	gray/black
Blue	f	0.25	2	green	gray
Bob	f	4	12	green	black
Boggie	m	3	10	green	pink
Boo	m	3.5	10.75	yellow/green	brown
Boots	m	0.25	3	brown	black
Bosley	m	0.33	1.5	yellow/brown	pink
Bradley	m	0.6	11	yellow	pink/gray
Buffy	m	0.75	8	blue/green	pink
Charcoal	m	11	12	yellow	black
Chelsea	f	2	9	yellow	black
Chessis	f	1.5	6	green	brown
Chubbs	m	1	7	green	pink
Cookie	f	4	9	gold	black
Dana	f	10	8	green	black
Diva	f	3.5	11	green	pink
Duffy	m	1	9	yellow/green	black
Ebony Kahlua	m	1.5	15	blue	brown
Elizabeth	f	10	9	green	pink
Emma	f	4	9.25	gold	pink
Emmie	f	4	7	green	black
Ethel	f	5	8	green	black
Feather	m	2.5	13	green	pink
Fire Smoke	f	0.25	2.5	green/brown	pink
Fluffy	f	5	10	green	pink
Fuzzy	f	1.25	2	green	pink
Gabriel	m	1	7	blue	white
George	m	12	14.5	green	black
Ginger	f	0.2	2	yellow/green	pink
Gizmo	m	4	10	yellow	black
Gracie	f	8	12	green	pink
Gray Kitty	f	3	9	green	gray

Cat	Gender	Age (yrs)	Weight (lbs)	Eye color	Pad color
Grey Boy	m	13	12	yellow	pink
Grey Girl	f	0.2	1.5	gold	pink/black
Grey Poupon	f	5	16	green	pink/black
Hanna	f	3.5	5	yellow	black
Harmony	m	3	12	yellow/green	black
Jinglebob	m	2	18.5	blue	pink
Kali	m	5	16	yellow	black
Kiki	f	1.5	6	green	black
Kitty	m	1.6	10	green	pink
Lady	f	10	8.5	yellow	black
Libby	f	4	8.5	yellow	gray
Lucky	m	4	5	green	pink
Lucy	f	5	10	green	pink
Matilda	f	4.5	9	yellow	pink
Melissa	f	8	11	yellow	pink
Mercedes	f	10	14	green	pink
Midnight	f	10	18	green	pink
Millie	f	10.5	5	blue	black
Miss Muppet	f	11	12	green	pink/black
Mittens	f	14	10.5	yellow	pink
Molly	f	15.5	10	amber	gray
Momma Kat	f	10	6	chartreuse	gray/white
Nancy Blue	f	0.6	5	blue	gray
Newton	m	5	18	yellow	pink
Peanut	f	15	7	green	pink
Peebles	f	5	9	green	black
Pepper	m	2	12	yellow	pink
Pink Lady	f	1.5	6.5	yellow	pink
Pip	m	1	9	yellow	pink
Precious	f	2	12	green	pink
Priscilla	f	3	8.5	green	pink/black
Prissy	f	4	9	green	pink
Ralph	m	3	9	yellow	black
Ravena	f	6	14	yellow	pink/black
Reebo	m	4	12	green	black
Samantha	f	0.2	2	yellow/green	pink
Sassy	f	3	8	yellow/green	gray
Scooter	m	7	16	gold	black
Sebastian	f	3	8	blue	black

Cat	Gender	Age (yrs)	Weight (lbs)	Eye color	Pad color
Seymour	m	0.25	1.5	gold	pink/black
Shiver	m	3	12	yellow/green	pink
Simon	m	0.25	2	green/brown	peach/gray
Skeeter	m	6	13	green	black
Smokey	f	2.5	8	green	black
Smudge	m	8	10	green	gray
Snowy	m	0.5	1.5	gray	gray
Sparky	m	7	12	green	pink
Speedy	m	3	12	blue	pink
Stinky	m	0.17	3.5	yellow	pink
Sweet Pea	f	16	14.5	green	black
Tabby	f	1.5	7	green	black
Tabby Burton	m	1	10	green	black
Terra	m	3	11	green	pink
Thomas	m	4	8	green	pink
Tiger	f	5	13	green	pink
Tigger	f	4	8	yellow	brown
Ting	f	0.25	2.5	green	pink/black
Tom	m	0.25	3	green	gray
Tomadachi	m	1	6.5	gold	pink
Treasure	f	4	8	green	pink
Wally	m	5	10	green	pink/black
Weary	m	8	15	green	pink
Ziggy	f	7	10	gold	pink/black

Did you know?

Ancient Egyptians considered cats to be sacred. Bastet, the Egyptian goddess of love and fertility, was represented as having the head of a cat and the body of a woman. Punishment for harming a cat was severe, and the sentence for killing a cat was usually death. When a cat died, Egyptians shaved their eyebrows as a sign of mourning. Dead cats were often mummified and buried in cat cemeteries.

To help them visualize the different characteristics of the cats in the database, the students made a hundredths grid with each cat's name in one of the squares.

Alex	Boots	Diva	Fuzzy	Hanna	Matilda	Newton	Ravena	Smokey	Thomas
Amanda	Bosley	Duffy	Gabriel	Harmony	Melissa	Peanut	Reebo	Smudge	Tiger
Augustus	Bradley	Ebony Kahlua	George	Jinglebob	Mercedes	Peebles	Samantha	Snowy	Tigger
Baguera	Buffy	Elizabeth	Ginger	Kali	Midnight	Pepper	Sassy	Sparky	Ting
Black Foot	Charcoal	Emma	Gizmo	Kiki	Millie	Pink Lady	Scooter	Speedy	Tom
Blacky	Chelsea	Emmie	Gracie	Kitty	Miss Muppet	Pip	Sebastian	Stinky	Tomadachi
Blue	Chessis	Ethel	Gray Kitty	Lady	Mittens	Precious	Seymour	Sweet Pea	Treasure
Bob	Chubbs	Feather	Grey Boy	Libby	Molly	Priscilla	Shiver	Tabby	Wally
Boggie	Cookie	Fire Smoke	Grey Girl	Lucky	Momma Kat	Prissy	Simon	Tabby Burton	Weary
Boo	Dana	Fluffy	Grey Poupon	Lucy	Nancy Blue	Ralph	Skeeter	Terra	Ziggy

Jane wondered what percent of the cats were female. To answer her question, she used the information in the database and shaded each square in the grid that represented a female cat.

Tang is interested in kittens. He wants to know what percent of the cats in the database are kittens (8 months old or younger) and what percent are adults (over 8 months old).

Problem 6.1

Using the database and Labsheet 6.1, mark all the cats that are female on one chart and all the cats that are kittens on another chart. When you are finished, answer the following questions.

A. What fraction of the cats are female? Write the fraction as a decimal and a percent.

B. What fraction of the cats are male? Write the fraction as a decimal and a percent.

C. What do you notice about the combined percentage of female and male cats?

D. What fraction of the cats are kittens? Write the fraction as a decimal and a percent.

E. What fraction of the cats are adults? Write the fraction as a decimal and a percent.

F. What do you notice about the combined percentage of kittens and adult cats?

■ Problem 6.1 Follow-Up

Make up another question that could be answered by looking at the database. Find the answer to your question.

6.2 Dealing with Discounts

Sometimes it is easier to think about a number in one representation than in another. For example, you would probably say that one computer screen is 34% larger than another, rather than saying it is $\frac{17}{50}$ larger than the other.

You will often find it helpful to be able to move among percents, decimals, and fractions. To do this you need to remember that percent means "out of 100," because this can help you to change a percent to a decimal. One way to think about changing representations is to write the percent as a fraction with 100 as its denominator.

When a store offers a discount, such as 20% off, it means that for every $100 an item costs, you get $20 off the price. It also means that for every dollar (100¢) an item costs, you get 20¢ off the price. In other words, you pay $80 for each $100 of the original cost, or, equivalently, 80¢ for each dollar of the original cost.

A pet store is having a big sale.

Problem 6.2

You may want to use fraction strips or hundredths squares to help you to think about these questions.

A. 1. Rewrite the text on the sign for leashes so that the discount is shown as a *fraction off* the original price of the leashes.

  2. What will a $10.00 leash cost after the discount?

B. 1. Rewrite the text on the sign for pet carriers so that the discount is shown as a *percent off* the original price of the carriers.

  2. What will a $10.00 pet carrier cost after the discount?

C. 1. Rewrite the text on the pet food sign so that the discount is shown as a *percent off* the original price of pet food.

  2. Now, write the discount as a *percent* of the original price customers will pay.

  3. Rewrite the discount as a *fraction* of the original price customers will pay.

  4. Rewrite the discount as a *fraction off* the original price customers will pay.

  5. What will $10.00 worth of pet food cost after the discount?

D. 1. Rewrite the text on the pet treats sign so that the discount is shown as a *decimal*.

  2. What will $10.00 worth of pet treats cost after the discount?

1. How can you change a percent to a fraction?
2. How can you change a percent to a decimal?
3. How can you change a decimal to a fraction?
4. How can you change a decimal to a percent?
5. How can you change a fraction to a decimal?
6. How can you change a fraction to a percent?

6.3 Changing Forms

There are many different ways to talk about number relationships. When you are telling a story with data, you have choices about how you express the relationships. Fractions or decimals or percents may be more suitable in certain situations. In this problem you will practice using what you know about changing between fractions, decimals, and percents.

A group of cat owners were asked this question: How much ransom would you be willing to pay if your pet was kidnapped? The table shows how the cat owners responded.

	Percent	Decimal	Fraction
$2000 and up	18%		
From $1500 to $1999		0.03	
From $1000 to $1499			$\frac{3}{100}$
From $500 to $999	25%		
From $1 to $499		0.31	
Nothing			$\frac{1}{5}$

Problem 6.3

Labsheet 6.3 contains the table above and a hundredths grid.

A. Fill in the missing information in your table.

B. Shade in the hundredths grid with different colors or shading styles to show the percent responding to each of the six choices. Add a key to your grid to show what each color or type of shading represents. When you finish, the grid should be completely shaded. Explain why.

■ **Problem 6.3 Follow-Up**
1. What percent of cat owners would pay less than $1000 ransom to get their pets back?
2. What percent of cat owners would pay less than $2000 ransom to get their pets back?

6.4 It's Raining Cats and Dogs

In a recent survey, 150 dog owners and 200 cat owners were asked what type of food their pets liked. Here are the results of the survey:

Preference	Out of 150 dog owners	Out of 200 cat owners
Human food only	75	36
Pet food only	45	116
Human and pet food	30	48

Problem 6.4

Consider the results of the survey.

A. What kind of food is favored by the greatest number of dogs, according to their owners? Write this number as a fraction, a decimal, and a percent of the 150 dog owners surveyed.

B. What choice is favored by the greatest number of cats, according to their owners? Write this number as a fraction, a decimal, and a percent of the 200 cat owners surveyed.

C. What percent of dog owners reported that their dogs liked either human food only or pet food only? Write this percent as a fraction and a decimal.

D. What percent of cat owners reported that their cats liked either human food only or pet food only? Write this percent as a decimal and a fraction.

■ Problem 6.4 Follow-Up

1. Suppose only 100 dog owners were surveyed, with similar results. Estimate how many would have answered in each of the three categories.

2. Suppose 400 cat owners were surveyed, with similar results. Estimate how many would have answered in each of the three categories.

3. Suppose 50 cat owners were surveyed, with similar results. Estimate how many would have answered in each of the three categories.

As you work on these ACE questions, use your calculator whenever you need it.

Applications

In 1–7, use the cat database on pages 69–71 to answer each question. You may want to use the grids on Labsheet 6.1 to help you.

1. What percent of the cats have green eyes (not mixed with green)?

2. What percent of the cats have yellow eyes (not mixed with yellow)?

3. What percent of the cats have eyes that are not yellow or green? How can you answer this question without looking at the database again?

4. What percent of the cats have only pink foot pads?

5. What percent of the cats have only black foot pads?

6. What percent of the cats have only pink/black foot pads?

7. What percent of the cats have foot pads that are not pink, black, or pink/black? How can you answer this question without looking at the database again?

8. 78% of pet owners surveyed say they live in a town where there is a pooper-scooper law in effect.

  a. How would you express this as a decimal?

  b. How would you express this as a fraction?

  c. What percent of people surveyed said they do not live in a town with a pooper-scooper law? Explain your reasoning. Express this percent as a decimal and a fraction.

  d. Can you determine how many people were surveyed? Why or why not?

In 9–11, use the following information to answer the questions. Jill noticed that 25% of all the cats in the database on pages 69–71 weigh less than 7 pounds. She also noticed that 72% of all the cats weigh less than 12 pounds.

9. What percent of the cats weigh 7 pounds or more? Explain your reasoning.

10. What percent of the cats weigh 12 pounds or more? Explain your reasoning.

11. What percent of the cats weigh 7 pounds or more and less than 12 pounds? Explain your reasoning.

12. When surveyed, 66% of dog owners who took their dog to obedience school said their dog passed with flying colors. What percent of dog owners said their dogs *didn't* perform up to par? Write an explanation for a friend about how to solve the problem and why your solution works.

13. Copy the table and fill in the missing information.

Percent	Decimal	Fraction
62%		
		$\frac{4}{9}$
	1.23	
		$\frac{12}{15}$

In 14 and 15, the large square represents one whole. Represent the shaded area as a fraction, a decimal, and a percent.

14.

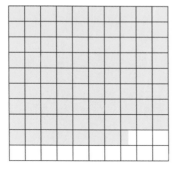

15.

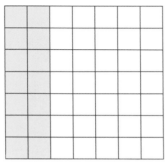

16. Trace the outline of your hand on a hundredths grid. (You can use a copy of Labsheet 4.2.) Estimate what percent of the grid is covered by the area of your hand. Explain how you made your estimate.

In 17–19, use Labsheet 6.ACE to *estimate* what portion of the square is shaded. Explain your reasoning.

17. What percent of this square is shaded? Explain your reasoning.

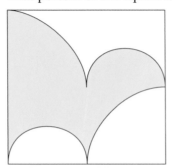

18. What fraction of this square is shaded? Explain your reasoning.

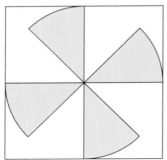

19. What part, in decimal form, of this square is shaded? Explain your reasoning.

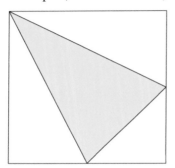

Connections

20. The following percents are a good set of benchmarks to know, because they have nice fraction equivalents and some nice decimal equivalents. The percents are spread out between 0 and 1. Copy the table, and enter the fraction and decimal equivalents for each percent. Use your table until you have learned these relationships.

Percent	10%	$12\frac{1}{2}$%	20%	25%	30%	$33\frac{1}{3}$%	50%	$66\frac{2}{3}$%	75%
Fraction									
Decimal									

Extensions

21. Below are the results when pet owners were asked what kinds of clothing or accessories their pets wear.

	Dogs	Cats
Ribbons	88%	90%
Sweater	65%	20%
Nail Polish	23%	6%
Jeweled Leash	17%	30%
Jewelry	12%	12%

a. Add the percents in the Dogs column. Write the total as a percent, a decimal, and a fraction.

b. Add the percents in the Cats column. Write the total as a percent, a decimal, and a fraction.

c. Why do the columns add to more than 100%?

In 22–25, make a copy of the number line below. Mark and label an approximate point on the number line for each fraction, decimal, and percent given. Use a different number line for each problem.

22. $\frac{3}{8}$, 72%, 1.9, $\frac{4}{3}$

23. 175%, $\frac{7}{9}$, 0.5, 120%

24. 1.35, 0.625, $\frac{8}{5}$, 25%

25. 34%, 0.049, 98%, 1.75

In 26–28, determine what fraction is the correct label for the mark halfway between the endpoints of the line segment. Write the fraction as a percent and a decimal.

26.

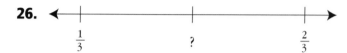

$\frac{1}{3}$? $\frac{2}{3}$

27.

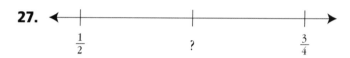

$\frac{1}{2}$? $\frac{3}{4}$

28.

$\frac{1}{6}$? $\frac{1}{5}$

Mathematical Reflections

In this investigation, you explored the relationships among fractions, decimals, and percents. These questions will help you summarize what you have learned:

1 What does *percent* mean?

2 How can you show a percent by using a drawing?

3 **a.** Describe how you can change a percent to a decimal and to a fraction.

b. Describe how you can change a fraction to a percent.

c. Describe how you can change a decimal to a percent.

4 Suppose 12% of students surveyed said they had tried rock climbing. If 100 students were surveyed, how many had tried rock climbing? If 200 students were surveyed? If 150 students were surveyed?

5 A store offers a discount of 30% on all reference books. If a dictionary costs $12.00, what is the amount of the discount? If a book on insect identification costs $15.00, how much will you have to pay for it?

Think about your answers to these questions, discuss your ideas with other students and your teacher, and then write a summary of your findings in your journal.

Unit Reflections

Working on the problems of this unit extended your knowledge of *fractions, decimals,* and *percents.* You learned how to relate fractions and decimals to their locations on a *number line.* You learned how fractions, decimals, and percents are related to each other. Finally, you learned how to *compare* and *order* fractions and decimals and how to identify *equivalent* fractions, decimals, and percents.

Using Your Number Sense—Test your understanding and skill working with fractions, decimals, and percents by solving the following problems.

1 *The diagram below shows a puzzle made up of different familiar shapes. Your challenge is to find a fraction name and a decimal name for the size of each piece.*

a. What fraction of the whole puzzle is covered by each piece? Use your measurement estimation skills and reasoning to find each fraction.

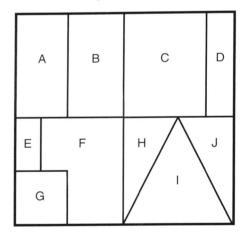

b. What decimal represents each part of the puzzle? The same puzzle is shown below, drawn on a 10-by-10 grid.

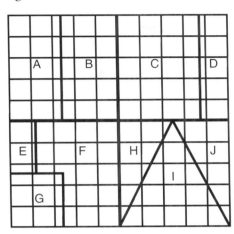

2 *Glenda drew eight cards from a deck of number cards. She was asked to show the position of each number on a number line and to write two equivalent names for each number.*

The fraction $\frac{1}{4}$ has already been located on the number line below, along with its percent and decimal equivalents. Copy the number line and show the placement of each of the other number cards. Write two equivalent names for each number.

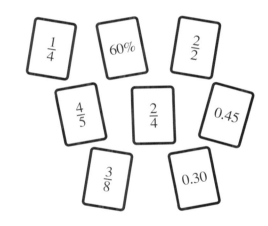

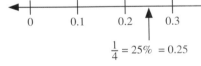

Explaining Your Reasoning—You have explored relationships among fractions, decimals, and percents in many different problems. There are some strategies for working with these *rational numbers* that apply in any situation.

1. Describe a strategy that can be used to find fractions equivalent to given fractions such as $\frac{3}{4}$, $\frac{8}{12}$, and $\frac{6}{4}$.

2. Describe a strategy that can be used to compare these pairs of fractions.

    a. $\frac{5}{8}$ and $\frac{7}{8}$ **b.** $\frac{3}{4}$ and $\frac{3}{5}$ **c.** $\frac{3}{4}$ and $\frac{5}{8}$

    d. $\frac{3}{8}$ and $\frac{2}{3}$ **e.** $\frac{3}{4}$ and $\frac{4}{5}$ **f.** $\frac{2}{3}$ and $\frac{5}{8}$

3. Describe a strategy that can be used to find decimal equivalents of fractions such as $\frac{5}{8}$, $\frac{3}{4}$, $\frac{3}{5}$, and $\frac{2}{3}$.

4. Describe a strategy that can be used to find fractions equivalent to decimals such as 0.5, 0.75, 0.14, 0.4, or 2.6.

5. Describe strategies that can be used to find

    a. the decimal and fraction equivalents of given percents such as 35% or 125%.

    b. the percent equivalents of given decimals and fractions such as 0.79 or $\frac{3}{4}$.

Fractions, decimals, and percents will be used in almost every future unit of *Connected Mathematics* and in applications of mathematics to problems in science, business, and personal life. You will use them in work on probability, geometry, measurement, and algebra. Another whole unit, *Bits and Pieces II*, deals with the operations of addition, subtraction, multiplication, and division of fractions and decimals.

Glossary

base ten number system The common number system we use. Our number system is based on the number 10 because we have ten fingers with which to group. In a number like 253, each place represents ten of the previous groups. By extending the place-value system to include places that represent fractions with 10 or powers of 10 in the denominator, we can represent quantities less than 1. Below is a graphic representation of the number 253 in the base ten number system.

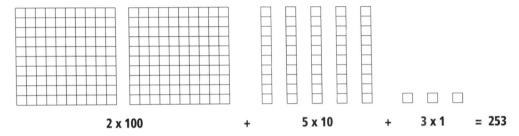

2 x 100   +   5 x 10   +   3 x 1   = 253

benchmark A "nice" number that can be used to estimate the size of other numbers. For work with fractions, 0, $\frac{1}{2}$, and 1 are good benchmarks. We often estimate fractions or decimals with benchmarks because it is easier to do arithmetic with them, and estimates often give enough accuracy for the situation. For example, many fractions and decimals—such as $\frac{37}{50}$, $\frac{5}{8}$, 0.43, and 0.55—can be thought of as being close to $\frac{1}{2}$. We also use benchmarks to help compare fractions such as $\frac{5}{8}$ and 0.43. For example, we could say that $\frac{5}{8}$ is larger than 0.43 because $\frac{5}{8}$ is larger than $\frac{1}{2}$ and 0.43 is smaller than $\frac{1}{2}$.

decimal A special form of a fraction. Decimals are based on the base ten place-value system. To write numbers as decimals, we use only 10 and powers of 10 as denominators. Writing fractions in this way saves us from writing the denominators because they are understood. When we write $\frac{375}{1000}$ as a decimal—0.375—the denominator of 1000 is understood. The digits to the left of the decimal point (period) show whole units, and the digits to the right of the decimal point show a portion of a whole unit. The diagram below shows the place value for each digit of the number 5620.301.

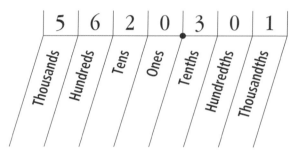

denominator The number written below the line in a fraction. In the fraction $\frac{3}{4}$, 4 is the denominator. In the part-whole interpretation of fractions, the denominator shows the number of equal-size parts into which the whole has been split.

equivalent fractions Fractions that are equal in value but have different numerators and denominators. For example, $\frac{2}{3}$ and $\frac{14}{21}$ are equivalent fractions. The shaded part of this rectangle represents both $\frac{2}{3}$ and $\frac{14}{21}$.

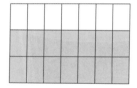

fraction   A number (a quantity) of the form $\frac{a}{b}$ where a and b are whole numbers. A fraction can indicate a part of a whole object or set, a ratio of two quantities, or a division. For the picture below, the fraction $\frac{3}{4}$ shows the part of the rectangle that is shaded: the denominator 4 indicates the number of equal-size pieces, and the numerator 3 indicates the number of pieces that are shaded.

The fraction $\frac{3}{4}$ could also represent three of a group of four items meeting a particular criteria; the ratio 3 to 4 (for example, when 12 students enjoyed a particular activity and 16 students did not); or the amount of pizza each person receives when three pizzas are shared equally among four people, which would be $3 \div 4$ or $\frac{3}{4}$ of a pizza per person.

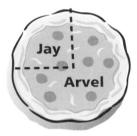 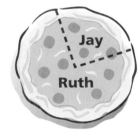 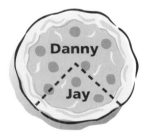

numerator   The number written above the line in a fraction. In the fraction $\frac{5}{8}$, 5 is the numerator. When you interpret a fraction such as $\frac{5}{8}$ as part of a whole, the numerator 5 tells that the fraction refers to 5 of the 8 equal parts.

percent A special decimal fraction in which the denominator is 100. Percent means "out of 100." When we write 68%, we mean 68 out of 100, $\frac{68}{100}$, or 0.68. We write the percent sign (%) after a number to indicate percent. 68 of the 100 squares in this rectangle are shaded, so we say 68% of the rectangle is shaded.

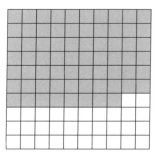

unit fraction A fraction with a numerator of 1. For example, in the unit fraction $\frac{1}{13}$, the part-whole interpretation of fractions tells us that 13 indicates the number of equal-size parts into which the whole has been split and that the fraction represents the quantity of 1 of those parts.

Index

Area model
ACE, 34–37
for fractions, 31–32

Benchmarks
ACE, 26–29, 63, 80
decimal, 43–44
fractional, 4, 23–24
percent, 80

Comparing decimals, 43–44, 54–56
ACE, 47–49, 51
Comparing fractions, 8–9, 19–25
ACE, 26–29, 47–49
to benchmarks, 23–24

Database, cat, 68–73
Decimal notation, 43
Decimals, 39–45, 53–57
ACE, 46–51, 58–65, 77–82
as benchmarks, 43–44
comparing, 43–44, 54–56
Dewey Decimal system, 51
estimation with, 54–56
fractions and, 4, 41–44, 53–57
on a hundredths grid, 42, 46–47
notation for, 43
ordering, 44, 54–56
percent and, 4, 67, 73–76
place value and, 45
on a tenths grid, 41

Denominator, 12
Dewey Decimal system, 51
Discounts, 73–74
Distinguishing Digits puzzles, 44–45
Division
decimals and, 57
fractions and, 4

Equivalent fractions, 4, 20–23
ACE, 26–29, 34–37
Estimation
with decimals, 43–44, 54–56
with fractions, 5–16, 54–56
with percent, 76, 79–80

Fraction, word origin, 3
Fractions, 4
ACE, 14–17, 25–29, 34–37, 46–51,
58–65, 77–82
area model for, 31–32
as benchmarks, 4, 23–24
comparing, 8–9, 19–30
cooking with, 31–37
decimals and, 4, 41–44, 53–57
division and, 4
early use of, 3, 20
equivalent, 4, 20–23
estimation with, 5–13, 54–56
fund raising and, 5–18
greater than one, 10–11, 24–25
on a hundredths grid, 42, 46–47

improper, 35
mixed number and, 35
on a number line, 22–23
ordering, 22–24
percent and, 4, 67, 73–76
of regions, 4, 5–13, 31–32
symbolic form, 12
on a tenths grid, 41
unit, 20
of a whole, 4, 5–13
Fraction strip model
for decimals, 54–57
for fractions, 4, 6–13, 22, 54–56

Hundredths grid, 42, 46–47

Improper fraction, 35
Investigations
Comparing Fractions, 19–30
Cooking with Fractions, 31–38
From Fractions to Decimals, 39–52
Fund-Raising Fractions, 5–18
introduction to, 2–3
Moving Between Fractions and
Decimals, 53–66
Out of One Hundred, 67–82

Looking Back and Looking Ahead:
Unit Reflections, 84–86

Mathematical Highlights, 4
Mathematical Reflections, 18, 30, 38, 52,
66, 83
Mixed number, 35

Model
area, 31–32, 34–37
fraction strip, 4, 6–13, 22, 54–57
hundredths grid, 42, 46–47
tenths grid, 41
Moscow Papyrus, 3

Napier, John, 43
Number line, fractions on, 22–23
Numerator, 12

Ordering decimals, 44, 54–56
ACE, 47–48, 51
Ordering fractions, 22–24
ACE, 26–29, 37, 47–48

Percent, 67–76
ACE, 77–82
decimals and, 4, 67, 73–76
discount and, 73–74
estimation with, 76
fractions and, 4, 67, 73–76
Place value, decimals and, 45

Region
ACE, 34–37
fractional parts of, 4, 5–18, 31–32

Stevinus, Simon, 43

Tenths grid, 41

Unit fractions, 20

Whole, fractional parts of , 4, 5–18

Connected   Mathematics™

Covering and Surrounding

Two-Dimensional Measurement

Student Edition

Glenda Lappan
James T. Fey
William M. Fitzgerald
Susan N. Friel
Elizabeth Difanis Phillips

Prentice
Hall

Glenview, Illinois
Needham, Massachusetts
Upper Saddle River, New Jersey

The Connected Mathematics Project was developed at Michigan State University with the support of National Science Foundation Grant No. MDR 9150217.

This project was supported, in part,
by the
National Science Foundation
Opinions expressed are those of the authors
and not necessarily those of the Foundation

The Michigan State University authors and administration have agreed that all MSU royalties arising from this publication will be devoted to purposes supported by the Department of Mathematics and the MSU Mathematics Education Enrichment Fund.

Contents

Mathematical Highlights   4

The Unit Project: Plan a Park   5

Investigation 1: Measuring Perimeter and Area   6
    1.1 Designing Bumper-Car Rides   6
    1.2 Decoding Designs   8
    1.3 Computing Costs   10
    1.4 Getting Your Money's Worth   12
    Applications—Connections—Extensions   13
    Mathematical Reflections   18

Investigation 2: Measuring Odd Shapes   19
    2.1 Making the Shoe Fit   19
    Applications—Connections—Extensions   21
    Mathematical Reflections   28

Investigation 3: Constant Area, Changing Perimeter   29
    3.1 Building Storm Shelters   29
    3.2 Stretching the Perimeter   30
    Applications—Connections—Extensions   32
    Mathematical Reflections   34

Investigation 4: Constant Perimeter, Changing Area   35
    4.1 Fencing in Spaces   35
    4.2 Adding Tiles to Pentominos   36
    Applications—Connections—Extensions   38
    Mathematical Reflections   45

Investigation 5: Measuring Parallelograms   46
    5.1 Finding Measures of Parallelograms   46
    5.2 Designing Parallelograms Under Constraints   48
    5.3 Rearranging Parallelograms   50
    Applications—Connections—Extensions   51
    Mathematical Reflections   55

Investigation 6: Measuring Triangles   56
    6.1 Finding Measures of Triangles   56
    6.2 Designing Triangles Under Constraints   58
    6.3 Making Parallelograms from Triangles   59
    Applications—Connections—Extensions   60
    Mathematical Reflections   68

Investigation 7: Going Around in Circles   69
    7.1 Pricing Pizza   70
    7.2 Surrounding a Circle   71
    7.3 Covering a Circle   72
    7.4 "Squaring" a Circle   73
    7.5 Replacing Trees   75
    Applications—Connections—Extensions   76
    Mathematical Reflections   81

The Unit Project: Plan a Park   82

Looking Back and Looking Ahead: Unit Reflections   84

Glossary   87

Index   90

Covering and Surrounding

Pizza parlors often describe their selections as 9-inch, 12-inch, 15-inch, or even 24-inch pizzas. What do these measurements tell you about pizza size? How does the size of a pizza relate to its price? Does a 24-inch pizza generally cost twice as much as a 12-inch pizza? Should price relate to size in that way?

You may know that China has the greatest population of any country. Which country do you think has the greatest land area? The longest borders? Which state in the United States the largest? Which state the smallest? How do you think land area, borders, and coastlines of states and countries are measured?

Carpet is commonly sold by the square yard. How would you estimate the cost of carpet for a room in your home? Base molding, which is used to protect the bases of walls, is usually sold by the foot. How would you estimate the cost of base molding for a room in your home?

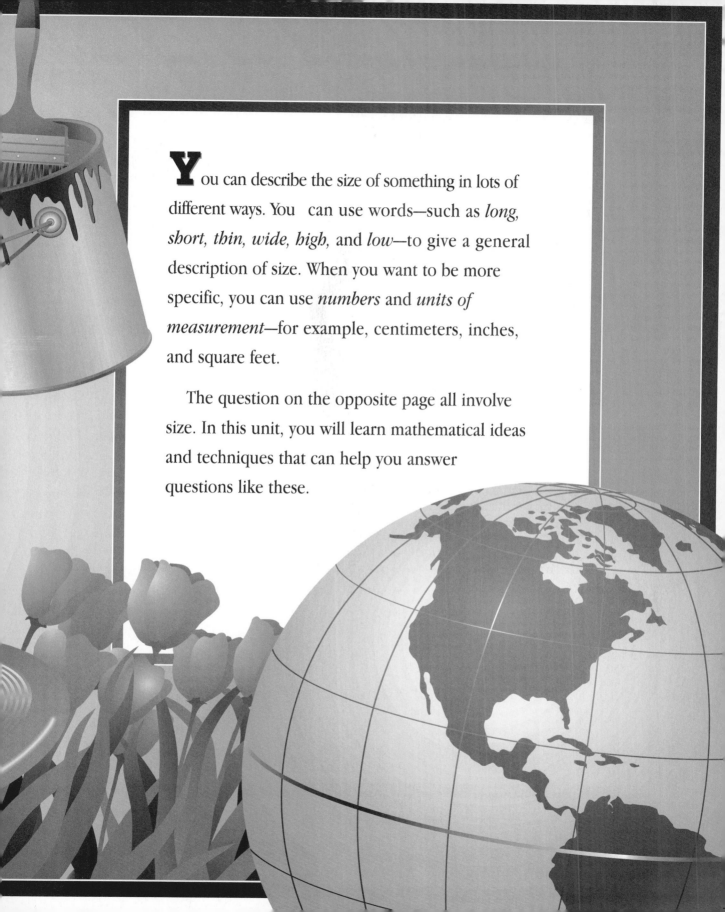

You can describe the size of something in lots of different ways. You can use words—such as *long, short, thin, wide, high,* and *low*—to give a general description of size. When you want to be more specific, you can use *numbers* and *units of measurement*—for example, centimeters, inches, and square feet.

The question on the opposite page all involve size. In this unit, you will learn mathematical ideas and techniques that can help you answer questions like these.

Mathematical Highlights

In *Covering and Surrounding,* you will explore area and perimeter of figures, in particular quadrilaterals, triangles and circles. The unit should help you to

● Understand area as a measure of *covering* a figure and perimeter as a measure of *surrounding* a figure;

● Explore whether perimeter and area are related and if so, how;

● Develop strategies for finding areas and perimeters of rectangular shapes and irregular shapes.

● Understand how the area of a rectangle is related to the area of a triangle and of a parallelogram;

● Develop formulas or procedures—stated in words and symbols—for finding areas and perimeters of rectangles, parallelograms, triangles, and circles; and

● Recognize situations in which measuring perimeter or area will answer practical questions.

As you work the problems in this unit, make it a habit to ask questions about situations involving area and perimeter. *What quantities are in the problem? How do I know which measures of a figure are involved—area or perimeter? Is an exact answer required? Is the figure an irregular or a regular shape? Is the shape made up of other shapes? What strategy or formula will help me find the area or the perimeter of the shape?*

Plan a Park

A local philanthropist, Dr. Doolittle, has just donated a piece of land to the city for a park. The plot of land is rectangular, and it measures 120 yards by 100 yards. Dr. Doolittle has also offered to donate money for construction of the park.

Dr. Doolittle wants the park to be a place that people of all ages would like to visit. She wants half of the park to be a picnic and playground area. She wants to leave the decision about what to do with the other half of the park area to someone else. She has decided to hold a design contest for the layout of the park.

Covering and Surrounding involves finding areas and perimeters of various figures and shapes. Dr. Doolittle's park design project will use the ideas you will study. After you finish the investigations in this unit, you will create a design for the park, including a scale drawing and a report that gives the dimensions of all the items you have included in your park.

As you work through each investigation, think about how you might use what you are learning to help you with your project. In particular, think about these things:

- How much space is needed for a swing set or a slide? You will need to measure one in a park or school yard near you so that your design is realistic.
- How big are tennis courts or basketball courts? You will need to find out their dimensions if you choose to put them into your park design.
- If you put in tennis courts or basketball courts, will you want a fence around them? You will need to answer this question to complete your design.

Measuring Perimeter and Area

Most Americans enjoy the rides at amusement parks and carnivals—from merry-go-rounds and Ferris wheels to roller coasters and bumper cars.

Let's suppose that a company called Midway Amusement Rides—MARs for short—builds and operates a variety of rides for amusement parks and carnivals. To do well in their business, MARs has to apply some mathematical thinking.

1.1 Designing Bumper-Car Rides

MARs sells many of its rides to traveling shows that set up their carnivals in parking lots of shopping centers and in community parks. Because they must be easy to take apart and transport, rides for traveling shows must be smaller than rides found in large amusement parks.

Bumper cars are one of the most popular rides in traveling shows. A bumper-car ride includes the cars and a smooth floor with bumper rails around it. MARs makes their bumper-car floors from tiles that are 1 meter by 1 meter squares. The bumper rail is built from sections that are 1 meter long.

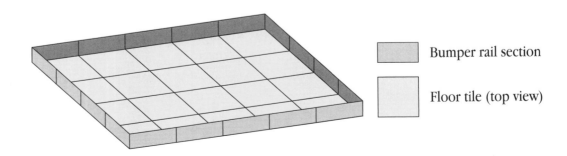

Bumper rail section

Floor tile (top view)

When MARs gets an order for a bumper-car ride, their designers sometimes use square tiles to model the possible floor plans, and then send sketches of their ideas to the customer for approval.

Problem 1.1

Solve these design problems by experimenting with square tiles.

A. Badger State Shows in Wisconsin requested a bumper-car ride with a total of 36 square meters of floor space and 26 rail sections. Sketch some possible designs for this floor plan.

B. Lone Star Carnivals in Texas wants a bumper-car ride that covers 36 square meters of floor space and has lots of rail sections for riders to bump against. Sketch some possible designs for this floor plan.

C. Design a bumper-car floor plan with 36 or more square meters of floor space that you think would make an interesting ride. Be prepared to share your design with the class and to explain why you like it.

■ Problem 1.1 Follow-Up

Two measures tell you important facts about the size of the bumper-car floor plans you have designed. The number of tiles needed to *cover* the floor is the **area** of the shape. The number of bumper rail sections needed to *surround* the floor is the **perimeter** of the shape.

1. Find the perimeter and area of each bumper-car floor plan you designed in Problem 1.1.

2. Which measure—perimeter or area—better indicates the size of a bumper-car floor plan?

The MARs company advertises its carnival rides in a catalog. One section of the catalog shows bumper-car floor plans. The catalog shows only outlines of the plans, not the grid of the floor tiles or the rail sections. Below are three of the designs shown in the catalog.

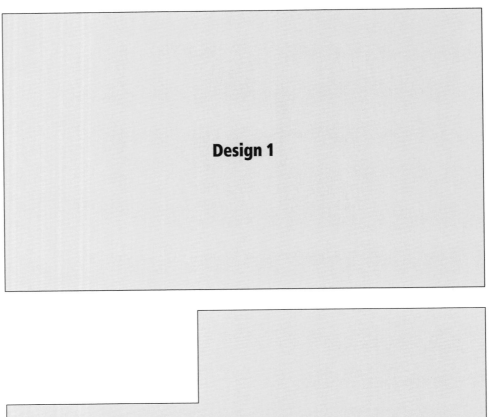

Design 1

Design 2

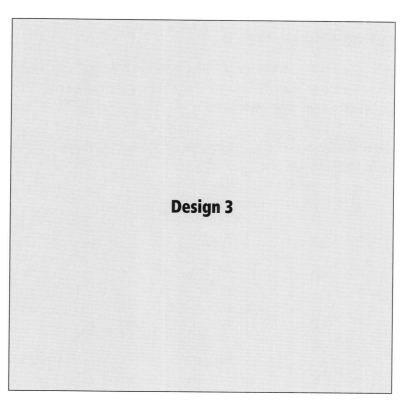

Design 3

Problem 1.2

Use the sample rail section and floor tile below to answer these questions.

A. Which of the three designs provides the greatest floor space (has the greatest area)?

B. Which of the three designs requires the most rail sections (has the greatest perimeter)?

Sample rail section   Sample floor tile section

■ **Problem 1.2 Follow-Up**

Choose the design you think is best, and explain how you would sell it to a customer.

Computing Costs

The designers at MARs specialize in creating unusual floor plans for bumper-car rides. But when it comes time to prepare estimates or bills for customers, they turn the plans over to the billing department.

The Buckeye Amusements company in Ohio wants some sample designs and cost estimates for small bumper-car rides designed for children in small cars. The MARs designers came up with the floor plans below.

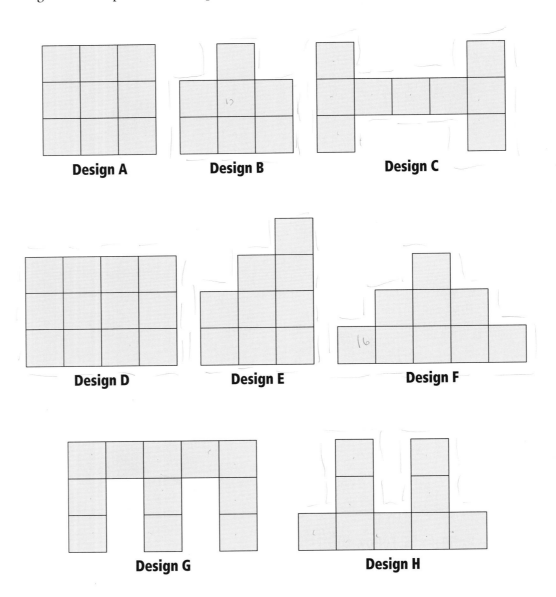

Design A   Design B   Design C

Design D   Design E   Design F

Design G   Design H

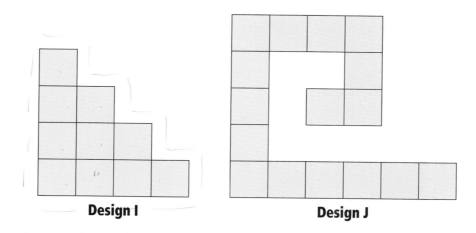

Design I   **Design J**

Problem 1.3

A. The MARs company charges $25 for each rail section and $30 for each floor tile. How much would each of the designs above cost? Record your data in a table with these column headings:

Design	Area	Perimeter	Cost of tiles	Cost of rail sections	Total cost

B. If you were the buyer for Buckeye Amusements, which design would you choose? Explain your choice.

■ **Problem 1.3 Follow-Up**

1. Of the designs above, which have an area of 9 square meters?

2. Give the price of each design you listed in question 1.

3. What accounts for the difference in the prices of the designs you listed in question 1?

Five of the bumper-car designs in Problem 1.3 had an area of 9 square meters. You found that these designs had different prices because their perimeters were different.

Problem 1.4

Questions A–E refer to the designs from Problem 1.3. Experiment with your tiles to try to answer the questions. Make sketches of your designs.

A. Build a design with the same area as design G, but with a smaller perimeter. Can you make more than one design that meets these requirements? Explain.

B. Design E can be made from design D by removing three tiles. How does the area of design D compare to the area of design E? How does the perimeter of design D compare to the perimeter of design E?

C. Design F and design I have the same perimeter. Can you rearrange the tiles of design F to make design I? Explain.

D. Design A and design C have the same area. Can you rearrange the tiles of design A to make design C? Explain.

E. Arrange your tiles to match design B. Now, move one tile to make a new design with a perimeter of 14 units. Sketch your new design.

■ Problem 1.4 Follow-Up

If two tile designs have the same area and the same perimeter, must they look exactly alike? Make a sketch to help explain your answer.

As you work on these ACE questions, use your calculator whenever you need it.

Applications

1. Cut out several 1-inch paper tiles. Cover this figure with your tiles. Record the area and the perimeter of the figure.

In 2–5, experiment with tiles or squares of grid paper. Sketch your final answers on grid paper.

2. Draw at least two shapes with an area of 6 square units and a perimeter of 12 units.

3. Draw at least two shapes with an area of 15 square units and a perimeter of 18 units.

4. Draw at least two shapes with an area of 12 square units and different perimeters.

5. Draw at least two shapes with a perimeter of 12 units and different areas.

In 6–9, find the area and perimeter of the shape.

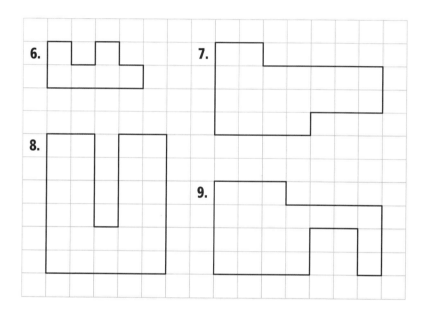

10. Look at this plan for design H.

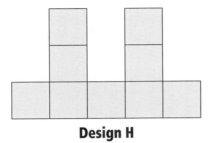

Design H

    a. If possible, design a figure with the same area as design H, but with a perimeter of 14 units. If this is not possible, explain why.

    b. If possible, design a figure with the same area as design H, but with a perimeter of 30 units. If this is not possible, explain why.

11.   **a.** Copy design J onto grid paper. Add six squares to make a new design with a perimeter of 22 units.

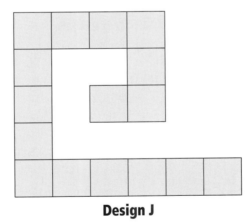

Design J

    b. Explain why the perimeters of your new design and design J are so different.

12. Carpet is commonly sold by the square yard. Base molding is commonly sold by the foot.

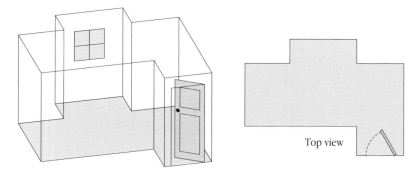

Top view

    a. Describe a method you could use to *estimate* the cost of carpet for the room sketched here.

    b. Describe a method you could use to *estimate* the cost of installing base molding around the base of the walls of this room.

Connections

13. Write a Logo program that will draw a rectangle with a perimeter of 200 turtle steps. Then, write a Logo program that will draw a *different* rectangle with a perimeter of 200 turtle steps.

You can describe the size and shape of a rectangle with just two numbers, *length* and *width*. In 14–16, sketch a rectangle on grid paper with the given area and with length and width that are whole numbers. Label each rectangle with its length and width.

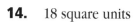

width

length

14. 18 square units

15. 20 square units

16. 23 square units

Extensions

In 17 and 18, experiment with tiles or squares of grid paper, then sketch your answers on grid paper.

17. Draw at least two shapes with a perimeter of 18 units but with different areas. Give the area of each shape.

18. Draw at least two shapes with an area of 25 square units but with different perimeters. Give the perimeter of each shape.

19. The figures drawn on the grid below are not made up entirely of whole squares.

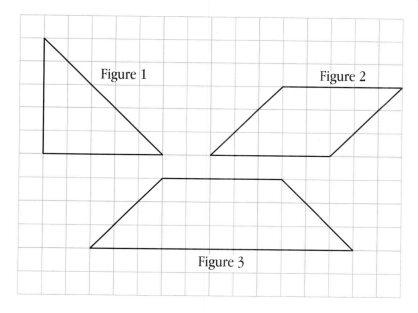

Figure 1

Figure 2

Figure 3

a. How would you find the area and perimeter of each figure?

b. For each figure, try your method, and record your estimates for area and perimeter.

Mathematical Reflections

In this investigation, you examined the areas and perimeters of figures made from square tiles. You found that some arrangements of tiles have large perimeters and some arrangements have smaller perimeters. These questions will help you summarize what you have learned:

1 Is it possible for two shapes to have the same area but different perimeters? Explain your answer by using words and drawings.

2 Is it possible for two shapes to have the same perimeter but different areas? Explain your answer by using words and drawings.

3 Can you figure out the perimeter of a figure if you know its area? Why or why not?

Think about your answers to these questions, discuss your ideas with other students and your teacher, and then write a summary of your findings in your journal.

At the end of this unit, you will be designing the layout for a city park. Start thinking now about what things you should consider as you create your layout. How could you apply what you know about area and perimeter to your park design?

Measuring Odd Shapes

It's not hard to find areas and perimeters of shapes made of complete squares. But measuring areas and perimeters of more interesting figures is not always easy.

2.1 Making the Shoe Fit

The clothes people wear come in many shapes and sizes. Shoes, for instance, are manufactured in thousands of types and styles. To make shoes that fit comfortably, shoe companies must know a lot about human feet.

In this problem, you will look at measures of feet and think about what measures a shoe company would need to know.

Did you know?

Although shoes are important to protect feet, for many people, they are also a fashion statement. In the 1300s, it was considered fashionable for European men to wear shoes with extremely long toes. On some of these shoes, called *crackowes,* the toe was so long that it had to be fastened to the knee with a chain so that the wearer would not trip. In the 1970s, *platform shoes,* with very thick soles, were popular. What shoe styles are popular today?

Problem 2.1

With your group, have a discussion about measuring feet. In what ways can you measure a foot? Which of these measurements would be of interest to shoe companies?

Have each person in your group trace one foot on a piece of grid paper.

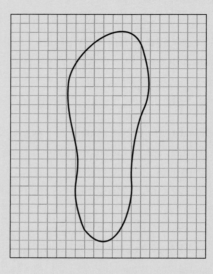

For each person's foot, estimate the length, width, area, perimeter, and any other measures your group thinks should be included. Record your data in a table with these column headings:

Student	Shoe size	Foot length	Foot width	Foot area	Foot perimeter

■ Problem 2.1 Follow-Up

Use the data from the whole class to answer these questions.

1. Does each of the data items seem reasonable? If there are outliers, do they indicate mistakes, or interesting feet?

2. a. What are the typical length, width, perimeter, and area of feet for students in your class?

   b. Explain how you organized the data and what measure(s) of center you used to decide what is typical.

3. Explain any patterns you see that would help you to predict shoe size from a particular foot measurement.

As you work on these ACE questions, use your calculator whenever you need it.

Applications

1. Below is a tracing of a student's hand on centimeter grid paper. The drawing has been reduced.

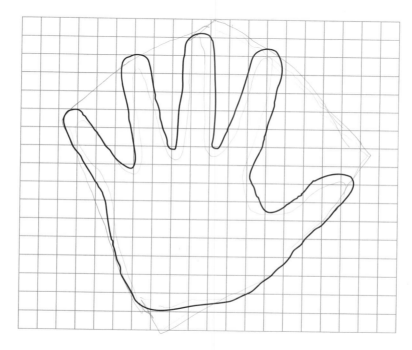

a. Estimate the area of the student's hand.

b. Use a piece of string or another method that makes sense to you to estimate the perimeter of the student's hand.

c. Explain how a company that makes gloves might be interested in area and perimeter of hands.

d. If the student's hand had been traced on half-centimeter grid paper, would your estimates be more precise, the same, or less precise? Explain.

In 2–7, use the map below. The Parks and Recreation Department bought a piece of property with two large lakes. Park planners proposed that one lake be used for swimming, fishing, and boating. The other lake would be a nature preserve with only hiking, tent camping, and canoes allowed.

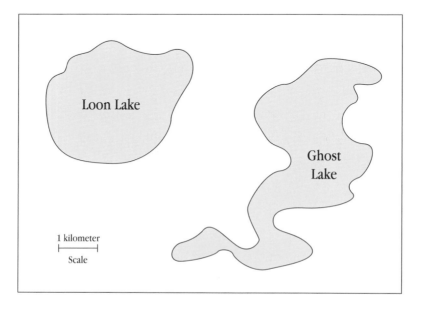

Loon Lake

Ghost Lake

1 kilometer

Scale

2. Naturalists claim that water birds need long shorelines for nesting and fishing. Which lake best meets this requirement? Explain your answer.

3. Boaters want a lake with a large area to give them space to cruise. Which lake best meets this requirement? Explain your answer.

4. Which lake has space for the greatest number of lakeside campsites? Explain your answer.

5. People who race powerboats like long stretches of water without turns. Which lake best meets this requirement? Explain your answer.

6. Sailors like lakes with long stretches to enable them to sail with any wind direction. Which lake best meets this requirement? Explain your answer.

7. Which lake do you think would be best to use for swimming, boating, and fishing, and which would be best for the nature preserve? Prepare an argument defending your choices.

Connections

8. The table below gives data on measures of head circumference (the distance around the head) and waist circumference (the distance around the waist) for 20 students.

Student	Head circumference (inches)	Waist circumference (inches)
M.S.	21.5	29.5
C.A.	23.5	32
P.B.	22	27.5
G.L.	23.25	26
K.B.	23	38.5
S.M.	21.5	23.5
K.E.	22.5	29.5
B.D.	23	27
J.G.	21	27
P.N.	21.5	28.5
L.C.	23	28
J.Y.	22	25
R.M.	21	26
J.H.	21.5	25
M.N.	23.5	25.5
M.L.	20.5	23
W.S.	20.5	31
J.J.	22	22
B.A.	23.5	31
C.F.	22.5	35

a. Make a coordinate graph with waist circumference on the horizontal axis and head circumference on the vertical axis.

b. Do you think there is a relationship between head circumference and waist circumference? Why or why not?

c. What would be a good estimate for the head circumference of a student with a waist circumference of 30 inches?

d. What would be a good estimate for the waist circumference of a student with a head circumference of 24 inches?

In 9–12, explain how perimeter is related to the size of each item.

9. Belts

10. Jeans

11. Hats

12. Shirts

In 13–15, explain how area or perimeter (or both) would be useful for the activity.

13. Painting a room or an entire house

14. Designing a parking lot

15. Designing a school playground surrounded by a fence

Extensions

16. Find a map of your city or state. Use the map's scale to estimate the area and the length of the border of your city or state.

In 17–21, use a world atlas or an encyclopedia to answer the question.

17. What is the world's longest river? What type of measurement was used to determine that it is the longest?

18. What is the world's largest lake? What type of measurement was used to determine that it is the largest?

19. Which country is the largest in the world? What type of measurement was used to determine that it is the largest?

20. What is the world's tallest mountain? What type of measurement was used to determine that it is the tallest?

21. What is the world's largest island? What type of measurement was used to determine that it is the largest?

In 22 and 23, use this map of Lake Okeehele and a centimeter grid transparency.

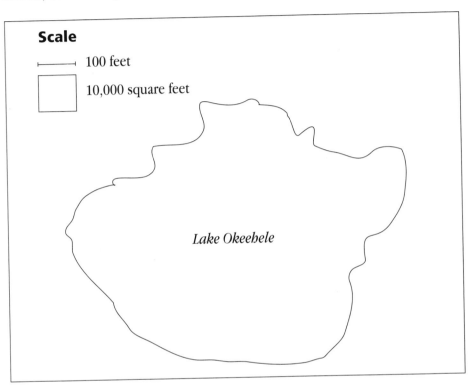

Scale

⊢────┤ 100 feet

☐ 10,000 square feet

Lake Okeehele

22. A developer plans to build houses around Lake Okeehele. If most of his customers want to buy about 100 feet of lakefront, how many lots can the developer build around the lake? Explain your answer.

23. The buyers want to know whether the lake has shrunk or grown over time. The developer found in the county records that the lake covered 500,000 square feet in 1920. What is happening to the lake? Give evidence to support your answer.

24. The state of Hawaii is a group of islands. Atlases and almanacs report the area of Hawaii as 6450 square miles and the shoreline as 1052 miles. How do you think these measurements were made? You might want to ask your geography teacher for more information.

Did you know?

The islands of Hawaii were formed from the eruptions of many volcanoes over tens of thousands of years. Volcanoes in the island chain are still erupting today—both above and below the water. Volcanoes continually add new land to Hawaii, so the area and perimeter of the state are increasing. Someday the buildup of hardened volcanic matter under the ocean will emerge as a new Hawaiian island.

Mathematical Reflections

In this investigation, you examined areas and perimeters of odd shapes using square grids and grid paper. These questions will help you summarize what you have learned:

1 Describe how you can find the area and perimeter of an odd shape such as a footprint.

2 If two odd shapes have the same perimeter, do they have the same area?

3 Can you figure out the perimeter of an odd shape if you know its area? Why or why not?

Think about your answers to these questions, discuss your ideas with other students and your teacher, and then write a summary of your findings in your journal.

What objects in a park might have odd shapes—a flower garden? A picnic area? A play area?

Constant Area, Changing Perimeter

In making floor plans for anything from a doghouse to a dream house, you have many options. Even when area and perimeter are fixed, there are lots of possible floor plans. Many factors—including the cost of materials and the purposes of the rooms—help to determine the best possible plan.

3.1 Building Storm Shelters

From March 12–14, 1993, a fierce winter storm hit the eastern United States from Florida to Maine. Thousands of people were stranded in the snow, far from shelter. A group of 24 Michigan students, who had been hiking in the Smoky Mountains of Tennessee, were among those stranded.

To prepare for this kind of emergency, parks often provide shelters at points along major hiking trails. Since the shelters are only for emergency use, they are designed to be simple and inexpensive buildings that are easily maintained.

Problem 3.1

The rangers in Great Smoky Mountains National Park want to build several inexpensive storm shelters. The shelters must have 24 square meters of floor space. Suppose that the walls are made of sections that are 1 meter wide and cost $125.

A. Use your tiles to experiment with different rectangular shapes. Sketch each possible floor plan on grid paper. Record your group's data in a table with these column headings:

Length   Width   Perimeter   Area   Cost of walls

B. Based on the cost of the wall sections, which design would be the least expensive to build? Describe what that shelter would look like.

C. Which shelter plan has the most expensive set of wall sections? Describe what that shelter would look like.

■ Problem 3.1 Follow-Up

Can you find a design—other than a rectangle—with 24 square meters of floor space and lower wall-section costs than any of the designs you have looked at so far? Experiment with your tiles to answer this question.

3.2 Stretching the Perimeter

In Problem 3.1, you worked with rectangles to help you understand the relationship between area and perimeter. In this problem, you will look at what happens when you cut an interesting part from a rectangle and slide that piece onto another edge. Look at these examples:

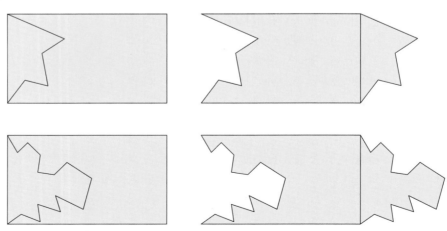

Can you use this technique to find a nonrectangular shape with an area of 24 square units and a larger perimeter than any of the rectangles you've found?

Problem 3.2

Draw a 4 × 6 rectangle on grid paper, and cut it out.

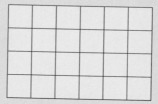

Starting at one corner, cut an interesting path to an adjacent corner.

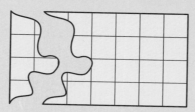

Slide the piece you cut out onto the opposite edge. Tape the two pieces together, matching the straight edges.

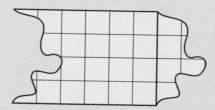

A. Find the area and the perimeter of your new figure.

B. Is the perimeter of the new figure larger than, the same as, or smaller than the perimeter of a 4 × 6 rectangle? Explain.

C. Could you make a figure with an area of 24 square units with a longer perimeter than you found in your first figure? Explain your answer.

Problem 3.2 Follow-Up

Summarize what you have discovered about figures with an area of 24 square units.

As you work on these ACE questions, use your calculator whenever you need it.

Applications

1. Sketch all the rectangles with an area of 30 square units and whole-number side lengths.

2. If the park rangers in Problem 3.1 wanted to build storm shelters with 20 square meters of floor space instead of 24, what design would be the least expensive?

3. Find the rectangle with an area 36 square units and whole-number side lengths that has the smallest perimeter possible.

4. Alyssa is designing a rectangular sandbox. The bottom is to cover 16 square feet. What shape will require the least amount of material for the sides of the sandbox?

5. Suppose you wanted to make a large banquet table from 36 square card tables. Four people can be seated at a card table, one person on each side. With two card tables put together to make a larger table, six people can be seated:

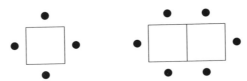

How would you arrange the 36 card tables to make the banquet table seat the greatest number of people? Explain your reasoning.

Connections

6. In a–c, find all rectangles that can be made from the given number of tiles.

    a. 60 square tiles   **b.** 61 square tiles   **c.** 62 square tiles

    d. How can you use your work in a–c to list the factors of 60, 61, and 62?

Extensions

7. A *pentomino* is a shape made of five identical squares that are connected along straight edges.

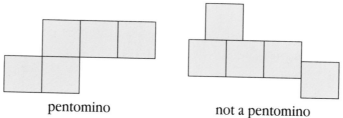

pentomino   not a pentomino

Turning or flipping a pentomino does *not* make a different pentomino.

a. Find all the possible pentominos. On grid paper, sketch each pentomino that you find.

b. Why do you think you have found all the possible pentominos?

c. Which pentomino has the smallest perimeter? Which pentomino has the largest perimeter?

8. a. On grid paper, design a 120-square-foot bedroom that you would enjoy having for your own. Draw in furniture on your floor plan. Measure real rooms, closets, and furniture to see whether your design is reasonable. Record the measurements you find. Include measures for a bed and a dresser.

     b. Describe why you think your design would be a good design for a bedroom. Include how you decided what would be reasonable for the shape of the room, the size of closets, and the other features of your design.

Mathematical Reflections

In this investigation, you designed storm shelters with an area of 24 square meters and determined which design would cost the least because it had the smallest perimeter. This problem helped you see how the perimeters of rectangles made from the same number of tiles can vary. You also looked at the perimeters of nonrectangular shapes with an area of 24 square units. These questions will help you summarize what you have learned:

1 If two rectangles have the same area, must they also have the same perimeter? Explain your answer.

2 Of all possible rectangles with a given area and whole-number side lengths, which has the smallest perimeter?

3 Of all possible rectangles with a given area and whole-number side lengths, which has the largest perimeter?

Think about your answers to these questions, discuss your ideas with other students and your teacher, and then write a summary of your findings in your journal.

Think about the city park you will be designing. You will have to use part of the area of the park for picnic tables, playground equipment, and other attractions. How could what you have learned about the relationship of perimeter and area be useful to you? You might want to visit some local parks to get more ideas for how you will design your city park. You may also want to measure some things in the parks you visit so you have a good idea about what size things in your design should be. Don't forget to record everything you find out!

Constant Perimeter, Changing Area

You often encounter situations in which you want to make the most of something. For example, suppose you were planning a party and had a set amount of money to spend on decorations and refreshments. Or, imagine that you were going on a trip and had a certain amount of spending money. In either situation, you would want to make the most of your budget.

Sometimes you want to make the least of something. If you were building a toy airplane or a racing bicycle, you would want to make it as lightweight as possible.

Mathematicians call these kinds of tasks finding the *maximum* or finding the *minimum*. In the last investigation, you found the maximum and minimum *perimeter* you could have for a rectangle with a fixed area of 24 square meters and whole-number side lengths. In this investigation, you will start with a fixed *perimeter* and try to find the maximum and minimum *area* that perimeter can enclose.

4.1 Fencing in Spaces

Americans have over 50 million dogs as pets. In many parts of the country—particularly in cities—there are laws against letting dogs run free. Many people build pens so their dogs have a chance to get outside for fresh air and exercise.

Problem 4.1

Suppose you wanted to help a friend build a rectangular pen for her dog, Shane. You have 24 meters of fencing, in 1-meter lengths, to build the pen. Which rectangular shape would be best for Shane?

Experiment with your square tiles to find all possible rectangles with a *perimeter* of 24 meters. Sketch each rectangle on grid paper. Record your data about each possible plan in a table with these column headings:

Length   Width   Perimeter   Area

■ **Problem 4.1 Follow-Up**

1. Which design would give Shane the best pen for running?

2. Which design would give Shane the most space for playing?

4.2 Adding Tiles to Pentominos

In Problem 4.1, you explored the relationship between area and perimeter by investigating the rectangles that could be made with a fixed perimeter of 24 units. In this problem, you will continue to investigate fixed perimeter by adding tiles to a pentomino.

Remember that a *pentomino* is a shape made from five identical square tiles connected along their edges. Here are some examples:

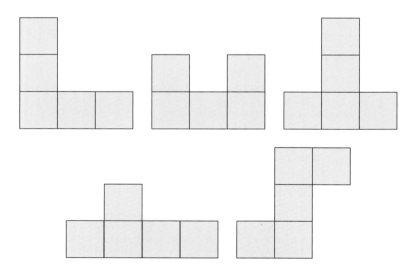

Problem 4.2

Make this pentomino with your tiles.

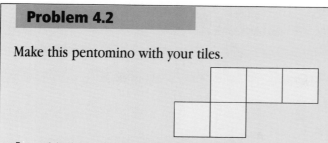

A. Add tiles to the pentomino to make a new figure with a perimeter of 18 units. Draw your new figure on grid paper. Show clearly where you added tiles to the pentomino.

B. What is the smallest number of tiles you can add to the pentomino to make a new figure with a perimeter of 18 units? Draw the new figure, showing where you would add tiles to the pentomino.

C. What is the largest number of tiles you can add to the pentomino to make a new figure with a perimeter of 18 units? Draw the new figure, showing where you would add tiles to the pentomino.

■ Problem 4.2 Follow-Up

How does adding one tile change the perimeter of a figure? Explain your answer. You might find it helpful to draw pictures.

As you work on these ACE questions, use your calculator whenever you need it.

Applications

1. Suneeta used square tiles to make rectangles with a perimeter of 8 units. On grid paper, draw all the possible rectangles Suneeta might have made.

2. Find a rectangle with whole-number side lengths, a perimeter of 20 units, and the largest possible area.

3. If you have 72 centimeters of molding to make a frame for a painting, how should you cut the molding to give the largest possible area for the painting?

4. On the next page is a diagram of the field next to Sarah's house. Each small square represents a space that is 1 foot on each side. Sarah wants to make a garden and a play area in the field.

    a. How much fencing does Sarah need to surround the field? Explain your answer.

    b. A box of grass seed plants an area of 125 square feet. How many boxes of seed would Sarah need to seed the entire field? Explain your answer.

    c. Sarah decides she wants to include some flower and vegetable plots and a small play area (a swing set and a sandbox) in the field. On Labsheet 4.ACE, make a design for Sarah that includes these items. Give the area and the dimensions of each part of your design.

    d. How many boxes of grass seed would Sarah need to seed the design you drew for part c?

Sarah's Field

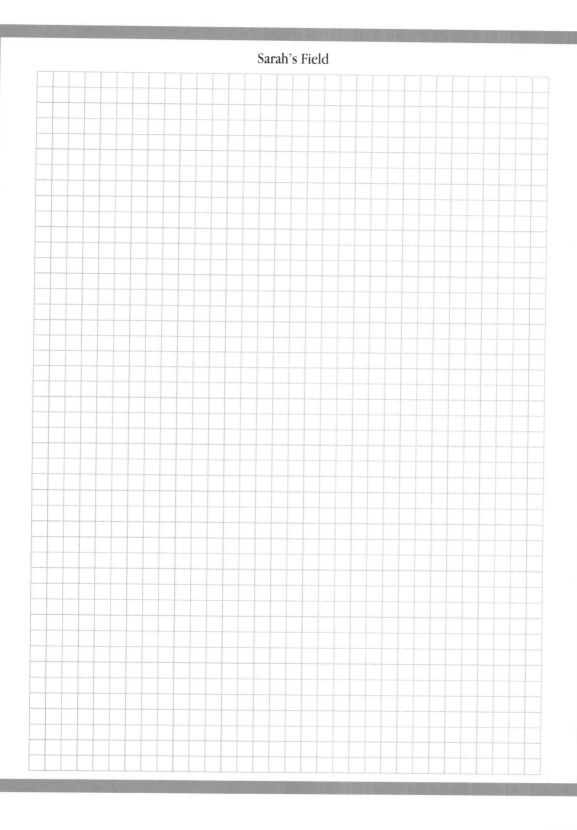

Connections

In 5–8, make any measurements you need to find the perimeter and area of the polygon in centimeters.

5.

6.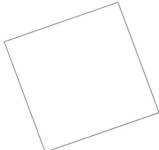

7.

8.

9. In *Shapes and Designs,* you found that if you make a rectangle out of Polystrips and press on the corners, the rectangle tilts out of a shape into a different parallelogram.

a. How does the perimeter of the original rectangle compare to the perimeter of the new parallelogram?

b. How does the area of the original rectangle compare to the area of the new parallelogram?

10. Kate and Eli want to design a garage with an area of 240 square feet.

   a. Make an organized list showing the dimensions (length and width), in feet, of all the possible rectangular garages they could make with whole-number dimensions.

   b. Which rectangles would be reasonable for a garage? Explain your answer.

   c. Which rectangle would you choose for a garage? Why?

11. a. Find the perimeter and area of the rectangle below.

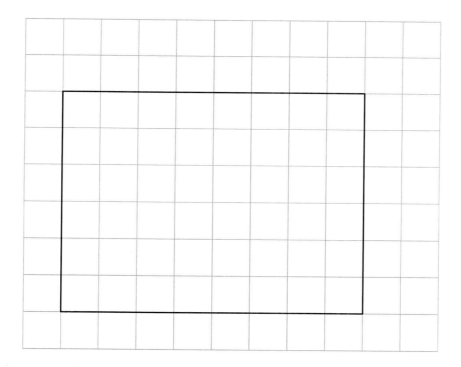

$\square$ = 1 square meter

b. On grid paper, draw a rectangle with the same area as the one shown on the previous page, but a different perimeter. Label its dimensions, and give its perimeter.

c. On your grid paper, draw a rectangle with the same perimeter as the rectangle you just drew, but a different area. Label its dimensions, and give its area.

In 12 and 13, give the area, in square inches, and the perimeter, in inches, of the rectangle.

12.

13.

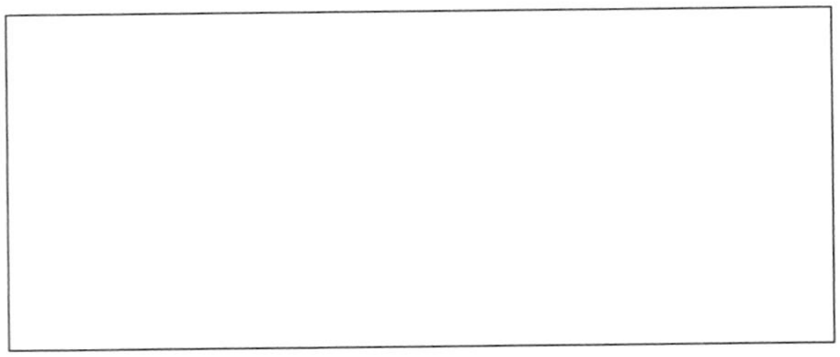

14. a. Find the area and perimeter of the rectangle below.

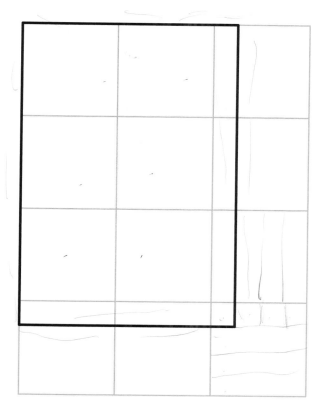

b. On inch grid paper, draw a rectangle with the same perimeter as the rectangle shown, but with a different area. Label the rectangle with its length and width, and give its area.

Extensions

15. Suppose a square sheet of paper has a perimeter of 1 meter.

a. What is the length of each side?

b. Suppose you folded the square sheet in half. What new shape would you have? What would the lengths of the shape's four sides be? What would the perimeter be?

c. Suppose you had folded over the top $\frac{1}{4}$ of the square. What new shape would you have? What would the lengths of the shape's four sides be? What would the perimeter be?

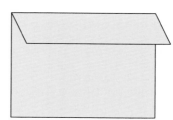

d. Suppose you had folded over only the top $\frac{1}{8}$ of the square. What new shape would you have? What would the lengths of the shape's four sides be? What would the perimeter be?

e. What would you predict for the perimeter of the shape you would get by folding over $\frac{1}{16}$ of the square?

Mathematical Reflections

In this investigation, you examined how the areas of shapes with the same perimeter could vary. First, you looked at rectangular pens with perimeters of 24 meters and decided which pens would give a dog the most room for running and for playing. Then you experimented with adding tiles to a pentomino, and you determined the smallest and the largest numbers of tiles you could add to the pentomino to make a shape with a perimeter of 18 units. These questions will help you summarize what you have learned:

1 Do all rectangles with the same perimeter have the same area? Explain your answer.

2 Of all rectangles with a given perimeter and whole-number side lengths, which rectangle has the smallest area?

3 Of all rectangles with a given perimeter and whole-number side lengths, which rectangle has the largest area?

Think about your answers to these questions, discuss your ideas with other students and your teacher, and then write a summary of your findings in your journal.

When you design the city park, how will these new ideas about perimeter and area help you? What things in a park would require information about area and perimeter? What areas might you want fencing around? Will you have sidewalks or paths in your park? You might want to start measuring some things like sidewalks and basketball courts now in preparation for designing the park. Remember to record in your journal all measurements that might help you with your project.

Measuring Parallelograms

You have found areas and perimeters of both rectangular and nonrectangular shapes. When a rectangle is displayed on a grid, you can find the area by counting the number of squares enclosed by the rectangle. You may have found that, once you counted the grid squares in one row, you could multiply by the number of rows to find the total number of squares in the rectangle. In other words, you can find the area of a rectangle by multiplying the length by the width.

For example, in this rectangle there are 5 squares in the first row and 7 rows in all. The area of the rectangle is $5 \times 7 = 35$ square units.

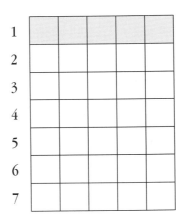

For a nonrectangular figure, you found that you could estimate the area by covering the figure with a grid and counting square units. In the next two investigations, you will find shortcuts for calculating areas of some special figures, including parallelograms. But don't forget that you can always cover a figure with a grid and count squares to find area.

5.1 Finding Measures of Parallelograms

On the next page are seven parallelograms drawn on a grid. Some of the parallelograms are not covered by whole squares. Even the two rectangles have sides that are not whole numbers of units long.

For parallelograms A–G, find the area and explain how you found it.

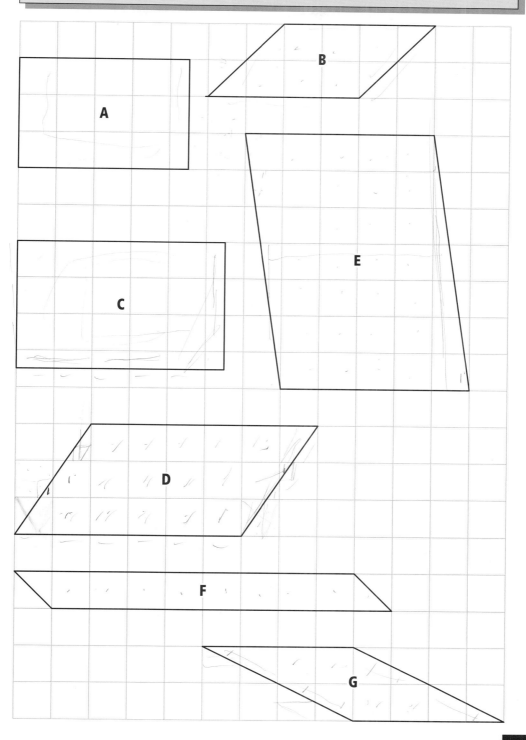

■ Problem 5.1 Follow-Up

Find the area and the perimeter of this parallelogram. Explain your reasoning.

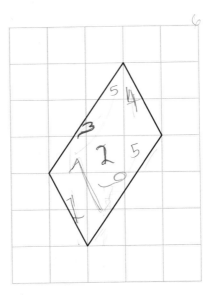

5.2 Designing Parallelograms Under Constraints

Parallelograms are often described by giving their **base** and **height.** The drawings illustrate the meanings of these terms.

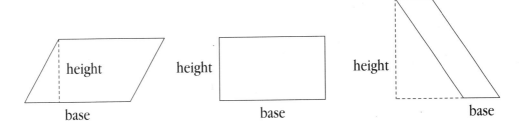

You can think of the height as the distance a rock would fall if you dropped it from a point at the top of a parallelogram down to the line that the base is on. In the first parallelogram, if we dropped the rock from the upper-left corner, it would fall inside the parallelogram. In the second parallelogram (a rectangle), the rock could fall along one of the sides. In the third parallelogram, if we dropped the rock from the upper-left corner, it would fall outside the parallelogram.

In the next problem, you will draw parallelograms that meet given requirements, or *constraints.* Sometimes you will be able to draw more than one parallelogram that satisfies the constraints.

Problem 5.2

In A–E, make your drawings on centimeter grid paper. Note that cm is the abbreviation for centimeters, and cm² is the abbreviation for square centimeters.

A. Draw a rectangle with an area of 18 cm². Then, try to draw a different rectangle with an area of 18 cm². Do the rectangles have the same perimeter? If you couldn't draw a different rectangle, explain why.

B. Draw a rectangle with the dimensions 3 cm by 8 cm. Then, try to draw a different rectangle with these same dimensions. Do the rectangles have the same area? If you couldn't draw a different rectangle, explain why.

C. Draw a parallelogram with a base of 7 cm and a height of 4 cm. Then, try to draw a different parallelogram with these same dimensions. Do the parallelograms have the same area? If you couldn't draw a different parallelogram, explain why.

D. Draw a parallelogram with all side lengths equal to 6 cm. Then, try to draw a different parallelogram with all side lengths equal to 6 cm. Do the parallelograms have the same area? If you couldn't draw a different parallelogram, explain why.

E. Draw a parallelogram with an area of 30 cm². Then, try to draw a different parallelogram with the same area. Do the parallelograms have the same perimeter? If you couldn't draw a different parallelogram, explain why.

■ Problem 5.2 Follow-Up

1. Summarize what you have discovered from making parallelograms that fit given constraints. Include your feelings about what kinds of constraints make designing a parallelogram easy and what kinds of constraints make designing a parallelogram difficult.

2. Have you discovered any shortcuts for finding areas of parallelograms? If so, describe them.

5.3 Rearranging Parallelograms

As you have probably discovered in your work, it would be useful to develop some easy ways to find perimeters and areas of common polygons without having to cover them with a grid and count squares. Let's do some exploring...

Problem 5.3

Draw two different nonrectangular parallelograms on a sheet of grid paper, and cut them out. Cut one of your parallelograms into two pieces so that the pieces can be reassembled to form a rectangle. Do the same for the second parallelogram. Use one of your parallelograms to complete parts A–C.

A. Record the base, height, perimeter, and area of the original parallelogram.

B. Record the length, width, perimeter, and area of the rectangle you made from the parallelogram pieces.

C. What relationships do you see between the measures for the rectangle and the measures for the parallelogram from which it was made?

■ Problem 5.3 Follow-Up

Use what you have learned to find the area and perimeter of this parallelogram.

As you work on these ACE questions, use your calculator whenever you need it.

Applications

In 1–7, find the area and perimeter of the polygon, and write a brief explanation of your reasoning for 2, 6, and 7.

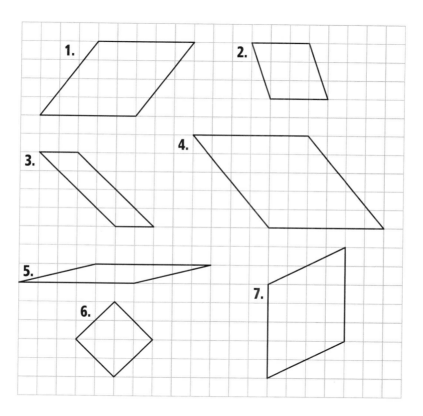

8. Below is a *family* of parallelograms.

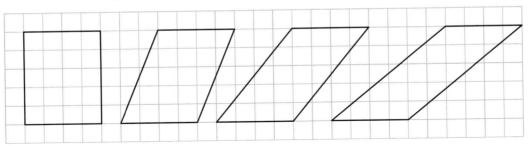

    a. Find the area of each parallelogram.

    b. What patterns do you see?

    c. Why do you think these parallelograms are called a family?

In 9–11, find the perimeter and area of the parallelogram.

9.

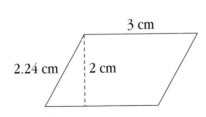

10.

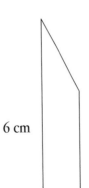

11.

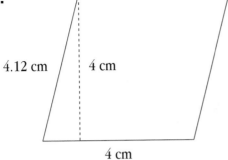

Connections

12. In *Shapes and Designs,* you found that if you make a rectangle out of Polystrips and press on the corners, the rectangle tilts out of a shape into a different parallelogram.

    a. How will the sides, angles, area, and perimeter of the new parallelogram compare to the original rectangle?

    b. What relations among the sides and angles of rectangles are also true of parallelograms?

13. In *Shapes and Designs,* you learned about shapes that can tile a flat surface.

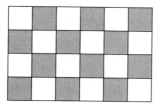  

    a. The floor plan on the following page is to be tiled with rectangular tiles like the one shown. Use your understanding of area and perimeter to calculate the number of tiles needed to cover the floor. Explain your reasoning.

    b. How would your reasoning change if you were to use nonrectangular parallelograms as tiles?

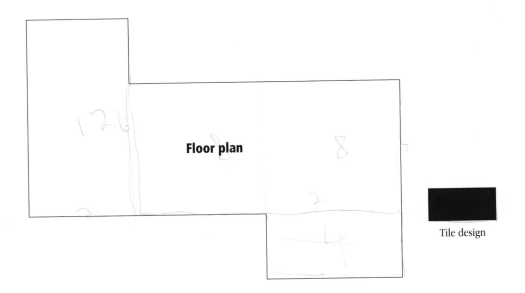

Floor plan

Tile design

14. Suppose you had a plot of land and you wanted to use what you have learned in this unit to design a garden. Design a parallelogram-shaped flower bed with an area of 24 square feet.

Extensions

15. Draw a parallelogram with a base of 6 centimeters and an area of 30 square centimeters. If possible, draw a second parallelogram with the same dimensions.

16. Design a rectangle with an area of 9 square centimeters. Make two sides a whole-number length, and two sides a length that is not a whole number. If possible, draw a second rectangle under these same constraints.

Mathematical Reflections

In this investigation, you invented strategies for finding areas and perimeters of parallelograms. These questions will help you summarize what you have learned:

1 Describe at least one efficient way to find the area of a parallelogram. Explain why it works.

2 Describe at least one efficient way to find the perimeter of a parallelogram. Explain why it works.

Think about your answers to these questions, discuss your ideas with other students and your teacher, and then write a summary of your findings in your journal.

How might your new knowledge about parallelograms help you in your park design? Have you thought about designing picnic areas or gardens in the shape of a parallelogram?

Measuring Triangles

You can always find the area of a figure by overlaying a grid and counting squares, but you probably realize that this can be very time-consuming. In Investigation 5, you discovered a shortcut for finding the area of a parallelogram without counting squares. In this investigation, you will estimate areas of triangles and look for patterns that might help you discover a shortcut for finding the area of a triangle.

6.1 Finding Measures of Triangles

On the next page are eight triangles drawn on a grid. The triangles are not covered by whole numbers of unit squares.

Problem 6.1

For triangles A–H on page 57, find the area and perimeter and explain how you found them.

■ Problem 6.1 Follow-Up

Find the area and perimeter of this triangle. Explain your reasoning.

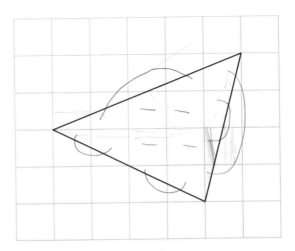

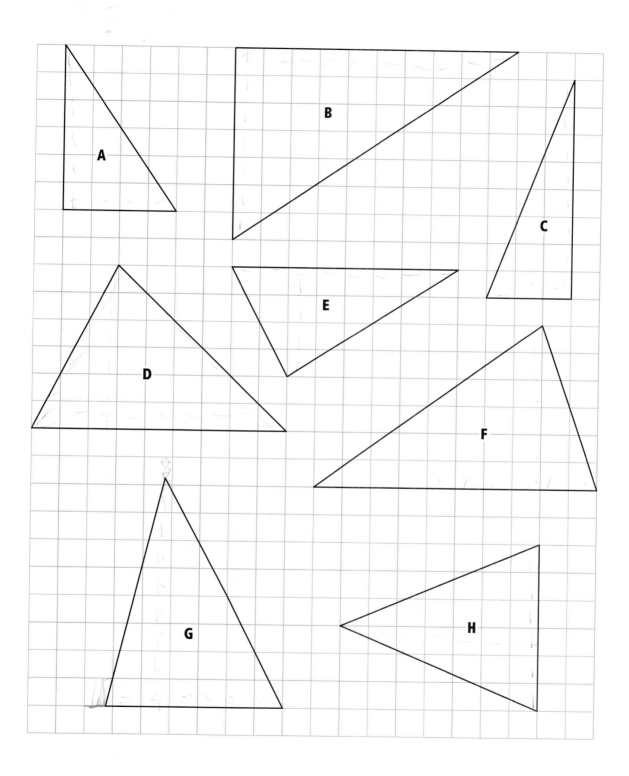

6.2 Designing Triangles Under Constraints

As with parallelograms, triangles are often described by giving their base and height. The drawings below illustrate what these terms mean.

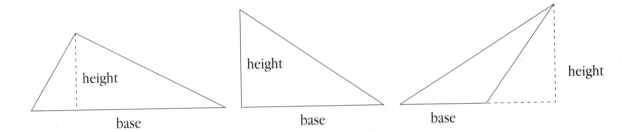

You can think of the height of a triangle as the distance a rock would fall if you dropped it from the top vertex of the triangle down to the line that the base is on. In the first triangle, the height falls inside the triangle. In the second triangle, the height is one of the sides. In the third triangle, the height falls outside the triangle.

In this problem, you will try to draw triangles that meet given constraints.

Problem 6.2

In A–D, make your drawings on centimeter grid paper. Remember that cm is the abbreviation for centimeters, and cm² is the abbreviation for square centimeters.

A. Draw a triangle with a base of 5 cm and a height of 6 cm. Then, try to draw a different triangle with these same dimensions. Do the triangles have the same area? If you couldn't draw a different triangle, explain why.

B. Draw a triangle with an area of 15 cm². Then, try to draw a different triangle with an area of 15 cm². Do the triangles have the same perimeter? If you couldn't draw a different triangle, explain why.

C. Draw a triangle with sides of length 3 cm, 4 cm, and 5 cm. Then, try to draw a different triangle with these same side lengths. Do the triangles have the same area? If you couldn't draw a different triangle, explain why.

D. A **right triangle** is a triangle that has a right angle. Draw a right triangle with a 30° angle. Then, try to draw a different right triangle with a 30° angle. Do the triangles have the same area? If you couldn't draw a different triangle, explain why.

■ **Problem 6.2 Follow-Up**

1. Summarize what you have discovered from making triangles that fit given constraints. Include your feelings about what kinds of constraints make designing a triangle easy and what kinds of constraints make designing a triangle difficult.

2. Have you discovered any shortcuts for finding areas of triangles? If so, describe them.

 ## 6.3 Making Parallelograms from Triangles

In *Shapes and Designs,* you discovered that triangles are useful for building because they are stable figures. If you make a triangle out of three Polystrips, you cannot "squish" it into a different shape. In this problem, you will experiment with paper triangles to try to discover a shortcut for finding the area of a triangle.

Problem 6.3

Draw two triangles on a sheet of grid paper. Make sure the triangles are very different from one another. For each triangle, complete parts A–C.

A. Record the base, height, area, and perimeter of your triangle.

B. Make a copy of your triangle, and cut out both copies. Experiment with putting the two triangles together to make new polygons. Describe and sketch the polygons that are possible.

C. Can you make a parallelogram by piecing together the two identical triangles? If so, record the base, height, area, and perimeter of the parallelogram. How do these measures compare to the measures of the original triangles?

D. Draw a parallelogram on grid paper, and cut it out. Can you cut the parallelogram into two triangles that are the same shape and size? Describe and sketch what you find.

■ **Problem 6.3 Follow-Up**

Use what you have learned to find the area and perimeter of this triangle.

As you work on these ACE questions, use your calculator whenever you need it.

Applications

In 1–6, calculate the area and perimeter of the polygon, and briefly explain your reasoning for figures 2, 4, and 6.

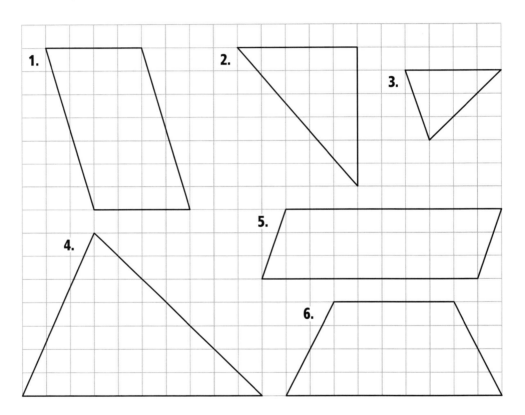

7. On the following page is a *family* of triangles.

  a. Find the area of each triangle.

  b. What patterns do you see?

  c. Why do you think these triangles are called a family?

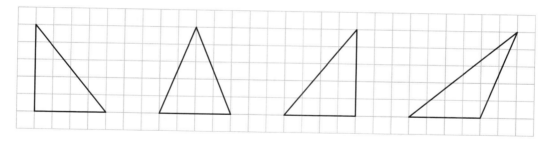

In 8–11, find the perimeter and area of the figure.

8.

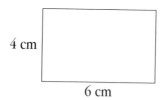

4 cm

6 cm

9.

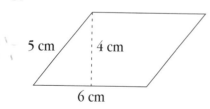

5 cm 4 cm

6 cm

10.

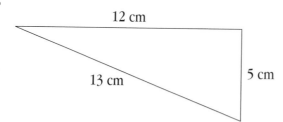

12 cm

13 cm 5 cm

11.

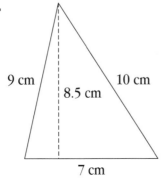

9 cm   8.5 cm   10 cm

7 cm

In 12–17, make whatever measurements you need to find the perimeter and area of the figure. Measure in centimeters.

12.

13.

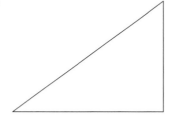

14.

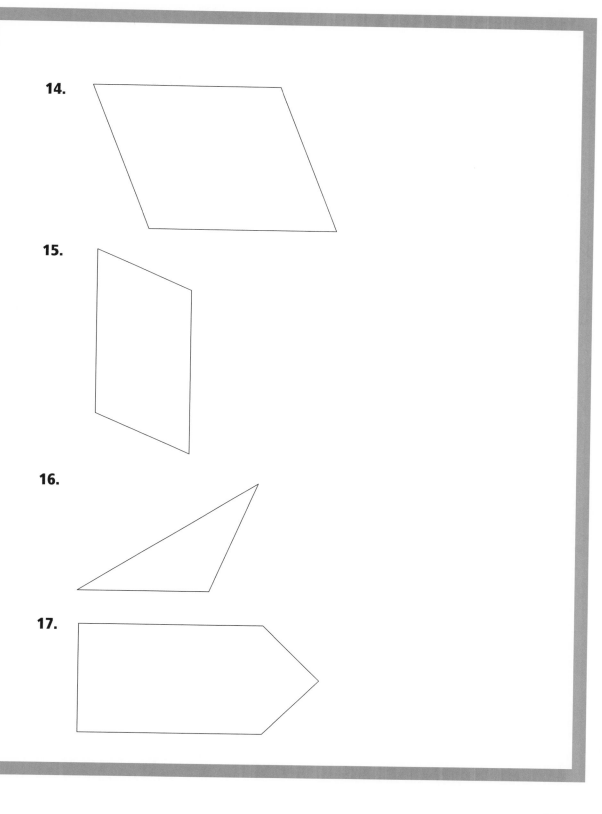

15.

16.

17.

Connections

18. **a.** Explain how the base and height could be measured in these figures.

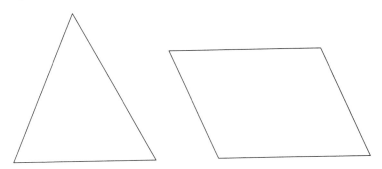

b. Explain how the base and height could be measured in this triangle.

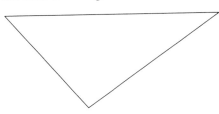

c. Explain how base and height are used to calculate area for parallelograms and triangles. Explain why this method works.

19. A **trapezoid** is a polygon with at least two opposite edges parallel. Below are two trapezoids drawn on grid paper.

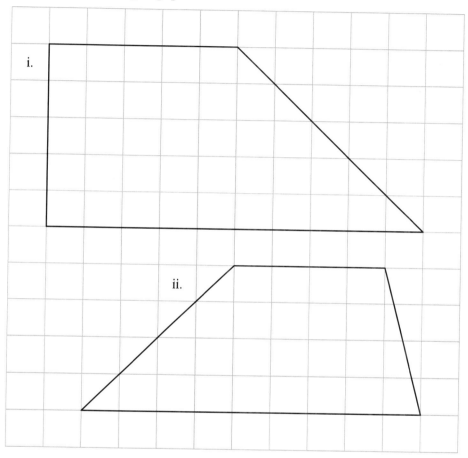

  a. Try to find a way to find the area of a trapezoid without having to count each square. Use your method to find the area for each trapezoid. Summarize your method as a rule or a description.

  b. How can you find the perimeter of a trapezoid? Use your method to calculate the perimeter of each trapezoid. Summarize your method as a rule or a description.

Extensions

20. Explain how you could calculate the area and perimeter of this hexagon.

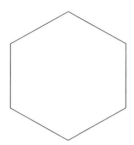

In 21 and 22, find the perimeter and area of the figure.

21.

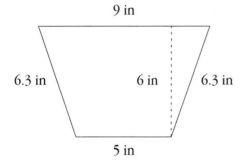

22.

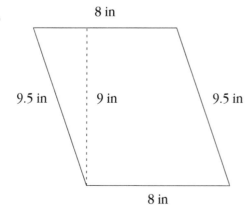

23. You saw earlier that in some parallelograms and triangles, the height falls outside of the shape being measured.

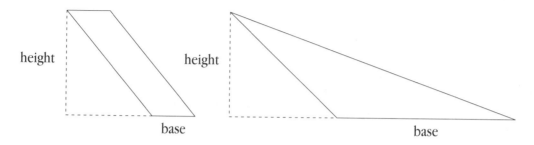

a. The area of the parallelogram can still be calculated by multiplying the base times the height. Write an explanation of why this is true.

b. The area of the triangle can still be calculated by multiplying $\frac{1}{2}$ times the base times the height. Write an explanation of why this is true.

Mathematical Reflections

In this investigation, you invented strategies for finding areas and perimeters of triangles by relating them to parallelograms and rectangles. These questions will help you summarize what you have learned:

1 Describe an efficient way to find the area of a triangle. Be sure to mention the measurements you would need to make and how you would use them to find the area.

2 Describe an efficient way to find the perimeter of a triangle. Be sure to mention the measurements you would need to make and how you would use them to find the perimeter.

3 Summarize what you have discovered about finding areas and perimeters of rectangles, parallelograms, and triangles. Describe the measures you need to make to find the area and perimeter of each figure.

Think about your answers to these questions, discuss your ideas with other students and your teacher, and then write a summary of your findings in your journal.

Are you finalizing your ideas for what you want to put in your park? Have you considered including a picnic area, a tennis court, a basketball court, a water fountain, or rest rooms? What kind of ground covering might you use for the playground area—concrete, sand, grass, wood chips? Keep track of your ideas in your journal.

Going Around in Circles

You encounter circles every day of your life. They are one of the most useful shapes. Circles are used for making things like tools, toys, and transportation vehicles, and everyday items like bottle caps, compact discs, and coins. Take a minute to think of how different your life would be without circles.

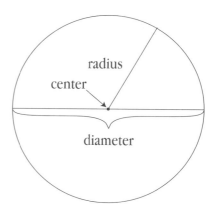

There are at least four measurements that are useful for describing the size of a **circle**: *diameter, radius, area,* and *circumference.* The **diameter** of a circle is any line segment that extends from a point on the circle, through the center, to another point on the circle. The **radius** is any line segment from the center to a point on the circle. **Circumference** means *perimeter* in the language of circles—it is the distance around the circle.

It is easy to measure the diameter and radius of a circle, but measuring the area and circumference is not as easy. You can't cover the circle with an exact number of square tiles to compute the area, and you can't easily use a ruler to measure its circumference.

As you work on the problems in this investigation, look for connections between a circle's diameter, radius, area, and circumference. Search for clues that tell when each of these measurements gives useful information about a circular object in a given situation.

7.1 Pricing Pizza

Many pizza restaurants sell small, medium, and large pizzas— usually measured by the diameter of a circular pie. Of course, the prices are different for the three sizes. Do you think a large pizza is usually the best buy?

Problem 7.1

The Sole D'Italia Pizzeria sells small, medium, and large pizzas. A small is 9 inches in diameter, a medium is 12 inches in diameter, and a large is 15 inches in diameter. Prices for cheese pizzas are $6.00 for small, $9.00 for medium, and $12.00 for large.

A. Draw a 9-inch, a 12-inch, and a 15-inch "pizza" on centimeter grid paper. Let 1 centimeter of the grid paper represent 1 inch on the pizza. Estimate the radius, circumference, and area of each pizza. (You may want to use string to help you find the circumference.)

B. Which measurement—radius, diameter, circumference, or area—seems most closely related to price? Explain your answer.

■ Problem 7.1 Follow-Up

Use your results to write a report about what you consider to be the best value of the pizza options at Sole D'Italia.

7.2 Surrounding a Circle

Mathematicians have found a relationship between the diameter and circumference of a circle. You can try to discover this relationship by measuring many different circles and looking for patterns. The patterns you discover can help you develop a shortcut for finding the circumference of a circle.

Problem 7.2

In this problem, you will work with a collection of circular objects.

A. Use a tape measure to find the diameter and circumference of each object. Record your results in a table with these column headings:

Object   Diameter   Circumference

B. Make a coordinate graph of your data. Use the horizontal axis for diameter and the vertical axis for circumference.

C. Study your table and your graph, looking for patterns and relationships that will allow you to predict the circumference from the diameter. Test your ideas on some other circular objects. Once you think you have found a pattern, answer this question: What do you think the relationship is between the diameter and the circumference of a circle?

■ Problem 7.2 Follow-Up

1. How can you find the circumference of a circle if you know its diameter?
2. How can you find the diameter of the circle if you know its circumference?
3. Use the relationships you discovered in the problem to calculate the circumferences of the pizzas from Problem 7.1. How do your calculations compare to your estimates?

7.3 Covering a Circle

In the last problem, you discovered a pattern for finding the circumference of a circle. Do you think there is a similar pattern for finding the area of a circle?

Problem 7.3

Find as many different ways as you can to estimate the area of the circle below. For each method, give your area estimate and carefully describe how you found it. Include drawings in your descriptions if they help show what you did.

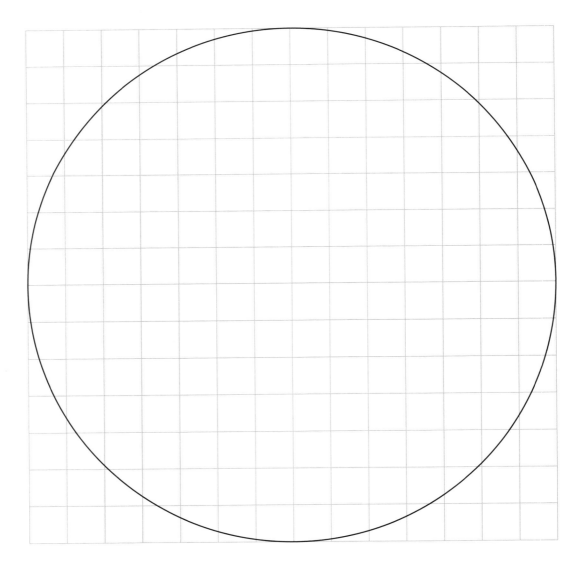

■ Problem 7.3 Follow-Up

Will a circle with a diameter equal to half the diameter of the circle in the problem have an area equal to half the area of that circle? Why or why not?

7.4 "Squaring" a Circle

In Investigations 5 and 6, you learned some things about parallelograms and triangles by comparing them to rectangles. Now you will find out more about circles by comparing them to squares.

Labsheet 7.4 shows the three circles that are drawn below. A portion of each circle is covered by a shaded square. The sides of each shaded square are the same length as the radius of the circle. We call such a square a "radius square."

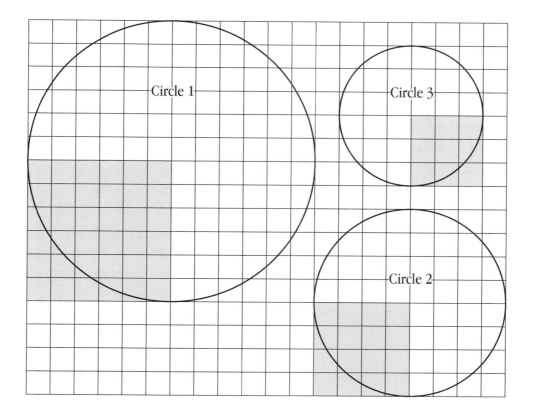

Problem 7.4

A. For each circle, cut out several copies of the radius square from a sheet of centimeter grid paper. Find out how many radius squares it takes to cover the circle. You may cut the radius squares into parts if you need to. Record your data in a table with these column headings:

Circle	Radius of circle	Area of radius square	Area of circle	Number of radius squares needed

B. Now draw a couple of your own circles on grid paper. You can use circles from the objects you measured in Problem 7.2 and from your Shapes Set. Make radius squares for each circle, and find out how many radius squares it takes to cover each circle. Add this data to your table.

C. Describe any patterns you see in your data.

D. If you were asked to estimate the area of any circle in "radius squares," what would you report as the best estimate?

■ **Problem 7.4 Follow-Up**

1. How can you find the area of a circle if you know the diameter or the radius?

2. How can you find the diameter or radius of a circle if you know the area?

Did you know?

You have discovered that the area of a circle is a *little more than 3* times the radius squared. You have also found that the distance around a circle is a *little more than 3* times the diameter. There is a special name given to this number that is a little more than 3.

In 1706, William Jones used π (pronounced "pi"), the Greek letter for *p*, to represent this number. He used the symbol to stand for the *periphery*, or distance around, a circle with a diameter of 1 unit.

As early as 2000 B.C., the Babylonians *knew* that π was more than 3! Their estimate for π was $3\frac{1}{8}$. By the fifth century, Chinese mathematician Tsu Chung-Chi wrote that π was somewhere between 3.1415926 and 3.1415927. From 1436 until 1874, the known value of π went from 14 places past the decimal to 707 places. Computers have been used to calculate millions more digits, and today we know that the digits will never repeat and will never end. This kind of number is called *irrational*.

7.5 Replacing Trees

In large cities filled with streets and concrete buildings, trees are a valuable part of the environment. In New York City, people who damage or destroy a tree are required by law to plant new trees as community service. Two replacement rules have been used:

Diameter rule: The total *diameter* of the new tree(s) must equal the diameter of the tree(s) that were damaged or destroyed.

Area rule: The total *area of the cross section* of the new tree(s) must equal the area of the cross section of the tree(s) that were damaged or destroyed.

Problem 7.5

The following diagram shows the cross section of a damaged tree and the cross section of the new trees that will be planted to replace it.

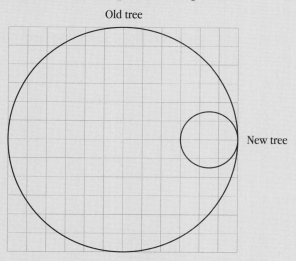

Old tree

New tree

A. How many new trees must be planted if the diameter rule is applied?

B. How many new trees must be planted if the area rule is applied?

Problem 7.5 Follow-Up
Which rule do you think is fairer? Use mathematics to explain your answer.

As you work on these ACE questions, use your calculator whenever you need it.

Applications

In 1–5, use the given measurements of a circle to find the other measurements. You may want to make scale drawings on grid paper to help find the missing measurements.

1. A dinner plate has a diameter of about 9 inches. Find its circumference and area.

2. A bicycle wheel is about 26 inches in diameter. Find its radius, circumference, and area.

3. A soft-drink can is about 2.25 inches in diameter. What is its circumference?

4. If the spray from a lawn sprinkler makes a circle 40 feet in radius, what are the approximate diameter, circumference, and area of the circle of lawn watered?

5. A standard long-playing record album has a 12-inch diameter; a compact disc has a 5-inch diameter. Find the radius, circumference, and area of each.

In 6–8, estimate, as accurately as possible, the area and perimeter of the figure. Make your measurements in centimeters.

6.

7.

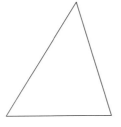

8.

[ ]

Connections

Some everyday circular objects are commonly described by giving their radius or diameter. In 9–12, explain what useful information (if any) you would get from calculating the area or circumference of the circle.

9. a 3.5-inch-diameter computer disk

10. a 21-inch-diameter bicycle wheel

11. a 12-inch-diameter water pipe

12. a lawn sprinkler that sprays a 15-meter-radius section of lawn

---

Did you know?

3.14159265358979323846264338327950288419716939937510 . . . How many places can you remember? One man was known to have memorized π to 50,000 places! How important is it to be exact about this number? Actually, precision engines can be built using an approximation of 3.1416. You can calculate the earth's circumference within a fraction of an inch by knowing π out to only 10 places. So unless you love to memorize, 3.14 or the fraction $\frac{22}{7}$ are close enough approximations to make pretty good measurements.

13. A large burner on a standard electric stove is about 8 inches in diameter.

   a. What are the radius, area, and circumference of the burner?

   b. How would the area and circumference of a smaller 4-inch-diameter burner compare to the area and circumference of the 8-inch burner? Check your answers with calculations.

14. Karl and Aimeé are building a playhouse for their little sister. The floor of the playhouse will be a rectangle that is 6 feet by $8\frac{1}{2}$ feet.

   a. How much carpeting will Karl and Aimeé need to cover the floor?

   b. How much molding will they need around the edges of the floor to hold the carpet in place?

   c. The walls will be 6 feet high. A pint of paint covers about 50 square feet. How much paint will they need to paint the inside walls? Explain your answer.

   d. Make your own plan for a playhouse. Figure out how much carpeting, wood, paint, and molding you would need to build the playhouse.

15. Which measurement of a circular pizza—diameter, radius, circumference, or area—best indicates its size?

16. The Logo instructions on the following page draw a polygon with so many sides that it looks like a circle.

   a. How many sides does this polygon have?

   b. What is the perimeter of the polygon, in turtle steps?

   c. *Approximately* how many turtle steps would it take for the turtle to walk the path from point A to point B? Explain your answer.

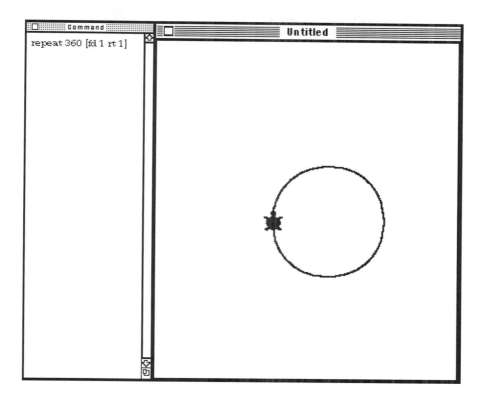

repeat 360 [fd 1 rt 1]

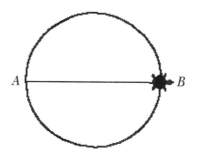

A |————————————| B

Extensions

17. Suppose you tie together the ends of a piece of string to form a loop that is 60 centimeters long.

    a. Suppose you arranged the string to form an equilateral triangle. What would the area of the enclosed space be? What would the area be if you formed square? A regular hexagon?

    Think back to the work you did in *Shapes and Designs.* Why do you think the surface of a honeycomb is covered with hexagons?

    b. Of all the rectangles with a perimeter of 60 centimeters, which has greatest area?

    c. Of all the triangles with a perimeter of 60 centimeters, which has greatest area?

    d. How does the area of a regular octagon with a perimeter of 60 centimeters compare to the areas of a triangle, a square, and a hexagon with perimeters of 60 centimeters?

    e. What happens to the enclosed area as the 60-centimeter perimeter is used to make regular polygons of more and more sides? (If you have access to a computer and the Logo programming language, you might use the computer to draw these figures.)

    f. As the number of sides of a polygon gets larger and larger, what shape does the polygon eventually resemble?

Mathematical Reflections

In this investigation, you discovered strategies for finding the area and circumference (perimeter) of a circle. You examined relationships between the circumference and the diameter of a circle and between the area and the radius of a circle. These questions will help you summarize what you have learned:

1 Describe how you can find the circumference of a circle by measuring the radius or the diameter. If you need to, explain your thinking by using a specific circle.

2 Describe how you can find the area of a circle by measuring its radius or its diameter. If you need to, explain your thinking by using a specific circle. Why is your method useful?

Think about your answers to these questions, discuss your ideas with other students and your teacher, and then write a summary of your findings in your journal.

You will soon be designing your layout for the city park. How might your new information about circles help you? What objects in your park might be in the shape of a circle—a flower garden, a water fountain?

Plan a Park

At the beginning of this unit, you read about Dr. Doolittle's donation of land to the city, which she designated as a new park. It is now time to design your plan for the piece of land. Use the information you have collected about parks, plus what you learned from your study of this unit, to prepare your final design.

Your design should satisfy the following constraints:

- The park should be rectangular with dimensions 120 yards by 100 yards.
- About half of the park should consist of a picnic area and a playground, but these two sections need not be located together.
- The picnic area should contain a circular flower garden. There should also be a garden in at least one other place in the park.
- There should be trees in several places in the park. Young trees will be planted, so your design should show room for the trees to grow.
- The park must appeal to families, so there should be more than just a picnic area and a playground.

Your design package should be neat, clear, and easy to follow. Your design should be drawn and labeled in black and white. In addition to a scale drawing of your design for the park, your project should include a report that gives:

1. the size (dimensions) of each item. These items should include gardens, trees, picnic tables, playground equipment, and anything else you included in your design.

2. the amount of land needed for each item and the calculations you used to determine the amount of land needed.

3. the materials needed. Include the amount of each item needed and the calculations you did to determine the amounts. Include the number and type of each piece of playground equipment, the amount of fencing, the numbers of picnic tables and trash containers, the amount of land covered by concrete or blacktop (so the developers can determine how much cement or blacktop will be needed), and the quantities of other items you included in your park.

4. a letter to Dr. Doolittle explaining why she should choose your design for the park. Include a justification for the choices you made about the size and quantity of items in your park.

Unit Reflections

Working on problems in this unit helped you to understand *area* and *perimeter*. You learned efficient strategies for estimating and calculating the area and perimeter of figures such as triangles, rectangles, parallelograms, and circles. You used these strategies to investigate the relationship between area and perimeter of simple polygons.

Using Your Understanding of Area and Perimeter—Test your understanding and skill in working with area and perimeter by solving the following problems.

1 *The diagram below shows a hexagon drawn on a grid.*

   a. Find the area of the hexagon.

   b. Describe two different strategies for calculating the area—one that makes use of area strategies for familiar polygons and another that does not.

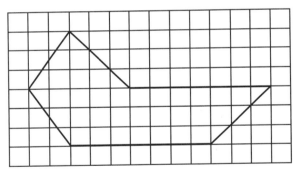

2 *In parts a–d, you are given directions for making different shapes. In each case, answer these questions.*

   i. Is it possible to make a shape with the specified properties? If so, sketch the shape.

   ii. If it is possible to make one shape with the specified properties, is it possible to draw different shapes with the same properties? If so, sketch some other possibilities.

a. a triangle with an area of 16 cm² and a height of 2 cm

b. a rectangle with a perimeter of 20 cm

c. a parallelogram with a pair of opposite sides of length 10 cm and an area of 96 cm²

d. a rectangle with perimeter of 24 cm and area of 20 cm²

3 *The Smith's living room floor is a square 20 feet by 20 feet that is covered with parquet wood. They have carpeted a quarter-circle region as shown in this diagram.*

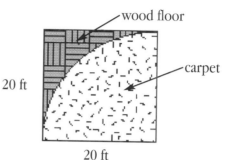

wood floor

carpet

20 ft

20 ft

a. What is the area of the **uncovered wood**, to the nearest square foot?

b. A 1-quart can of floor wax covers 30 square feet of wood flooring. How many cans of floor wax are needed to wax the uncovered wood?

c. A special finishing trim was placed along the curved edge of the carpet. How much trim, to the nearest tenth of a foot, was needed?

Explaining Your Reasoning—To answer questions about area and perimeter you have to apply properties of geometric figures and then use strategies to make numerical estimates or calculations.

1. How would you explain the difference between area and perimeter to a younger student who has not yet studied those mathematical ideas?

2. Describe calculation strategies that can be used to find the area of each shape and be prepared to justify each procedure.

a. Rectangle

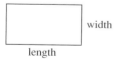

width

length

b. Triangle

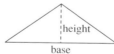

height

base

c. Parallelogram

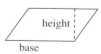

height

base

d. Circle

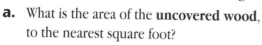

radius

diameter

3. How would you estimate the area and perimeter of an irregular figure such as the one drawn on the grid below? What is a reasonable estimate for the area of this particular figure?

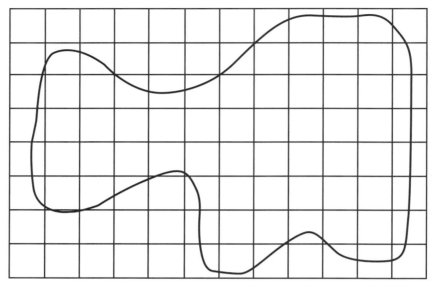

Area and perimeter are among the most useful concepts for measuring the size of geometric figures. You will use strategies for estimating and calculating the size of geometric figures in many future units of *Connected Mathematics*, especially those that deal with surface area and volume of solid figures, similarity, and the Pythagorean Theorem. You will also find that area and volume estimates and calculations are required in a variety of practical and technical problems.

area The measure of the amount of surface enclosed by the sides of a figure. To find the area of a figure, you can count how many unit squares it takes to cover the figure. You can find the area of a rectangle by multiplying the length by the width. This is simply a shortcut method for finding the number of unit squares it takes to cover the rectangle. If a figure has curved or irregular sides, you can estimate the area by covering the surface with a grid and counting whole grid squares and parts of grid squares. When you find the area of a shape, write the units, such as square feet or cm², to indicate the unit square that was used to find the area. The area of the square below is 9 square units, and the area of the rectangle is 6 square units.

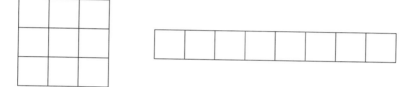

circle A two-dimensional object in which every point is the same distance from a point (not on the circle) called the *center*. Point C is the center of the circle below.

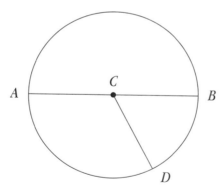

circumference The distance around (or perimeter of) a circle. It takes slightly more than three diameters to match the circumference of a circle. More formally, the circumference of a circle is pi (π) times the diameter of the circle. Pi is the mathematical name for the ratio of a circle's circumference to its diameter. This ratio is the same for every circle, and is approximately equal to 3.1416.

diameter A segment that goes from one point on a circle, through the center, to another point on the circle. The length of this segment is also called the diameter. In the definition of circle on page 87, segment *AB* is a diameter.

linear dimensions Linear measurements, such as length, width, base, and height, which describe the size of figures. The longest dimension or the dimension along the bottom of a rectangle is usually called the *length*, and the other dimension is called the *width*, but it is not incorrect to reverse these labels. The word *base* is used when talking about triangles and parallelograms. The *base* is usually measured along a horizontal side, but it is sometimes convenient to think of one of the other sides as the base. For a triangle, the height is the perpendicular distance from the vertex opposite the base to the base. For a parallelogram, the height is the perpendicular distance from a point on the side opposite the base to the base. You need to be flexible when you encounter these terms, so you are able to determine their meanings from the context of the situation.

perimeter The measure of the distance around a figure. Perimeter is a measure of length. To find the perimeter of a figure, you count the number of unit lengths it takes to surround the figure. When you find the perimeter of a shape, write the units (such as centimeters, feet, or yards) to indicate the unit that was used to find the perimeter. The perimeter of the square on page 87 is 12 units, because 12 units of length surround the figure. The perimeter of the rectangle is 18 units. Notice that the rectangle has a larger perimeter, but a smaller area, than the square.

perpendicular lines Lines that meet at right angles. The length and width of a rectangle are perpendicular to each other and the base and height of a triangle are perpendicular to each other. In diagrams, perpendicular lines are often indicated by drawing a small square where the lines meet.

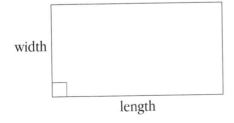

width

length

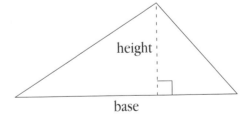

height

base

radius A segment from the center of a circle to a point on the circle. The length of this segment is also called the radius. The radius is half of the diameter. In the definition of circle on page 87, *CD* is one radius. The plural of radius is radii. All the radii of a circle have the same length.

Index

Area, 4
  ACE, 13–17, 21–27, 32–33, 38–44,
    60–67, 76–80
  changing with constant perimeter,
    35–37
  of a circle, 4, 69–75
  constant with changing perimeter,
    29–31
  estimating, 16, 17, 19–27
  of irregular shapes, 19–27
  measuring, 6–12
  of a parallelogram, 4, 40
  perimeter and, 6–12
  of a rectangle, 30–31, 35–37, 46
  of a trapezoid, 65
  of a triangle, 4

Base
  of a parallelogram, 48
  of a triangle, 58

Circle
  ACE, 76–80
  area of, 4, 69–75
  circumference of, 69–75
  diameter of, 69
  perimeter of, 4
  radius of, 69
  square and, 73–74

Circumference, 4, 23–24, 69–75
  ACE, 76–80
  diameter and, 71
Constraints
  parallelogram design under, 48–49
  park design under, 5, 82–83
  triangle design under, 58–59

Diameter, 69
  circumference and, 71

Estimation
  ACE, 21–27
  area, 16, 17, 19–27
  perimeter, 16, 17, 19–27

Family
  of parallelograms, 52
  of triangles, 60–61

Height
  of a parallelogram, 48
  of a triangle, 58

Investigations
  Constant Area, Changing Perimeter,
    29–34
  Constant Perimeter, Changing Area,
    35–45

Going Around in Circles, 69–81
Measuring Odd Shapes, 19–28
Measuring Parallelograms, 46–55
Measuring Perimeter and Area, 6–18
Measuring Triangles, 56–68
Irrational number, 74
Irregular shape
area of, 19–27
perimeter of, 19–27, 30–31

Jones, William, 74
Journal, 18, 28, 34, 45, 55, 68, 81

Length, of a rectangle, 16
**Looking Back and Looking Ahead:
Unit Reflections**, 84–86

Mathematical Highlights, 4
Mathematical Reflections, 18, 28, 34,
45, 55, 68, 81
Maximum area, 35–44
Maximum perimeter, 29–33
Measurement *See also* **Area**; **Perimeter**
earth, 25
foot, 20
hand, 21
head, 23–24
precision in, 21
waist, 23–24
Minimum area, 35–44
Minimum perimeter, 29–33

Outliers, in measurements, 20

Parallelogram
ACE, 51–55
area estimation, 17
area of, 4, 40, 46–50
base of, 48
height of, 48
perimeter estimation, 17
perimeter of, 4, 40, 49–50
from triangles, 59
Pentomino, 33, 36–37
Perimeter, 4
ACE, 13–17, 21–27, 32–33, 38–44,
51–52, 60–67
area and, 6–12
changing with constant area, 29–31
circumference and, 69
constant with changing area,
35–37
estimation, 16, 17, 19–27
of irregular shapes, 19–27
measuring, 6–12
of a parallelogram, 4, 40, 49–50
stretching, 30–31
of a trapezoid, 65
Pi, 74, 77
Precision, in measurement, 21

Radius, 69
Radius square, 73–74
Rectangle
ACE, 32–33, 38–44
area of, 30–31, 35–37, 46
length of, 16

parallelogram and, 46–50
   perimeter of, 30–31, 35–37
   width of, 16
Right triangle, 58

Size
   area and, 6–12
   of a circle, 69
   describing, 3
   perimeter and, 6–12
Square, circle and, 73–74

Trapezoid
   area estimation, 17
   area of, 65

perimeter estimation, 17
   perimeter of, 65
Triangle
   ACE, 60–67
   area estimation, 17
   area of, 4, 56–59
   base of, 58
   height of, 58
   perimeter estimation, 17
   right, 58
Tsu Chung-Chi, 74

Unit project, 5, 82–83

Width, of a rectangle, 16

Connected Mathematics

Probability

Student Edition

Glenda Lappan
James T. Fey
William M. Fitzgerald
Susan N. Friel
Elizabeth Difanis Phillips

Prentice
Hall

Glenview, Illinois
Needham, Massachusetts
Upper Saddle River, New Jersey

The Connected Mathematics Project was developed at Michigan State University with the support of National Science Foundation Grant No. MDR 9150217.

This project was supported, in part,
by the
National Science Foundation
Opinions expressed are those of the authors
and not necessarily those of the Foundation

The Michigan State University authors and administration have agreed that all MSU royalties arising from this publication will be devoted to purposes supported by the Department of Mathematics and the MSU Mathematics Education Enrichment Fund.

Contents

Mathematical Highlights — 4

Investigation 1: A First Look at Chance — 5
    1.1 Flipping for Breakfast — 5
    1.2 Analyzing Events — 7
    Applications—Connections—Extensions — 9
    Mathematical Reflections — 13

Investigation 2: More Experiments with Chance — 14
    2.1 Tossing Marshmallows — 14
    2.2 Pondering Possible and Probable — 16
    Applications—Connections—Extensions — 17
    Mathematical Reflections — 21

Investigation 3: Using Spinners to Predict Chances — 22
    3.1 Bargaining for a Better Bedtime — 22
    Applications—Connections—Extensions — 24
    Mathematical Reflections — 28

Investigation 4: Theoretical Probabilities — 29
    4.1 Predicting to Win — 29
    4.2 Drawing More Blocks — 32
    4.3 Winning the Bonus Prize — 33
    Applications—Connections—Extensions — 35
    Mathematical Reflections — 41

Investigation 5: Analyzing Games of Chance — 42
    5.1 Playing Roller Derby — 42
    Applications—Connections—Extensions — 44
    Mathematical Reflections — 48

Investigation 6: More About Games of Chance — 49
    6.1 Scratching Spots — 49
    Applications—Connections—Extensions — 51
    Mathematical Reflections — 56

Investigation 7: Probability and Genetics — 57
    7.1 Curling Your Tongue — 57
    7.2 Tracing Traits — 58
    Applications—Connections—Extensions — 61
    Mathematical Reflections — 64

Looking Back and Looking Ahead: Unit Reflections — 65

Glossary — 68

Index — 70

How Likely Is It?

Imagine that you are one of four contestants on a game show. The host is holding a bucket containing red, yellow, and blue blocks. You cannot see the blocks. Each contestant guesses a color and then draws a block from the bucket. A contestant who correctly predicts the color of the block wins $500. After each draw, the block is returned to the bucket. What are your chances of winning the game? Is there an advantage to choosing first? Is there an advantage to choosing last?

Suppose you have a scratch-off game card with five spots. Each spot covers the name of a prize. The names under two of the spots match. You are allowed to scratch off two spots. If the names under the spots match, you win the prize. How likely is it that you will win?

Some people can curl their tongues into a U shape; other people can't. What are the chances that a person can curl her or his tongue?

How do you make decisions? If you are deciding whether or not to carry an umbrella to school, you might ask yourself, "How likely is it that it will rain today?" If you are deciding whether to buy a lottery ticket, you might ask yourself, "What are the chances that I will win the lottery?" These questions are asking about the *probability* that a particular event will occur.

Determining probabilities can help you understand past events and make decisions about future events. In this unit, you will look at many questions that involve probability, including the three questions on the opposite page.

Mathematical Highlights

In *How Likely Is It?*, you will explore concepts related to *chance* and *probability* applied to situations that have uncertain outcomes. This unit will help you to

● Become acquainted with probability through experiments;

● Understand the concepts of equally likely and not equally likely;

● Understand that there are two ways to build probability models: by gathering data from experiments (experimental probability) and by analyzing the possible equally likely outcomes (theoretical probability);

● Develop strategies for finding both experimental and theoretical probabilities;

● Understand that experimental probabilities are better estimates of theoretical probabilities when they are based on larger numbers of trials;

● Understand that probabilities are useful for predicting what will happen over the long run; and

● Determine and critically interpret statements of probability.

As you work on the problems of this unit, make it a habit to ask questions about situations that involve probability and uncertainty: *What are the possible outcomes that can occur for the event in this situation? How could I determine the experimental probability of each of the outcomes? Is it possible to determine the theoretical experimental probability of each of the outcomes? If so, what are these probabilities? How can I use the probabilities I have found to answer questions or make decisions about this situation?*

A First Look at Chance

One way to make a decision about something is to do an experiment to see what is likely to happen. In this investigation, you will experiment with flipping a coin.

1.1 Flipping for Breakfast

Kalvin, an eighth grader, always has cereal for breakfast. He likes Cocoa Blast cereal so much that he wants to eat it every morning. Kalvin's mother wants him to eat Health Nut Flakes at least some mornings because it is more nutritious than Cocoa Blast.

Kalvin and his mother have come up with a fun way to determine which cereal Kalvin will have for breakfast. Each morning, Kalvin flips a coin. If the coin comes up heads, he will have Cocoa Blast. If he flips a tail, he will have Health Nut Flakes.

Problem 1.1

How many days in June do you think Kalvin will eat Cocoa Blast?

Explore this question by flipping a coin 30 times to determine Kalvin's cereal for each morning in June. Use Labsheet 1.1 to help you collect your data.

June						
1	**2**	**3**	**4**	**5**	**6**	
7	**8**	**9**	**10**	**11**	**12**	**13**
14	**15**	**16**	**17**	**18**	**19**	**20**
21	**22**	**23**	**24**	**25**	**26**	**27**
28	**29**	**30**				

For each day, record the result of the flip (H or T) and the percent of heads so far. Use the data to make a coordinate graph with the days from 1 to 30 on the *x*-axis and the percent of heads so far on the *y*-axis.

■ Problem 1.1 Follow-Up

Work with your teacher to combine the results from all the groups.

1. a. What fraction of the entire class's flips were heads?
   b. As you added more and more data, did the fraction of heads get closer to or further from $\frac{1}{2}$?
2. a. Based on what you found for June, how many times would you expect Kalvin to eat Cocoa Blast cereal in July?
   b. How many times would you expect Kalvin to eat Cocoa Blast cereal in a year?
3. Kalvin's mother told him that the chances of getting a head when you flip a coin are $\frac{1}{2}$. Does this mean that every time you flip a coin twice you will get one head and one tail? Explain your reasoning.

1.2 Analyzing Events

Kalvin found a penny near a railroad track. It looked flattened and a bit bent, so Kalvin assumed it must have been run over by a train. He decided to use this unusual penny for determining his breakfast.

Kalvin's mother became suspicious of the penny at the end of June because Kalvin had eaten Health Nut Flakes only seven times. She explained why she was suspicious. "With a fair coin, heads and tails are **equally likely** results. This means that you have the same chance of getting a head as a tail. I just don't think your coin is fair!"

Think about this!

Do you think heads and tails are equally likely with Kalvin's penny? How could Kalvin find out whether his coin is fair?

Kalvin was not quite sure what his mother meant by *equally likely,* so she made up an example to help explain it.

"Suppose everyone in our family wrote his or her name on a card and put the card in a hat. If you mixed up the cards and pulled one out, each name would have an equally likely chance of being picked. But suppose I put my name in the hat ten times. Then when you picked one card out of the hat, our names wouldn't all have an equal chance of being picked—my name would have a greater chance of being chosen than everyone else's name."

Problem 1.2

In A–H, decide whether the possible resulting events of each action are equally likely, and briefly explain your answer.

Action	Possible resulting events
A. You toss a soda can.	The can lands on its side, the can lands upside down, or the can lands right side up.
B. You roll a number cube.	1, 2, 3, 4, 5, or 6
C. You check the weather in Alaska on a December day.	It snows, it rains, or it does not rain or snow.
D. The Pittsburgh Steelers play a football game.	The Steelers win, the Steelers lose, or the Steelers tie.
E. A baby is born.	The baby is a boy or the baby is a girl.
F. A baby is born.	The baby is right-handed or the baby is left-handed.
G. You guess on a true/false question.	The answer is right or the answer is wrong.
H. You shoot a free throw.	You make the basket or you miss.

■ Problem 1.2 Follow-Up

1. Describe three other situations in which the possible resulting events are equally likely.

2. Describe three other situations in which the possible resulting events are not equally likely.

As you work on these ACE questions, use your calculator whenever you need it.

Applications

1. **a.** Sarah flipped a coin 50 times, and heads turned up 28 times. What fraction of the 50 flips of the coin turned up heads?

   b. If the coin is fair, and Sarah flips it 500 times, how many times should she expect it to come up heads?

2. Suppose Kalvin flipped a coin to determine his breakfast cereal every day starting on his twelfth birthday and continuing until his eighteenth birthday. How many times would you expect him to eat Cocoa Blast cereal?

3. Kalvin flipped a coin five days in a row and got tails every time. He told his mother there must be something wrong with the coin he was using. Do you think there is something wrong with the coin? How could Kalvin find out?

4. Len flipped a coin three times and got a head each time. What are the chances he will get a tail on his next toss? Explain your reasoning.

5. Is it possible to flip a coin 20 times and have it turn up heads 20 times? Is this likely to happen? Explain your reasoning.

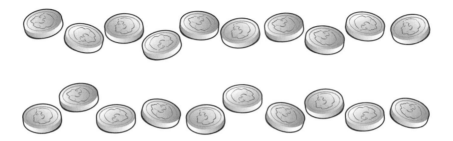

Connections

In 6–10, decide whether the resulting events are equally likely, and briefly explain your answer.

Action	Possible resulting events
6. Your phone rings at 9:00 P.M.	The caller is your best friend, the caller is a relative, or the caller is someone else.
7. You check the temperature in your area tomorrow.	The temperature is over 30°F or the temperature is under 30° F.
8. You spin this spinner.	The spinner lands on stripes, the spinner lands on hearts, or the spinner lands on dots.
9. Your teacher arrives at school in the morning.	Your teacher arrives on time or your teacher is late.
10. You find out how many car accidents occurred in your city or town yesterday.	There were fewer than five accidents, there were exactly five accidents, or there were more than five accidents.

In 11–14, use this graph, which shows the average number of tornadoes per year in several states:

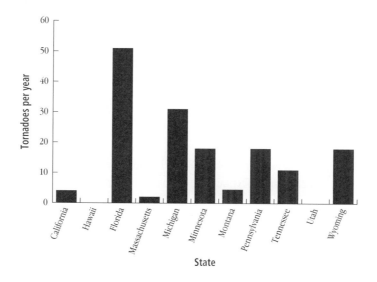

11. Is it equally likely for a tornado to hit somewhere in California as for a tornado to hit somewhere in Florida?

12. Is it equally likely for a tornado to hit somewhere in Minnesota as for a tornado to hit somewhere in Pennsylvania?

13. Is it equally likely for a tornado to hit somewhere in Massachusetts as for a tornado to hit somewhere in California?

14. Based on these data, is a person living in Montana in more danger of being hit by a tornado than a person living in Massachusetts? Explain your reasoning.

Extensions

15. Monday was the first day Kalvin flipped a coin to determine his cereal. During his first five days of flipping, he only had Cocoa Blast twice. One way that Kalvin could have done this was to have flipped heads on Monday and Tuesday and tails on Wednesday, Thursday, and Friday. We can write this as:

Monday	Tuesday	Wednesday	Thursday	Friday
H	H	T	T	T

Find every other way Kalvin could have flipped the coin during the week and had Cocoa Blast cereal twice. Explain how you know that you have found every way.

Mathematical Reflections

In this investigation, you experimented with coins to determine the fraction of heads and tails that occurred when you tossed a coin 30 times and when you combined the tosses from all the students in your class. You also investigated other situations to evaluate whether the possible resulting events were equally likely. These questions will help you summarize what you have learned:

1 What does it mean to say that the chances of getting a head when a coin is tossed are $\frac{1}{2}$?

2 If you experiment by tossing a coin and tallying the results, are 30 tosses as good as 500 tosses to predict the chances of a coin landing tails up? Explain why or why not.

3 a. What does it mean for the results of some action to be equally likely?

b. Give an example of an action in which the possible resulting events are equally likely.

c. Give an example of an action in which the possible resulting events are not equally likely.

4 If you toss a fair coin, is it *possible* to get 25 heads in a row? Is this *likely* to happen?

Think about your answers to these questions, discuss your ideas with other students and your teacher, and then write a summary of your findings in your journal.

More Experiments with Chance

Kalvin loves Cocoa Blast cereal so much that he wants to find something else to flip that will give him a better chance of eating it each morning.

2.1 Tossing Marshmallows

Kalvin looked through the kitchen cupboard and found a bag of large marshmallows and a bag of small marshmallows. He thought that a marshmallow might be a good thing to flip, and wondered which size would be better. Since Kalvin wants to eat Cocoa Blast most of the time, he needs to find a marshmallow that lands in one position—either on its side or on one of its flat ends—most of the time. Once he decides which type of marshmallow is better, he will ask his mother if he may use the marshmallow instead of a coin for deciding his cereal each morning.

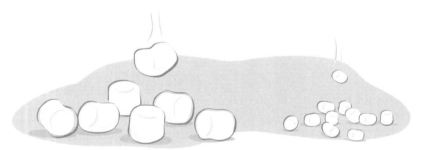

Did you know?

Originally, marshmallows were made from the root of the marsh mallow, a pink-flowered European perennial herb. Today, most marshmallows are made from corn syrup, sugar, albumen, and gelatin.

Problem 2.1

Experiment with large and small marshmallows to help you answer these questions:

A. Which size marshmallow should Kalvin use to determine which cereal he will eat? Explain your answer.

B. Which of the marshmallow's landing positions—end or side—should Kalvin use to represent Cocoa Blast? Explain your answer.

To conduct your experiment, toss each size of marshmallow 50 times. Keep track of your data carefully. Here is an example of how you might want to organize your data:

	Lands on an end	Lands on side
Large marshmallow	~~HHH~~ I	IIII
Small marshmallow		

Use the results of your experiment to help you answer questions A and B.

■ **Problem 2.1 Follow-Up**

Work with your teacher to combine results from all the groups.

1. a. For what fraction of your 50 tosses did the large marshmallow land on one of its ends? On its side?

   b. For what fraction of the class's tosses did the large marshmallow land on one of its ends? On its side?

   c. If you toss a large marshmallow once each day for a year, how many times would you expect it to land on its side?

2. a. For what fraction of your 50 tosses did the small marshmallow land on one of its ends? On its side?

   b. For what fraction of the class's tosses did the small marshmallow land on one of its ends? On its side?

   c. If you toss a small marshmallow once each day for a year, how many times would you expect it to land on its side?

3. Suppose Kalvin uses the marshmallow you chose—large or small—to decide his cereal each morning. He tosses the marshmallow twice, and it lands on an end once and on its side once. He says, "This marshmallow isn't any better than the penny—it lands on an end 50% of the time!" How would you convince Kalvin that the marshmallow is better for him to use than a penny?

Pondering Possible and Probable

Jon and Tat Ming are playing a coin-tossing game. To play the game, they take turns tossing three coins. If all three of the coins match, Jon scores a point. If only two of the coins match, Tat Ming scores a point. The first player to get 5 points wins. Both players have won the game several times, but Tat Ming seems to be winning more often. Jon says that he thinks the game is unfair. Tat Ming claims that the game is fair because both of them have a chance to win.

What do you think? Is the game fair as long as it is possible for each player to win?

Problem 2.2

Conduct an experiment to help you answer these questions:

A. Is it possible for Jon to win the game? Is it possible for Tat Ming to win the game? Explain your reasoning.

B. Who is more likely to win? Why?

C. Is this a fair game of chance? Explain.

To conduct your experiment, toss three coins 30 times. Keep track of the number of times three coins match and the number of times only two coins match. Be sure to organize your data and give reasons for your conclusions.

■ Problem 2.2 Follow-Up

1. If you tossed the coins 30 more times, how many times would you expect the three coins to match?

2. Toss the coins 30 more times. Compare this set of results to your first set of results. Did the three coins match about the same number of times in each experiment?

As you work on these ACE questions, use your calculator whenever you need it.

Applications

1. When you toss a marshmallow, are the chances that it will land on an end the same as the chances that it will land on its side? That is, are the two events equally likely? Explain your reasoning.

2. If Kalvin uses the size marshmallow that you chose in Problem 2.1, how many times a month would you expect him to eat Cocoa Blast? How many times a year? Explain your reasoning.

3. Dawn tossed a pawn from her chess set 5 times. It landed on its base 4 times and on its side only once. Dawn decided that the pawn lands on its base more often than on its side.

Andre tossed the same pawn 100 times. It landed on its base 28 times and on its side 72 times. Andre decided the pawn lands on its side more often than its base.

Based on Andre and Dawn's data, if you toss the pawn one more time, do you think it would be more likely to land on its base or its side? Why?

Connections

4. Meteorologists make many claims about the chances of rain, sun, and snow occurring. Waldo, the meteorologist from WARM radio, claims he is the best weather predictor in Sunspot, South Carolina. On the day before Sunspot High's graduation ceremony, Waldo said: "There is only a 10% chance of rain tomorrow!"

a. Ask at least two adults what they think Waldo's statement means, and write down their explanations.

b. Explain what you think Waldo's statement means.

c. If it rains on the graduation ceremony, was Waldo wrong? Why or why not?

You can use a fraction or a percent to indicate the chances that a particular event will occur. The larger the fraction or percent, the greater the chances that the event will happen. If an event is impossible, the chances that it will occur are 0, or 0%. If an event is sure to happen, the chances that it will occur are 1, or 100%.

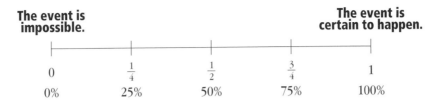

In 5–12, assign a number from 0 to 1 to indicate the chances that the event will occur, and explain your reasoning. For example, if the event is, "You will watch television tonight," your answer might be this:

I watch some television every night unless I have too much homework. So far today I do not have much homework. Therefore, I am about 95% sure that I will watch television tonight.

5. You will be absent from school at least one day during this school year.

6. You will have pizza for lunch one day this week.

7. It will snow on July 4 this year in Mexico.

8. You will get all the problems on your next math test correct.

9. The next baby born in your local hospital will be a girl.

10. The sun will set tonight.

11. You will win a coin-tossing game by tossing four coins, all of which must land heads.

12. You will toss a coin and get 100 tails in a row.

13. Make up two of your own events, and then estimate the chances that each event will happen.

In 14–16, use the chart below, which shows the percent of people who have been fired from a job for various reasons.

Reasons People Are Fired

Source: Michael D. Shook and Robert L. Shook, *The Book of Odds* (New York: Penguin books, 1991), p. 53.

14. If this chart represents 5000 people, about how many of these people were fired because they could not get along with others? Explain your reasoning.

15. What fraction of the people represented in the chart were fired for reasons other than incompetence? Explain more than one way that you could find the answer to this question.

16. If the chart represents 5000 people, about how many were fired for dishonesty or lying? Explain.

Extensions

17. While Yolanda was at a carnival, she watched a game in which a paper cup was tossed. If the cup landed upright, the player won $5. It cost $1 to play the game. Yolanda watched the cup being tossed 50 times. The cup landed on its side 32 times, upside down 13 times, and upright 5 times.

    a. If Yolanda plays the game 10 times, about how many times can she expect to win? How many times can she expect to lose?

    b. Would you expect Yolanda to have more or less money at the end of 10 games than she had before? Why?

Mathematical Reflections

In this investigation, you conducted an experiment that involved tossing marshmallows. You also experimented with a coin-tossing game to determine whether it was fair. These questions will help you summarize what you have learned:

1 When you toss a large marshmallow, is it equally likely to land on an end as its side? What evidence can you use to help you answer this question?

2 How would you use the results of your work in Problem 2.1 to predict how many times a small marshmallow would land on its side if you tossed it 1000 times?

3 What does it mean for a two-person game of chance to be fair?

4 In a–f, give an example of an event that would have about the given chances of occurring.

a.	0%	**b.**	10%
c.	25%	**d.**	50%
e.	75%	**f.**	100%

Think about your answers to these questions, discuss your ideas with other students and your teacher, and then write a summary of your findings in your journal.

INVESTIGATION 3

Using Spinners to Predict Chances

School is out for the summer! Kalvin thinks he should be allowed to stay up until midnight every night since he doesn't have to get up for school in the morning. His father disagrees; he thinks Kalvin will have more energy for all the things he plans to do in the summer if he goes to bed earlier.

3.1 Bargaining for a Better Bedtime

Kalvin decided to make a spinner that he hopes his father will let him use to determine his bedtime each night. To encourage his father to go for his idea, Kalvin put three 10:00 and three 11:00 spaces on the spinner. However, he used the biggest space for 12:00, and he hopes the spinner will land on that space most often. Kalvin's spinner is shown on the next page.

Problem 3.1

Conduct an experiment to help you answer these questions.

A. Kalvin prefers to go to bed at midnight, so he wants his spinner to land on 12:00 more often than anywhere else. Is it likely that this spinner will allow him to achieve this goal? Explain.

B. Suppose Kalvin's father lets him use this spinner to determine his bedtime. What are Kalvin's chances of going to bed at 12:00? Explain how you determined your answer.

To conduct your experiment, use Labsheet 3.1 and a bobby pin or paper clip to make a spinner like Kalvin's. Spin the spinner, and keep track of the data you collect. Continue spinning the spinner and recording data until you are confident about your answers to the questions above.

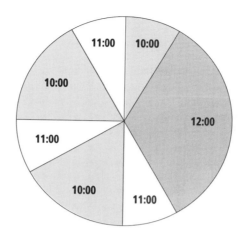

■ Problem 3.1 Follow-Up

1. After how many spins did you decide to stop spinning? Why? If you continued to spin the spinner, do you think your answers to Problem 3.1 would change? Why or why not?

2. a. How many times did you spin the spinner? How many times did the spinner land on 10:00? On 11:00? On 12:00?

  b. Based on your data, what fraction of the time will Kalvin go to bed at 10:00? At 11:00? At 12:00?

  c. Summer vacation is 90 days long. If Kalvin uses this spinner every night, how many nights do you think he will go to bed at 10:00? At 11:00? At 12:00? Explain your reasoning.

3. In a–c, use your angle ruler or other ways of reasoning to analyze Kalvin's spinner. You can set your angle ruler on the spinner to measure the angle of each section.

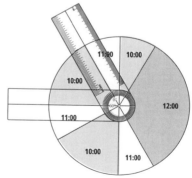

  a. What fraction of the area of the spinner is made up of 10:00 spaces? Of 11:00 spaces? Of 12:00 spaces?

  b. How do the fractions from part a compare with the fractions you found in part b of question 2?

  c. How do the fractions from part a compare with the fractions from the data your entire class collected for Problem 3.1?

As you work on these ACE questions, use your calculator whenever you need it.

Applications

1. In a–g, use the spinner on Labsheet 3.ACE.

a. Use a paper clip or bobby pin to spin the spinner 30 times. What fraction of your spins landed on a space with hearts? With dots? With stripes?

b. Use your angle ruler or another method to analyze the spinner. What fraction of the spinner is covered with hearts? With dots? With stripes? Explain how you found each fraction.

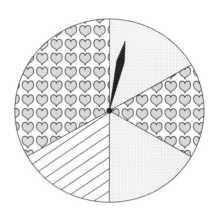

c. Compare your answers to parts a and b. Would you expect these answers to be the same? Why or why not?

d. If you were to spin the spinner 300 times instead of 30 times, do you think your answers would become closer to or further from the fractions you found in part b? Explain your reasoning.

e. When you spin the spinner, are the three possible outcomes—landing on a space with hearts, landing on a space with dots, and landing on a space with stripes—equally likely? Explain.

f. Suppose you use the spinner to play a game with a friend. Your friend scores a point every time the spinner lands on a space with hearts. What spaces should you score on to make the game fair? Explain your reasoning.

g. Suppose you use this spinner to play a three-person game. Player A scores if the spinner lands on stripes. Player B scores if the spinner lands on hearts. Player C scores if the spinner lands on dots. How could you allocate points so the game would be fair?

2. Mollie is designing a game for a class project. She made the three spinners shown here and experimented with them to see which one she liked best for her game. She spun each spinner 20 times and wrote down her results, but she forgot to record which spinner gave which set of data. Which spinner most likely gave each data set? Explain your answer.

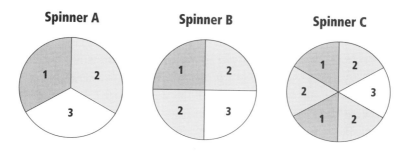

Spinner A **Spinner B** **Spinner C**

First data set

1 2 3 2 1 1 2 1 2 2 2 3 2 1 2 2 2 3 2 2

Second data set

2 3 1 1 3 3 3 1 1 2 3 2 2 2 1 1 1 3 3 3

Third data set

1 2 3 3 1 2 2 2 3 2 1 2 2 2 3 2 2 3 2 1

3. Three people play a game on each of the spinners in question 2. Player 1 scores a point if the spinner lands on an area marked 1, player 2 scores a point if the spinner lands on an area marked 2, and player 3 scores a point if the spinner lands on an area marked 3.

a. On which spinner or spinners would the game be a fair game of chance? Why?

b. Choose a spinner that you think would not make a fair game of chance with these rules. Then, change the scoring rules to make the game fair by assigning different points for landing on the different numbers. Explain why your point system works.

4. a. Create a spinner and a set of rules for a two-person game that would be a fair game.

b. Create a spinner and a set of rules for a two-person game that would not be fair. Explain how you could change the rules to make the game fair.

Connections

In 5–9, use the data below to answer the question. If there is not enough information to answer a question, explain what additional information you would need.

- In 1988, 47,093 people were killed in car crashes and 3486 people were killed in motorcycle crashes in the United States.
- In the U.S., 40% of all deaths of people between the ages of 15 and 19 result from motor-vehicle crashes. Alcohol is involved in about half of these crashes.
- Males outnumber females as fatal-crash victims by an average of 2 to 1.
- 55% of motorcycle deaths occurred on weekends.
- In 1988, the car with the lowest death rate was the Volvo 740/760 four-door, while the car with the highest death rate was the Chevrolet Corvette.

Source: Michael D. Shook and Robert L. Shook, *The Book of Odds* (New York: Penguin Books, 1991), p. 90.

---

5. Which is safer to drive, a car or a motorcycle?

6. What percent of all deaths of 15-year-olds to 19-year-olds result from alcohol-related motor-vehicle crashes?

7. Is a particular motorcycle rider more likely to be in a fatal crash during the week or during the weekend?

8. Are males worse drivers than females?

9. Your family is trying to decide which used car to buy. Are you less likely to have an accident if you buy a Volvo 740 or Volvo 760 than if you buy a Chevrolet Corvette?

Extensions

10. Design a spinner with five spaces so that the chances of landing in each space are equally likely. Give the number of degrees in the central angle of each space.

11. Design a spinner with five spaces so that the chances of landing in each space are not equally likely. Give the number of degrees in the central angle of each space.

12. Design a spinner with five spaces so that the chances of landing in one space are twice the chances of landing in each of the other four spaces. Give the number of degrees in the central angle of each space.

Mathematical Reflections

In this investigation, you experimented with spinners. When you spin a spinner, you cannot know in advance which section it will land on, but you can conduct an experiment to gather data that will help you to predict what will happen over many trials. These questions will help you summarize what you have learned:

1. Suppose that out of 400 spins, a spinner lands 306 times on region A and 94 times on region B. What can you say about the spinner? What might the spinner look like? How confident are you in your answer? Explain.

2. Suppose that out of 20 spins, a spinner lands 13 times on region A and 7 times on region B. What can you say about the spinner? What might the spinner look like? How confident are you in your answer? Explain.

3. Describe how you could construct a spinner with four equally likely outcomes.

4. Look back at Kalvin's bedtime spinner for Problem 3.1. Is it possible that the spinner will land on 12:00 each night for a month? Is it likely?

Think about your answers to these questions, discuss your ideas with other students and your teacher, and then write a summary of your findings in your journal.

Theoretical Probabilities

In the last three investigations, you worked with problems involving the chances that a particular event would occur. Another word for chance is *probability*. So far, you have determined probabilities by doing experiments and collecting data. For example, you flipped a coin many times and found that the probability of getting a head is $\frac{1}{2}$. You also discovered that the more trials that were done, the better the probabilities that you found could predict future outcomes.

The results of the coin-flipping experiment probably did not surprise you. You already knew that when a coin is flipped there are two possible outcomes—heads and tails—and that each outcome is equally likely. In fact, you could have found the probability of getting a head by *analyzing* the possible outcomes instead of by *experimenting*. Since there are two equally likely outcomes, and one of these outcomes is a head, the probability of getting a head is 1 out of 2, or $\frac{1}{2}$.

In this investigation, you will look at some other situations in which you can find the probabilities both by experimenting and by analyzing the possible outcomes.

4.1 Predicting to Win

In the last 5 minutes of the Gee Whiz Everyone Wins! television game show, all the members of the studio audience are called to the stage to select a block randomly from a bucket containing an unknown number of red, yellow, and blue blocks. Before drawing, each contestant is asked to predict the color of the block he or she will draw. If the guess is correct, the contestant wins a prize. After each draw, the block is put back into the bucket.

Think about this!

Suppose you are a member of the audience. Is there an advantage to being called to the stage first? Is there an advantage to being called last? Why?

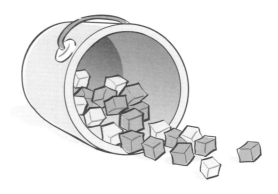

Problem 4.1

Play the block-guessing game with your class. Your teacher will act as the host of the game show, and you and your classmates will be the contestants. Keep a record of the number of times each color is drawn. Play the game until you think you can predict with certainty the chances of each color being drawn.

A. In your class experiment, how many blue blocks were drawn? Red blocks? Yellow blocks? What was the total number of blocks drawn?

B. The probability of drawing a red block can be written as P(red). Find all three probabilities based on the data you collected in your experiment.

   P(red) =   P(yellow) =   P(blue) =

Now, your teacher will dump out the blocks so you can see them.

C. How many of the blocks are red? Yellow? Blue? How many blocks are there altogether?

D. Find the fraction of the total blocks that are red, the fraction that are yellow, and the fraction that are blue.

■ **Problem 4.1 Follow-Up**

The probabilities you computed in part B are called **experimental probabilities** because you found them by experimenting. The fractions you found in part D are called **theoretical probabilities.** You find theoretical probabilities by analyzing the possible outcomes rather than by experimenting.

If all the outcomes of an action are equally likely, then the theoretical probability of an event is computed with this formula:

$$\frac{\text{number of favorable outcomes}}{\text{number of possible outcomes}}$$

where *favorable outcomes* are the outcomes in which you are interested.

For example, if you want to find the probability of drawing a red block, a red block is a favorable outcome. If a bucket has a total of six blocks, and two of the blocks are red, the theoretical probability of drawing a red block is $\frac{2}{6}$.

6 possible outcomes (blocks)
2 favorable outcomes (red blocks)

Theoretical probability
of drawing a red block $= \frac{2}{6}$

1. Compare the *experimental probabilities* you found in part B to the *theoretical probabilities* you found in part D. Are the experimental and theoretical probabilities for each color of block close to each other? Do you think they should be close? Why or why not?

2. **a.** When you drew a block from the bucket, did each *block* have an equally likely chance of being chosen? Explain.
   b. When you drew a block from the bucket, did each *color* have an equally likely chance of being chosen? Explain.

3. Look back at the "Think about this!" on page 30. Is there an advantage to being the first person to draw from the bucket? To being the last person to draw?

4. In the Gee Whiz Everyone Wins! game show, contestants select a block randomly from the bucket. What do you think *random* means?

4.2 Drawing More Blocks

Your teacher put eight blocks in a bucket. All the blocks are the same size. Three are yellow, four are red, and one is blue.

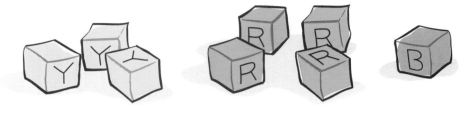

Problem 4.2

A. When you draw a block from the bucket, are the chances equally likely that it will be yellow, red, or blue? Explain your answer.

B. What is the total number of blocks? How many blocks of each color are there?

C. What is the *theoretical probability* of drawing a blue block? A yellow block? A red block? Explain how you found each answer.

Now, as a class or in groups, take turns drawing a block from the bucket. After each draw, return the block to the bucket. Keep a record of the blocks that are drawn. If you work in a group, take turns drawing blocks until you have 40 trials.

D. Based on your data, what is the *experimental probability* of drawing a blue block? A yellow block? A red block?

E. Compare the theoretical probabilities you found in part C to the experimental probabilities you found in part D. Are the probabilities for each color close? Are they the same? If not, why not?

■ Problem 4.2 Follow-Up

Suppose you and your classmates each took three turns drawing a block from the bucket, replacing the block each time, and then used the large amount of data you collected to find new experimental probabilities for drawing each color. You found the theoretical probability of drawing each color in part C. Do you think these new experimental probabilities would be closer to the theoretical probabilities than the experimental probabilities you found in part D were? Explain your reasoning.

Winning the Bonus Prize

All the winners from the Gee Whiz Everyone Wins! game show get an opportunity to compete for a bonus prize. Each winner draws one block from each of two bags, both of which contain one red, one yellow, and one blue block. The contestant must predict which color she or he will draw from each of the two bags. If the prediction is correct, the contestant wins a $10,000 bonus prize!

Bag 1   Bag 2

Problem 4.3

What are a contestant's chances of winning?

Conduct an experiment to help you answer this question. Keep track of the pairs of colors that are drawn, and make sure you collect enough data to give you good estimates of the probability of drawing each pair. Remember, contestants must guess the color of the block they will pick from each bag. That means you will have to count (a blue from bag 1, a red from bag 2) as a different pair from (a red from bag 1, a blue from bag 2).

A. Based on your experiment, what are a contestant's chances of winning?

B. List all the possible pairs that can be drawn from the bags. Are each of these pairs equally likely? Explain your answer.

C. What is the theoretical probability of each pair being drawn? Explain your answer.

D. How do the theoretical probabilities compare with your experimental probabilities? Explain any differences.

■ Problem 4.3 Follow-Up

Suppose you are a contestant on the show, and you have already won a mountain bike, a fantastic portable CD player, a vacation to Hawaii, and a one-year supply of Glimmer toothpaste. You have just played the bonus round and lost, but the host makes the following offer: you can draw from the two bags again, but this time you do not need to predict the color. If the two colors match, you will win $5000. If the two colors do not match, you must return all the prizes you have won. Would you accept this offer? Explain why or why not.

As you work on these ACE questions, use your calculator whenever you need it.

Applications

1. A bucket contains one green block, one red block, and two yellow blocks.

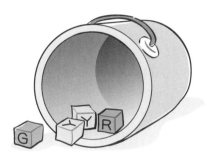

a. Find the theoretical probability of choosing each color.

P(green) = _____   P(yellow) = _____   P(red) = _____

b. Find the sum of the probabilities in part a.

c. What is the probability of *not* drawing a red block? Explain how you found your answer.

d. What do you get when you add the probability of *getting* a red to the probability of *not getting* a red?

e. What happens to the probability of drawing a red block if the number of blocks of each color is doubled?

f. What happens to the probability of drawing a red block if two more blocks of each color are added to the original bucket?

g. How many blocks of which colors would you have to add to the original bucket to make the probability of drawing a red block $\frac{1}{2}$?

2. A bag contains exactly three blocks, all blue.

    a. What is the probability of drawing a blue block?

    b. What is the probability of *not* drawing a blue block?

    c. What is the probability of drawing a yellow block?

3. A bubble-gum machine contains 25 gum balls. There are 12 green, 6 purple, 2 orange, and 5 yellow gum balls.

    a. Find the theoretical probability of getting each color.

        P(green) = _____   P(purple) = _____

        P(orange) = _____   P(yellow) = _____

    b. What is the sum of the probabilities for all the possible colors?

        P(green) + P(purple) + P(orange) + P(yellow) = _____

    c. Write each of the probabilities in part a as a percent.

        P(green) = _____   P(purple) = _____

        P(orange) = _____   P(yellow) = _____

    d. What is the sum of all the probabilities as a percent?

    e. What do you think the sum of the probabilities for all possible outcomes must be for any situation?

4. **a.** What do you think the word *probability* means?

    b. Describe some situations in which probability is important.

5. a. If two people do an experiment to estimate the probability of a particular event occurring, will they get the same result? Explain why or why not.

b. If two people analyze a situation to find the theoretical probability of an event occurring, and each person does a correct analysis, will they get the same result? Explain why or why not.

c. If one person uses an experiment to estimate the probability of an event occurring and another person analyzes the situation to find the theoretical probability of the event occurring, will they get the same result? Explain why or why not.

Connections

6. A bag contains several marbles. Some are red, some are white, and some are blue. Carlos counted the marbles and found that the theoretical probability of drawing a red marble is $\frac{1}{6}$ and the theoretical probability of drawing a white marble is $\frac{1}{3}$.

a. What is the smallest number of marbles that could be in the bag?

b. Could the bag contain 48 marbles? If so, how many of each color must it contain?

c. If the bag contains 4 red marbles and 8 white marbles, how many blue marbles must it contain?

d. How can you tell what the probability of a drawing a blue marble is?

7. Katherine's class made this line plot of the first letters in the first names of all the students in her class.

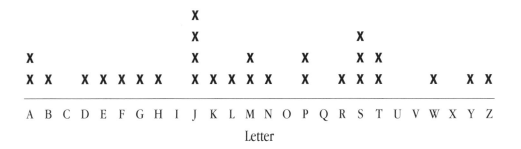

                               X
                               X   X
X   X   X   X   X X
X X   X X X X   X X X X   X   X X X   X   X X

A B C D E F G H I J K L M N O P Q R S T U V W X Y Z

Letter

    a. If you randomly select a student from Katherine's class, what is the probability you will choose someone whose first name begins with J?

    b. If you randomly select a student from Katherine's class, what is the probability you will choose someone whose first name begins with a letter that occurs after F in the alphabet, but before T?

    c. If you randomly select a student from Katherine's class, what is the probability that you will choose Katherine?

    d. Suppose two more people joined the class, Melvin and Theo. Now if you randomly select a student from the class, what is the probability you will choose someone whose first name begins with J?

8. Suppose you were to spin this spinner and then roll this six-sided number cube.

a. Make an organized list of the possible outcomes of a spin of the spinner and a roll of the number cube. For example, the outcome that is showing is this:

Spinner   Number cube

2   2

b. What is the probability you would get a 2 on both the number cube and the spinner? Explain your reasoning.

c. What is the probability you would get a *factor* of 2 on both the number cube and the spinner?

d. What is the probability you would get a *multiple* of 2 on both the number cube and the spinner?

Extensions

9. The cook in the Casimer Middle School cafeteria is in a bad mood! When Jonalyn went through the lunch line, she tried to tell the cook what she wanted, but the cook just mumbled, "Appreciate what you get!" Jonalyn thinks some of the things on the menu are really gross. Her favorite lunch is a grilled cheese sandwich, carrots, and a chocolate chip cookie.

Lunch at Casimer consists of one sandwich, one vegetable, and one cookie. The cook has an equal number of each kind of sandwich, vegetable, and cookie. She is not paying any attention to how she puts the lunches together.

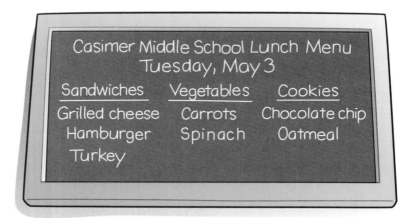

Casimer Middle School Lunch Menu
Tuesday, May 3

Sandwiches	Vegetables	Cookies
Grilled cheese	Carrots	Chocolate chip
Hamburger	Spinach	Oatmeal
Turkey		

a. How many different lunches are possible? Explain your answer.

b. What is the probability that Jonalyn will get her favorite lunch? Explain your reasoning.

c. What is the probability that Jonalyn will get at least *one* of her favorite things? Explain your reasoning.

10. Make up a bag containing 12 objects—such as blocks or marbles—of the same size and shape. Use three or four different colors.

a. Describe the contents of your bag.

b. Determine the *theoretical probability* of drawing each color by analyzing the bag's contents.

c. Conduct an experiment to determine the *experimental probability* of drawing each color. Carefully describe how you did your experiment and recorded your results.

d. How do the two types of probability you found compare?

Mathematical Reflections

In this investigation, you studied a new way to find probabilities. You now have two ways to get information about the chances, or probability, that something will occur. You can design an experiment and collect data (to find experimental probabilities), or you can think about a situation, analyzing the outcomes carefully to see exactly what might happen (to find theoretical probabilities). These questions will help you summarize what you have learned:

1 How can you find the experimental probability of an event? Why is this called an *experimental probability?*

2 How can you find the theoretical probability of an event? Why is this called a *theoretical probability?*

3 When you tossed coins to figure out which cereal Kalvin would have for breakfast, you found experimental probabilities by counting heads and tails. You might have noticed that the more trials you did, the closer your experimental probability came to the theoretical probability of $\frac{1}{2}$. Do you think that conducting more trials will always bring your experimental probability closer to the theoretical probability? Why or why not?

4 Think of some situations in which it would be easier to find theoretical probabilities than experimental probabilities. Explain your reasoning.

5 Think of some situations in which it would be easier to find experimental probabilities than theoretical probabilities. Explain your reasoning.

Think about your answers to these questions, discuss your ideas with other students and your teacher, and then write a summary of your findings in your journal.

Analyzing Games of Chance

Have you ever figured out a strategy for winning a game? In this activity, you will play a two-team game called Roller Derby. As you play, think about strategies for winning and the probabilities associated with those strategies.

5.1 Playing Roller Derby

In a game of Roller Derby, two teams compete. Each team needs a game board with columns numbered 1 through 12, a pair of number cubes, and 12 markers (like pennies, buttons, or small blocks).

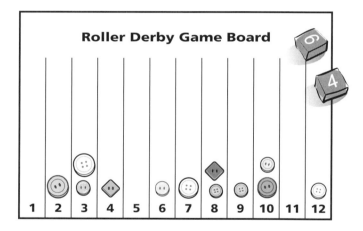

Roller Derby Rules

1. Each team places its 12 markers into the columns in any way it chooses.
2. Each team rolls a number cube. The team with the highest roll goes first.
3. Teams take turns rolling the two number cubes and removing a marker from the column with the same number as the total shown on the cubes. If the column is empty, the team does not get to remove a marker.
4. The first team to remove all the markers from its board wins.

Problem 5.1

What is a good strategy for placing your markers in the 12 columns on the game board?

Play the game at least twice before answering this question. As you play, keep a record of the strategies you use.

■ Problem 5.1 Follow-Up

1. a. Find a systematic way to list all the possible outcomes (number pairs) of rolling two number cubes and the sums for each of these outcomes. Analyze your list carefully before answering b–e.

   b. What sums are possible when you roll two cubes?

   c. Which sum or sums occur most often?

   d. How many ways can you get a sum of 6? A sum of 2?

   e. Are all the sums equally likely? Explain.

2. Now that you have analyzed the possible outcomes, do you have any new ideas for a strategy for winning Roller Derby? Explain. If time allows, play the game again using your new strategy.

As you work on these ACE questions, use your calculator whenever you need it.

Applications

1. Eleanor is playing Roller Derby with Carlos. Eleanor placed all of her markers in column 1, and Carlos placed all of his markers in column 12. What is the probability that Eleanor will win? What is the probability that Carlos will win? Explain your reasoning.

2. When you play the game of Monopoly®, you sometimes end up in "jail." One way to get out of jail is to roll a double (two cubes that match). What is the probability of getting out of jail on your turn by rolling a double? Use your list of possible outcomes of rolling two number cubes to help you answer this question. Explain your reasoning.

Connections

In 3–9, use your list of possible outcomes of rolling two number cubes to help you answer the question.

3. When two number cubes are rolled, what is the probability that their sum will be 3?

4. When two number cubes are rolled, what is the probability that their sum will be greater than 9?

5. When two number cubes are rolled, what is the probability that their sum will be a multiple of 4?

6. When two number cubes are rolled, what is the probability that their sum will be a common multiple of 2 and 3?

7. When two number cubes are rolled, what is the probability that their sum will be a prime number? Explain.

8. Which has a greater probability of being rolled on a pair of number cubes—a sum that is a factor of 6 or a sum that is a multiple of 6? Explain.

9. Humberto and Kate are playing a game called Odds and Evens. To play the game, they roll two number cubes. If the sum is odd, Humberto scores a point. If the sum is even, Kate scores a point. Is this a fair game of chance? Why or why not?

10. Suppose that Humberto and Kate play a game called Evens and Odds. (This game is similar to the game in question 9, except it involves *products* instead of *sums*.) To play the game, they roll two number cubes. If the product is odd, Kate scores a point. If the product is even, Humberto scores a point.

    a. Make an organized table of the possible products of two number cubes.

    b. What is the probability that Kate will win? What is the probability that Humberto will win? Explain your reasoning.

    c. Is this a fair game? If it is fair, explain why. If it is not fair, tell how you could change the points scored by each player so that it would be fair.

    d. What is the probability that the product rolled will be a prime number?

    e. What is the probability that the product rolled will be a factor of 30?

    f. What is the probability that the product rolled will be greater than 18?

11. The cooks at Kyla's school made the spinners shown below to help them determine the lunch menu. They let the students take turns spinning to determine the daily menu. In a–c, decide which spinner you would choose, and explain your reasoning.

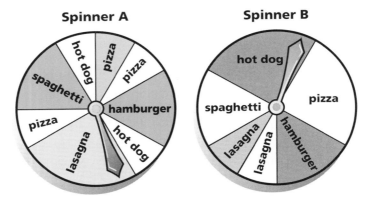

Spinner A   **Spinner B**

a. Your favorite lunch is pizza.

b. Your favorite lunch is lasagna.

c. Your favorite lunch is hot dogs.

12. Abigail and Christopher are playing a game with two coins. To play the game, they each flip a coin at the same time. If the two coins match, Christopher gets a point; if they do not match, Abigail gets a point. Is this a fair game of chance? Explain your reasoning.

13. Alex and Fumi are playing a game with three coins. To play the game, they flip all three coins at the same time. If the three coins match, Fumi gets a point. If they do not all match, Alex gets a point. Is this a fair game of chance? Explain your reasoning.

Extensions

14. Make up three probability questions that can be answered by looking at your list of possible outcomes of rolling two number cubes. Then answer your own questions.

In 15–18, suppose Selina has just rolled three number cubes.

15. What is the probability that all three cubes match? Explain your reasoning.

16. What is the probability that the sum of the cubes is less than 5? Explain your reasoning.

17. What is the probability that the sum of the cubes is more than 2? Explain your reasoning.

18. What is the probability that the product of the cubes is prime? Explain your reasoning.

Mathematical Reflections

In this investigation, you played a game of chance that involved rolling a pair of number cubes and computing the sum of the cubes. These questions will help you summarize what you have learned:

1. What are the possible outcomes when you roll one number cube? Is each of these outcomes equally likely?

2. When you roll a pair of number cubes, how many different pairs of numbers can occur? Is each pair equally likely?

3. In the Roller Derby game, you added the numbers on the faces of two number cubes. How many different sums were possible? Were they all equally likely? Explain.

4. Suppose you roll two number cubes and add the results. What is the sum of the probabilities of all of these outcomes? Explain your answer.

Think about your answers to these questions, discuss your ideas with other students and your teacher, and then write a summary of your findings in your journal.

More About Games of Chance

Have you ever tried to win a contest? Stores and restaurants often have contests to attract customers. Knowing something about probability can often help you figure out your chances of winning these contests.

6.1 Scratching Spots

Tawanda's Toys is having a contest! Any customer who spends at least $10 receives a scratch-off game card. Each card has five gold spots that reveal the names of video games when they are scratched. Exactly two spots match on each card. A customer may scratch off only two spots on a card; if the spots match, the customer wins the video game under those spots.

Problem 6.1

If you play this game once, what is your probability of winning? To answer this question, do the following two things:

A. Create a way to simulate Tawanda's contest, and find the experimental probability of winning.

B. Analyze the different ways you can scratch off two spots, and find the theoretical probability of winning a prize with one game card.

■ Problem 6.1 Follow-Up

1. a. If you play Tawanda's scratch-off game 100 times, how many video games would you expect to win?

b. How much money would you have to spend to play the game 100 times?

2. Tawanda wants to be sure she will not lose money on her contest. The video games she gives as prizes cost her about $15 each. Will Tawanda lose money on this contest? Why or why not?

3. Suppose you play Tawanda's game 20 times and never win. Would you conclude that the game is unfair? For example, would you think that there were not two matching spots on every card? Why or why not?

As you work on these ACE questions, use your calculator whenever you need it.

Applications

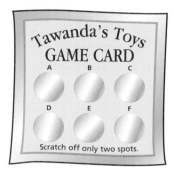

1. Tawanda thinks there should be fewer winners in her contest. She has decided to order new cards with six spots. Two of the spots on each card match. What is the probability that a person who plays the game once will win a prize?

2. The Kalikak High School Science Club is hosting a carnival to raise money for a trip to the national science fair in San Diego, California. They will have a game called Making Purple at the carnival. The game involves the two spinners below. A player spins spinner A and spinner B. If the player gets red on spinner A and blue on spinner B, the player wins, because red and blue together make purple.

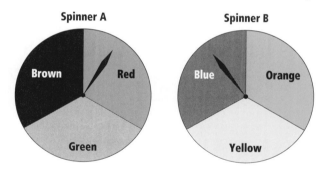

a. List the outcomes that are possible when both spinners are spun. Are these outcomes equally likely? Explain your reasoning.

b. What is the theoretical probability that a player will "make purple"? Explain.

c. If 100 people play this game, how many people would you expect to win? Explain your reasoning.

d. The science club will charge $1.00 per spin. A player who makes purple wins $5.00. If 100 people play, how much money would you expect the science club to make?

Connections

3. The Federal Trade Commission is the part of the U.S. government that makes rules for businesses that buy and sell things. The Federal Trade Commission Act states that an advertisement may be found unlawful if it could deceive someone.

The FTC doesn't need to prove that anyone was actually deceived by an advertisement to decide that it is deceptive and unlawful. To decide whether an ad is deceptive, the FTC considers the "general impression" it makes on a "reasonable person." So even if every statement in an ad is true, the ad is deceptive if it gives an overall false impression. (For example, companies cannot show cows in margarine commercials, because it gives the false impression that margarine is a dairy product.)

a. Suppose Tawanda placed this advertisement in the newspaper.

According to the Federal Trade Commission Act, do you think it is legal for Tawanda to say that "every card is a winner"? Explain your answer.

b. Design a better advertisement for Tawanda that will make people excited about the contest but will not lead some to think they will win every time they play.

4. A sugarless gum company used to have an advertisement that stated:

> *Nine out of ten dentists surveyed recommend sugarless gum for their patients who chew gum.*

Do you think this statement means that 90% of dentists think their patients should chew sugarless gum? Explain your reasoning.

5. Suppose you are the coach of the U.S. all-star baseball team. You need to pick someone to pinch hit for the pitcher. You look over the records of your players and narrow your choices to these three:

Player	At bats	Hits
George Brett	9789	3005
Kirby Puckett	5645	1812
Wade Boggs	6213	2098

Source: Mike Meserole (ed.) *1993 Sports Almanac* (Boston: Houghton Mifflin), p. 109.

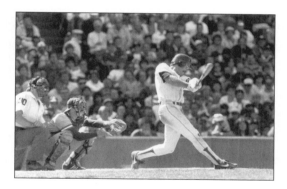

a. What percent of Brett's at bats were hits? Puckett's? Boggs'?

b. Which player has the greatest chance of getting a hit on his next turn at bat? Explain your reasoning.

6. Willie Mae has flown over a million miles as an airline passenger without ever being in an accident. Kobie has never flown in an airplane. Both are planning to take a trip in an airplane.

    a. Who do you think is more likely to be in an airplane accident? Why?

    b. Does your answer to part a make sense if Willie Mae and Kobie get on the same airplane? Explain.

7. A-1 Trucks used this graph to show that their trucks last longer than other companies' trucks. A-1 Trucks is company A on the graph.

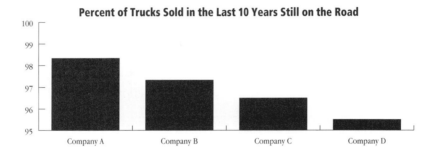

Percent of Trucks Sold in the Last 10 Years Still on the Road

    a. The bar for company A is about six times as tall as the bar for company D. Does this mean that the chances of one of company A's trucks lasting 10 years are about six times as great as the chances of one of company D's trucks lasting 10 years? Explain your reasoning.

    b. If you wanted to buy a truck, would this graph convince you to buy a truck from company A? Why or why not?

Extensions

8. Refer to the discussion of the Federal Trade Commission Act in question 3 above. Find an advertisement that might be deceptive, and bring it in to discuss with your class. You might consider contacting the company, telling them why you think the ad might be deceptive, and asking for proof of their claims. The company is required by law to respond.

In 9–11, imagine that you help businesses by designing promotional contests. Design a contest for each company. Each contest should help the company attract customers, but not make the company lose money. For each contest, explain the rules, including any requirements for entering the contest, and design an advertisement for the contest.

9. The Fashion Gallery is a small clothing store. Its manager would like you to design a contest in which 1 of every 30 players wins a prize.

10. Supermart Superstores is a chain of supermarkets with over 100 locations. The director of operations would like to have a contest with a $100,000 grand prize!

11. Ally's AutoWorld sells new and used cars. Ally would like to have a contest with lots of winners and fairly big prizes. She would like about one out of every ten players to win a $500 prize.

Mathematical Reflections

In this investigation, you examined what you might *expect* to gain or lose when you play a game of chance. These questions will help you summarize what you have learned:

1 How can you find the number of times you would expect to win if you play Tawanda's game on a five-spot card 1000 times?

2 How can you find the number of times you would expect to win if you play Tawanda's game on a six-spot card 1000 times?

3 Suppose that your probability of winning a game at the school fair is $\frac{1}{6}$. It costs 10¢ to play the game, and the prize for winning is 50¢. Describe how you could decide whether this is a fair game of chance. (A *fair game of chance* is one in which you would expect to break even in the long run.)

Think about your answers to these questions, discuss your ideas with other students and your teacher, and then write a summary of your findings in your journal.

Probability and Genetics

Have you ever wondered why your eyes and your hair are the color they are? Scientists who study traits such as eye and hair color are called *geneticists*. Geneticists use probabilities to predict the occurrence of certain traits in children based on the traits of their parents, grandparents, and other relatives.

One interesting genetic trait is the ability to curl the tongue into a U shape. In this investigation you will explore the question, What are the chances that someone can curl his or her tongue?

7.1 Curling Your Tongue

One day Kalvin was teasing his little sister Kyla, and he stuck his tongue out at her. She noticed that his tongue was curled into a U shape. Kyla said, "That's weird, Kalvin—your tongue looks goofy!"

Kalvin looked in the mirror and noticed that he *could* curl his tongue. He wondered how many other people can curl their tongues.

Problem 7.1

What fraction of students in your class can curl their tongues?

With your class, conduct a survey of the students in the class to investigate tongue curling and to answer this question.

■ Problem 7.1 Follow-Up

What is the probability that a student you choose randomly from the hallway of your school will be able to curl his or her tongue?

7.2 Tracing Traits

Surveys are often used to gather information about a group of people, or a *population.* For example, if scientists want to find out the percent of people in a population that have a certain disease, they might conduct a survey of a large number of people. Sometimes scientists are interested in the probability that a *specific person* has a certain trait or will have a particular disease. In these situations, geneticists study the traits of the person's parents, grandparents, and other family members.

Have you ever heard of *genes?* (We don't mean the kind you wear!) Your parents gave you a unique set of genes that determines many of your traits, such as your eye color, whether you are color blind, whether you will be bald someday, and whether you can curl your tongue.

Did you know?

Psychologists have long been interested in investigating how great a part genes play in determining human intelligence. One way of learning more about this topic is by studying identical twins who have been separated at a young age and raised in very different kinds of homes. Studies have shown that such twins showed remarkable similarities in intelligence. One study showed that twins raised in different home environments had IQ scores almost as close as those of identical twins raised in the same home. Since identical twins have the exact same set of genes, these results support the idea that genes play a key role in human intelligence.

Even more surprising was learning that these twins also were very similar in physical appearance, dress, mannerisms, preferences, attitudes, and even personality. Many of the twins had similar hairstyles, moved their hands in similar ways, or had the same attitude toward their jobs.

Geneticists use the word *allele* to mean a special form of a gene. For example, you have two alleles that determine whether or not you can curl your tongue. Each of your parents also has two alleles for tongue curling. You received one of your alleles from your mother and one from your father. Each of your mother's two alleles had an equal chance of being passed on to you, and each of your father's two alleles had an equal chance of being passed on to you.

Let's let a capital T stand for the allele for tongue curling, and a small t stand for the allele for non-tongue curling. If a person receives a T allele from each parent, his tongue-curling alleles will be TT, and he will be able to curl his tongue. If a person receives a t allele from each parent, his tongue-curling alleles will be tt, and he won't be able to curl his tongue. What if a person receives one T allele and one t allele? Nature has figured out a way to break this tie. In the case of tongue curling, the T allele is *dominant,* and the t allele is *recessive.* This means that if a person has a Tt allele combination, the T allele dominates, and the person has the tongue-curling trait.

If your tongue-curling alleles are TT or Tt, you can curl your tongue. If your tongue-curling alleles are tt, you won't be able to curl your tongue—no matter how hard you try!

An Example: Bonnie and Ebert's Baby

Bonnie and Ebert are going to have a baby. Bonnie's tongue-curling alleles are Tt, and Ebert's tongue-curling alleles are tt. You can determine the probability that their baby will be able to curl his or her tongue. Here is a diagram of the allele possibilities for the baby:

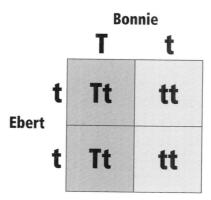

Ebert's alleles are shown at the left side, and Bonnie's alleles are shown at the top. The Tt in the upper-left square is the combination of Bonnie's T allele and Ebert's t allele.

You can see that there are four possible allele pairs (outcomes). Two of these pairs—Tt and Tt—result in the tongue-curling trait. So, the probability that Bonnie and Ebert's baby will have the tongue-curling trait is $\frac{2}{4}$ or $\frac{1}{2}$.

The probability of a child being able to curl his or her tongue will not always be $\frac{1}{2}$. If the parents' alleles are different from Ebert and Bonnie's, the probability will be different.

Problem 7.2

Kalvin's mother is pregnant with her third child. Kalvin figured out from studying his family for several generations that his mother and father both have the tongue-curling alleles Tt. Based on what you know about his parent's alleles, what is the probability that Kalvin's new sibling will be able to curl his or her tongue?

■ Problem 7.2 Follow-Up

1. Neither of Eileen's parents can curl their tongues. What is the probability that Eileen can curl her tongue?
2. Suppose that Geoff's tongue-curling alleles are TT and Mali's tongue-curling alleles are Tt. What is the probability that their child will be able to curl his or her tongue?
3. Marc can curl his tongue, and he wonders whether his parents can. He asks his mother to try it, and she can't curl hers. Do you think Marc's father can curl his tongue? Why or why not?
4. If Rodney's mother and father can both curl their tongues, can you conclude that Rodney can curl his tongue? Explain.

There are many other dominant traits that you can study in the way you have just studied tongue curling. For example, brown eyes are dominant over blue eyes, having a hairy head as an adult is dominant over having a bald head as an adult, and having a "hitchhiker's thumb" (also called a double-jointed thumb) is dominant over not having it.

As you work on these ACE questions, use your calculator whenever you need it.

Applications

In 1–6, use the following information about the genetics of eye color to answer the question. The alleles for blue eyes and brown eyes work similarly to tongue-curling alleles. Let B stand for the brown-eyes allele, and let b stand for the blue-eyes allele. B is dominant, so a person with BB or Bb will have brown eyes, while a person with bb will have blue eyes. (You may have noticed that we have not talked about green eyes and other variations. These things can get pretty complicated—you might learn more about this in your high-school science classes.)

1. Suppose two blue-eyed people are expecting a baby. What is the probability that their child will have brown eyes? Explain.

2. Suppose a brown-eyed person with alleles BB and a blue-eyed person are expecting a baby. What is the probability that the baby will have brown eyes? Explain.

3. If Laura has brown eyes, could both of her parents have blue eyes? Why or why not?

4. If Katrina has blue eyes, could both of her parents have brown eyes? Why or why not?

5. Suppose Ken and Andrea both have brown eyes. They are wondering how many of their children will have brown eyes.

   a. Andrea's mother has brown eyes, and her father has blue eyes. What are Andrea's eye-color alleles? Explain.

   b. Ken's mother has blue eyes, and his father has brown eyes. What are Ken's eye-color alleles? Explain.

   c. What is the probability that Ken and Andrea's first child will have brown eyes?

   d. If their first child has brown eyes, what is the probability that their second child will also have brown eyes?

   e. Suppose Ken and Andrea have ten children. How many of their children would you expect to have brown eyes? Why?

6. Suppose you are a geneticist and you are trying to determine Dawn and Tomas's eye-color alleles. Here is the information you have:

- Dawn has blue eyes.

- Tomas has brown eyes.

- Their two daughters have brown eyes.

- Their son has blue eyes.

  a. What are Dawn's eye-color alleles?

  b. What are Tomas's eye-color alleles?

  c. If they have another child, what is the probability that he or she will have blue eyes?

Connections

7. Write your own definition for the word *probability.* In your definition, show what you have learned about probability during this unit.

8. **a.** Write your own explanation about how experimental and theoretical probabilities are alike and different.

  b. When you surveyed your classmates to find the probability that a student has the tongue-curling trait, were you finding an experimental or a theoretical probability? Explain.

  c. When you found the probability that Kalvin's new sibling would have the tongue-curling trait, were you finding an experimental or theoretical probability? Explain.

Extensions

9. Pick one of the following two options:

a. Investigate tongue curling in your family. Make a family tree that shows the tongue-curling alleles that you can figure out for each person. Trace back as many generations as you can. (If you'd like, you may do this for eye color instead.)

b. Survey a large number of people to estimate the percent of people in the population who can curl their tongues. Represent the data in a graph. How do these data compare with your class's data?

Mathematical Reflections

In this investigation, you studied an example of a way that probabilities are used to predict a person's characteristics, such as eye color or tongue curling. These questions will help you summarize what you have learned:

1 How was probability used in your class's tongue-curling experiment?

2 How was probability used in your theoretical analysis of tongue curling?

3 If both parents of a child can curl their tongues, will the child be able to curl his or her tongue? Explain.

Think about your answers to these questions, discuss your ideas with other students and your teacher, and then write a summary of your findings in your journal.

Looking Back and Looking Ahead

Unit Reflections

Working on problems in this unit, you explored some of the big ideas in *probability*. You learned how to think about *chance* in activities for which individual trials have uncertain outcomes but patterns of outcomes emerge after many trials. You learned how to use *experimental* and *theoretical probabilities* to predict outcomes when tossing number cubes or flipping coins. You found that some events are *equally likely* while other events are not. Most important of all, you learned what makes outcomes of some activities uncertain and how to use mathematics to describe the probabilities of those outcomes.

Using Your Probability Reasoning—To test your understanding and skill in the use of probability ideas and techniques, consider examples of how probability is involved in designing and playing carnival games.

1 *Joanna designed a game for the school carnival. She prepared two bags of marbles.*

Bag A contains 3 marbles: one red, one blue, and one green.

Bag B contains 4 marbles: two reds and two blues.

To play the game, a contestant picks one marble from each bag. If the colors of the marbles match, the contestant wins a prize.

a. These are the win/loss results for the first 30 games.

W L L W W L L W W L L W W L L
L W L L L L W L W L L L L W W

What do these data suggest about the experimental probability of winning the game?

b. What is the theoretical probability of winning the game?

c. What explains the difference between your answers to part a and part b?

2 *David designed a different game for the carnival. His game uses the spinner pictured at the right. If the spinner lands on a GOLD section, then the player gets a prize.*

   a. Does the player have a better chance of winning the bag game or the spinner game?

   b. Is it more likely that the spinner will land on GOLD in 2 of the first 3 trials or that the spinner will land on GOLD in 20 of the first 30 trials?

3 *David also created the five spinners shown below for the carnival. The spinners are shown below. He used one of the spinners 100 times and recorded the results.*

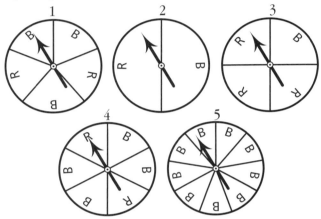

   a. Which spinner is most likely the one he used?

Outcome	Blue	Red
Frequency	28	72

   b. On which spinner(s) do you have the same chance of getting red or blue?

Explaining Your Reasoning—When you use mathematical calculations or diagrams to solve a problem or make a decision, it is important to justify your reasoning. Answer these questions about your work on Problems 1–3.

1. When studying activities with uncertain outcomes like games of chance or genetic inheritance,

   a. how do you calculate experimental probabilities for the possible outcomes?

   b. how do you calculate theoretical probabilities for the possible outcomes?

2. What relationship would you expect between experimental and theoretical probabilities for an uncertain event in a case where the experimental probability is based on

   a. 5 trials?

   b. 50 trials?

   c. 500 trials?

3. Suppose that three friends play a game in which a nickel and a dime are tossed. If neither coin shows heads up, Aisha wins; if two coins show heads up, Billie wins; if one coin shows heads up, Caitlin wins. Caitlin says that this is a fair game because each player has a chance to win.

   a. How would you convince her otherwise?

   b. What would you say to Caitlin if each player has one win in the first three plays and she says, "See, the game is fair"?

4. If you were asked to give five examples of situations in which probability can be used to predict outcomes of uncertain events, what examples would you choose?

The ideas of probability will be used and developed further in several other units of *Connected Mathematics*, especially *Bits and Pieces II* and *What Do You Expect?* You will also find that you can apply probability ideas and reasoning in science and in questions about personal health care, safety, and games of chance.

Glossary

certain event An event that is bound to happen—for example, the sun rising tomorrow. The probability of a certain outcome is 1.

chances The likelihood that something will happen. For example, "What are the chances that it will rain tomorrow?"

equally likely events Two or more events that have the same chance of happening. For example, when you toss a fair coin, heads and tails are equally likely. Each has a 50% chance of happening.

event A set of outcomes. For example, when two coins are tossed, getting two matching coins is an event consisting of the outcomes HH and TT.

experimental probability A probability that is found by experimenting. Experimental probabilities are used to predict what might happen over the long run. For example, you could find the experimental probability of getting a head when you toss a coin by tossing the coin several times and keeping track of the outcomes. The experimental probability would be the ratio of the number of heads to the total number of trials.

fair game A game in which each player has the same chance of winning. A game that is not fair can be made fair by adjusting the scoring system. For example, suppose you play a game in which two coins are tossed. You score one point when the coins both land heads up. Otherwise, your opponent scores one point. The probability that you will score is $\frac{1}{4}$ and the probability that your opponent will score is $\frac{3}{4}$. To make the game fair, you should get three points each time you score, and your opponent should get only one point for a score.

favorable outcome An outcome in which you are interested. A favorable outcome is sometimes called a success. For example, when you toss two coins to find the probability of the coins matching, then HH and TT would be favorable outcomes.

impossible event An event that cannot happen. For example, the probability of putting a quarter in a gumball machine and getting the moon is zero.

outcome A possible result of an action. For example, when one number cube is rolled, the possible outcomes are 1, 2, 3, 4, 5, and 6.

possible A word used to describe an event that can happen. "Possible" does not imply anything about how likely the outcome is. For example, it is *possible* to toss a coin 200 times and get heads every time, but it is not at all likely.

probability A number between 0 and 1 that describes the likelihood that an event will occur. For example, if a bag contains a red marble, a white marble, and a blue marble, then the probability of drawing a red marble is $\frac{1}{3}$.

probable Another way to say likely. An event that is probable is likely to happen.

random events Events that are uncertain when viewed individually but which may exhibit a regular pattern over many trials. For example, when you roll a number cube, you have no way of knowing what the next roll will be, but you know that, over the long run, you will roll each number about the same number of times.

theoretical probability A probability found by analyzing a situation mathematically. If all the outcomes are equally likely, you can first list all the possible outcomes, and then find the ratio of the number of outcomes you are interested in to the total number of outcomes. For example, there are 36 possible equally likely outcomes (number pairs) when two number cubes are rolled. Of these outcomes, 6 have a sum of 7, so the probability of rolling a sum other than 7 is $\frac{30}{36}$, or $\frac{5}{6}$.

trial One round of an experiment. For example, if you are interested in the behavior of a coin, you might flip the coin 50 times and record the results. Each toss would be a trial, and so this experiment would consist of 50 trials.

Index

Angle measurement, 23

Bar graph, prediction from, 19

Certain event, 18
Chance *See* **Probability**

Equally likely events, 4, 7–8
  ACE, 9–12, 24–25
Experiment
  block drawing, 29–34
  coin flip, 5–8, 16
  game simulation, 49–50
  marshmallow toss, 14–15
  spinner, 22–23
  tongue curling, 57–60
Experimental probability, 5–7, 14–16,
    22–23, 29–34
  ACE, 9–12, 17–20, 24
  computing, 31–34
  theoretical probability and, 31–34,
    49–50

Fair
  coin toss game, 5–7, 16
  spinner, 22–23

Games of chance, 4
  ACE, 44–47
  analyzing, 42–43
  coin toss, 5–8, 16
  drawing, 29–34

  number cube, 42–43
  scratch off, 4, 49–50
  spinner, 22–23
Genetics
  ACE, 61–63
  probability and, 57–60

Impossible event, 18
Investigation
  A First Look at Chance, 5–13
  Analyzing Games of Chance, 42–48
  More About Games of Chance, 49–56
  More Experiments with Chance, 14–21
  Probability and Genetics, 57–60
  Theoretical Probabilities, 29–41
  Using Spinners to Predict Chances,
    22–28

Journal, 13, 21, 28, 41, 48, 56, 64

Line plot, prediction from, 38
Looking Back and Looking Ahead:
  Unit Reflections, 65–67

Mathematical Highlights, 4
Mathematical Reflections, 13, 21, 28, 41,
  48, 56, 64

Outcome, 31

Possible event, 16
Possible outcome, 4, 31

Prediction, 4

ACE, 26–27, 35–40, 44–47, 51–55, 61–63

from a bar graph, 19

from a line plot, 38

using experimental probability, 22–23, 29–34

using theoretical probability, 29–34, 42–43, 49–50, 57–60

Probability, 29

ACE, 9–12, 17–20, 26–27, 35–40, 44–47, 51–55, 61–63

certain event, 18

computing, 31–34

equally likely events, 4, 7–8

experimental, 5–7, 14–16, 22–23, 29–34

flipping a coin, 5–8

game analysis, 42–43

genetics and, 4, 57–60

impossible event, 18

from a line plot, 38

outcome, 31

possible outcomes, 4

prediction with, 22–23, 29–34, 42–43, 49–50, 57–60

theoretical, 29–34, 42–43, 49–50, 57–60

tossing a marshmallow, 14–15

Probable event, 16

Simulation, scratch-off game, 4, 49–50

Theoretical probability, 29–34

ACE, 35–40, 44–47, 51–55, 61–63

computing, 31–34

experimental probability and, 31–34. 49–50

for game analysis, 42–43, 49–50

genetics and, 57–60

prediction with, 29–34, 42–43, 49–50, 57–60

Connected  Mathematics™

Using Rational Numbers

Student Edition

Glenda Lappan
James T. Fey
William M. Fitzgerald
Susan N. Friel
Elizabeth Difanis Phillips

Prentice
Hall

Glenview, Illinois
Needham, Massachusetts
Upper Saddle River, New Jersey

The Connected Mathematics Project was developed at Michigan State University with the support of National Science Foundation Grant No. MDR 9150217.

This project was supported, in part,
by the
National Science Foundation
Opinions expressed are those of the authors
and not necessarily those of the Foundation

The Michigan State University authors and administration have agreed that all MSU royalties arising from this publication will be devoted to purposes supported by the Department of Mathematics and the MSU Mathematics Education Enrichment Fund.

Contents

Mathematical Highlights   4

Investigation 1: 1.1 Taxing Tapes   5
     1.2 Computing Tips   7
     1.3 Finding Bargains   9
     1.4 Spending Money   10
     Applications—Connections—Extensions   12
     Mathematical Reflections   17

Investigation 2: 2.1 Finding Percents   18
     2.2 Finding a General Strategy   19
     2.3 Clipping Coupons   20
     2.4 Making Circle Graphs   21
     Applications—Connections—Extensions   24
     Mathematical Reflections   30

Investigation 3: 3.1 Getting Close   31
     3.2 Getting Even Closer   33
     Applications—Connections—Extensions   35
     Mathematical Reflections   42

Investigation 4: 4.1 Dividing Land   43
     4.2 Redrawing the Map   44
     4.3 Pirating Pizza   46
     4.4 Designing Algorithms   48
     Applications—Connections—Extensions   49
     Mathematical Reflections   53

Investigation 5: 5.1 Selling Brownies   54
     5.2 Discounting Brownies   56
     5.3 Buying the Biggest Lot   58
     5.4 Designing a Multiplication Algorithm   59
     Applications—Connections—Extensions   60
     Mathematical Reflections   63

Investigation 6: 6.1 Buying School Supplies   64
     6.2 Moving Decimal Points   66
     6.3 Multiplying Decimals   68
     6.4 Shifting Decimal Points   70
     6.5 Fencing a Yard   71
     Applications—Connections—Extensions   72
     Mathematical Reflections   76

Investigation 7: 7.1 Fractions in Fund-raising   77
     7.2 Share and Share Alike   80
     7.3 Summer Work   81
     Applications—Connections—Extensions   83
     Mathematical Reflections   87

Looking Back and Looking Ahead: Unit Reflections   88

Glossary   91

Index   95

Bits and Pieces II

You and two friends are at a pizza parlor. The total cost for your drinks and a large pizza is $14.90 before tax. The tax rate is 5%. Your group wants to leave a 15% tip. If you want to share the bill equally, how much should each person pay?

If each person in North America throws away $3\frac{2}{3}$ pounds of garbage every day, how many pounds of garbage does each person throw away in a year?

During their Season's End clearance, a store offers an additional 25% discount on items that have already been reduced by 30%. After both discounts are applied, will the cost of an item be the same as if the original price were discounted 55%?

How many bows can you make from 5 meters of ribbon if making a bow takes $\frac{1}{4}$ of a meter of ribbon?

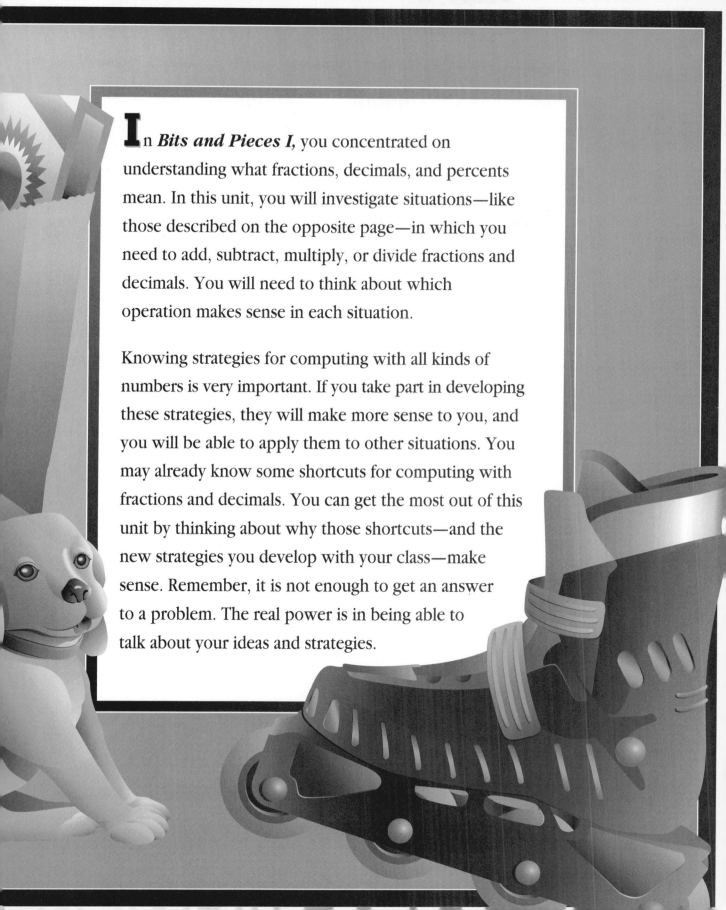

In *Bits and Pieces I,* you concentrated on understanding what fractions, decimals, and percents mean. In this unit, you will investigate situations—like those described on the opposite page—in which you need to add, subtract, multiply, or divide fractions and decimals. You will need to think about which operation makes sense in each situation.

Knowing strategies for computing with all kinds of numbers is very important. If you take part in developing these strategies, they will make more sense to you, and you will be able to apply them to other situations. You may already know some shortcuts for computing with fractions and decimals. You can get the most out of this unit by thinking about why those shortcuts—and the new strategies you develop with your class—make sense. Remember, it is not enough to get an answer to a problem. The real power is in being able to talk about your ideas and strategies.

Mathematical Highlights

In *Bits and Pieces II* you will develop understanding of and algorithms for operations with fractions, decimals and percents. The unit should help you to

- Use benchmarks and other strategies to estimate sums, differences, products and quotients;

- Develop ways to model sums, differences, products and quotients, including strip models, number line models and area models;

- Understand when addition, subtraction, multiplication, or division is the appropriate operation to solve a problem;

- Develop strategies and algorithms for adding, subtracting, multiplying and dividing fractions and decimals;

- Become fluent at changing a fraction to a decimal and a percent and at estimating what fraction a given decimal is near;

- Use percents to estimate or compute taxes, tips, and discounts;

- Look for and generalize patterns in numbers; and

- Solve problems involving fractions, decimals, or percents.

As you work on the problems in this unit, make it a habit to ask questions about situations that involve fractions, decimals, or percents: *What models or diagrams might be helpful in understanding the situation and the relationships among the quantities in the problem? Will it be useful to express the quantities in the problem as fractions? As percents? As decimals? What models or diagrams might help decide which operation is useful in solving a problem? What is a reasonable estimate for the answer?*

Using Percents

In *Bits and Pieces I,* you discovered that percents are useful for reporting the results of surveys. Percents are also helpful in situations involving money. Discounts, taxes, and tips are all described with percents. Understanding what these percents mean and how they are used can make you a smarter consumer.

1.1 Taxing Tapes

Remember that a percent is a special way of representing a fraction with a denominator of 100. You can think of percent as meaning "out of 100."

Let's begin by looking at sales tax. A sales tax of 6% means that for every dollar an item costs, a person needs to pay an additional six hundredths of a dollar, or $0.06:

$1.00 + (6\% \text{ of } \$1.00) = \$1.00 + \$0.06 = \$1.06$

Or, since $1.00 is 100 pennies:

100 pennies + (6% of 100 pennies) = 100 pennies + 6 pennies = 106 pennies = $1.06

Problem 1.1

Jill wants to buy a cassette tape that is priced at $7.50. The sales tax is 6%. What will be the total cost of the tape? Try to find more than one way to solve this problem. Be prepared to explain the different methods you find.

■ Problem 1.1 Follow-Up

Developing shortcuts can help make estimating tax easier. To find a shortcut, you can begin by examining a way to mark hundredths grids to show percents. The grids below show what an item would cost if the price were $1.00 and the tax were 6%.

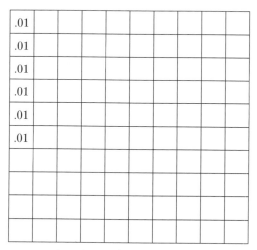

.01	.01	.01	.01	.01	.01	.01	.01	.01	.01
.01	.01	.01	.01	.01	.01	.01	.01	.01	.01
.01	.01	.01	.01	.01	.01	.01	.01	.01	.01
.01	.01	.01	.01	.01	.01	.01	.01	.01	.01
.01	.01	.01	.01	.01	.01	.01	.01	.01	.01
.01	.01	.01	.01	.01	.01	.01	.01	.01	.01
.01	.01	.01	.01	.01	.01	.01	.01	.01	.01
.01	.01	.01	.01	.01	.01	.01	.01	.01	.01
.01	.01	.01	.01	.01	.01	.01	.01	.01	.01
.01	.01	.01	.01	.01	.01	.01	.01	.01	.01

This shows 100% of the whole, which is $1.00.

This shows 6% of the whole, which is $0.06.

You would pay $1.06 for the item.

1. Use what you have discovered about percents to help you solve these problems. Explain your reasoning.

    a. What is the total price for a magazine that costs $2.00 plus 6% tax?

    b. What is the total price for a book on dogs that costs $5.00 plus 6% tax?

    c. What is the total price for a comic book that costs $0.50 plus 6% tax?

2. Solve each problem. When you finish, describe any patterns you observe.
   - **a.** What is the total price for a balloon that costs $1.00 plus 5% tax?
   - **b.** What is the total price for a balloon that costs $1.00 plus 6% tax?
   - **c.** What is the total price for a balloon that costs $1.00 plus 7% tax?
   - **d.** What is the total price for a balloon that costs $1.00 plus 8% tax?

3. Use what you learned in questions 1 and 2 to help you answer these questions. Explain your reasoning.
   - **a.** What is the total price of a pack of tennis balls that costs $5.00 plus 3% tax?
   - **b.** What is the total price of a calculator that costs $19.50 plus 8% tax?

4. Kiah bought a portable cassette player. She does not remember the price, but she does know that the 6% sales tax was $4.80. What was the price of the portable cassette player? Explain your reasoning.

5. Frank bought a new video game. The 5% sales tax was $0.75. What was the price of the game? Explain your reasoning.

1.2 Computing Tips

At most restaurants, customers pay their server a tip for providing good service. A typical tip is 15% to 20% of the cost of the meal. Some people calculate the tip based on the cost of the meal *before* the tax is added, and others use the cost of the meal *after* the tax is added.

You have just finished lunch at Larry's Lunch Place. The food was delicious, and the service was excellent! The bill has just arrived.

Problem 1.2

Have each member of your group use the menu your teacher provides to make up a lunch order. Write all the items ordered by your group on the order check. Total the bill, and add your local sales tax.

A. What is your total bill for food and tax?

B. How much will you leave for the tip? (The tip must be between 15% and 20%.)

C. The members of your group decide to share the cost of the meal equally. About how much would each person need to contribute to pay the bill as well as the tip?

Try to find more than one way to solve parts A and B. Be prepared to explain the different methods you used.

---

1. Many people use benchmarks for determining tips. Jim explains his strategy for finding a tip: "I always figure out 10% of the bill, and then I use this information to calculate a 15% or 20% tip."

    a. Find 10% and 5% of $20.00. Explain how the two percents are related.

    b. Find 10% and 20% of $24.50. Explain how the two percents are related.

    c. Find 10% of $17.35. Use this to find 15% and 20% of $17.35. Explain your reasoning.

2. The sales tax in Kadisha's state is 5%. Kadisha says she computes a 15% tip by multiplying the tax shown on her bill by 3. For the bill shown here, Kadisha's tip would be $0.38 × 3 = $1.14.

Garden Cafe	
ITEM	AMOUNT
Food	$7.55
5% Tax	.38
TOTAL	$7.93

    a. Why does Kadisha's method work?

    b. Use a similar method to compute a 20% tip on Kadisha's bill. Explain your answer.

    c. Does Kadisha's method give 15% of the *entire bill* (including tax) or 15% of the cost *before* tax is added? Explain your thinking.

3. When people leave a 15% or 20% tip, they often round up to the nearest multiple of 5 or 10 cents. For example, in question 2, Kadisha might leave a tip of $1.15 rather than $1.14.

    a. If Kadisha always rounds up, what would she likely leave for a 20% tip on her bill?

    b. Omar always leaves a 20% tip based on the meal price before tax is added. Find a meal price for which Omar would leave a tip of $1.00 after rounding up to the nearest multiple of 5 or 10 cents.

    c. Marlene always leaves a 15% tip based on the meal price before tax is added. Find a meal price for which Marlene would leave a tip of $4.50 after rounding up to the nearest multiple of 5 or 10 cents.

    d. Customers left Jerome $2.50 as a tip for service. The tip was 20% of the bill for their food. How much was the bill?

1.3 Finding Bargains

At Loud Sounds Music Warehouse, CDs are regularly priced at $9.95 and tapes are regularly priced at $6.95. Every day this month, the store is offering a 10% discount on all CDs and tapes.

Problem 1.3

Joshua and Jeremy go to Loud Sounds to buy a tape and a CD. They do not have much money, so they have pooled their funds. When they get to the store, they find that there is another discount plan available just for that day—if they buy three or more items, they can save 20% (instead of 10%) on each item.

A. If they buy a CD and a tape, how much money will they spend after the store adds a 6% sales tax on the discounted prices?

B. Jeremy says he thinks they can buy three tapes for less money than the cost of a tape and a CD. Is he correct? Explain your reasoning.

Try to find more than one way to solve these problems. Be prepared to explain the different methods you discover.

■ Problem 1.3 Follow-Up

1. Mr. Knapp wants to take advantage of the day's special to fill out his CD collection. There are 15 CDs he wants to buy.
   a. What is the total amount of the discount he will receive?
   b. What will the 15 CDs cost after a 6% sales tax has been added?

2. Look back at question 1.

    a. If the discount were only 1%, what total discount amount would Mr. Knapp receive on the 15 CDs?

    b. What is the relationship between 1% of the cost of 15 CDs and 20% of the cost of 15 CDs?

    c. If the discount were 10%, what total discount amount would Mr. Knapp receive for the 15 CDs?

    d. How is a 10% discount related to a 20% discount?

    e. How is a 10% discount related to a 1% discount?

    f. How could you use what you know about a 10% discount on the cost of the 15 CDs to find a 15% discount on the cost of the CDs?

    g. How could you use what you found out above to find a 16% discount on the cost of the 15 CDs? Can you find another way to compute 16% of the cost of the CDs? Explain your methods and how they are related.

3. You have been finding percents of numbers to compute taxes and tips. Explain how you can find *any* percent of a given number.

1.4 Spending Money

Do you ever keep track of what you spend for an evening out? Are you sometimes surprised to find that you have very little money left when you get home? Danny wanted to pay more attention to where her money goes, so she decided to keep track of what she spent for an evening.

Problem 1.4

At the beginning of the evening, Danny had a twenty-dollar bill, five quarters, seven dimes, three nickels, and eight pennies.

A. Danny went to the Friday night school dance, which cost $2.50 to attend. How much money did she have left after paying for the dance?

B. After the dance, Danny and three friends bought a pizza for $6.99 and four soft drinks for 89¢ each. The bill for the pizza and drinks included a sales tax of 7%. How much was the bill? Show how you found your answer.

C. If Danny and her friends shared the cost of the pizza and drinks equally, how much was Danny's share of the bill?

D. On the way home, Danny stopped at a newsstand and bought a copy of *Stars and Planets* magazine for $2.50 plus 7% sales tax. How much had she spent for the evening?

E. How much money did Danny have left at the end of the evening?

■ Problem 1.4 Follow-Up

1. About what fraction of her money did Danny spend during the evening?

2. About what fraction of her money did Danny have left at the end of the evening?

3. About what percent of her money did Danny spend during the evening?

4. About what percent of her money did Danny have left?

As you work on these ACE questions, use your calculator whenever you need it.

Applications

1. Find three examples of advertisements, news reports, or other information in which percents are used. Store windows, newspapers, magazines, radio, and television are good places to look. Write down each example, or cut it out and tape it to your paper. For each example, describe how percents are used and what they mean.

2. Faaiz and Tat Ming go to a restaurant for dinner. Their meals total $13.75.

    a. The local sales tax is 5%. How much tax will be added to the bill?

    b. They want to leave a 15% tip based on the bill and the tax combined. How much should they leave? Explain.

    c. If Faaiz decides he should pay $2.75 more than Tat Ming because he ordered the more expensive dinner, how much should each pay? Explain.

3. Jeremy and Jessica are at a carnival.

    a. At the food stand, hot dogs cost 99¢ each plus 7% tax. How much will Jeremy and Jessica be charged for one hot dog?

    b. They stop at a ball-toss game. The sign reads, "Get three balls for 50¢ or six balls for 80¢." What percent would they save by buying one set of six balls instead of two sets of three balls? Explain.

4. **a.** Roller blades are on sale for 35% off the regular price. What fraction off is this discount?

    b. If the original price of roller blades is $124.99, what is the sale price?

    c. If a tax of 5% is computed on the sale price, what will the roller blades cost?

5. **a.** Ted has done $\frac{3}{10}$ of his homework. What percent is this?

 b. What percent does he still have to do?

6. In a survey, 75% of 400 parents said yes, they give their children fruit as a snack. How many answered yes to the survey?

7. In a survey, 50% of 150 kindergarten teachers said yes, they give their students crackers as a snack. How many answered yes to the survey?

8. In a survey, 50% of 50 grandparents said yes, they give their grandchildren candy as a snack. How many answered yes to the survey?

9. In a survey, 5% of 100 children said yes, they get popcorn as a snack. How many answered yes to the survey?

10. Four friends ordered a square pizza. Maryann said she wasn't hungry and only wanted 10% of the pizza. Bill was very hungry and said he would eat 50% of the pizza. Jon said he would eat 35%, and Kwan thought she could eat 15%. Will this be possible? Explain your reasoning.

11. Science fiction books at the Book Bonanza are marked $\frac{1}{3}$ off. What percent is this?

12. A certain bean plant grows 15% of its height each day. Express this percent growth as a decimal.

13. The purchase of a new mountain bike at Ike's Bikes requires 25% of the cost as a down payment. What fraction of the cost is this percent?

14. A fifty-cent piece is $\frac{50}{100}$ of a dollar, or half of a dollar, or 50% of a dollar, or $0.50.

 a. Find three different ways to represent 30% of a dollar.

 b. Find three different ways to represent 120% of a dollar.

In 15–17, list the smallest number of coins needed to make each amount.

15. 4% of a dollar

16. 20% of a dollar

17. 137% of a dollar

Connections

18. Anna, Brenda, and Carma each sent an entry to the Spartan Running Shoe contest. The Spartan Company advertised that they would award prizes for 1% of the total number of entries. They reported that 1600 entries were received. How many prizes did they award?

In 19–22, ink has been spilled on the page, covering up part of the fraction strips. Use what is showing to reason about each set of strips, and to find fractions equivalent to those marked.

19.

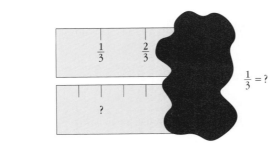

$\frac{2}{3} = ?$

20.

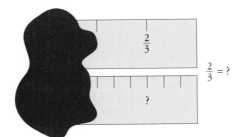

$\frac{1}{3} = ?$

21.

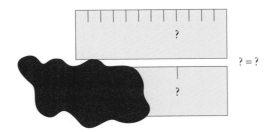

$? = ?$

22.

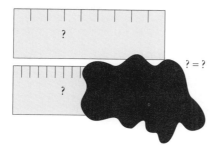

$? = ?$

In 23–26, replace the question marks with numbers that will make the sentence true. There may be more than one solution. If so, show at least two solutions.

23. $\frac{4}{9} = \frac{?}{?}$

24. $\frac{?}{?} = \frac{3}{5}$

25. $\frac{?}{3} = \frac{8}{?}$

26. $\frac{5}{?} = \frac{?}{18}$

27. **a.** Write two fractions that are equivalent. Explain how you know that they are equivalent.

    b. Look at the fractions you wrote in part a. Write two other fractions, one that is equivalent to your first fraction and one that is equivalent to your second fraction.

    c. Are the four fractions you have written equivalent to each other? Why or why not?

28. **a.** Write two fractions that are not equivalent. Tell which is larger, and explain how you know.

    b. Look at the fractions you wrote in part a. Write two other fractions, one that is *not* equivalent to your first fraction and one that is *not* equivalent to your second fraction. Show which fraction is larger in each pair.

    c. Order the four fractions you have written from smallest to largest, and explain how you know the order is correct.

Extensions

29. Write a percent problem that involves discounts on food, cars, books, clothes, or other items. Solve your problem.

In 30–32, copy the number line (including all the labeled marks), and mark it to show where 1 would be. Rewrite each fraction, including 1, as a decimal and a percent.

30.

0                    $\frac{3}{4}$

31.

0 $\frac{7}{8}$

32.

0 $\frac{5}{3}$

33. In a–d, replace the question marks with numbers that will make the sentence true.

a. $\frac{1}{3} = \frac{?}{9} = \frac{?}{6}$ **b.** $\frac{?}{18} = \frac{8}{12} = \frac{4}{?}$

c. $\frac{3}{?} = \frac{12}{?} = \frac{9}{?}$ **d.** $\frac{?}{3} = \frac{?}{21} = \frac{?}{7}$

e. Which problems have more than one possible answer? Why do you think this is so?

Mathematical Reflections

In this investigation, you solved problems that involved finding percents of numbers. You computed discounts, sale prices, tips, and sales taxes. These questions will help you summarize what you have learned:

1 If 1% of your bill for lunch at Pizza Muncho is 18¢, and you want to leave a 15% tip, how much money should you leave? How much money would you leave for a 20% tip? Explain how you got your answers and why your method works.

2 A sports outlet is having a 20% off sale on all merchandise. Describe a procedure you can use to find the sale price for any item in the store.

3 If you bought a calendar that was marked down by 30%, what percent of the original price did you pay? Explain your answer.

4 A store advertises an everyday discount of $\frac{1}{8}$ off the retail price of any item. Write an advertising slogan for the store that gives the everyday discount as a percent. Explain why the percent you have used in your slogan is equivalent to $\frac{1}{8}$.

Think about your answers to these questions, discuss your ideas with other students and your teacher, and then write a summary of your findings in your journal.

More About Percents

In the last investigation, you found percents of numbers. For example, you started with the price of an item and the percent discount offered on the item, and you computed how much money you would save.

In this investigation, you will begin with two numbers and find a percent that describes how they are related. For example, suppose that 50 out of 100 sixth graders surveyed said they liked to play basketball. You could say that 50% of the sixth graders surveyed liked to play basketball.

2.1 Finding Percents

It was easy to determine that 50% of the sixth graders liked to play basketball because exactly 100 people were surveyed, and percent means "out of 100." Often, though, surveys involve more than or less than 100 people.

Problem 2.1

A survey asked cat owners, Does your cat have bad breath? Out of the 200 cat owners surveyed, 80 answered yes to this question. What *percent* of the cat owners answered yes?

Try to find more than one way to solve this problem. For example, you might begin by asking yourself what *fraction* of the cat owners surveyed said their cats have bad breath. Be prepared to explain the different methods you use to solve the problem.

1. If you survey 500 cat owners, about how many would you expect to say their cats have bad breath? Explain your reasoning.

2. If you survey 75 cat owners, about how many would you expect to say their cats have bad breath? Explain your reasoning.

2.2 Finding a General Strategy

One of the powerful things about mathematics is that you can often find a way to solve one problem that will also work for solving similar problems.

Problem 2.2

Here are more questions that involve figuring out what percent of people have answered yes to a survey question. As you work on these questions, try to find a way to describe a general strategy you can use for solving these kinds of problems.

A. If 80 out of 400 cat owners surveyed said their cats have bad breath, what percent of the cat owners is this? Is this percent greater than, equal to, or less than the percent represented by 80 out of 200 cat owners? Explain.

B. If 120 out of 300 seventh graders surveyed said math is their favorite subject, what percent of these seventh graders is this?

C. If 30 out of 50 adults surveyed said they enjoy their jobs, what percent of these adults is this?

D. If 34 out of 125 sixth graders surveyed said they would like to try hang gliding, what percent of these sixth graders is this?

E. If 5 out of 73 middle-school students said they look forward to fire drills, what percent of these middle-school students is this?

F. Write an explanation for how to solve these kinds of problems.

■ **Problem 2.2 Follow-Up**

1. For each part of Problem 2.2, how would you find the *fraction* of people surveyed that answered in the given way? How does finding a fraction help you find a percent?

2. a. A pet store sells a new digestible mouthwash for cats. To promote the new product, the store is offering $0.50 off of the regular price of $2.00 for an 8-ounce bottle. Use the explanation you wrote in question 1 to find the percent of the discount.

b. Change the dollar amounts in part a to numbers of pennies. Now find the percent discount on the mouthwash. How do your answers compare?

2.3 Clipping Coupons

Newspapers often have coupons for discounts on many different things. For example, the pet store mentioned in Problem 2.2 Follow-Up had a coupon for $1.50 off a 20-ounce bottle of mouthwash for cats. The regular price for the mouthwash is $5.00. Alicia wanted to figure out what percent discount this is. She thought about the problem this way:

"I need to find what percent $1.50 is of $5.00. I can think of these amounts in pennies. The fraction I want to represent as a percent is $\frac{150}{500}$, which is equivalent to $\frac{30}{100}$. As a decimal, this fraction is 0.3. This means that the discount is 30%!"

Coupons for cat mouthwash may not interest you, but you may be interested in coupons, like the one below, that give discounts for purchases of food at your favorite restaurant:

Problem 2.3

What percent discount do you get with the coupon above?

Try to find more than one way to solve this problem. Be prepared to explain the different methods you discover.

Problem 2.3 Follow-Up

1. For the sale below, estimate the percent discount you get. Explain your reasoning.

Regular price: $4.50
Today only: $4.00

2. For the sale below, estimate the percent discount you get. Explain your reasoning.

BIG SALE ON
BINOCULARS!
Regular price: $29.50
Now pay just: $17.70

3. The discount on a skateboard is $24.75, which is 25% of the original cost. What was the original cost?

4. The regular price for the sneakers that Kelly wants is $68.98. The sneakers are on sale for 20% off. A sales tax of 6% will be computed on the sale price. How much will Kelly pay for the shoes?

2.4 Making Circle Graphs

Circle graphs, or *pie charts,* are special kinds of graphs used to show how a whole (100%) is divided into several categories. For example, dog and cat owners who said their pets had bad breath were asked, Which of these methods do you use most frequently to take care of your pet's bad breath? Here are the results of the survey:

	Dog owners	Cat owners
Toothpaste	54%	53%
Mouthwash	16%	14%
Dental floss	7%	24%
Other	23%	9%
Total	**100%**	**100%**

Notice that when you add the percents in each column, you get a total of 100%.

This information is represented below in two circle graphs.

Methods Used by Dog Owners

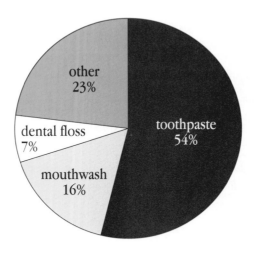

Methods Used by Cat Owners

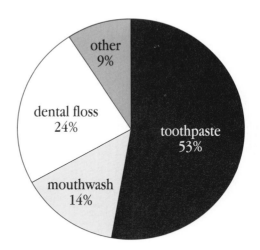

Problem 2.4

Study the circle graphs above. Use what you know about angle measures, circles, and percents to figure out how they were created. Then work on the problem below.

Cat and dog owners were asked, Do you let your pet lick your face? Here are the results of the survey:

	Cat owners	Dog owners
Yes	40%	75%
No	60%	25%
Total	**100%**	**100%**

Create two circle graphs to display this information.

■ Problem 2.4 Follow-Up

1. Cat and dog owners were asked, Does your pet sleep in the same room with you? The results are shown in the table. Make two circle graphs to display these results.

	Cat owners	Dog owners
Yes	73%	47%
No	27%	53%
Total	**100%**	**100%**

2. How do the answers of the cat owners and dog owners compare?

As you work on these ACE questions, use your calculator whenever you need it.

Applications

1. Suppose 43 out of 100 cat owners surveyed said their cats weigh under 10 pounds. What percent of cat owners surveyed is this?

2. Suppose 18 out of 200 race car owners surveyed said their cars are green. What percent of race car owners surveyed is this?

3. Suppose 15 out of 25 skydivers surveyed said they had never had a skydiving accident. What percent of skydivers surveyed is this?

4. Suppose 30 out of 40 private investigators surveyed said their jobs are exceedingly dull. What percent of private investigators surveyed is this?

5. What is 5% of 40? Show how you found your answer.

6. What is 75% of 80? Show how you found your answer.

7. What is 22% of 220? Show how you found your answer.

8. 5 is what percent of 40? Show how you found your answer.

9. 75 is what percent of 80? Show how you found your answer.

10. 22 is what percent of 220? Show how you found your answer.

11. In 1991, about 15 bike thefts were reported for every 100 people who owned bikes. What percent of the bike owners had their bikes stolen?

12. As part of a probability activity, Jack is counting the occurrence of different letters in a paragraph in his biology book. In the first 1000 letters in the paragraph, he found 50 b's. What percent of the letters were b's?

13. Estimate what percent discount Janey will receive if she buys the microscope kit advertised below. Explain.

MICROSCOPE KITS

Customers *usually* pay: $7.95
Students *save* by paying only: $6.76

14. The auto shop class conducted a survey to determine which math teacher's car was the most popular with the students. These were the results:

Ms. Grant's car   48 votes
Ms. Dole's car   35 votes
Mr. Manzine's car   12 votes
Ms. Block's car   75 votes

a. What percent of the votes did Mr. Manzine's car receive? Explain.

b. What percent of the votes did Ms. Dole's car receive? Explain.

c. One student said Ms. Grant's car received 48% of the votes. Is he correct? Explain.

15. Bob, Sally, and Chi belong to an after-school youth group. They joined the group at different times after the beginning of school. The chart shows their attendance so far at the various events, including meetings, held by the youth group.

Member	Events attended since joined	Total events held since joined
Bob	20	30
Sally	11	18
Chi	7	12

a. If the attendance pattern of all three students remains about the same for the next 30 events, who will have the highest percent of attendance at the 30 events? Explain your reasoning.

b. Out of the 120 events planned for the rest of the year, how many would you expect each of the students to attend if they kept the same percent of attendance? Explain your reasoning.

16. a. Dog and cat owners were asked, How often do you feed your pet? The results are shown in the table below. Make two circle graphs of the results.

	Cat owners	Dog owners
Night only	4%	2%
Morning only	6%	10%
Morning and night	42%	46%
Anytime	48%	42%
Total	**100%**	**100%**

b. Compare the feeding patterns of dog owners to cat owners.

Connections

17. In a survey of 100 dog owners about their pets' habits, 39% said that their dogs eat bugs. How many dog owners surveyed said this?

18. When 300 tarantula owners were surveyed, 26% said they let their spiders crawl on them. How many tarantula owners surveyed said this?

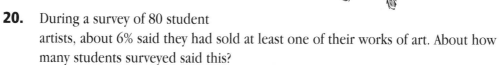

19. In a survey of 80 students, 40% said they had a savings account of their own. How many students surveyed said this?

20. During a survey of 80 student artists, about 6% said they had sold at least one of their works of art. About how many students surveyed said this?

21. a. Janelle said, "The median divides a set of data in half." What does she mean?

   b. Randy added, "If the median divides a set of data in half, you always know what percent of the data is below the median and what percent of the data is above the median." Is Randy correct? Justify your answer.

22. In a–e, use the line plot to answer the question.

How Many Pets Does Your Family Have?

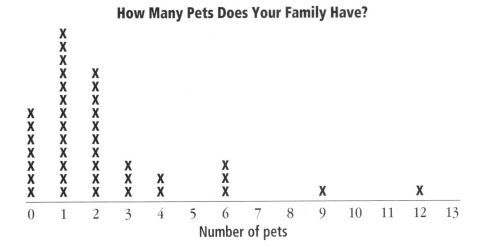

   a. What percent of the 40 people surveyed have more than two pets? Explain how you found your answer.

   b. What percent of the 40 people surveyed have fewer than three pets? Explain how you found your answer.

   c. What is the median of the distribution?

   d. What percent of the people surveyed are below the median?

   e. What percent of the people surveyed are above the median?

Extensions

23. 80 is 40% of what number? Explain.

24. 220 is 20% of what number? Explain.

25. A circle graph is not always useful when you are working with percents. For example, when people are allowed to choose more than one answer to a survey question, the percents for the categories may add to *more than* 100%. For example, in one survey people were asked why they owned a pet. They were given several choices and were allowed to mark off more than one reason. Because multiple answers were allowed, the percents add to more than 100%.

	Dog owners	Cat owners
Love/companionship	88%	93%
Security	39%	0%
Protection	35%	0%
Entertainment	26%	33%
Catching rodents	0%	16%
Breeding (to make money)	16%	6%
Children grown/spouse died	4%	10%
Total	**208%**	**158%**

You can make a circle graph only when the percents add to 100%. When they add to more than 100%, you can make a bar graph to show the information.

a. Make bar graphs to display the data shown in the table. Before you make your bar graphs, think about these questions:

- What kind of data will you display in your graphs?
- What information will you show on the horizontal axis (the *x*-axis)?
- What information will you show on the vertical axis (the *y*-axis)?
- What scale will you use for the *y*-axis?

b. Write a paragraph comparing the responses of dog owners to cat owners in this survey.

In 26–30, replace the question marks with numbers that make the sentence true.

26. $\frac{6}{?} = \frac{18}{?} = \frac{?}{20}$

27. $\frac{12}{?} = \frac{?}{36} = \frac{?}{12}$

28. $\frac{2}{3} < \frac{?}{9}$

29. $\frac{2}{3} = \frac{?}{9}$

30. $\frac{2}{3} > \frac{?}{9}$

Mathematical Reflections

In this investigation, you studied situations for which you needed to find the percent one number is of another number so that you could describe the situation or compare it to another situation. These questions will help you summarize what you have learned:

1 Describe at least two ways to find what percent 30 is of 120. Explain why each method works.

2 Describe how to find what percent 34 is of 135. Explain your method.

3 Explain how you would find what part of a circle graph should be shaded to show 23%.

Think about your answers to these questions, discuss your ideas with other students and your teacher, and then write a summary of your findings in your journal.

Estimating with Fractions and Decimals

Sometimes when you need to find an amount of something, you will not need or will not be able to get an exact answer. In these situations, you can estimate an answer. This investigation will give you practice in making estimates with fractions and decimals.

3.1 Getting Close

Getting Close is a game that will sharpen your skills at estimating with fractions and decimals. In *Bits and Pieces I*, we developed a set of *benchmarks* for estimating fractions and decimals. You learned to find which benchmark a number is nearest. Look at this set of benchmarks:

$$0 \qquad \frac{1}{4} \qquad \frac{1}{2} \qquad \frac{3}{4} \qquad 1 \qquad 1\frac{1}{4} \qquad 1\frac{1}{2} \qquad 1\frac{3}{4} \qquad 2$$

Which benchmark is $\frac{5}{8}$ nearest? Five eighths is larger than $\frac{1}{2}$, because it is larger than $\frac{4}{8}$. Five eighths is smaller than $\frac{3}{4}$, because it is smaller than $\frac{6}{8}$. In fact, $\frac{5}{8}$ is exactly halfway between $\frac{1}{2}$ and $\frac{3}{4}$.

Think about this!

How could you use benchmarks to help you quickly estimate the sum of two fractions? For example, think about this sum:

$$\frac{1}{8} + 1\frac{5}{7}$$

Is this sum larger or smaller than 2? Now, look at this sum:

$$\frac{1}{2} + \frac{5}{8}$$

Is this sum closest to 0, to 1, or to 2?

When you play Getting Close, you will use benchmarks and other methods to estimate the sum of two numbers.

Getting Close Rules

Getting Close is played by two to four players.

Materials
- A set of Getting Close game cards
- A set of three number squares—0, 1, and 2 (1 set per player)

Playing
- All players hold their 0, 1, and 2 number squares in their hands, hidden from view of the other players.

- The game cards are placed face down in a pile in the center of the table.

- For a *round of play,* one player turns over two game cards from the pile. Each player mentally estimates the sum of the numbers on the two game cards, and puts the number square (0, 1, or 2) he or she thinks is closest to the sum face down in the center of the table.

- After each player has played a number square, find the actual sum by using a calculator or some other method.

- The first player who put the correct number square in the center of the table collects the two game cards. If there is a tie, all players who tied get one game card. Players who have tied may take game cards from the deck if necessary.

- Each player who chose the wrong number square must return one game card (if he or she has one) to the bottom of the pile.

- The player who wins the round turns over the next two game cards.

- When all of the game cards have been used, the player with the most game cards wins.

Problem 3.1

Play Getting Close once or twice. Keep a record of the estimation strategies you find useful. You may find benchmarks, fraction strips, number lines, hundredths grids, or changing a fraction to a decimal or a decimal to a fraction helpful in making estimates. You may discover other ways of thinking that help. As you play the game, your group may use a calculator to check whether a player is correct—but not to estimate the sums!

■ Problem 3.1 Follow-Up

Describe or illustrate one estimation strategy that you found useful in the game.

3.2 Getting Even Closer

Now you will play the game Getting Even Closer, which requires you to estimate sums to the nearest 0.5. The rules are the same as for Getting Close, and the same game cards are used. However, each player will now have six number squares: 0, 0.5, 1, 1.5, 2, and 2.5.

Problem 3.2

Play Getting Even Closer once or twice. Keep a record of your strategies for estimating the sums. As before, your group may use a calculator to check whether a player is correct, but not to estimate the sums.

After a round of play, the player who won should explain the strategy he or she used to estimate the sum.

■ Problem 3.2 Follow-Up

1. a. The following fractions occur so often that it is useful to be able to recall their decimal and percent equivalents quickly:

$$\frac{1}{2} \qquad \frac{1}{3} \qquad \frac{1}{4} \qquad \frac{2}{3} \qquad \frac{3}{4} \qquad \frac{1}{6} \qquad \frac{1}{5}$$

For each of these important fractions, give the decimal and percent equivalents.

b. Draw a number line. On your number line, label the point corresponding to each fraction listed in part a.

2. Suppose you played Getting Close with only these game cards:

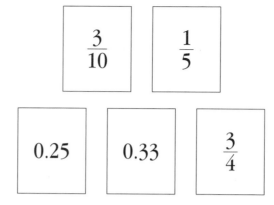

a. What is the largest sum possible?

b. What is the smallest sum possible?

3. a. If you add two numbers and the sum is closest to 1.5 (using the set of benchmarks 0, 0.5, 1, 1.5, 2, and 2.5), what is the largest the sum could actually be?

b. If you add two numbers and the sum is closest to 1.5 (using the set of benchmarks 0, 0.5, 1, 1.5, 2, and 2.5), what is the smallest the sum could actually be?

As you work on these ACE questions, use your calculator whenever you need it.

Applications

1. Ask an adult to describe some situations in which a very close estimate is needed and some situations in which an estimate can just be "in the ballpark."

2. Ask an adult to describe some situations in which an overestimate is needed.

3. Ask an adult to describe some situations in which an underestimate is needed.

4. Many sewing patterns have a $\frac{5}{8}$-inch allowance for sewing the seam. Is this allowance closer to 0, $\frac{1}{2}$, or 1 inch? Explain your reasoning.

In 5–10, tell whether the fraction is closest to 0, $\frac{1}{2}$, or 1. Explain your reasoning.

5. $\frac{4}{9}$

6. $\frac{9}{16}$

7. $\frac{4}{7}$

8. $\frac{500}{1000}$

9. $\frac{5}{6}$

10. $\frac{48}{100}$

In 11–19, find two fractions with a sum that is between the two given numbers.

11. 0 and 1

12. 0 and $\frac{1}{2}$

13. $\frac{1}{2}$ and 1

14. 1 and 2

15. 1 and $1\frac{1}{2}$

16. $1\frac{1}{2}$ and 2

17. 2 and 3

18. 2 and $2\frac{1}{2}$

19. $2\frac{1}{2}$ and 3

In 20–23, the sum is a student's solution to the problem: "Find two fractions with a sum greater than $\frac{3}{4}$." Tell whether the solution is correct and explain your reasoning.

20. $\frac{1}{8} + \frac{2}{4}$

21. $\frac{3}{6} + \frac{2}{4}$

22. $\frac{5}{12} + \frac{5}{6}$

23. $\frac{5}{10} + \frac{3}{8}$

In 24–29, tell whether the number is closest to 0, 0.5, 1, or 1.5, and explain your reasoning.

24. 0.67

25. 1.15

26. 0.000999

27. 0.78

28. 0.26

29. 1.90

30. Janine is having seven friends over for breakfast. Of the eight people who will be eating breakfast, six like orange juice best, and two prefer grapefruit juice. Both kinds of juice cost $2.89 for a half gallon, $2.09 for a quart ($\frac{1}{4}$ of a gallon), and $1.29 for a pint ($\frac{1}{8}$ of a gallon). How many of each size container of each type of juice should Janine buy? Use estimation to help you decide. Explain your reasoning.

In 31–34, fill in each blank with 1, 2, or 3 to form decimal numbers so that each sum is as close as possible to the given number. You may use the same digit twice in one number. For example, you may write 0.33. The symbol ≈ means "is approximately equal to."

31. 0.____ ____ + 0.____ ____ ≈ 0.5

32. 0.____ ____ + 0.____ ____ ≈ 0.25

33. 0.____ ____ + 0.____ ____ ≈ 0.75

34. 0.____ ____ + 0.____ ____ ≈ 0.4

Connections

35. If you sleep about 30% of each day, estimate how many hours you have slept by the time you are 12 years old. Explain your reasoning.

36. Order these decimals from largest to smallest.

5.693   5.639   5.96   5.67   5.599

37. Julio is at the grocery store near his apartment. He has $10.00, but no calculator or paper and pencil. At right is a list of the items he would like to buy.

Item	Price
Milk	$2.47
Eggs	$1.09
Cheese	$1.95
Bread	$0.68
Honey	$1.19
Cereal	$3.25
Avocado	$0.50

Use mental computation and estimation to answer questions a–c.

a. Can Julio buy all the items with the money he has? Explain your reasoning.

b. If Julio had only $5.00, what could he buy? Give two possibilities.

c. What different items could Julio buy to come as close as possible to spending $5.00?

In 38–40, copy the figure onto your paper and shade about $\frac{1}{3}$ of the figure.

38.

39.

40.

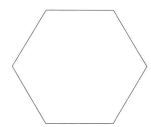

In 41–43, copy the figure onto your paper and shade about $\frac{1}{4}$ of the figure.

41.

42.

43.

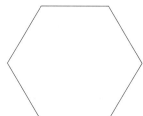

Extensions

44. Here is a map of the area where Seth is hiking.

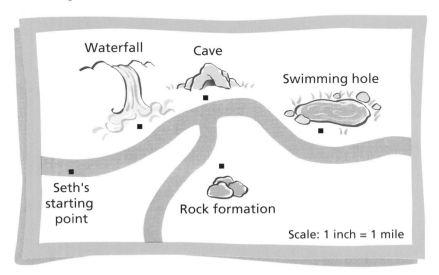

Waterfall

Cave

Swimming hole

Seth's starting point

Rock formation

Scale: 1 inch = 1 mile

a. The distance from where Seth starts to the waterfall is $\frac{7}{8}$ of an inch. The distance from the waterfall to the mouth of the cave is $\frac{3}{4}$ of an inch. Will Seth's trip to the waterfall and then the cave be shorter or longer than a mile? Explain.

b. When Seth gets to the cave, he decides to take a side trip to see the rock formation. On the map, the rock formation is about 75% of an inch from the cave. After visiting the rock formation, Seth retraces his steps to return to the main trail. When he gets back to the main trail, about how many miles has he hiked since he started his travels?

c. After the side trip, Seth heads for the swimming hole. On the map, this is about $1\frac{1}{4}$ inches from the cave. When he arrives at the swimming hole, about how many miles has he walked altogether?

d. Seth's buddy, who lives on the other side of the swimming hole, meets him for a swim. Late in the day, they retrace Seth's steps to where Seth started. They do not make the side trip to the rock formation. About how many miles has Seth now walked altogether?

In 45–48, tell what percent of the whole rectangle each numbered section represents.

45.

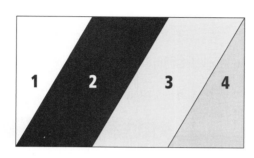

46.

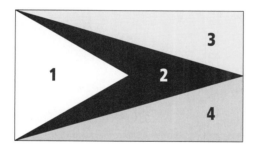

47.

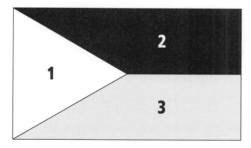

48.

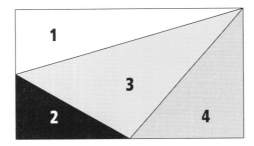

49. The table below lists the abundance of the eight most common elements in the earth's crust.

Element	Portion of earth's crust
Oxygen	0.4660
Iron	0.0500
Silicon	0.2772
Aluminum	0.0813
Sodium	0.0283
Calcium	0.0363
Potassium	0.0259
Magnesium	0.0209

a. Order the elements in the earth's crust from most abundant to least abundant.

b. Estimate how much of the earth's crust is made up of the *three* most abundant elements.

c. About what percent of the crust is made up of these three elements?

d. About what percent of the crust is made up of the three least abundant elements listed in the table?

In 50–54, find a decimal number in the given interval.

50. between $\frac{1}{2}$ and 1

51. between $\frac{1}{3}$ and $\frac{1}{2}$

52. between $\frac{1}{4}$ and $\frac{1}{3}$

53. between $\frac{1}{5}$ and $\frac{1}{4}$

54. between $\frac{1}{6}$ and $\frac{1}{5}$

55. In 50–54, can you find another decimal in each interval? Why or why not?

In 56 and 57, ink has been spilled on the page, concealing part of the fraction strips. Use what is showing to reason about each pair of strips, and find the equivalent fractions indicated by the question marks.

56.

57.

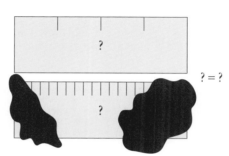

Mathematical Reflections

In this investigation, you played two games that helped you develop strategies for estimating the sum of two fractions or decimals. These questions will help you summarize what you have learned:

1 Describe one strategy that you found helpful in estimating sums. Explain why it was helpful to you.

2 If the two game cards turned up are both between 0.5 and 0.75, what is the smallest the sum could be? What is the largest the sum could be? Explain your reasoning.

3 If you are estimating the sum of two numbers and one is nearest the benchmark $\frac{1}{4}$ and the other is nearest the benchmark $1\frac{1}{2}$, what estimate would you give? Why?

Think about your answers to these questions, discuss your ideas with other students and your teacher, and then write a summary of your findings in your journal.

Adding and Subtracting Fractions

Knowing how to combine and remove quantities is a skill that is helpful for understanding the world around you. The mathematical names for combining and removing are adding and subtracting. For example, if you owned two lots of land and you bought another half a lot, you could combine the two lots and the half lot to determine that you owned $2 + \frac{1}{2}$, or $2\frac{1}{2}$, lots of land.

The problems in this investigation require you to add and subtract fractions. As you work on these problems, use what you have learned in earlier investigations about finding equivalent fractions and rewriting fractions as decimals.

4.1 Dividing Land

When Tupelo township was founded, the land was divided into sections that could be farmed. Each *section* is a square that is 1 mile long on each edge—that is, each section is 1 square mile of land. There are 640 acres of land in a 1-square-mile section.

The diagram on the next page shows two *adjacent* sections of land, sections 18 and 19. Each section is divided among several owners. The diagram shows the part of the land each person owns.

Problem 4.1

Determine what fraction of a section each person owns. Explain your reasoning.

■ Problem 4.1 Follow-Up

Determine how many acres of land each person owns. Explain your reasoning.

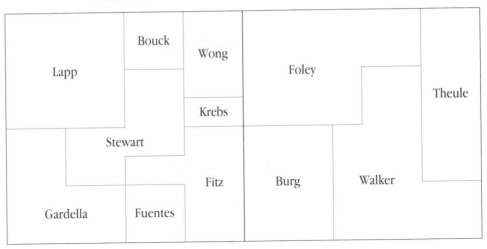

Section 18   **Section 19**

Bouck	Wong	Foley	Theule
Lapp	Krebs		
Stewart	Fitz	Burg	Walker
Gardella	Fuentes		

Redrawing the Map

As time goes by, some people in sections 18 and 19 want to sell their farms, and other people want to buy more land to expand their farms. In the real world, transactions to buy and sell land occur every day.

Some of the owners of land in sections 18 and 19 sold their land to other people who already owned land in these sections. The clues below describe the results of several transactions.

Clue 1 When all the sales are completed, four people—Theule, Fuentes, Wong, and Gardella—own all of the land in the two sections.

Clue 2 Theule bought from one person and now owns land equivalent to $\frac{1}{2}$ of one section.

Clue 3 Fuentes bought from three people and now owns the equivalent of $\frac{13}{32}$ of one section.

Clue 4 Gardella now owns the equivalent of $\frac{1}{2}$ of a section.

Clue 5 Wong now owns all of the rest of the land in the two sections.

Clue 6 Each of the four owners can walk around all of their land without having to cross onto another person's land.

A. Use the clues to determine what transactions took place. Determine exactly which pieces of land Theule, Fuentes, Wong, and Gardella bought, and explain how you know you are correct.

B. Draw a new map of the two sections, outlining the land belonging to each of the four owners. Tell how many acres each person now owns.

■ Problem 4.2 Follow-Up

After a few years, Fuentes wants to acquire more land to put in new pastures for his livestock. Gardella sells $\frac{1}{2}$ of a section to Fuentes, Theule sells $\frac{1}{8}$ of a section to Fuentes, and Wong sells $\frac{1}{16}$ of a section to Fuentes. What fraction of a section does each person now own?

4.3 Pirating Pizza

In this problem, you can use what you have discovered about adding and subtracting fractions to make sense of the havoc that the infamous Pizza Pirate is causing! As you work on the problem, look for patterns that can help you to solve it.

Problem 4.3

Courtney's class made a gigantic square pizza for a class party to be held the day after the final exam. They made it a week before the party so they would have time to study. To keep the pizza fresh, they stored it in the cafeteria freezer.

Unfortunately, the notorious Pizza Pirate was lurking in the area. That night, the Pizza Pirate disguised himself as a janitor, tiptoed into the cafeteria, and gobbled down half of the pizza! On the second night, he ate half of what was left of the pizza. Each night after that, he crept in and ate half of the pizza that remained.

After the final exam, Courtney's class went to get their pizza to start their celebration—and were stunned by what they found!

What fraction of the pizza was left for the party?

To help you answer this question, make a table or chart showing

- the fraction of the pizza the Pizza Pirate ate each day
- the fraction of the pizza he had eaten so far at the end of each day
- the fraction of the pizza that remained at the end of each day

Write a summary of how your group solved this problem. Draw any diagrams that will help you to show your thinking.

Problem 4.3 Follow-Up

1. a. Make a graph of the total amount eaten so far by the Pizza Pirate for each of the seven days.

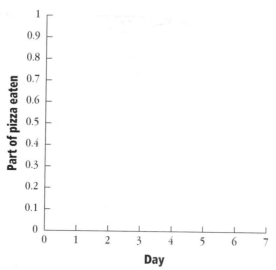

b. Make a graph of how much pizza remains at the end of the day for each of the seven days.

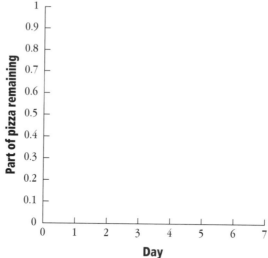

c. How are the graphs you made in parts a and b related?

2. If the students canceled the party and left the pizza in the freezer for a long time, would the Pizza Pirate ever eat all of the pizza?

4.4 Designing Algorithms

To become skillful at handling situations that call for the addition and subtraction of fractions, you need a good plan for carrying out your computations. In mathematics, a plan—or a series of steps—for doing a computation is called an **algorithm.** For an algorithm to be useful, each step should be clear and precise so that other people will be able to carry out the steps and get correct answers.

In this problem, you will work with your group to develop algorithms for adding and subtracting fractions. Your group may develop more than one algorithm for each computation. What is important is that each member of your group understands and feels comfortable with at least one algorithm for adding fractions and at least one algorithm for subtracting fractions.

Problem 4.4

Work with your group to develop at least one algorithm for adding fractions and at least one algorithm for subtracting fractions. You might want to look back over the first three problems in this investigation and discuss how each person in your group thought about them. Look for ideas that you think will help you develop algorithms for adding and subtracting fractions that will always work, even with mixed numbers.

Test your algorithms on a few problems, such as these:

$$\frac{5}{8} + \frac{7}{8} \qquad \frac{3}{5} + \frac{5}{3} \qquad 3\frac{3}{4} + 7\frac{2}{9}$$

$$\frac{3}{4} - \frac{1}{8} \qquad 5\frac{4}{6} - 2\frac{1}{3} \qquad \frac{5}{6} - \frac{1}{4}$$

If necessary, make adjustments to your algorithms until you think they will work all the time. Write up a final version of each algorithm. Make sure they are neat and precise so others can follow them.

■ Problem 4.4 Follow-Up

1. Exchange your addition algorithm with that of another group. Test the other group's plan. Write a paragraph explaining how your algorithm and the other group's algorithm are alike and how they are different.

2. Exchange your subtraction algorithm with that of another group (a different group from the group you exchanged with in part 1). Test the other group's plan. Write a paragraph explaining how your algorithm and the other group's algorithm are alike and how they are different.

As you work on these ACE questions, use your calculator whenever you need it.

Applications

1. A local magazine sells advertising space. It charges advertisers according to the fraction of a page their ad will fill.

   a. For page 20 in the magazine, advertisers have purchased $\frac{1}{8}$ of the page and $\frac{1}{16}$ of the page. What fraction of the page will be used for ads? What fraction of the page will remain for other uses? Explain your reasoning.

   b. The Cool Sub Shop is having its grand opening and has purchased several ads. They buy three $\frac{1}{4}$-page ads, four $\frac{1}{8}$-page ads, and ten $\frac{1}{16}$-page ads. What is the total amount of space that they have bought? Explain your reasoning.

   c. The magazine wants to make $160 for each page of advertising sold. What might the magazine charge for each size ad if ads can be any of the following sizes: $\frac{1}{32}, \frac{1}{16}, \frac{1}{8}, \frac{1}{4}, \frac{1}{2}$, or a whole page? Explain your reasoning.

   d. Using the pricing scheme you developed in part c, what would the bill for the Cool Sub Shop be for the ads they purchased in part b? Explain your reasoning.

   e. For an upcoming issue, a local promoter has purchased a total of $2\frac{3}{4}$ pages of ads to promote two concerts. Now, one of the concerts must be canceled because the lead guitarist broke her finger. The promoter calls to cancel $1\frac{5}{8}$ pages of ads for that concert. How much advertising space does the promoter want to keep? Explain your reasoning.

   f. The senior class is having a fund-raiser to help raise money for their senior trip. They have $80 dollars to spend on advertising. Geraldo says they can purchase two $\frac{1}{8}$-page ads and four $\frac{1}{16}$-page ads for their money. According to your answer to part c, is he correct? Explain your reasoning.

   g. Give four different sets of ad sizes that the senior class could purchase with their $80 (using your pricing scheme from part c). Show why your answers work.

2. The Pizza Pirate and a friend broke into the school cafeteria and ate part of the huge sheet cake that was being stored for a party. The Pizza Pirate ate $\frac{1}{16}$ of the cake, and the accomplice ate $\frac{1}{32}$ of the cake. How much cake was left?

3. If you eat $\frac{3}{4}$ of a pizza and then eat $\frac{1}{8}$ of another pizza of the same size, how much of a whole pizza have you eaten altogether?

4. On the stock market report yesterday, the price of a stock that Ms. Jennings is watching was $27\frac{3}{4}$ dollars. Today the stock is reported at $26\frac{1}{8}$ dollars. How much did the stock price decline?

5. Ms. Jennings is watching another stock. These are the prices reported for a week in March: $1\frac{15}{16}$ on Monday, $2\frac{1}{8}$ on Tuesday, $2\frac{3}{8}$ on Wednesday, $2\frac{3}{16}$ on Thursday, and $2\frac{1}{4}$ on Friday. For each day of the week, beginning with Tuesday, how much did the stock go up or down?

In 6–9, tell which sum or difference is larger. Show your work.

6. $\frac{2}{3} + \frac{5}{6}$ or $\frac{3}{4} + \frac{4}{5}$

7. $\frac{7}{6} - \frac{2}{3}$ or $\frac{3}{5} - \frac{5}{10}$

8. $\frac{1}{4} + \frac{5}{6}$ or $\frac{1}{5} + \frac{7}{8}$

9. $\frac{1}{16} + \frac{1}{12}$ or $\frac{5}{4} - \frac{4}{5}$

Connections

In 10–15, replace the question mark with a number that will make the sentence true.

10. $\frac{3}{12} = \frac{?}{8}$

11. $\frac{?}{4} = \frac{6}{8}$

12. $\frac{1}{2} = \frac{?}{12}$

13. $\frac{?}{12} = \frac{2}{3}$

14. $\frac{?}{8} = \frac{14}{16}$

15. $\frac{5}{12} = \frac{10}{?}$

In 16–18, ink has spilled on the page, obscuring part of the fraction strips. Use what is showing to reason about each set of strips and to find the equivalent fractions indicated by the question marks.

16.

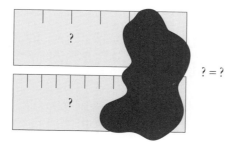

17.

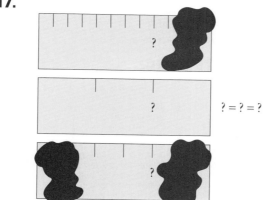

18.

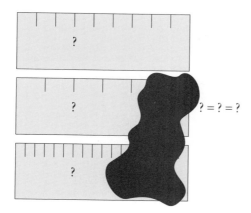

In 19–22, insert <, =, or > to make a true statement.

19. 18.156 _____ 18.17

20. 3.184 _____ 31.84

21. 5.78329 _____ 5.78239

22. 4.0074 _____ 4.0008

In 23–26, express the fraction as a decimal.

23. $\frac{3}{5}$

24. $\frac{18}{12}$

25. $\frac{5}{8}$

26. $\frac{15}{16}$

Extensions

27. **a.** Find three numbers for the denominators to make the sentence true.

$$\frac{1}{?} - \frac{1}{?} = \frac{1}{?}$$

b. Can you find another set of numbers that works?

Mathematical Reflections

In this investigation, you explored ways to add and subtract fractions. These questions will help you summarize what you have learned:

1 Describe how you can add or subtract two fractions that have the same denominator. Explain why your method makes sense.

2 Describe and illustrate with an example your algorithm for adding two fractions that have different denominators. Do the same for your algorithm for subtracting two fractions with different denominators.

3 Describe how you can use what you know about adding and subtracting fractions to add or subtract mixed numbers.

Think about your answers to these questions, discuss your ideas with other students and your teacher, and then write a summary of your findings in your journal.

Finding Areas and Other Products

Sometimes rather than adding or subtracting fractions, you need to multiply them. For example, suppose you are taking inventory at the sporting goods store where you work. There are $13\frac{1}{2}$ boxes of footballs in the stock room, and there are 12 footballs in a full box. How can you find the total number of footballs without opening all the boxes? Or, suppose $\frac{1}{4}$ of a pizza was left over and you ate $\frac{1}{2}$ of this amount. What number shows the amount of pizza you ate?

In this investigation, you will see how you can relate what you already know about multiplication to situations involving fractions. Remember, to make sense of a situation, you can draw a model or change a fraction to an equivalent fraction or an equivalent form.

5.1 Selling Brownies

Paulo and Paula are tending the brownie booth at the school fair. All evening long they have run into interesting situations in which they have to find fractional parts of other fractions.

Think about this!

What operation is called for when you find a fractional part of another fraction: $+, -, \times,$ or $\div$? For example, how much is $\frac{1}{2}$ of $\frac{1}{4}$? How could you write this problem using a mathematics operation sign?

Let's look at some of the problems Paulo and Paula had to solve while they were selling brownies.

Problem 5.1

The brownies are baked in square pans, and they are sold as fractional parts of a pan. A whole pan of brownies costs $24 dollars. The cost of any fractional part of a pan is that fraction of $24.

A. One pan of brownies was $\frac{2}{3}$ full. Mr. Sims bought $\frac{1}{2}$ of what was in the pan. What fraction of a full pan did Mr. Sims buy? How much did he pay?

B. Paulo's aunt Serena asked to buy $\frac{3}{4}$ of what was left in another pan. The pan was half full. How much of a whole pan did Aunt Serena buy? How much did she pay?

Problem 5.1 Follow-Up

For A and B above, draw a picture to show what each brownie pan looked like before Mr. Sims and Aunt Serena bought part of what remained. Then draw a picture that shows how much of each pan the customer got and how much was left. Mark your drawings so that someone else can easily see what fraction of the pan each customer bought.

Model of a Brownie Pan

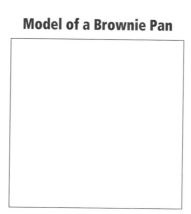

Use the drawings to check your computations in A and B for the fraction of the brownie pan and the price each customer paid.

5.2 Discounting Brownies

There are many occasions in which you will want to find a fraction times a fraction or a fraction times a whole number. When you solve problems involving multiplication with fractions, it helps to remember that finding a fraction *times* a number is the same as finding a fraction *of* a number. It is also helpful to draw models to show fractions and fraction operations.

At the brownie booth, a customer wanted to buy $\frac{1}{3}$ of a pan that was $\frac{1}{3}$ full. Paula said that they had to find $\frac{1}{3}$ of $\frac{1}{3}$. Paulo said that this is the same as $\frac{1}{3} \times \frac{1}{3}$. They decided to make a drawing to figure out how much the customer would get.

First, they made a drawing to show how much was in the pan:

Then, they showed how much the customer wanted, which was $\frac{1}{3}$ of $\frac{1}{3}$ of a pan:

They extended the horizontal lines to form nine equal parts. They then figured out that the customer would buy $\frac{1}{9}$ of a pan:

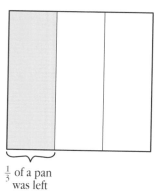

$\frac{1}{3}$ of a pan was left

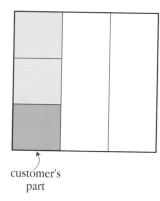

customer's part

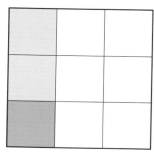

From inspecting their drawing, Paula and Paulo figured out that they should charge the customer $\frac{1}{9}$ of $24, or $2.67.

Think about this!

Why does it make sense that $\frac{1}{3}$ of $\frac{1}{3}$, or $\frac{1}{3} \times \frac{1}{3}$, is $\frac{1}{9}$?

Problem 5.2

The school fair was almost over. Paulo and Paula wanted to sell all the remaining brownies in a hurry, so they decided to offer a discount of 20% on all sales. They had $2\frac{1}{4}$ pans of brownies left. Remember, they originally sold a pan of brownies for $24.

Mr. Vargas offered to buy half of all that they had left.

A. How much will Mr. Vargas purchase?

B. How much should Paulo and Paula charge Mr. Vargas?

■ Problem 5.2 Follow-Up

When Mr. Vargas got his bill, he realized he had only $20 in his wallet, so he said, "I guess I'll only buy $\frac{1}{3}$ of what you have left."

1. Now how much will Mr. Vargas buy?

2. Can he afford this much? Explain your reasoning.

5.3 Buying the Biggest Lot

In the area where Miguel lives, land is expensive because many people want to live there. The lots for houses are small compared to the lots needed for farmland.

Miguel's mother builds and sells houses. She wants to buy a piece of land in their area on which to build several houses. There are two large lots for sale. One is a rectangular plot that is $\frac{3}{8}$ of a mile by $\frac{2}{3}$ of a mile. The other is a square plot that is $\frac{2}{5}$ of a mile by $\frac{2}{5}$ of a mile.

Problem 5.3

A. Which lot should Miguel's mother buy if she wants the biggest lot? Explain your reasoning.

B. If land in this area sells for $750,000 a square mile, about how much should Miguel's mother expect to pay?

■ Problem 5.3 Follow-Up

Miguel's mother has an idea for a beautiful trailer park. The trailer park would have lots of open areas for children to play in and a set of shops. She finds a farm for sale that is $1\frac{1}{4}$ miles × $2\frac{1}{5}$ miles. The farm has a pretty lake and lots of trees. She thinks it would be perfect for her trailer park.

1. How many square miles does the farm cover?

2. If land costs $750,000 a square mile, how much should she expect to pay?

3. If Miguel's mother receives a 7% discount because she is buying a large lot, how much will she have to pay?

5.4 Designing a Multiplication Algorithm

In Investigation 4, you wrote algorithms for adding and subtracting fractions. Recall that an *algorithm* is a plan, or a series of steps, for doing a computation. In this problem, you will work with your group to develop an algorithm for multiplying fractions.

Your group may develop more than one algorithm. What is important is that each member of your group understands and feels comfortable with at least one algorithm for multiplying fractions. Remember, for an algorithm to be useful, each step should be clear and precise so that other people will be able to carry out the steps and get correct answers.

Problem 5.4

Work with your group to develop at least one algorithm for multiplying fractions. You might want to look back over the first three problems in this investigation and discuss how each person in your group thought about them. Look for ideas that you think will help you develop an algorithm for multiplying fractions that will always work, even with mixed numbers.

Test your algorithm on a few problems, such as these:

$$\frac{1}{5} \times 25 \qquad 24 \times \frac{2}{3} \qquad \frac{5}{8} \times 12$$

$$\frac{3}{8} \times \frac{3}{4} \qquad \frac{1}{2} \times 2\frac{2}{3} \qquad 3\frac{1}{3} \times 2\frac{4}{5}$$

If necessary, make adjustments to your algorithm until you think it will work all the time. Write up a final version of the algorithm. Make sure it is neat and precise so others can follow it.

■ Problem 5.4 Follow-Up

Exchange your algorithm with that of another group. Test the other group's plan. Write a paragraph explaining how your algorithm and the other group's algorithm are alike and how they are different.

As you work on these ACE questions, use your calculator whenever you need it.

Applications

1. Ms. Guerdin owns $\frac{4}{5}$ of a section of land in Tupelo township. She wants to sell $\frac{2}{3}$ of her land to her neighbor. What fraction of a section does she want to sell?

2. **a.** Sarah uses balsa wood to build airplane models. After completing a model, she had a strip of balsa wood measuring $\frac{7}{8}$ of a yard left over. Shawn wants to buy half of the strip from Sarah. What fraction of a yard does Shawn want to buy?

   b. If Sarah paid $2.00 for each yard, how much should she charge Shawn for the strip he buys?

3. A recipe for a large batch of cookies calls for $3\frac{1}{4}$ cups of flour. Amos wants to make half of a batch of cookies. How much flour should he use?

4. Murphy's department store is having a two-week sale during which all prices are reduced by $\frac{1}{3}$. Ophelia wants to buy the following items for her new apartment:

Item	Regular price
Vacuum cleaner	$120
Microwave oven	$240
Television	$330
4 CDs	$15 each
2 Speakers	$75 each

   a. Ophelia has $500 saved for the purchases. Can she buy everything on her list?

   b. There is a 5% sales tax. What is the most Ophelia could spend and on which items?

5. Rubin and Lea went to the amusement park on Saturday. Lea spent $\frac{1}{2}$ of her money, and Rubin spent $\frac{1}{4}$ of his money. Is it possible for Rubin to have spent more money than Lea? Explain your reasoning.

6. Mr. Jones' garden has an area of 21 square meters. He wants to increase its size by $\frac{1}{2}$. Draw a picture to show what his new garden might look like. Be sure to give the new area and dimensions, and show your reasoning.

7. Find a fraction and a whole number with a product that is a whole number.

8. Find a fraction and a whole number with a product less than $\frac{1}{2}$.

9. Find a fraction and a whole number with a product between $\frac{1}{2}$ and 1.

10. Find a fraction and a whole number with a product greater than 1.

Connections

11. Write a fraction between $\frac{1}{2}$ and $\frac{2}{3}$. Explain how you know your fraction is between $\frac{1}{2}$ and $\frac{2}{3}$.

12. The following table shows the number of people surveyed that intend to vote for each of the candidates for president. Make a circle graph for this data.

Candidate	Expected votes
Murningham	31
Graves	58
McKane	91

13. Inflation has caused a store owner to decide that she must increase all prices by 8%. What should she charge for the following items?

Item	Current price
basketball	$30
skateboard	$50
roller blades	$110
tennis racket	$75

In 14–16, insert <, >, or = to make the statement true.

14. $\frac{3}{5}$ _____ $\frac{7}{8}$

15. $\frac{12}{15}$ _____ $\frac{3}{4}$

16. $\frac{5}{8}$ _____ $\frac{10}{16}$

17. Order these decimals from greatest to least.

0.302   0.1   0.099   0.167   0.32   0.4

Extensions

18. The Pizza Pirate has been up to new tricks. The archery club put two pizzas in the freezer for a party. Of the two pizzas, the Pizza Pirate ate $\frac{1}{2}$ of a pizza, then $\frac{1}{3}$ of a pizza, then $\frac{1}{4}$ of a pizza, and then $\frac{1}{6}$ of a pizza. How much pizza is left?

19. On a map of the city of Detroit, the library is $\frac{5}{12}$ of an inch from the post office. On the map, 1 inch represents 5 miles.

   a. What fraction of an inch represents 1 mile?

   b. How far apart are the post office and the library?

20. While traveling in Mexico, Samantha found some beautiful ceramic tiles. The tiles are square, $6\frac{1}{2}$ inches on each side. Samantha wants to buy enough tiles to cover the floor of her sun room. The sun room is also square, 108 inches on each side. How many tiles does Samantha need?

Mathematical Reflections

In this investigation, you explored situations in which you need to find a fraction of another fraction or a fraction of a whole number. You discovered that $\frac{2}{3}$ *of* $\frac{1}{2}$ is the same as $\frac{2}{3} \times \frac{1}{2}$. **These questions will help you summarize what you have learned:**

1 You can model the product of whole numbers by thinking of multiplication as finding area. For example, you can think of 6×7 as the area of a rectangle with dimensions of 6 and 7. Describe and show how you can mark a square to show $\frac{2}{3} \times \frac{1}{2}$.

2 Look back over all of the examples of multiplying fractions—or finding a fractional part of another fraction—that you worked with in this investigation. What patterns do you see that helped you develop an algorithm for multiplying fractions?

3 When you multiply two whole numbers, the product is larger than the factors. Is the product of two fractions larger than the fractions? Explain your reasoning.

Think about your answers to these questions, discuss your ideas with other students and your teacher, and then write a summary of your findings in your journal.

Computing with Decimals

Nearly every day of your life, you use or interpret *decimal* quantities. Because our system of currency is based on the decimal system, you deal with decimals every time you buy something. You use decimals when you measure things in metric units. When you read the newspaper, you often have to interpret statements that involve decimal numbers such as, "The new baseball stadium will cost 7.5 million dollars." or "The average working week in Finland is 38.1 hours."

The problems in this investigation involve adding, subtracting, and multiplying decimals. As you work through the problems, you will learn to make sense of operations with decimals.

6.1 Buying School Supplies

The School Supply game will give you practice in estimating and calculating with decimals. The game involves the prices of items at a school store.

Items Sold at the School Store

Divider page	$0.07	Roll of tape	$0.84
Pencil	$0.28	Pen	$0.98
Eraser	$0.35	Highlighter	$1.05
Note paper	$0.42	Notebook	$2.24
Ruler	$0.70	Scissors	$3.15

School Supply Game Board

$2.24	$1.33	$0.35	$2.31	$1.68	$0.07
$3.43	$0.28	$3.08	$2.59	$1.05	$1.47
$1.26	$1.75	$1.12	$1.61	$1.54	$1.96
$1.40	$3.57	$2.80	$1.89	$0.91	$2.66
$2.03	$0.84	$2.87	$2.73	$0.70	$2.52
$3.15	$0.77	$2.45	$0.98	$0.63	$0.42

Rules for the School Supply Game

Materials

- Labsheet 6.1 (1 per pair)
- Markers, such as squares of paper, marked with each player's initials (about 15 per person)

Playing

- Each player begins each turn assuming he or she has $4.20.

- In turn, each player makes up an addition, subtraction, or multiplication problem that uses the prices of some of the items from the school store. (Assume there is no sales tax.)

- If the answer to the problem is on the grid, the player who made up the problem covers the answer with one of his or her markers. If the answer is not on the grid, the player does not get to cover a square, and the next player takes a turn.

- The first player with four markers in a row—horizontally, vertically, or diagonally— wins the game.

Problem 6.1

Play the School Supply game once or twice with your partner. Keep track of any strategies you find that help you win the game.

Problem 6.1 Follow-Up

1. If you wanted to spend as much of your $4.20 as possible on rulers, how many rulers could you buy and how much money would you have left?
2. Tell what operations you used to do question 1, and explain why you used each operation.

6.2 Moving Decimal Points

In a decimal number, the location of the decimal point tells you the place value of every digit in the number. For example, in the numbers 236.5 and 23.65, the 2, 3, 6, and 5 mean different things. The 2 in the first number means 2 hundreds; in the second number, it means 2 tens.

In this problem you will explore the possible sums and differences you can make with the same two sets of digits. You might be surprised by all the possibilities you can make just by changing the location of the decimal point!

To keep the number of possibilities reasonable, the constraint is added that you may place the decimal point just before, between, or just after the given digits. After placing the decimal point, you may add zeros only if they do not change the value of your number. For example, using the numbers 2, 3, 6, and 5, the numbers 0.002365 and 236,500 are not allowed, but 2.3650 is allowed.

Think about this!

Alice is trying to create different sums by moving the decimal points in two numbers: 236 and 89. Here is her work so far:

a.
$$
\begin{array}{r}
236 \\
+ 89 \\
\hline
325
\end{array}
$$

b.
$$
\begin{array}{r}
23.6 \\
+ 8.9 \\
\hline
32.5
\end{array}
$$

c.
$$
\begin{array}{r}
23.6 \\
+89.0 \\
\hline
112.6
\end{array}
$$

d.
$$
\begin{array}{r}
23.6 \\
+ 0.089 \\
\hline
23.689
\end{array}
$$

Bill says that the 0 added in problem c is all right, but the 0 added after the decimal point in problem d does not fit the constraint. Bill is correct. Why?

Bill says that she could have written this problem:
$$
\begin{array}{r}
23.60 \\
+ 0.89 \\
\hline
24.49
\end{array}
$$

Why does Bill's problem fit the constraints?

Problem 6.2

Work with the digits 2365 and 894. You may insert a decimal point just before, between, or just after the given set of digits, but you cannot change the order of the digits. After placing the decimal point, you may add zeros only if they do not change the value of your number.

A. Find ways to insert decimal points so you get five different *sums* using these two numbers.

B. Find ways to insert decimal points so you get five different *differences* using these two numbers.

C. What is the largest sum that you can make that fits the constraints of the problem? What is the smallest sum?

D. What is the largest difference that you can make that fits the constraints of the problem? What is the smallest difference?

Problem 6.2 Follow-Up

Suppose you can put the digits *in any order* and insert a decimal point at any position, but you cannot add zeros after a decimal point in front of the digits.

1. What is the largest sum you can make? What is the smallest sum?

2. What is the largest difference you can make? What is the smallest difference?

6.3 Multiplying Decimals

You can think of decimals as fractions with denominators of 10, 100, 1000, and so forth. For example, $\frac{1}{10}$ can be written as 0.1 and $\frac{37}{100}$ can be written as 0.37. To write $\frac{2}{5}$ as a decimal, first rewrite it as the equivalent fraction $\frac{4}{10}$, and then write it as the decimal 0.4. Since decimal numbers are fractions, you can use what you know about multiplying fractions to help you think about how to multiply decimals.

The grid on the left is a tenths grid with one strip shaded. This strip represents $\frac{1}{10}$, or 0.1. On the right, the strip representing 0.1 is shown divided into 10 squares, with one of the squares shaded darkly. This single square is $\frac{1}{10}$ of $\frac{1}{10}$, or 0.1×0.1.

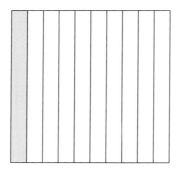 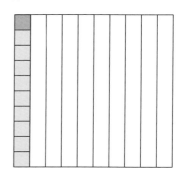

Below the horizontal lines have been extended to make a hundredths grid. This shows that $\frac{1}{10}$ of $\frac{1}{10}$ is one square out of a hundred squares, which is $\frac{1}{100}$, or 0.01 of the whole.

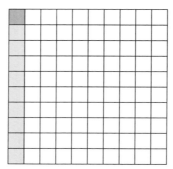

When you multiply 0.1 by 0.1 on your calculator, you get 0.01. What is the fraction name for 0.01? It is $\frac{1}{100}$, as you saw with the grid model.

In the next problem, you explore what happens when you multiply decimals on your calculator. Before you use a calculator to find an exact answer, think about how big you expect the answer to be.

Problem 6.3

A. Look at each set of multiplication problems below. Estimate how large you expect the answer to each problem to be. Will the answer be larger or smaller than 1? Will it be larger or smaller than $\frac{1}{2}$?

Set 1	Set 2	Set 3	Set 4
$21 \times 1 =$	$2.1 \times 1 =$	$0.21 \times 1 =$	$2.1 \times 11 =$
$21 \times 0.1 =$	$2.1 \times 0.1 =$	$0.21 \times 0.1 =$	$2.1 \times 1.1 =$
$21 \times 0.01 =$	$2.1 \times 0.01 =$	$0.21 \times 0.01 =$	$2.1 \times 0.11 =$
$21 \times 0.001 =$	$2.1 \times 0.001 =$	$0.21 \times 0.001 =$	$2.1 \times 0.011 =$
$21 \times 0.0001 =$	$2.1 \times 0.0001 =$	$0.21 \times 0.0001 =$	$2.1 \times 0.0011 =$

B. Use your calculator to do the multiplication, and record the answers in an organized way so that you can look for patterns. Describe any patterns that you see.

C. In a multiplication problem, there is a relationship between the number of decimal places in the factors and the number of decimal places in the product. Summarize what you think this relationship is. Show your reasoning.

Problem 6.3 Follow-Up

1. Test the relationship you discovered in part C on these two problems:

$0.5 \times 4 = \qquad 5 \times 0.4 =$

Now do the two problems on your calculator. What does the calculator show? Why?

2. When you multiply a number by 10, do you get a larger number or a smaller number? Why? Give three examples to support your answer.

3. When you multiply a number by 0.1, do you get a larger number or a smaller number? Why? Give three examples to support your answer.

Shifting Decimal Points

Now that you have seen how the positions of decimal points affect products, you can use these ideas to build a deeper understanding of multiplication. In this problem, you will work backward to find numbers with products that fit certain constraints.

Problem 6.4

A. **1.** Find two numbers with a product of 1344.

2. Find two numbers with a product of 134.4.

3. Find two numbers with a product of 1.344.

4. Find two numbers with a product of 0.1344.

5. Explain how you got your answers and why you think they are correct.

B. **1.** Find two numbers with a product between 2000 and 3000.

2. By moving decimal points, change the value of each of the numbers you found in part 1 so that their product is between 200 and 300.

3. By moving decimal points, change the value of each of the numbers you found in part 1 so that their product is between 20 and 30.

4. By moving decimal points, change the value of each of the numbers you found in part 1 so that their product is between 2 and 3.

5. Explain what you did to get your answers and why you think they are correct.

■ Problem 6.4 Follow-Up

1. What number times 6 gives the product 0.36? Explain.

2. What number times 0.9 gives the product 2.7? Explain.

3. What number times 1.5 gives the product 0.045? Explain.

4. What number times 0.12 gives the product 24? Explain.

6.5 Fencing a Yard

Kelly has a new Golden Retriever. The dog is full of energy and needs some safe space in which to exercise. Kelly has several friends who have agreed to help her fence in part of her yard—she just needs to buy the materials for the fence.

Problem 6.5

Kelly wants to fence in a rectangular space in her yard, 9 meters by 7.5 meters. The salesperson at the supply store recommends that she put up posts every $1\frac{1}{2}$ meters. The posts cost $2.19 each. Kelly will also need to buy wire mesh to string between the posts. The wire mesh is sold by the meter from large rolls and costs $5.98 a meter. A gate to fit in one of the spaces between the posts costs $25.89. Seven staples are needed to attach the wire mesh to each post. Staples come in boxes of 50, and each box costs $3.99.

A. How much will the materials Kelly needs cost before sales tax? Show how you arrived at your answer.

B. Local sales tax is 7%. How much will Kelly's total bill be?

■ **Problem 6.5 Follow-Up**

Using centimeter grid paper, draw a diagram of the fence. Draw the diagram carefully and accurately, and mark the position of each post and the gate.

As you work on these ACE questions, use your calculator whenever you need it.

Applications

In 1–3, estimate the answer, and explain how you made your estimate.

1. $23.54 + $7.98 + $3.45 + $13.03 ≈

2. $119.56 − $22.90 ≈

3. $15.10 × 12 ≈

4. Mr. Sandival's class is growing a plant. Each of the five teams in his class measured the height of the plant at the end of the first week and at the end of the second week. Here is a table of their measurements.

	Team 1	Team 2	Team 3	Team 4	Team 5
First week	3.4 cm	3.25 cm	3.3 cm	3.5 cm	3.35 cm
Second week	7.95 cm	7.8 cm	8 cm	8.15 cm	8.2 cm

a. All the teams measured the same plant. Why are the measures different?

b. Find the mean of the teams' measures for each week.

c. Using the means, how much did the plant grow from the first week to the second week?

5. Samuel buys the following at the grocery store:

> two dozen eggs at $0.75 a dozen
>
> one pound of butter at $1.39
>
> a 5-pound bag of sugar for $1.79
>
> two 5-pound bags of flour at $1.19 each
>
> an 8-ounce package of unsweetened chocolate for $1.64

If Samuel pays 3% sales tax, how much is his bill?

6. Loren is laying decorative brick along both edges of the 21-meter walkway up to his house. Each brick is 0.26 meters long. He is placing the bricks end to end. How many bricks does he need to do the job?

7. Lynette has a beautiful box that she wants to protect. She has been advised to put a strip of molding along each edge of the box to protect it. She measures the edges and finds that the length is 0.75 meters, the width is 0.4 meters, and the height is 0.22 meters.

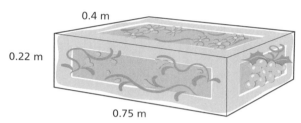

0.4 m

0.22 m

0.75 m

a. Lynette decides she needs four of each of these lengths. Is she correct? Explain.

b. How much molding does Lynette need in all?

c. If the molding costs $0.90 a meter, how much will Lynette's bill be without sales tax?

d. If the sales tax is 4%, how much will her final bill be?

Connections

8. What happens to a decimal number when you multiply it by 10 repeatedly? Use an example to explain your thinking.

9. What happens to a decimal number when you multiply it by 5 repeatedly? Use an example to explain your thinking.

10. Use your calculator to explore what happens to a decimal number when you divide it by 10 repeatedly. Use an example to explain your thinking.

11. In a–d, each mark on the number line is spaced so that the distance between two consecutive marks is the same. Copy each number line and label the marks.

a.

       1.8   2

b.

      1   1.1

c.

    2.93   2.95

d.

    1.99   2.01

e. Explain how you figured out what the labels should be.

Extensions

12. The table on the next page lists the winners of the gold medal in nine consecutive Olympic meets in men's springboard diving. The points are awarded for the difficulty and the execution of the dive.

In a–c, give evidence to support your conclusion. You may want to make a table of the differences between each pair of years.

a. Between what two years did the greatest change in winning score occur?

b. Between what two years did the next greatest change in winning score occur?

c. Between what two years did the least change in winning score occur?

d. What is the average of Greg Louganis's scores?

Men's Springboard Diving

Year	Winner (country)	Score
1960	Gary Tobian (USA)	170
1964	Kenneth Stizberger (USA)	150.9
1968	Bernie Wrightson (USA)	170.15
1972	Vladimir Vasin (USSR)	594.09
1976	Phil Boggs (USA)	619.52
1980	Aleksandr Portnov (USSR)	905.02
1984	Greg Louganis (USA)	754.41
1988	Greg Louganis (USA)	730.8
1992	Mark Lenzi (USA)	676.53

13 **a.** Show four *different* ways to fill in the missing numbers on the number line.

2.1

b. Add the five numbers in each of your answers in part a. Do you see a pattern?

c. Can you find four numbers for the blanks on this number line so that the sum of the five numbers will be 10? Why or why not?

2.1

Mathematical Reflections

In this investigation, you explored adding, subtracting, and multiplying decimals. You looked for relationships between whole-number and decimal computation. These questions will help you summarize what you have learned:

1 Describe in words, and illustrate with one or more examples, how to add two decimal numbers without using a calculator. Explain why your method makes sense.

2 Test your method from part 1 on this sum: 23.0574 + 11.99. Does your method tell you how to handle this case? If not, adjust your description so that someone reading it would know how to add these two decimals.

3 Describe in words, and illustrate with one or more examples, how you subtract two decimal numbers without using a calculator. Explain why your method makes sense.

4 Test your method from part 3 on this difference: 23.05 − 11.9863. Does your method tell you how to handle this case? If not, adjust your description so that someone reading it would know how to subtract these two decimals.

5 How is the number of decimal places in the product of two decimal numbers related to the number of decimal places in each of the numbers? Why is this so?

6 **a.** Find or create an example in which the product of two decimals is smaller than either of the numbers that are multiplied.

  b. Find or create an example in which the product of two decimals is smaller than one of the numbers multiplied but larger than the other.

  c. Find or create an example in which the product of two decimals is larger than either of the numbers multiplied.

  d. Look for patterns that will help you predict which of these results—a, b, or c—will be the case with any multiplication problem that you do.

Think about these questions, discuss your ideas with other students and your teacher, and then write a summary of your findings in your journal.

Dividing Fractions

Have you ever been with a group of your friends and shared a pizza or cookies or some other kind of food? Perhaps you looked for a way to share the food so that all portions were equal. For a similar type of situation, suppose a large supply of new math books is delivered to your school. The assistant principal hires you and a friend to assemble groups of 30 books to be delivered to each classroom. He asks you to figure out how many classroom sets you can make with the supply you have.

Mathematics can be used in such situations to help determine what an equal share is and how many rooms can receive a set of 30 books. In each of these situations, you can use the operation of division to help find an answer. As you explore the problems in this investigation, you will learn to decide when division is useful, and you will learn to make sense of division of fractions.

Fractions in Fund-Raising

7.1

In earlier investigations of this unit, you've learned how to use the operations of addition, subtraction, and multiplication of fractions to solve a variety of problems. Sometimes problems involving fractions can be solved by using the operation of division. Reviewing the meaning of division in problems involving only whole numbers will help to develop ideas about when and how to divide fractions.

Students at Spartan Middle School take a special field trip each spring. But they must raise funds to support the trip. Write number sentences showing the calculations required to solve some of the problems that occurred in one year's plans for fund-raising. Then explain how you recognized what operations to use in each case.

- The 24 members of the school swim team planned to raise money by getting pledges for miles in a swim marathon. If the team goal is to swim 120 miles, how many miles should each swimmer swim?
- Members of the school band plan to sell 600 boxes of cookies in the fund-raising project. There are 20 members in the band. How many boxes should each member sell to reach the goal if all members sell the same number of boxes?
- There will be 360 students going on the field trip, and each school bus carries 30 students. How many buses will be needed?
- Fifteen students in one homeroom earned money for the trip by helping their teacher pick apples in her orchard. She gave them one bushel of apples to split equally. The students counted 125 apples in their bushel. How many apples should each student get?

Compare your number sentences and reasoning about these problems with the ideas of others. If there are different ideas for solving the problems, decide which are correct and why.

Sometimes the amounts given in a situation are not whole numbers but fractions. To deal with those problems, you need to understand what division of fractions means and how to calculate the quotients when a fraction appears as the divisor or the dividend or both. The following problems challenge you to use your understanding of division with whole numbers to make sense of situations involving fractions.

Problem 7.1

In preparing food for sale at a school fund-raising event, several students faced questions that involved fractions. Answer the questions and give written explanations or diagrams that show your reasoning. Write a number sentence that shows all calculations that you performed to find your solution.

A. Naylah plans to make small cheese pizzas to sell at the fund-raiser. She has 9 packages of cheddar cheese. How many pizzas can she make if each uses

1. $\frac{1}{3}$ package of cheese?   **2.** $\frac{1}{6}$ package of cheese?

3. $\frac{1}{4}$ package of cheese?   **4.** $\frac{3}{4}$ package of cheese?

B. A local coffeehouse donated twelve pounds of fresh-roasted gourmet coffee. The students running the fund-raiser decided to sell the coffee in small bags. How many bags can be made if each contains

1. $\frac{1}{5}$ pound?   **2.** $\frac{3}{5}$ pound?

3. $\frac{1}{8}$ pound?   **4.** $\frac{5}{8}$ pound?

■ Problem 7.1 Follow-Up

1. Use ideas from your work on the questions about cheese pizzas and coffee bags to complete the following calculations

  a. $12 \div \frac{1}{4} =$ **b.** $12 \div \frac{1}{3} =$

  c. $12 \div \frac{2}{3} =$ **d.** $15 \div \frac{5}{3} =$

  e. $18 \div \frac{5}{6} =$ **f.** $21 \div \frac{7}{1} =$

  g. Explain in words why $8 \div \frac{1}{3} = 24$ and $8 \div \frac{2}{3} = 12$. How are these two calculations related? Why is the answer to $8 \div \frac{2}{3}$ exactly half of the answer to $8 \div \frac{1}{3}$?

2. Describe a procedure that seems to make sense for dividing any whole number by any fraction.

3. Write a story problem that can be solved by the division $12 \div \frac{2}{3}$, and explain why the calculation matches the story.

Share and Share Alike

At their special fund-raising event, Spartan Middle School students operated a number of games. Figuring prize amounts for the games led to more questions involving fractions.

> ### Problem 7.2
>
> Answer the following questions and give written explanations or diagrams that show your reasoning. Write a number sentence that shows the calculations that you performed to find your solution.
>
> **A.** Ms. Phillips brought jars of jellybeans to be shared by members of the student teams winning each game. How much of a pound of candy will each student get if
>
>   **1.** a four-person team wins $\frac{1}{2}$ pound of jellybeans?
>
>   **2.** a three-person team wins $\frac{1}{4}$ pound of jellybeans?
>
>   **3.** a three-person team wins $\frac{1}{3}$ pound of jellybeans?
>
>   **4.** a two-person team wins $\frac{1}{5}$ pound of jellybeans?
>
> **B.** A local candy store donated long chocolate bars that were used for prizes in a team competition. What fraction of a whole bar will each team member get if
>
>   **1.** a two-person team wins $\frac{3}{4}$ of a bar as a prize and shares it equally?
>
>   **2.** a four-person team wins $\frac{7}{8}$ of a bar and shares it equally?
>
>   **3.** a four-person team wins $1\frac{1}{2}$ bars and shares the prize equally?

■ **Problem 7.2 Follow-Up**

1. Complete the following calculations based on your work on the questions about jellybeans and chocolate bars. Be prepared to explain how you thought about each problem.

    a. $\frac{1}{2} \div 4 =$ **b.** $\frac{3}{2} \div 2 =$

    c. $\frac{2}{5} \div 3 =$ **d.** $\frac{4}{5} \div 4 =$

    e. $\frac{7}{10} \div 2 =$ **f.** $1\frac{4}{5} \div 3 =$

2. What procedure seems to make sense for dividing a fraction by a whole number?

3. Write a story problem that can be solved by the division $\frac{8}{3} \div 4$, and explain why the calculation matches the story.

7.3 Summer Work

In Problems 7.1 and 7.2, you developed ways of thinking about and solving division problems involving a whole number and a fraction. The questions in this problem involve dividing a fraction by another fraction. Use what you have learned to answer the questions.

Problem 7.3

Rasheed and Jade have a summer job at a kiosk called *Ribbon Remnants.* They sell small amounts of ribbon very inexpensively from end-of-bolt pieces of ribbon. In each situation that follows, give written explanations or diagrams that show your reasoning, and write a number sentence that shows the calculations that you performed to find your solution.

A. Rasheed takes a customer order to provide ribbons for conference badges. Each badge requires $\frac{1}{6}$ of a yard of ribbon. How many badge ribbons can he make from the given remnants of ribbon? For each answer that has a remainder, tell what fractional part of another badge ribbon he could make with that leftover amount of ribbon.

  1. $\frac{1}{2}$ yard

  2. $\frac{3}{4}$ yard

  3. $\frac{5}{8}$ yard

  4. $2\frac{2}{3}$ yards (Remember, $2\frac{2}{3} = \frac{8}{3}$.)

B. Jade is working on an order for bows for the conference workers to wear. She uses $\frac{2}{3}$ of a yard of ribbon to make one bow. How many bows can Jade make from each of the following remnants?

  1. $\frac{4}{5}$ yard

  2. $\frac{8}{9}$ yard

  3. $1\frac{3}{4}$ yards

  4. $2\frac{1}{3}$ yards

■ Problem 7.3 Follow-Up

1. Based on your work in Problems 7.1–7.3, what general procedure makes sense for division of fractions? Remember that a set of steps to do a computation is called an *algorithm.* So this procedure should be your algorithm for dividing fractions.

2. Test your algorithm on these division calculations.

    a. $\frac{2}{5} \div 2$ **b.** $6 \div \frac{2}{3}$ **c.** $\frac{3}{4} \div \frac{2}{3}$

    d. $1\frac{3}{4} \div \frac{1}{2}$ **e.** $7 \div 3$ **f.** $\frac{2}{3} \div 1\frac{1}{4}$

3. Write a story problem that can be solved by the division $1\frac{3}{4} \div \frac{1}{2}$, and explain why the calculation matches the story.

Applications

Lee's group in Home Arts class purchased ingredients in large quantities to make different sizes of muffins for a bake sale. Each bag of sugar contains approximately 20 cups. In 1–7, find how many muffins can be made from a bag of sugar if each of the different-sized muffins needs the amount of sugar given.

1. $\frac{1}{4}$ cup of sugar

2. $\frac{1}{8}$ cup of sugar

3. $\frac{1}{16}$ cup of sugar

4. $\frac{1}{5}$ cup of sugar

5. $\frac{2}{5}$ cup of sugar

6. $\frac{2}{7}$ cup of sugar

7. $\frac{4}{9}$ cup of sugar

8. Explain in words how the answers for $20 \div \frac{1}{5}$ and $20 \div \frac{2}{5}$ are related. Show why this makes sense.

Sam is in charge of awarding prizes to teams that win medals at an all-state mathematics competition. He decided to give each team member a little bag of chocolate drops with each prize. In 9–13, find how many pounds of candy each member on each of the winning teams receives.

9. The team of 8 students shares $\frac{1}{2}$ pound of the chocolate drops.

10. The team of 4 students shares $\frac{1}{4}$ pound of the chocolate drops.

11. The team of 3 students shares $\frac{3}{4}$ pound of the chocolate drops.

12. The team of 10 students shares $\frac{4}{5}$ pound of the chocolate drops.

13. The team of 2 students shares $1\frac{1}{2}$ pound of the chocolate drops.

A latte is the most popular coffee drink made at Jean's Beans Coffee Shop. Each latte requires $\frac{1}{3}$ cup of milk. In 14–16, find how many lattes can be made with the given amounts of milk. Be sure to explain what the remainder means in each case.

14. $\frac{7}{9}$ cup of milk

15. $\frac{5}{6}$ cup of milk

16. $3\frac{2}{3}$ cups of milk

Solve 17–19 and show why your answer is correct. Drawings may be used to explain your reasoning. Write a number sentence that can be used to solve each problem.

17. It takes $18\frac{2}{3}$ inches of molding to make a small picture frame for a snapshot. Ms. Jones has 3 yards of molding. How many small picture frames can she make? If there is a remainder, tell what this remainder means.

18. At the pet store, there are 12 cages with a rabbit in each. Sarah's mother owns the pet store and allows Sarah to feed the rabbits special treats. She has $1\frac{1}{3}$ pounds of treats for today. How much should Sarah give to each rabbit?

19. Bill wants to make 22 small pizzas for a party. He has 16 cups of flour, and $\frac{3}{4}$ cup of flour is needed for each crust. Does he have enough flour? Explain your answer.

In 20–25, complete each division. If there is a mixed number equivalent to your quotient, find it.

20. $10 \div \frac{2}{3} =$ **21.** $5 \div 37 =$ **22.** $\frac{6}{7} \div 4 =$

23. $\frac{3}{10} \div 2 =$ **24.** $\frac{2}{5} \div \frac{1}{3} =$ **25.** $2\frac{1}{2} \div 1\frac{1}{3} =$

26. Choose any two of ACE 20–25 and write a story problem to fit the computation.

Connections

27. Betty jogged $2\frac{2}{5}$ km on a trail and then sat down to wait for her friend, Glenda. Glenda has jogged $1\frac{1}{2}$ km on the trail. How much farther will Glenda have to jog to reach Betty?

28. John is scheduled to work at the car wash for 3 hours. He has already worked $1\frac{3}{4}$ hours. How many more hours must he work?

29. Jenny and her sister are paid to mow their lawn. Jenny mowed $\frac{2}{5}$ of the lawn and her sister mowed $\frac{1}{4}$ of it. How much of the lawn is left to be mowed?

Add or subtract. Write another fraction that is equivalent to each answer.

30. $\frac{9}{10} + \frac{1}{5} =$ **31.** $\frac{5}{6} + \frac{7}{8} =$ **32.** $\frac{2}{3} - \frac{5}{12} =$

33. $\frac{3}{4} - \frac{1}{3} =$ **34.** $2\frac{2}{3} + 1\frac{1}{3} =$ **35.** $2\frac{5}{6} - 1\frac{1}{4} =$

In 36–41, compute each product.

36. $\frac{1}{2} \times 7 =$ **37.** $4 \times \frac{3}{5} =$ **38.** $\frac{2}{7} \times \frac{1}{3} =$

39. $\frac{3}{4} \times \frac{7}{8} =$ **40.** $1\frac{1}{2} \times \frac{1}{3} =$ **41.** $4\frac{2}{3} \times 2\frac{3}{4} =$

42. Choose any two of ACE 36–41 and explain why your answer makes sense. You may use a drawing to support your answer.

43. Show how multiplication and division are connected. Use the multiplication fact that $\frac{1}{3} \times \frac{3}{5} = \frac{1}{5}$ to write two division statements that use the same three numbers.

44. You learned in *Bits and Pieces I* that every fraction can be written in many equivalent forms. For example, the fraction $\frac{12}{15}$ is equivalent to any other fraction that results from multiplying the numerator and the denominator by the same number. If we multiply the numerator and the denominator by 2, we get $\frac{24}{30}$, which is equivalent to $\frac{12}{15}$. When we multiply the numerator by 2 and the denominator by 2, we are multiplying the fraction by $\frac{2}{2}$, which is equal to 1.

Write two fractions that are equivalent to each of the following fractions. Find one with a greater numerator and one with a smaller numerator.

a. $\frac{4}{6}$ **b.** $\frac{10}{12}$ **c.** $\frac{12}{9}$

Extensions

45. When working with fractions, you sometimes need to find what to multiply a given number by to get a product of 1. For example, you multiply $\frac{1}{6}$ by 6 to get a product of 1. We can show this in symbols as $\frac{1}{6} \times 6 = 1$ or, since $6 = \frac{6}{1}$, we could write $\frac{1}{6} \times \frac{6}{1} = 1$.

In a-i write a factor that will make each number sentence true.

a. $2 \times \underline{\quad} = 1$ **b.** $\frac{1}{2} \times \underline{\quad} = 1$ **c.** $3 \times \underline{\quad} = 1$

d. $\frac{1}{3} \times \underline{\quad} = 1$ **e.** $\underline{\quad} \times \frac{2}{3} = 1$ **f.** $\frac{3}{4} \times \underline{\quad} = 1$

g. $\underline{\quad} \times \frac{5}{2} = 1$ **h.** $1\frac{1}{4} \times \underline{\quad} = 1$ **i.** $\frac{7}{12} \times \underline{\quad} = 1$

In each case, the factor by which you multiply a number so their product is 1 is called the **reciprocal** of the number.

For example, $\frac{1}{2}$ is the **reciprocal** of 2 and 2 is the **reciprocal** of $\frac{1}{2}$ because $\frac{1}{2} \times 2 = 1$ and $2 \times \frac{1}{2} = 1$.

46. Find a number by which to multiply the numerator and the denominator of the fraction so that the resulting denominator equals 1.

a. $\dfrac{1}{\frac{1}{2}}$ **b.** $\dfrac{\frac{2}{3}}{3}$

47. Find a number by which to multiply the numerator and the denominator of the fraction so that the resulting numerator equals 1.

a. $\dfrac{\frac{2}{4}}{\frac{3}{5}}$ **b.** $\dfrac{\frac{5}{2}}{\frac{1}{3}}$

48. Find the missing numbers in each number sentence. Describe the relationship between each pair of number sentences.

a. $3 \div \underline{\quad\quad} = 9$ $3 \times \underline{\quad\quad} = 9$

b. $3 \div \underline{\quad\quad} = 12$ $3 \times \underline{\quad\quad} = 12$

c. $2\frac{1}{2} \div \underline{\quad\quad} = 5$ $2\frac{1}{2} \times \underline{\quad\quad} = 5$

Mathematical Reflections

In this investigation, you explored situations in which you needed to divide fractions. You developed an algorithm for dividing fractions and used division to solve problems. These questions will help you to summarize what you have learned.

1. Explain your algorithm for dividing fractions. Demonstrate the algorithm on a problem for each situation given.

   a. a whole number divided by a fraction

   b. a fraction divided by a whole number

   c. a fraction divided by a fraction

   d. a mixed number divided by a fraction

2. How is the quotient of $20 \div \frac{1}{5}$ related to the quotient of $20 \div \frac{3}{5}$? Explain your answer.

3. You considered two different types of situations that call for division—sharing and grouping. Write a story problem for each type of situation and explain why you think it is a sharing problem or a grouping problem.

4. Can the answer to a division problem be greater than, less than, or between the two numbers you are dividing? In each case explain why or why not and show an example to illustrate your answer.

Unit Reflections

*R**ational numbers*** can be expressed in several forms—*fractions, decimals,* and *percents.* In this unit, you learned how to choose the form that will be most useful in a given situation and how to draw *diagrams* or *pictures* to make sense of those situations. You learned how to identify situations that call for *computation* with rational numbers. You developed *algorithms* for adding, subtracting, multiplying, and dividing fractions and decimals, and you have learned how to compute and solve problems with percents.

Using Your Quantitative Reasoning—To test your understanding and skill in using rational numbers, consider the following examples of ways that fractions, decimals, and percents occur in everyday situations.

1 *A local department store offered a scratch-off coupon to attract customers. Shoppers received a discount of 5%, 10%, 15%, and 25% off the list prices of any collection of items in the store. (Typically, sales tax and discounts are computed on the original price and rounded up to the nearest cent.)*

a. What were the least and the greatest possible costs, including 6% sales tax, for a shirt listed at $24.99?

b. Joey decided to buy the shirt in part a in three different colors. At the checkout, he scratched the coupon, and 15% appeared. How much did he actually pay for the shirts?

c. The store conducted a survey to find out whether the scratch-off coupons had influenced customers to buy. At the end of the day, they tallied these results.

- Would have purchased the items without the coupon—556

- Were strongly influenced by the coupon—378

- Were somewhat influenced by the coupon—137

i. What percent of customers was influenced by the coupon?

ii. Make a graph to show the percent of customers in each category.

2 *The Sweet Shop sells jellybeans in many different flavors. One day Jane asked for this mix:*

$\frac{1}{2}$ pound of cinnamon apple $\frac{1}{6}$ pound of bubble gum

$\frac{1}{3}$ pound of lemon $\frac{3}{4}$ pound of coconut

$\frac{1}{4}$ pound of licorice

a. What was Jane's bill, including sales tax, if jellybeans cost $4.98 per pound? There is a 2% tax on candy and snack food in her state.

b. What percent of Jane's mix did each flavor of jellybean represent?

c. Make a graph to show the percent of each flavor of jellybean in Jane's order.

d. Sammy hates coconut jellybeans, so he asked for Jane's mix without the coconut. What was his bill?

e. Shaquile likes fruit flavors. He wanted a mix of peach, mango, blueberry, and strawberry. The following chart shows how much the Sweet Shop still had of each flavor and how much Shaquile ordered.

Sweet Shop's Stock	**Shaquile's Order**
$1\frac{1}{2}$ pounds of peach	$\frac{1}{3}$ of what is left
$\frac{2}{3}$ pound of mango	$\frac{1}{2}$ of what is left
$\frac{3}{4}$ pound of blueberry	$\frac{1}{4}$ of what is left
$2\frac{1}{4}$ pounds of strawberry	$\frac{3}{5}$ of what is left

i. What was the bill for Shaquile's mix?

ii. What percent of his mix was strawberry?

Explaining Your Reasoning—When you use mathematical calculations to solve a problem or make a decision, it is important to be able to justify each step in your reasoning.

1. Explain how you found the least and greatest possible costs for a shirt in Problem 1.

2. How did you find the percent of customers in each category in Problem 1c? Explain why you chose the particular type of graphic display that you used. Explain how you constructed that display.

3. What operations did you use to find the cost for Jane's jellybeans?

4. How did you find the percent of the mix for each flavor in Jane's order?

5. Do you agree with these computations: $4 \div \frac{1}{3} = 12$ and $4 \div \frac{2}{3} = 6$? If so, why is the second answer half of the first?

6. Use the following problems to show the steps involved in algorithms for adding, subtracting, multiplying and dividing fractions and decimals. Be prepared to explain your reasoning in each case.

a. $\frac{5}{6} + \frac{1}{4}$ **b.** $\frac{3}{4} - \frac{2}{3}$ **c.** $\frac{2}{5} \times \frac{3}{8}$ **d.** $\frac{3}{8} \div \frac{3}{4}$

e. $23.4 + 17.42$ **f.** $43.09 - 17.62$ **g.** 350.5×12.4 **h.** $15.6 \div 9$

7. Explain the general procedures you use to answer these questions about percents. Give specific numerical examples that illustrate your answers.

a. How do you find the percent equivalent to a given decimal number?

b. How do you find what percent one number is of another?

c. How do you find a given percent of a number?

The ideas and techniques you've used in this unit will be applied and expanded in many future units of *Connected Mathematics* and in other mathematics work on problems that lie ahead in school and in your future work. Fractions, decimals, and percents are used in measuring and calculating quantities of all kinds—from length, area, and volume to time, money, test scores, and weights.

Glossary

algorithm A set of rules for performing a procedure. Mathematicians invent algorithms that are useful in many kinds of situations. Some examples of algorithms are the rules for long division or the rules for adding two fractions. The following algorithm was written by a middle-grades student.

> *To add two fractions, first change them to equivalent fractions with the same denominator. Then add the numerators and put the sum over the common denominator.*

base ten number system The common number system we use. Our number system is based on the number 10 because we have ten fingers with which to group. In a number like 253, each place represents ten of the previous groups. By extending the place-value system to include places that represent fractions with 10 or powers of 10 in the denominator, we can represent quantities less than 1. Below is a graphic representation of the number 253 in the base ten number system.

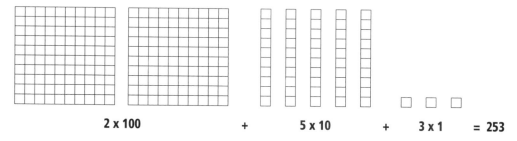

2 x 100   **+**   **5 x 10**   **+**   **3 x 1**   **= 253**

benchmark A "nice" number that can be used to estimate the size of other numbers. For work with fractions, 0, $\frac{1}{2}$, and 1 are good benchmarks. We often estimate fractions or decimals with benchmarks because it is easier to do arithmetic with them, and estimates often give enough accuracy for the situation. For example, many fractions and decimals—such as $\frac{37}{50}$, $\frac{5}{8}$, 0.43, and 0.55—can be thought of as being close to $\frac{1}{2}$. We also use benchmarks to help compare fractions such as $\frac{5}{8}$ and 0.43. For example, we could say that $\frac{5}{8}$ is greater than 0.43 because $\frac{5}{8}$ is greater than $\frac{1}{2}$ and 0.43 is less than $\frac{1}{2}$.

decimal A special form of a fraction. Decimals, or decimal fractions, are based on the base ten place-value system. To write numbers as decimals, we use only 10 and powers of 10 as denominators. Writing fractions in this way saves us from writing the denominators because they are understood. When we write $\frac{375}{1000}$ as a decimal—0.375—the denominator of 1000 is understood. The digits to the left of the decimal point (period) show whole units, and the digits to the right of the decimal point show a portion of a whole unit. The diagram below shows the place value for each digit of the number 5620.301.

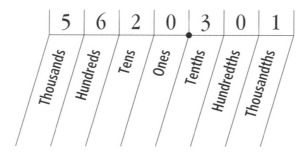

denominator The number written below the line in a fraction. In the fraction $\frac{3}{4}$, 4 is the denominator. In the part-whole interpretation of fractions, the denominator shows the number of equal-size parts into which the whole has been split.

equivalent fractions Fractions that are equal in value but have different numerators and denominators. For example, $\frac{2}{3}$ and $\frac{14}{21}$ are equivalent fractions. The shaded part of this rectangle represents both $\frac{2}{3}$ and $\frac{14}{21}$.

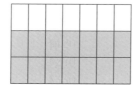

fraction   A number (a quantity) of the form $\frac{a}{b}$ where a and b are whole numbers. A fraction can indicate a part of a whole object or set, a ratio of two quantities, or a division. For the picture below, the fraction $\frac{3}{4}$ shows the part of the rectangle that is shaded: the denominator 4 indicates the number of equal-size pieces, and the numerator 3 indicates the number of pieces that are shaded.

The fraction $\frac{3}{4}$ could also represent three of a group of four items meeting a particular criteria; the ratio 3 to 4 (for example, when 12 students enjoyed a particular activity and 16 students did not); or the amount of pizza each person receives when three pizzas are shared equally among four people, which would be $3 \div 4$ or $\frac{3}{4}$ of a pizza per person.

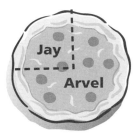
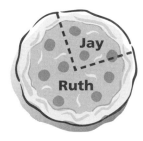
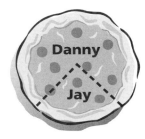

numerator   The number written above the line in a fraction. In the fraction $\frac{5}{8}$, 5 is the numerator. When you interpret fractions as a part of a whole, the numerator tells the number of parts in the whole.

percent A special decimal fraction in which the denominator is 100. Percent means "out of 100." When we write 68%, we mean 68 out of 100, $\frac{68}{100}$, or 0.68. We write the percent sign (%) after a number to indicate percent. 68 of the 100 squares in this rectangle are shaded, so we say 68% of the rectangle is shaded.

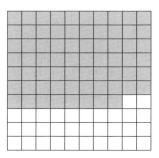

reciprocal A factor by which you multiply a given number so that their product is 1. For example, $\frac{3}{5}$ is the reciprocal of $\frac{5}{3}$ and $\frac{5}{3}$ is the reciprocal of $\frac{3}{5}$ because $\frac{3}{5} \times \frac{5}{3} = 1$. Note that the reciprocal of $1\frac{2}{3}$ is $\frac{3}{5}$ because $1\frac{2}{3} \times \frac{3}{5} = 1$.

unit fraction A fraction with a numerator of 1. For example, in the unit fraction $\frac{1}{13}$, the part-whole interpretation of fractions tells us that 13 indicates the number of equal-size parts into which the whole has been split and that the fraction represents the quantity of 1 of those parts.

Index

Addition
    ACE, 35–41, 49–52, 72–75
    algorithm, 48
    decimal, 4, 31–34, 64–68
    estimation, 4, 31–34
    of fractions, 4, 31–34, 43–48
Algorithm, 48
    for adding fractions, 48
    for dividing fractions, 82
    for multiplying fractions, 4, 59
    for subtracting fractions, 48
Area, 54–59

Benchmark
    ACE, 35–41
    decimal, 31–34
    fraction, 31–34

Circle graph, 4
    making, 21–23

Decimals
    ACE, 12–16, 35–41, 72–75
    adding, 4, 31–34, 64–68
    benchmarks, 31–34
    estimating with, 4, 31–34, 64–66
    fractions and, 16, 47, 68–69
    multiplying, 4, 5–11, 64–71
    place value, 66–67
    subtracting, 4, 64–68
Discount, percent, 4, 9–11, 20–21

Division
    ACE, 83–86
    algorithm, 82
    with fractions, 77–87

Estimation
    ACE, 35–41, 72–73
    with decimals, 4, 31–34, 64–66
    with fractions, 4, 31–34

Fractions
    ACE, 14–16, 29, 35–41, 49–52, 60–62, 83–86
    adding, 4, 43–48
    addition and subtraction algorithms for, 48
    benchmarks, 31–34
    decimals and, 16, 47, 68–69
    division, 77–82
    equivalent, 14–15, 43–45
    estimating with, 4, 31–34
    multiplication algorithm for, 59
    multiplying, 54–59
    percent and, 5, 16, 18–19
    subtracting, 4, 43–48

Graph, circle, 4, 21–23
Graphing, nonlinear, 47

Investigation
    Adding and Subtracting Fractions, 43–53

Computing with Decimals, 64–76

Dividing Fractions, 77–87

Estimating with Fractions and Decimals, 31–42

Finding Areas and Other Products, 54–63

More About Percents, 18–30

Using Percents, 5–17

Journal, 17, 30, 42, 53, 63, 76, 87

Looking Back and Looking Ahead: Unit Reflections, 88–90

Mathematical Highlights, 4
Mathematical Reflections, 17, 30, 42, 53, 63, 76, 87
Multiplication
ACE, 12–16, 60–62, 72–75
algorithm, 59
with decimals, 5–11, 64–71
with fractions, 54–59
pattern, 69–70
reasonable answers, 66–68

Nonlinear graphing, 47

Pattern
ACE, 61, 73–75
decimal product, 69–70
Percent
ACE, 12–16, 24–29, 61
discount, 4, 9–11, 20–21
fractions and, 5, 16, 18–19
of a number, 5–11
one number is of another, 18–23
sales tax, 4, 5–7
tip, 4, 7–8
Pie chart, making, 21–23
Place value, decimal, 66–67
Prediction, using percent, 18–19

Reciprocal, 86, 94

Sales tax, 5–7
Subtraction
ACE, 49–52, 72–75
algorithm, 48
with decimals, 64–68
with fractions, 43–48

Connected Mathematics™

Ruins of Montarek

Spatial Visualization

Student Edition

Glenda Lappan
James T. Fey
William M. Fitzgerald
Susan N. Friel
Elizabeth Difanis Phillips

Prentice
Hall

Glenview, Illinois
Needham, Massachusetts
Upper Saddle River, New Jersey

The Connected Mathematics Project was developed at Michigan State University with the support of National Science Foundation Grant No. MDR 9150217.

This project was supported, in part,
by the
National Science Foundation
Opinions expressed are those of the authors
and not necessarily those of the Foundation

The Michigan State University authors and administration have agreed that all MSU royalties arising from this publication will be devoted to purposes supported by the Department of Mathematics and the MSU Mathematics Education Enrichment Fund.

Photo Acknowledgements: 7 (architect) © Spencer Grant/FPG International; 7 (construction) © Norman R. Rowan/Stock, Boston; 10 © Gene Ahrens/FPG International; 13 © George Holton/Photo Researchers, Inc.; 26 © Arvind Garg/Photo Researchers, Inc.; 35 © Roy Bishop/Stock, Boston; 52 © T. Holton/Superstock, Inc.; 67 © Sam C. Pierson Jr./Photo Researchers, Inc.; 68 © S. Vidler/Superstock, Inc.; 79 © C. Orrico/Superstock, Inc.

Contents

Mathematical Highlights   6

Investigation 1: Building Plans   7
   1.1 Building from Base Plans   8
   1.2 Reflecting Figures   10
   1.3 Making Drawings of Cube Models   13
   1.4 Unraveling Mysteries   14
   1.5 Matching a Building to Its Plans   15
   1.6 Which Building Is Which?   16
   Applications—Connections—Extensions   19
   Mathematical Reflections   25

Investigation 2: Making Buildings   26
   2.1 Reconstructing Ruins   26
   2.2 Constructing Buildings from Plans   28
   2.3 Building from Incomplete Plans   30
   Applications—Connections—Extensions   33
   Mathematical Reflections   39

Investigation 3: Describing Unique Buildings   40
   3.1 Finding All the Possibilities   40
   3.2 Finding Maximal and Minimal Buildings   41
   3.3 Unraveling an Ancient Mystery   43
   Applications—Connections—Extensions   45
   Mathematical Reflections   51

Investigation 4: Isometric Dot Paper Representations   52
   4.1 Drawing a Cube   53
   4.2 Drawing a Cube Model   54
   4.3 Drawing More Complex Buildings   56
   4.4 Creating Your Own Building   57
   Applications—Connections—Extensions   58
   Mathematical Reflections   61

Investigation 5: Ziggurats   62
   5.1 Building Ziggurats   62
   5.2 Representing Ziggurats   64
   Applications—Connections—Extensions   65
   Mathematical Reflections   71

Investigation 6: Seeing the Isometric View   72
   6.1 Viewing a Building   72
   6.2 Removing Cubes   74
   6.3 Adding Cubes   75
   6.4 Putting the Pieces Together   76
   Applications—Connections—Extensions   77
   Mathematical Reflections   81

The Unit Project: Design a Building   82

Looking Back and Looking Ahead: Unit Reflections   83

Glossary   85

Index   86

Ruins of Montarek

What are some situations in which a three-dimensional model is used to represent a three-dimensional object? What are some situations in which a two-dimensional image or drawing is used to represent a three-dimensional object?

How would you make a drawing to represent a cube building so that a person looking at your drawing would know exactly what the building looks like?

How do you think architects communicate information about three-dimensional buildings with a set of two-dimensional drawings?

We live in a three-dimensional world. You and the objects around you can be measured in three different directions. We call these measures length, width, and height. You can look at any object and ask, "How wide is it?" "How long is it?" and "How tall is it?" Objects from our three-dimensional surroundings are often represented with only two dimensions. For example, when you watch television or look at a photograph, you are seeing two-dimensional images of three-dimensional objects. As an experiment, pick up a book and hold it so that you can only see the front cover. From this view, the book looks two-dimensional; you can see its width and height, but not its depth. Just as 3-D is short for "three-dimensional," 2-D is a short way of saying "two-dimensional."

Sometimes we have to make decisions or gather information about three-dimensional objects from two-dimensional representations. Architects create plans for buildings on paper, which serve as a guide to builders during construction. Some video games require making judgments about moves based on the depth of objects as well as their length and width.

In this unit, you will learn about relationships between two-dimensional building plans and three-dimensional buildings. The plans will help you solve problems and make models of the buildings you encounter. You also learn to make a set of plans to describe a particular building.

As you develop your spatial skills, you will solve problems like those on the opposite page.

• Here are the *base outline, front view,* and *right view* of a cube
building. Can you make a model of the building from cubes?

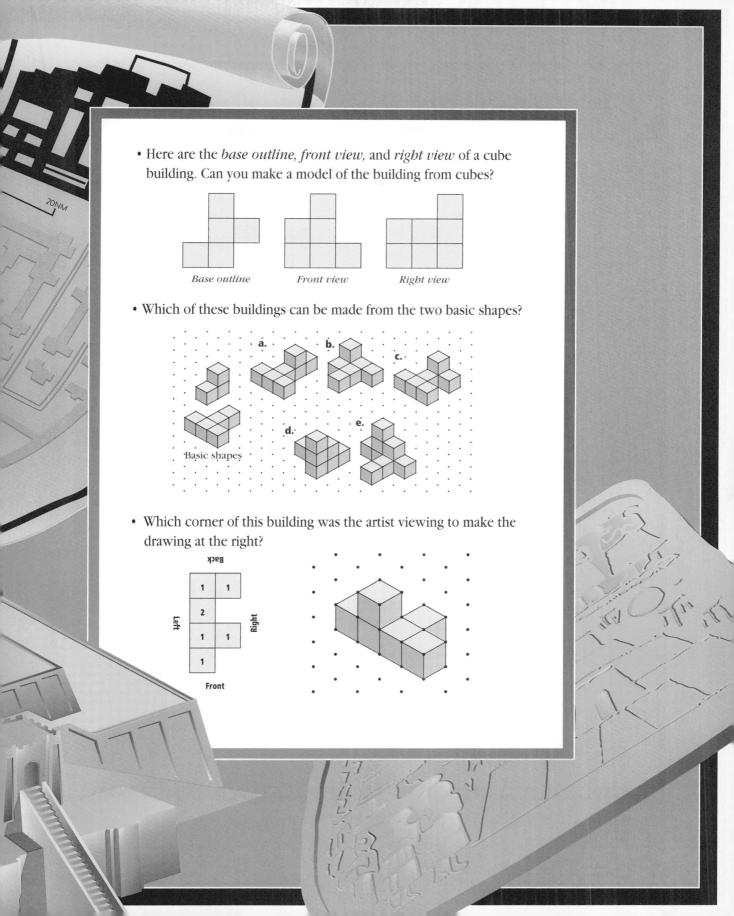

Base outline   Front view   Right view

• Which of these buildings can be made from the two basic shapes?

a.   b.   c.

d.   e.

Basic shapes

• Which corner of this building was the artist viewing to make the
drawing at the right?

Back

1	1
2	
1	1
1	

Left   Right

Front

Mathematical Highlights

In *Ruins of Montarek*, you will explore relationships between three-dimensional objects and two-dimensional representations of those objects. The unit should help you to

- Create two-dimensional representations of cube buildings in three different ways;

- Understand and recognize line symmetry;

- Read information from two-dimensional drawings and create examples of cube buildings that fit the drawings;

- Understand that a set of drawings or plans can have more than one building that fits the given information and learn to find the maximal and minimal buildings for the plans;

- Visualize transformations of cube buildings and make isometric drawings of the transformed buildings;

- Reason about and communicate spatial relationships; and

- Use models and representations of models of cube buildings to solve problems.

As you work on the problems in this unit, make it a habit to ask questions about situations that involve visualizing and reasoning about three-dimensional objects in space: *What kind of representations might be helpful in understanding the given situation and the relationships among the sets of plans and the buildings in the problem? Will it be useful to look for lines of symmetries in the plans? Are there cubes that are hidden in the buildings that will not be seen in the sets of plans? Do I know where some of the hidden cubes must be in reconstructing the building? Can I visualize what the building looks like from the front and the right side? Can I rotate the building in my head and visualize the other views?*

Building Plans

Have you ever seen a building under construction? As a building crew is constructing a building, they use a set of building plans. *Building plans* show how the different parts of the building—such as the foundation, walls, and ceilings—fit together. Building plans are created by architects and used by building crews and construction supervisors.

In this unit, you will learn about drawings that show what the base and the outside of a building look like. You will also use sets of building plans to construct models of buildings out of cubes. Models tell you how much space is in the building and what it looks like from the outside.

In this unit, Emily Hawkins, a famous explorer and adventurer, investigates the ancient ruins of the lost city of Montarek. As she explores the ruins, Emily finds it helpful to make models of the buildings from cubes. Some of the buildings that once existed in the city are now gone, so making models from the clues that remain is the *only* way to study them.

1.1 Building from Base Plans

The following problems will introduce you to how Emily Hawkins uses sets of plans to describe buildings. You will need 15 cubes and a building mat. A *building mat* is a sheet of paper labeled "Front," "Back," "Left," and "Right" as shown below.

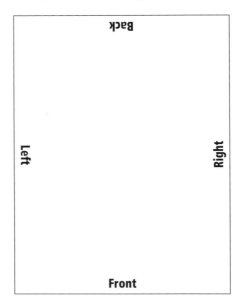

When you make your building mat, put the labels near the edges so there is a large area inside the labels. Always have the building mat on your desk so that the word "Front" is toward you.

One important piece of information to have about a building is the base outline. A *base outline* is a drawing of the building's base. The base outline tells you the shape of the building's base and how many cubes are in the bottom layer. In Problem 1.1, you will be working with a building with this base outline:

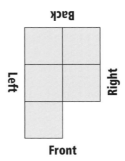

One kind of plan for a building is a simple base plan. A **base plan** is a drawing of the base with numbers on the squares to show how high each stack of cubes is. The building you will be working with in Problem 1.1 has this base plan:

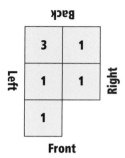

Back

Left | Right

Front

| Problem 1.1 |

The drawings above show the base outline and the base plan for a building. Use the base outline to construct the first layer of the building on your building mat.

How many cubes do you need to construct the bottom layer?

Now use the base plan to complete the building.

If you turn the building mat so that you look at the front, back, left, or right side of your cube building straight on, you will see a two-dimensional pattern of squares. Turn the building on your mat and decide which side of the building (front, back, left, or right) Emily was looking at when she made these diagrams:

A.

B.

C.

D.

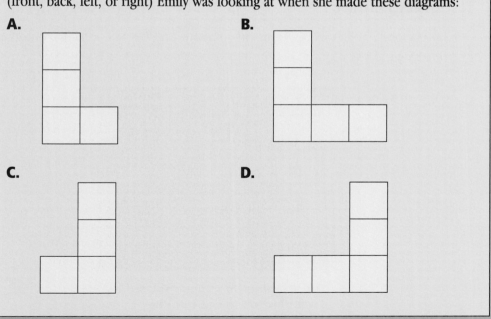

1. Compare the four views. What relationships do you see among them? How are they alike and how are they different?

2. If you are on one side of a cube model of a building and your friend is on the opposite side, how do your views of the cube model compare?

3. If your friend shows you a drawing of the back view of a cube model of a building, can you draw the front view? Why or why not?

4. Below is the view of a cube model of a building from the right. What does the left view look like?

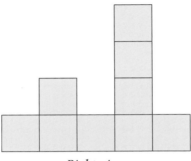

Right view

5. Create a building on your building mat that has the right view shown in question 4. Draw the views from the other three sides of your building. Have your partner check your building and views while you check your partner's.

1.2 Reflecting Figures

A small mirror is useful for visualizing the opposite sides of cube models. You can use a mirror to see the reflection, or *mirror image,* of a given view of a building.

**The Washington Monument and its
reflection in the Tidal Basin**

Problem 1.2

Labsheet 1.2A shows the figures below. For each drawing, set the edge of a mirror on the mirror line so that the reflecting surface is facing the cube diagram. Sketch the mirror image on the other side of the mirror line, and label the image. If the image is the opposite of the *front*, it must be the *back*. If it is the opposite of the *right*, it must be the *left*.

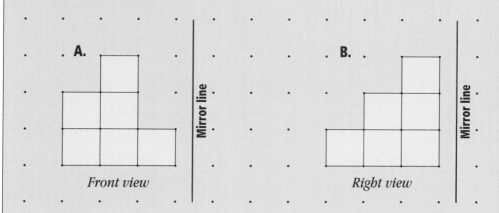

A. *Front view*

B. *Right view*

Labsheet 1.2A also shows the polygons below. Try to imagine what the mirror image of each figure would look like. On the labsheet, draw what you think the image will look like. Use a mirror to check your prediction.

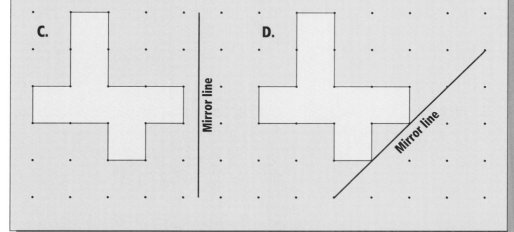

C.

D.

■ Problem 1.2 Follow-Up

If you made the drawings in Problem 1.2 correctly, they will show *line symmetry* around the mirror line. This means that if you fold your paper on the mirror line, the figure fits exactly on top of its image. Sometimes you can draw a mirror line on the figure itself. If you fold the figure on the mirror line, its two parts fall exactly on top of each other.

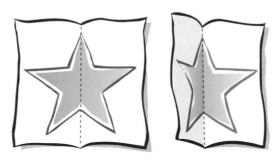

1. On Labsheet 1.2B, see if you can draw mirror lines on the figures shown below.

   a.   **b.**

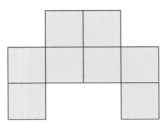   

2. How many different mirror lines can you find for this figure? Use the figure on Labsheet 1.2B and a mirror to test your ideas.

1.3 Making Drawings of Cube Models

You can represent a cube building by drawing the base outline and the front, back, left, and right views of the building.

Problem 1.3

Construct this building on your building mat.

A. Draw the base outline of the building on a piece of grid paper. Remember that the base outline shows the cubes that touch the building mat. Then, draw and label the front, back, left, and right views.

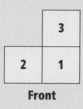

Front

B. Remove a cube from the building. Draw a base outline and a set of views for the new building.

C. Return the cube you removed so that you again have the original building. Now, add three more cubes to the building. Draw a base outline and a set of views for the new building.

■ Problem 1.3 Follow-Up

Look carefully at your views for each building. For each set of views, do you see any relationships that would let you use fewer views to represent the same information about the building?

Did you know?

The area that is now Central America and southern Mexico was once the home of an ancient people called the Maya. The Mayan civilization flourished between A.D. 250 and A.D. 900. The Maya made extraordinary advancements in astronomy, mathematics, and architecture. Mayan architects created remarkable buildings, including tall limestone pyramids topped by temples, like the one shown at right. Priests climbed the stairs of these pyramids and performed ceremonies in the temples.

1.4 Unraveling Mysteries

Emily Hawkins is trying to unravel some old mysteries about the ruins of the ancient city of Montarek (pronounced *mon tar´ek*). At the site of the ruins, she discovered pieces of broken stone tablets that have parts of sketches and diagrams etched on them. Emily needs to decipher the etchings to reconstruct the entire set of diagrams and sketches.

Problem 1.4

Some of the stone fragments show the front and right views of a building from the ancient city of Montarek.

A. The etchings show this front view of the building:

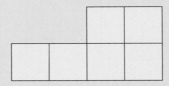

On your grid paper, draw the back view.

B. The etchings show this right view of the building:

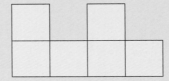

On your grid paper, draw the left view.

C. Use your cubes to build a building that matches your four views.

D. Do you think there is more than one building with the front and right views etched on the tablets and the back and left views you have sketched on grid paper? Explain your answer.

■ **Problem 1.4 Follow-Up**

Describe in *words* how what you see looking at a cube building from the front compares to what you see looking at the cube building from the back.

1.5 Matching a Building to Its Plans

In the last problem, you found that the right view of a cube building is the mirror image of the left view. Once you see the right view of a cube building, the left view does not give you any new information. Therefore, the plans for a cube building need only contain one of these views. For the same reason, a set of plans need only contain the front view or the back view, not both.

When Emily refers to a **set of building plans,** she is talking about a set of three diagrams—the front view, the right view, and the base outline.

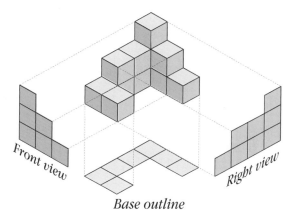

Base outline

Problem 1.5

Emily found a fragment of a stone tablet with this base plan etched on it:

Front

On your building mat, construct the building represented by the base plan.

Emily also found the three sets of building plans shown on the next page on stone tablets. Does one of the three sets of plans correspond to the building you made using the base plan? If so, which one?

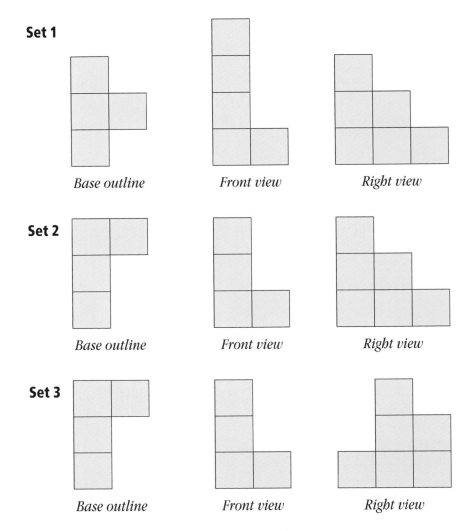

Set 1

Base outline   Front view   Right view

Set 2

Base outline   Front view   Right view

Set 3

Base outline   Front view   Right view

■ **Problem 1.5 Follow-Up**

Examine the sets of plans that do not match the building. Explain why each of these sets of plans does not match.

1.6 Which Building Is Which?

In this problem, you will have a chance to test your observation skills. You will try to match four different buildings with their building plans. In order to "read" information about buildings from drawings, you need to be very observant and look carefully at both the drawings and the building.

Problem 1.6

Below are base plans for four different buildings. With your group, construct a model of each building on a building mat.

A.

2	1	2
2	3	
2	1	

Front

B.

1	1	2
3	1	
2	1	

Front

C.

2	1	1
3	2	
1	1	

Front

D.

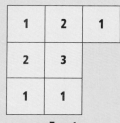

1	2	1
2	3	
1	1	

Front

Now, use your observation skills to match your buildings with the drawings on the next page. When you are finished, discuss your ideas with your group and try to reach consensus about which views go with which building.

■ Problem 1.6 Follow-Up

1. Can you remove cubes from the building in part A without changing its building plans? Explain your answer.

2. Can you remove cubes from the building in part B without changing its building plans? Explain your answer.

3. Can you remove cubes from the building in part C without changing its building plans? Explain your answer.

4. Can you remove cubes from the building in part D without changing its building plans? Explain your answer.

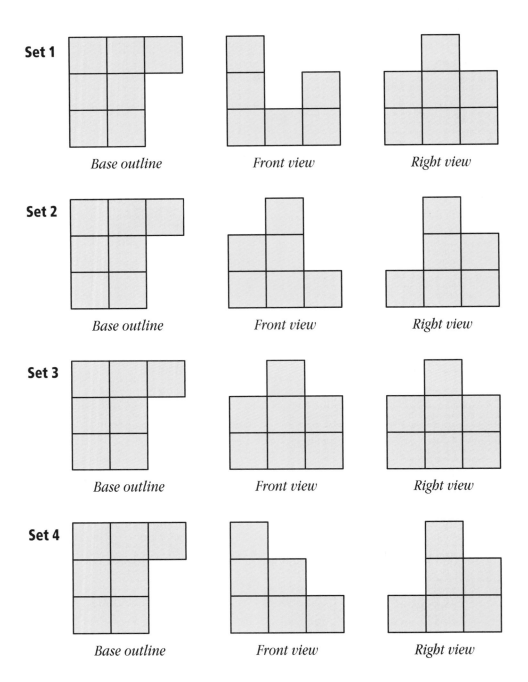

Set 1

Base outline   *Front view*   *Right view*

Set 2

Base outline   *Front view*   *Right view*

Set 3

Base outline   *Front view*   *Right view*

Set 4

Base outline   *Front view*   *Right view*

As you work on these ACE questions, use your calculator whenever you need it.

Applications

In 1–4, make a cube model of the building represented by the base plan. Then, make a set of building plans for the building on grid paper. Remember that a *set of building plans* includes a base outline and the front and right views of the building.

1.

1	1	1
1	1	
2		

Front

2.

2	2	1
	3	1
		1

Front

3.

2	1	1
	3	1
	2	

Front

4.

2	3	1
	1	2
	1	

Front

In 5–7, make a cube model of the building represented by the base plan. Then, match the building with the correct set of plans.

5.

1	1	1	1
2	3	3	
	2		

Front

6.

1	3	2	3
1	2	1	
	1		

Front

7.

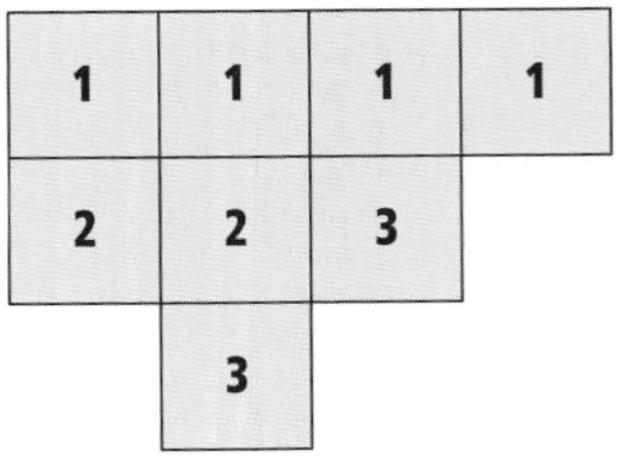

1	1	1	1
2	2	3	
	3		

Front

Set A

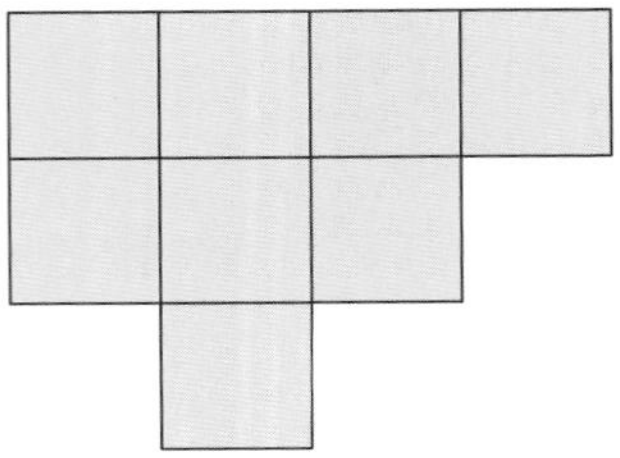

Base outline 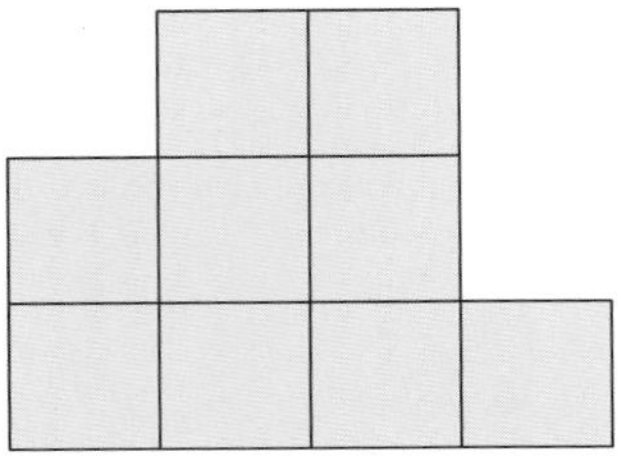 *Front view* 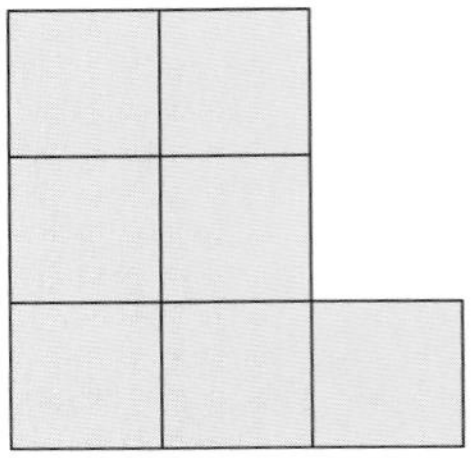 *Right view*

Set B

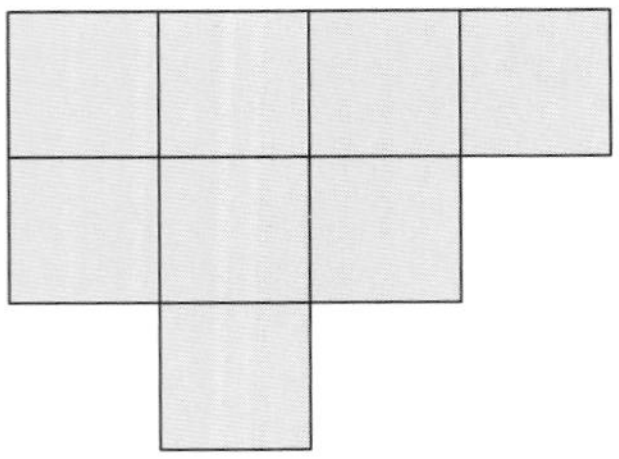

Base outline 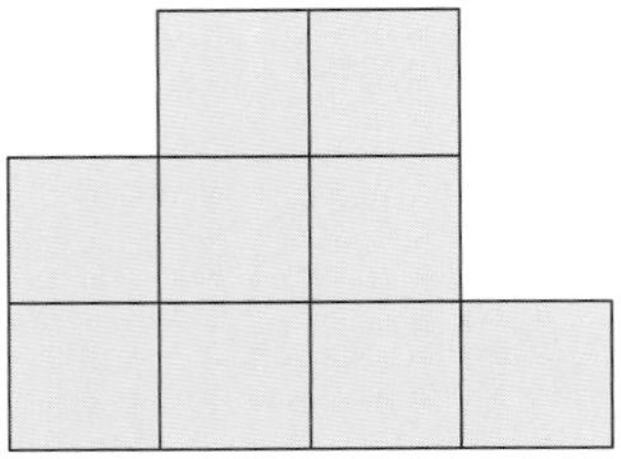 *Front view* 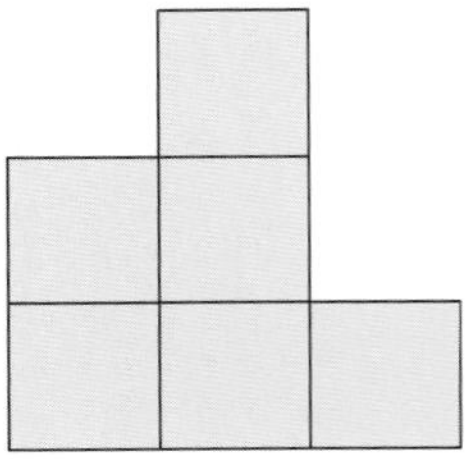 *Right view*

Set C

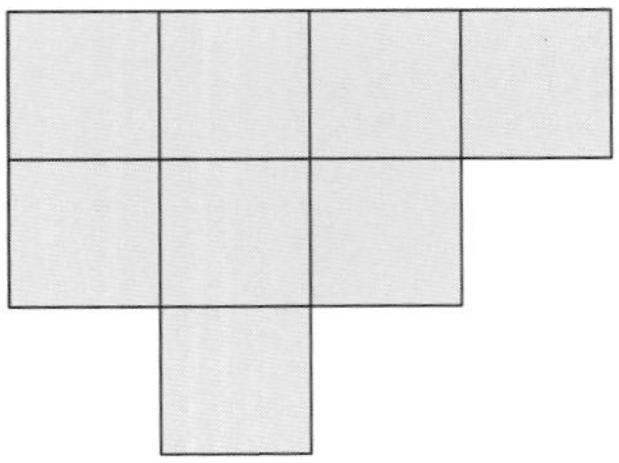

Base outline 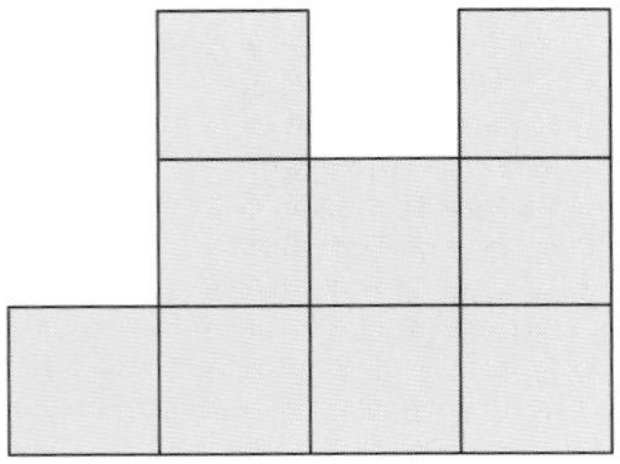 *Front view* 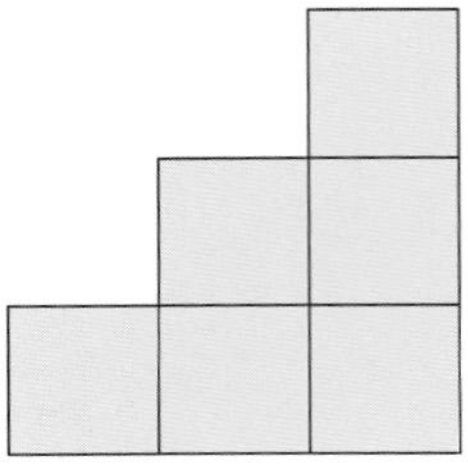 *Right view*

8. Each side of a number cube is numbered 1, 2, 3, 4, 5, or 6. The numbers are placed so that opposite sides add to 7. Below is the outline of a number cube with some values marked. What should the values of a, b, and c be so that the outline will fold up into a number cube?

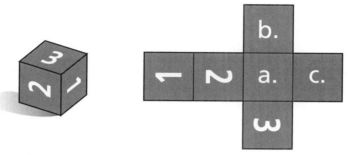

Connections

In 9 and 10, look back at the building plans you made in ACE questions 1 and 3.

9. If the length of a side of each square shown on your building plans is 1 unit, what is the perimeter of each of the three diagrams—base outline, front view, and right view—in each set of building plans for ACE questions 1 and 3?

10. If you were to paint the *top* of each exposed cube on the cube model in ACE question 1, how many square units would you have to paint?

Extensions

11. Emily Hawkins says that in the ancient city of Montarek, different kinds of buildings served different purposes. For example, some buildings were constructed to be garden houses, and others were built to be watchtowers.

   a. Garden houses needed lots of floor space so plants could be displayed and people would have room to walk through the gardens. Draw a base plan for a building that uses eight cubes that you think best meets this requirement for lots of floor space.

   b. Watchtowers needed to be tall but did not need much floor space. Draw a base plan for a building that uses eight cubes that you think would best suit the requirements for a watchtower.

In 12–14, three views of a cube and a sketch of a flattened cube are shown. Copy the sketch of the flattened cube on a sheet of grid paper. Then, use information from the pictures to mark the squares so that, if you folded the sketch into a cube, it would match the drawings.

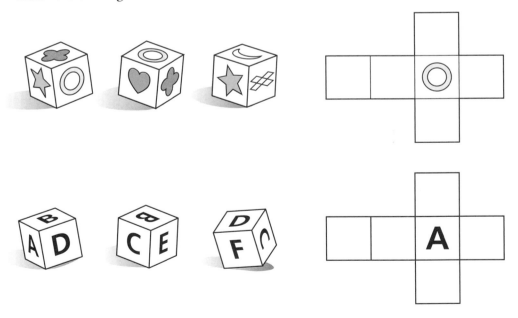

14.

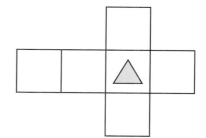

15. Design a cube puzzle of your own.

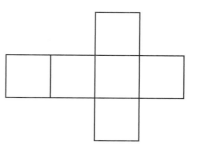

In 16 and 17, use Labsheet 1.ACE. Complete each diagram so that it has line symmetry around the mirror line shown.

16.

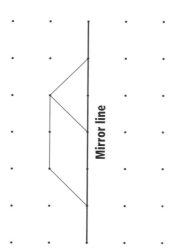

17.

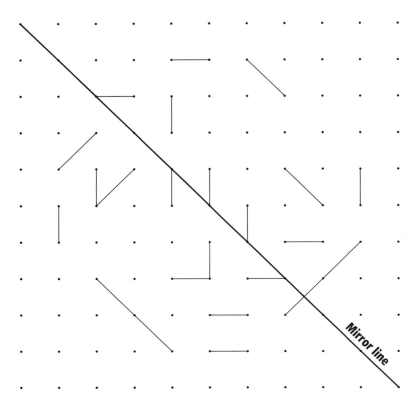

Mirror line

18. Design a figure on dot paper that has at least one line of symmetry.

Mathematical Reflections

In this investigation, you have been learning to read information about three-dimensional buildings from two-dimensional drawings. These questions will help you summarize what you have learned:

1 How does what you see looking at the front of a cube model compare to what you see looking at the back of the cube model?

2 What does it mean for a figure to have *line symmetry?* Give an example as a part of your explanation.

3 How many lines of symmetry does a 3-sided regular polygon have? A 4-sided regular polygon? A 5-sided regular polygon? A 12-sided regular polygon? How do you know your answers are correct?

4 Why is it possible to describe a building with a set of only three drawings—the base outline, the front view, and the right view—rather than a set of views showing each of the four sides and a base outline?

Think about your answers to these questions, discuss your ideas with other students and your teacher, and then write a summary of your findings in your journal.

Making Buildings

In the last investigation, you learned how to draw plans for cube buildings. In this investigation, you will begin by solving mysteries about some ancient buildings. Then, you will construct buildings based on complete and incomplete sets of building plans. By comparing your buildings with those of your classmates, you will determine whether more than one building can be constructed from a set of plans.

2.1 Reconstructing Ruins

For an explorer like Emily Hawkins, carefully analyzing plans of ancient buildings is one way of learning about the culture of the people who once inhabited a city. In this problem, Emily is trying to answer some questions about two buildings that were discovered among the ruins of Montarek.

Did you know?

People lived in "modern" cities over 4000 years ago. In 1922, archaeologists discovered the ruins of the ancient city of Mohenjo-Daro in Pakistan. This city was laid out on a grid containing broad central boulevards with shops. In the city was a huge building where wheat and barley were stored. Some archaeologists believe this building was similar to a modern bank. Many of the estimated 40,000 residents of Mohenjo-Daro lived in private houses with indoor plumbing. This luxury was made possible by an extensive sewer system, which was maintained by public workers.

Problem 2.1

In A and B, construct the building represented by the base plan. Then, make a set of building plans for each building on grid paper. Remember that a set of building plans consists of the base outline, the front view, and the right view.

A.

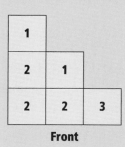

Front

B.

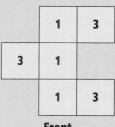

Front

C. Emily has studied some ancient writings she found among the ruins of Montarek. She thinks that one of the two buildings was used as a lookout post to watch for the approach of enemies or friendly travelers. Look at your building plans of the two buildings. Which do you think might have been used as a lookout post? Write at least two or three sentences to explain your answer.

D. Emily has discovered part of a diary kept by one of the residents of ancient Montarek. The diary indicates that the resident lived in the building from part A. Emily shows you a translated entry from the diary:

> *After dinner I went upstairs to my room. The stars were very bright, so I made my way to the tower from where I gazed at the stars. I can look down on the roof of my room from the tower, but I cannot see the tower from the windows of my room.*

By examining your cube model from part A, the building plans you made for the building, and clues from the diary entry, identify which cube(s) on the building might have been the location of the resident's room. Write an explanation for your answer.

■ Problem 2.1 Follow-Up

Design a building and imagine that your room is in one of the cubes. Write a diary entry that could be used to figure out where your room is located.

2.2 Constructing Buildings from Plans

So far, you have been drawing sets of building plans by looking at cube models of buildings. Sometimes it is necessary to work the other way. In the next problem, you get to be the explorer and make cube models of buildings from sets of building plans.

Problem 2.2

Emily Hawkins uncovered six ancient stone tablets in her last expedition to the ruins of Montarek. A set of building plans is drawn on each tablet. The plans are shown below and on the next page. Use cubes to make a model of a building corresponding to each set of plans.

As you make each building, compare your models with those of other students in your class. Note how the other cube models are like yours and how they are different. Record a base plan for each building so that you can share what you did with the class.

Set A

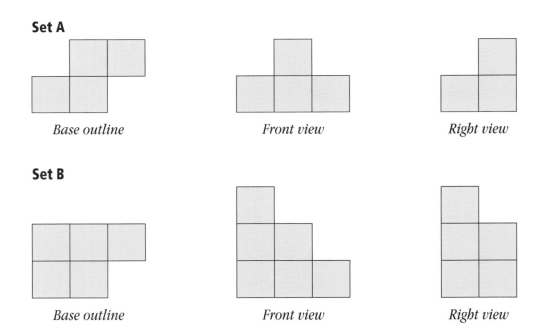

Base outline   Front view   Right view

Set B

Base outline   Front view   Right view

Set C

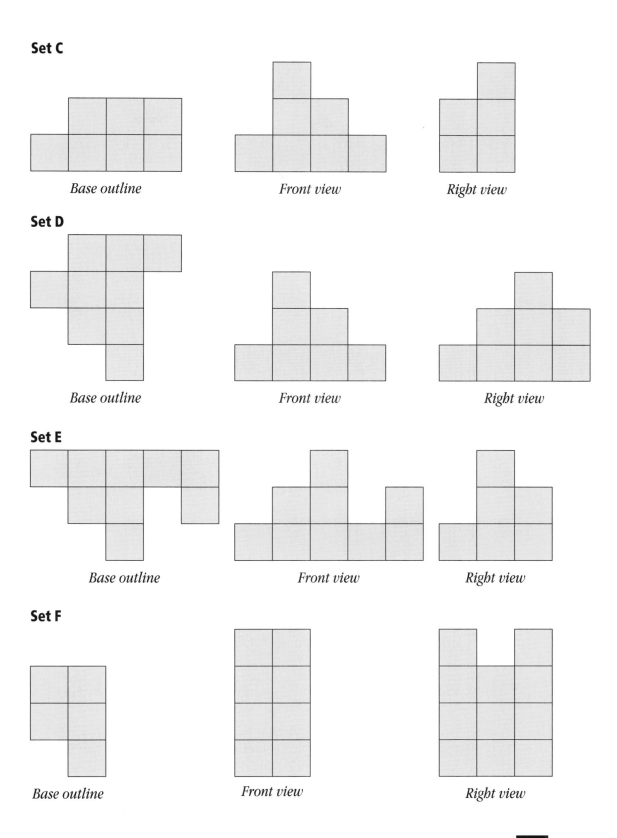

Base outline

Front view

Right view

Set D

Base outline

Front view

Right view

Set E

Base outline

Front view

Right view

Set F

Base outline

Front view

Right view

1. Did you find any differences between the cube buildings you made from the building plans and the buildings others in your class made? If so, describe the differences.

2. Do you think that more than one building can be made from a set of building plans? Explain your answer.

2.3 Building from Incomplete Plans

Often Emily finds only partial sets of building plans. She uses these incomplete plans to construct *possible* buildings. In the next problem, you will be working from some of Emily's incomplete sets of building plans.

Did you know?

Architects often prepare blueprints of building plans. A *blueprint* is like a combination of a drawing and a photograph. An architect or builder draws his plans in pencil or India ink on special paper that lets light pass through. This drawing is placed on blueprint paper and exposed to strong light. Special chemicals on the blueprint paper react with the light and turn blue. Because the light does not pass through the lines drawn in pencil or ink, they stay white on the blueprint paper. Before the blueprint is used, it is washed in water to remove the chemicals. This ensures that the white lines do not turn blue when the blueprint is used in the light. Blueprints allow architects and builders to make hundreds of exact copies of building plans for clients and workers.

Problem 2.3

Emily discovered some pieces of pottery among the ruins of Montarek. Each piece of pottery has an incomplete set of building plans painted on it.

An incomplete set of plans is shown in A–C. In each case, one of the three diagrams is missing—either the base outline, the front view, or the right view. On grid paper, draw the missing view and a base plan for each building.

A.

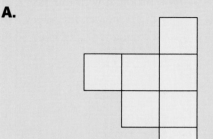

Base outline   *Right view*

B.

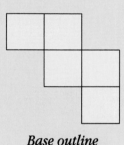

Base outline   *Front view*

C.

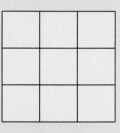

Front view   *Right view*

D. What is the greatest number of cubes you can use and still fit the plans given in part C? Make a base plan for a building with the greatest number of cubes.

E. What is the least number of cubes you can use and still fit the plans given in part C? Make a base plan for a building with the least number of cubes.

■ Problem 2.3 Follow-Up

1. Which incomplete set of building plans was easiest to use to create a base plan? Why do you think this is so?

2. Which incomplete set of building plans was hardest to use to create a base plan? Why do you think this is so?

3. Do you think there is more than one base plan possible for a set of incomplete building plans? Why or why not?

4. Compare the base plans you made in part C of the problem with the base plans made by other students in your class. Are your base plans the same or different? Explain your thinking.

As you work on these ACE questions, use your calculator whenever you need it.

Applications

1. Using your cubes, construct the building shown by this base plan:

3	2	2
2	1	2
2	2	3

Front

    a. Draw a set of building plans for the building on grid paper. Remember that a set of building plans includes the base outline, the front view, and the right view.

    b. Modify your cube building to make a different building with the same building plans. Make the base plan for your new building.

    c. Explain how your new building can have the same building plans as the original building even though it has a different base plan.

2. Record a base plan for this building:

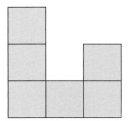
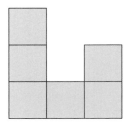
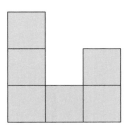

        Base outline   *Front view*   *Right view*

In questions 3–5, an incomplete set of building plans is given. On grid paper, draw the missing part of the plans—front view, right view, or base outline—and record a base plan for your building.

3.

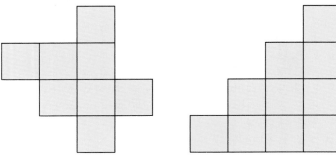

Base outline   *Right view*

4.

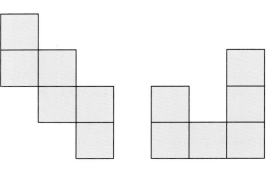

Base outline   *Front view*

5.

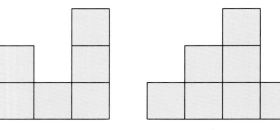

Front view   *Right view*

**Ruins of the Propylaea and the Temple of
Athena Nike (427–424 B.C.) in Athens, Greece**

6. Use your cubes to construct the building shown in this base plan:

3	1	1
1	1	2
1		

Front

a. Draw a set of building plans for the building on grid paper.

b. Remove two cubes from the building so that the front view is unchanged. Make a base plan of the new building.

c. Rebuild the original building. Remove one cube so that the right view *and* the front view are unchanged. Make a base plan of the new building.

d. Rebuild the original building. What is the greatest number of cubes you can remove so that the base outline is unchanged? Explain your answer, and make a base plan of the new building.

Connections

7. The *average height* of a cube building is the mean of the numbers of cubes that are stacked on each square of the building's base outline. Look at this base plan:

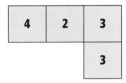

Front

a. Find the average height of this building. Explain how you found your answer.

b. Is it necessary to construct the building with cubes to find the average height? Why or why not?

c. If you multiply the average height of the building by the number of squares in the base outline, what is the result? Is anything special about this number?

d. Find the average height of the building shown in ACE question 2. What does your answer mean?

In 8–10, make a drawing that shows all lines of symmetry for the figure.

8.

9.

10.

Extensions

11. Emily Hawkins has uncovered a stone tablet that describes an ancient building. Emily asks you to help her figure out what the building may have looked like. She shows you this passage, which has been translated from the writing on the tablet:

A building stands at the border of Montarek. The building is made from 12 cubic blocks of stone. Its foundation occupies a rectangular area of 6 square units. Two towers, each made from 4 cubic blocks of stone, reach into the air from opposite corners of the building.

a. Use cubes to make a model of what the building might have looked like. Assume that each face of a cube is 1 square unit of area. Make a base plan of your building, and describe how you figured out how to make your building.

b. Are you sure your building is exactly what the ancient building looked like, or are there other possibilities? Explain your answer.

12. Design a building with no more than 15 cubes. Try to make your building a challenge. Draw a set of plans for your building, including a base outline, a front view, and a right view. Also make a base plan for your building. If there is more than one building that fits your plans, draw a base plan for at least one of these buildings.

Mathematical Reflections

In this investigation, you have learned to use building plans—the base outline, the front view, and the right view—to construct a cube model of a building. Sometimes you made a building from a complete set of plans; other times, one of the views was missing. When you constructed a building from a set of building plans, your building was sometimes different from the buildings made by other students. These questions will help you summarize what you have learned:

1 When you are building from an incomplete set of plans, which piece of information is the hardest to do without: the base outline, the front view, or the right view? Why?

2 If you are given the front view and the right view but not the base outline, how can you always figure out what is the largest possible base that will fit the two views? Explain. Use an example if it helps to explain your thinking.

3 Fatima thinks she has found a good way to build a cube building from a complete set of plans. She builds the base, the right side, and the front side separately and then tries to put them together. What do you think of her method? Will it always work? Why or why not?

Think about your answers to these questions, discuss your ideas with other students and your teacher, and then write a summary of your findings in your journal.

Describing Unique Buildings

In the last investigation, you found that it is sometimes possible to construct more than one building from a set of building plans. We need a way to interpret building plans so that they specify only one building. That way, if you and a friend work independently but use the same set of building plans as a guide, you will construct identical buildings.

3.1 Finding All the Possibilities

In this problem, you will work with your group to find all the buildings that fit a set of building plans.

Problem 3.1

With your cubes, make a building that corresponds to this set of building plans:

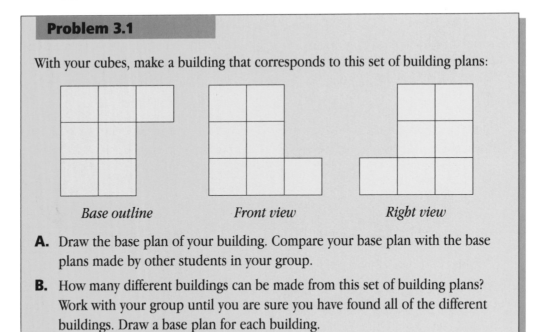

Base outline   *Front view*   *Right view*

A. Draw the base plan of your building. Compare your base plan with the base plans made by other students in your group.

B. How many different buildings can be made from this set of building plans? Work with your group until you are sure you have found all of the different buildings. Draw a base plan for each building.

■ **Problem 3.1 Follow-Up**

1. Of the different base plans you made in Problem 3.1, are there any squares with numbers that do not change? If so, identify the squares with numbers that always remain the same.

2. Look carefully at the base plans for the different buildings you found in Problem 3.1.

   a. What is the least number of cubes used for any of the buildings?

   b. How many different buildings can be made from the least number of cubes?

   c. What is the greatest number of cubes used for any of the buildings?

   d. How many buildings can be made from the greatest number of cubes?

3.2 Finding Maximal and Minimal Buildings

Emily Hawkins has translated some interesting facts about the way buildings were constructed in ancient Montarek. For a set of building plans, buildings made using the *least* number of cubes are called **minimal buildings**. Buildings made with the *greatest* number of cubes are called **maximal buildings**.

In Problem 3.1, you discovered that the *maximal building is unique* and *the minimal building is not necessarily unique.* This means that only one maximal building can be made from a set of building plans. However, using the same plans, it may be possible to construct more than one minimal building.

Problem 3.2

The plans in A–C were discovered by Emily among the ruins of Montarek. For each set of plans, find a minimal building and the maximal building. Record the base plans for your minimal building and the maximal building on grid paper. For each part, compare your minimal and maximal base plans with those of others in your class or group.

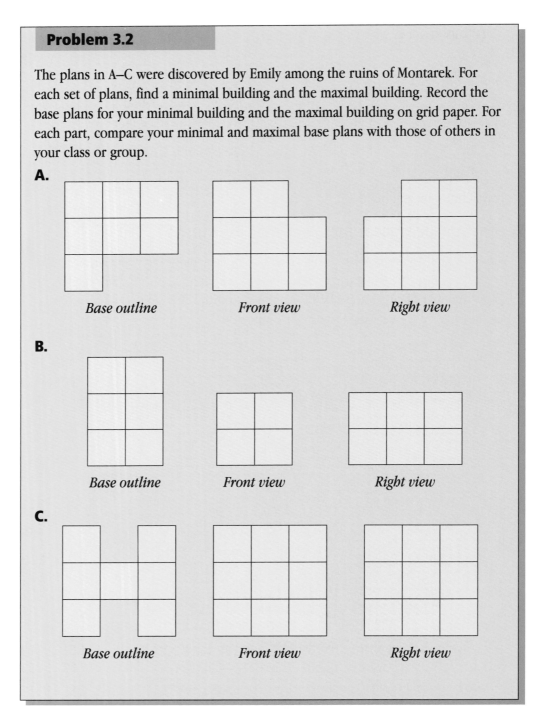

A.

Base outline   Front view   Right view

B.

Base outline   Front view   Right view

C.

Base outline   Front view   Right view

■ **Problem 3.2 Follow-Up**

Create a set of building plans for which the minimal building is the same as the maximal building.

3.3 Unraveling an Ancient Mystery

Emily Hawkins' explorations of the ruins of Montarek have helped her to make an important discovery! She discovered that when making a building from a set of building plans, the people of Montarek always constructed the maximal building. Emily feels that this discovery can be useful in solving another ancient mystery about the ruins of Montarek.

In her explorations, Emily came across the following set of building plans for a large and mysterious ancient building:

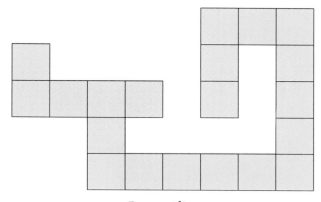

Base outline

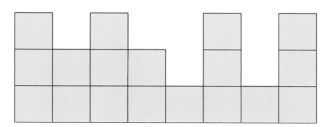

Front view

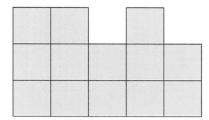

Right view

Problem 3.3

A. Work with your group to construct a minimal building from the set of building plans. Make a base plan of your building on grid paper.

B. Work with your group to construct the maximal building from the set of building plans. Make a base plan of your building on grid paper.

■ Problem 3.3 Follow-Up

Recall that the people of Montarek always constructed maximal buildings. How might the people of Montarek have used this ancient building? Explain your reasoning.

As you work on these ACE questions, use your calculator whenever you need it.

Applications

1. Look carefully at this set of building plans:

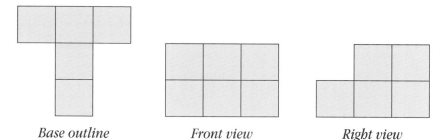

Base outline   *Front view*   *Right view*

a. Construct a minimal building from the building plans. Make a base plan of the building.

b. Suppose it costs $5 to put a special glaze on the top of each exposed cube in a building. How much would it cost to put the glaze on the exposed top of your minimal building?

c. Now construct the maximal building from the building plans. Make a base plan of the building.

d. How much will it cost to glaze the exposed top of the maximal building?

e. How do the costs of glazing the roofs of the minimal and maximal buildings compare? Will the relationship between the cost of glazing the roof of a minimal building and the cost of glazing the roof of a maximal building always be the same as what you found here? Why or why not?

In 2 and 3, make base plans for a minimal building and the maximal building with the given set of building plans. Tell how many cubes are needed for each building.

2.

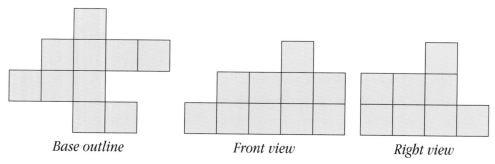

Base outline   Front view   Right view

3.

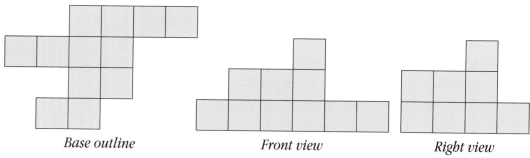

Base outline   Front view   Right view

Connections

4. Use your cubes to construct a maximal building that has a roof area of 12 square units.

   a. On grid paper, make a base plan of your maximal building, and draw a set of building plans for it.

   b. How many cubes did you use to construct your building?

5. Construct a building with 10 cubes.

   a. On grid paper, make a base plan for your building, and draw a set of building plans for it.

   b. Do you think your building is a minimal building, the maximal building, or neither? Explain your reasoning.

6. Here is a set of incomplete plans for a building.

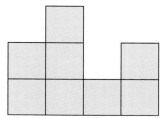

Base outline

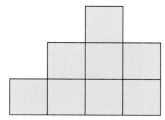

Front view

   a. Build every possible building that will fit these plans. Make base plans to record each possible building.

   b. Explain how you know you have found every possible building.

Extensions

7. Emily Hawkins has uncovered another mystery among the ruins of Montarek. She is trying to reconstruct an ancient building that has completely disappeared—no trace of it remains. One of the clues that Emily has is that the building was a maximal building made from 13 cubes. Emily also has a piece of ancient parchment that shows the front view of the building:

Front view

a. Using your cubes, construct a building that fits the clues. Draw a base plan of the building on grid paper.

b. Make a set of building plans for your building.

c. Do you think the building you have constructed is a model of the same building that once existed in Montarek, or do you think there are other possibilities? Explain your reasoning.

8. a. For each of the regular polygons shown below, find the number of lines of symmetry. Organize your data into a table.

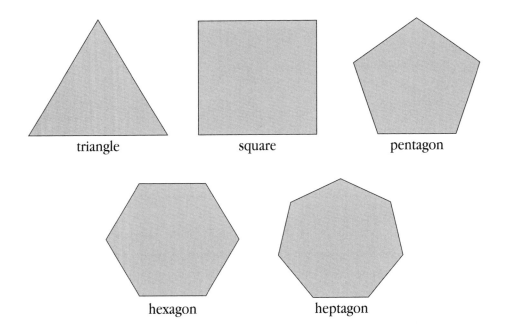

triangle   square   pentagon

hexagon   heptagon

b. Find a pattern in your data that will help you predict how many lines of symmetry a regular polygon with 20 sides will have. Describe your method of predicting.

c. How many lines of symmetry will a regular polygon with 101 sides have?

In 9 and 10, a set of plans for a building is given. The buildings are unusual in that some of the cubes on certain levels fit on half of a cube in the level below. This means that if you look at the building from the top, what you see is not a picture of the base outline. For each building, try to construct the maximal building that fits the plans. Find a way to record your building on paper.

9.

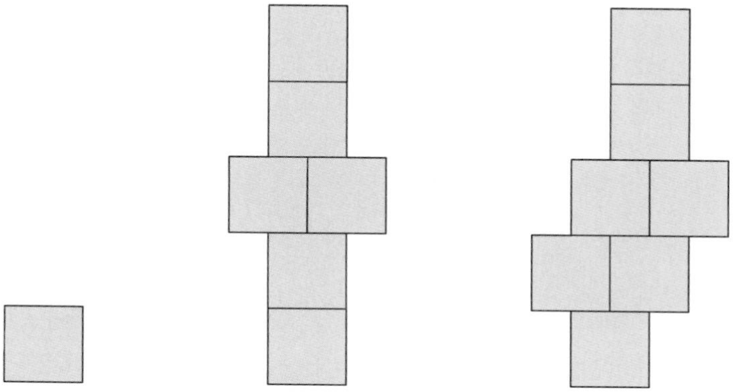

Base outline   Front view   Right view

10.

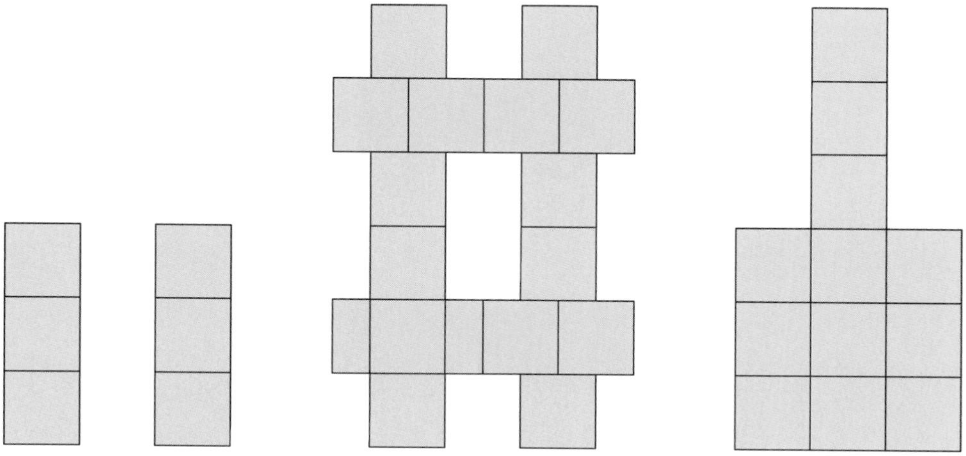

Base outline   Front view   Right view

11. Use exactly 20 cubes to make a model from the building plans below. Record a base plan for your building.

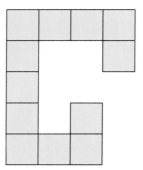

Base outline

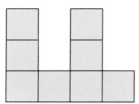

Front view

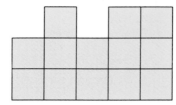

Right view

Mathematical Reflections

In this investigation, you have built models to consider what additional constraint, or requirement, can be added to a set of building plans so it will specify only one building. These questions will help you summarize what you have learned:

1 Is it possible to build several buildings that fit a set of plans made up of a base outline, a front view, and a right view? Explain and illustrate your answer.

2 Is it possible for there to be a set of plans with the three views—base outline, front view, and right view—that has only one possible building? If so, how is this building different from the example you gave in question 1?

3 What can you require that will make every set of plans specify only one building? Explain why this requirement will give a unique building.

Think about your answers to these questions, discuss your ideas with other students and your teacher, and then write a summary of your findings in your journal.

Isometric Dot Paper Representations

In the last investigation, you learned how a set of building plans represents a unique maximal building. You also found that a set of building plans may correspond to several different minimal buildings.

In this investigation, you will learn about another way to represent three-dimensional cube buildings on paper. You will learn how to look at a cube building from a corner and make a drawing that shows three of its faces.

The Flat Iron building in New York City has an interesting corner.

You have used grid paper and dot paper in your mathematics classes to help you make graphs, record rectangles, and find areas. In this investigation, you will use a new kind of dot paper that will help you make drawings of the way buildings look from their corners. This new paper is called *isometric dot paper.* The word *isometric* comes from the Greek language and has two parts: "iso" meaning "the same," and "metric" meaning "measure." So isometric means "same measure."

4.1 Drawing a Cube

Below is part of a sheet of isometric dot paper. Take a few minutes to study the paper. Why do you think it is called isometric dot paper?

Think about this!

- Describe the pattern of dots on isometric dot paper. How is it different from the pattern on the usual kind of dot paper?

- Focus on a dot and the six dots that are its "nearest neighbors." You may want to mark your center and the six surrounding dots so that you can find them easily. Find the number of degrees in each of the angles that you can form with any three of the dots that you marked (one of the dots must serve as the vertex of the angle).

- What are the side lengths of the smallest equilateral triangle you can make by connecting three dots?

- What other patterns do you see in the way the dots are arranged or in the measures of angles on isometric dot paper?

Problem 4.1

Hold a cube level with your eyes. Look at the cube carefully. Turn it to see each of its corners. Tip the cube so that you see the corner nearest you in the center with six vertices evenly spaced around this center corner. Your challenge is to find a way to draw the cube in exactly this position on a sheet of isometric dot paper.

When you and your partner have each successfully drawn the cube, try to find a way to show a different view of the cube in a picture on the dot paper. The two pictures should look quite different. One should show the top of the cube and one should show the bottom.

■ Problem 4.1 Follow-Up

What is the measure of each angle of the cube drawn on dot paper? How do these measures compare to the measures on the real cube?

4.2 Drawing a Cube Model

Some people find it very hard to visualize cube models as they are pictured on isometric dot paper. To help you investigate drawing cube models on isometric dot paper, cut out the 2-D models of cubes on Labsheet 4.2. Store the models in an envelope so you don't lose them.

These models are like the drawing you made on isometric dot paper. If you turn a 2-D model upside down, you should see the drawing you made of the bottom of a cube. You can use the models to help you in Problem 4.2. Notice how the 2-D model can be placed to fit the dots on the isometric dot paper.

 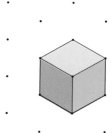

Problem 4.2

Make a stack using three cubes. Hold the stack in the air and turn it, observing it from many different views.

 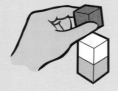 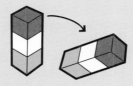

Your challenge is to find every way this stack of three cubes can be pictured on isometric dot paper.

You can use your 2-D cube models to help you draw your pictures. Be sure you stack the models in the same way that the real cubes are stacked. You can place the 2-D models on the dot paper so you can better see where to draw the lines.

Talk to your partner and check each other's work so that you can both get better at drawing models of cube arrangements on isometric dot paper.

■ Problem 4.2 Follow-Up

Describe any patterns you see in the isometric drawings of the stack of three cubes.

4.3 Drawing More Complex Buildings

Now that you have an idea of how to draw stacks of cubes and how to use your 2-D cube models to help you make drawings, you can try your skills on more complicated arrangements of cubes. In this problem, you will make drawings of cube buildings made from four cubes.

Problem 4.3

A. Use four cubes to make the building shown below. On isometric dot paper, make as many drawings of this cube building, turned in the air in different ways, as you can.

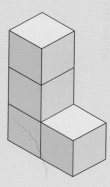

B. Explain why you think you have found all possible ways to draw the building on isometric dot paper.

■ Problem 4.3 Follow-Up

Now, make a different arrangement with four cubes. On dot paper, draw as many pictures as you can of your cube arrangement turned in different ways. Remember that the 2-D cube models can help you figure out what lines to connect on the dot paper.

4.4 Creating Your Own Building

Now it is your turn to be the architect. As you make drawings of your own building, think about what information someone else will be able to tell about your building from your drawings.

Problem 4.4

A. On your building mat, create a building using at least 7 cubes but no more than 12 cubes. Make a drawing of it on isometric dot paper. Label the drawing to indicate which corner the building is being viewed from (front right, right back, back left, or left front).

B. Now turn the building and make a drawing from the opposite corner. Label the view to indicate the corner.

C. If you give a friend just these two drawings, do you think he or she will be able to construct the building exactly as you have made it? Explain.

D. Exchange the isometric dot paper drawings that you made with the drawings that your partner made. Construct a cube building from your partner's drawings.

E. Were you able to get enough information from the drawings to re-create the building your partner constructed? Explain why or why not.

F. Was your partner able to re-create your building from your drawings? Why or why not?

G. In the last investigation, you found that a set of building plans does not always allow you to construct a unique building. However, if you specify that the building must be maximal, it will be unique. Do you think a set of two diagrams on isometric dot paper corresponds to a unique building? Or, is it possible that more than one building can be made from a set of two diagrams on isometric dot paper?

■ Problem 4.4 Follow-Up

Would a set of diagrams showing all four corners of a building determine a unique building? Explain your reasoning.

As you work on these ACE questions, use your calculator whenever you need it.

Applications

In 1–4, a view is shown from the front right corner of a building.

- Copy each building, exactly as it appears, on isometric dot paper.
- Make a cube model of the building. Then, make a drawing from the back left corner of the building.

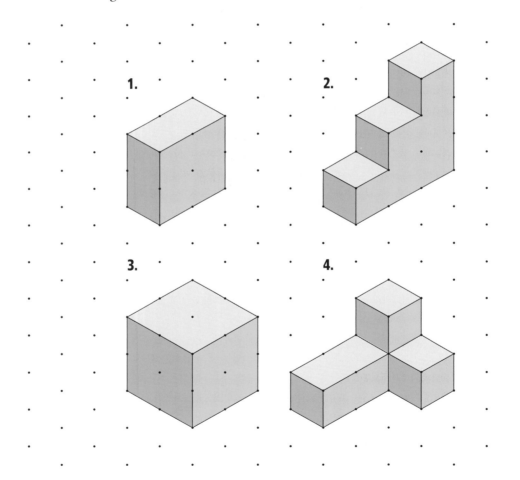

1.

2.

3.

4.

Connections

5. a. Use cubes to construct a model of each building in questions 1–4. For each building, draw a set of building plans on a sheet of grid paper.

b. Is there more than one building that will fit the building plans you have made? Why or why not?

Extensions

6. How many cubes touch the orange cube face to face?

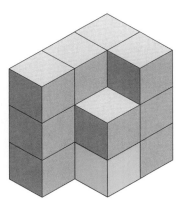

7. How many cubes are needed to build this rectangular solid?

Mathematical Reflections

In this investigation, you used isometric dot paper to learn a new way to make representations, or drawings, of cube buildings. These questions will help you summarize what you have learned:

1. Explain, in your own words, how isometric dot paper is arranged so that it is possible to draw cube buildings from the corners.

2. **a.** What are the measures of the angles formed by the edges of a face of a *real* cube?

   b. On isometric dot paper, what are the measures of the angles formed by the edges of a cube?

   c. Explain any differences or similarities in the measures you found.

3. Imagine that your friend gives you isometric drawings from all four corners of a cube building. Will you be able to read enough information to construct a building exactly like the original? Why or why not?

   Think about your answers to these questions, discuss your ideas with other students and your teacher, and then write a summary of your findings in your journal.

Ziggurats

In this unit, you have learned three different ways to represent cube buildings with drawings. You can draw a *base plan* to record a building you have made; then, a friend can use your base plan to construct a replica of your building. You have also learned to make *a set of building plans*, which includes the base outline, the front view, and the right view of a building. Finally, you have learned to represent a building with an *isometric dot paper drawing*, which shows three sides of the building at once. In this investigation, you will use what you have learned to explore a special kind of pyramid that Emily Hawkins discovered among the ancient ruins of Montarek.

5.1 Building Ziggurats

Emily Hawkins found several pyramids among the ruins. She made a sketch of one of the pyramids using isometric dot paper.

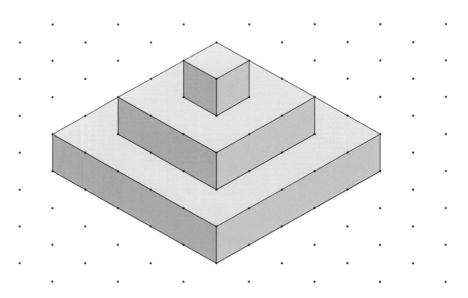

Notice that the pyramid has a square layer for each of its stories and that each layer is smaller than the layer beneath it. This kind of pyramid is called a *ziggurat* (pronounced *zig´-gu-rat*). Look up the word in your dictionary.

Did you know?

Archaelogists have uncovered over 30 ziggurats, some dating back to 3000 B.C., at sites in every important ancient Mesopotamian city. Ziggurats were built through great communal efforts as artificial mountains to house their local gods. Most of the ziggurats contained from three to seven levels. Sometimes the walls were painted different colors and plants and trees were grown on the terraces. This five-layer ziggurat built in the 13th century B.C. in the city of Tchoga Zanbil had a base of 350 square feet and was 174 feet high.

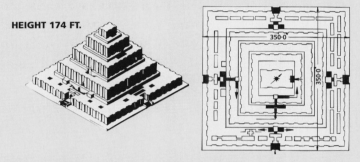

HEIGHT 174 FT.

Used with permission from the British Architectural Library, RIBA, London.

Problem 5.1

A. Make the base plan for the ziggurat shown on page 62.

B. Working with a partner, build the ziggurat with cubes, and make a set of building plans for it.

C. Why do you suppose people from ancient Montarek would build such pyramids? Explain your thoughts.

■ Problem 5.1 Follow-Up

1. List the numbers of cubes in each layer of the ziggurat from the top layer to the bottom layer. Is there a pattern in this sequence? Explain your answer.

2. If the ziggurat in Problem 5.1 had a fourth and fifth layer of cubes added to the bottom, how many cubes would be needed for each of these new layers? Explain your reasoning.

Representing Ziggurats

Emily Hawkins found that the ziggurat pyramids of Montarek were not all the same size. Some were small; others were quite huge. She has uncovered different base plans of two ziggurats.

Problem 5.2

Below are sketches of base plans that Emily Hawkins found in the diary of an architect who was a citizen of ancient Montarek.

1	1	1
1	2	1
1	1	1

Front

3	3	3	3	3
3	5	5	5	3
3	5	6	5	3
3	5	5	5	3
3	3	3	3	3

Front

A. Construct a model of the first ziggurat from cubes. Then, use your model to sketch a set of building plans for the ziggurat on grid paper.

B. Use cubes to construct a model of the second ziggurat. Make a sketch of the ziggurat on isometric dot paper. Look back at the ziggurat from Problem 5.1 if you are unsure of how to begin.

C. Compare the representations you have made of the two ziggurats. Write a short paragraph explaining to Emily which of the three representations—the cube model, the building plans, or the sketch on isometric dot paper—is the most useful for describing a ziggurat.

■ **Problem 5.2 Follow-Up**

Design a ziggurat in which each layer is more than one cube thick. Draw a base plan for your ziggurat.

As you work on these ACE questions, use your calculator whenever you need it.

Applications

1. Some of the buildings in Montarek are shaped something like a ziggurat, but not exactly. Here is a sketch from the front right corner of an ancient Montarek building:

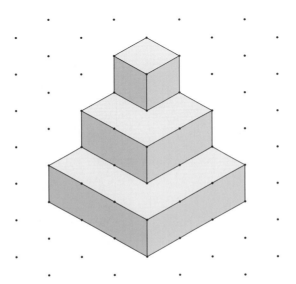

a. Make a cube model of the building and draw a base plan of your model on grid paper.

b. Make a set of building plans for the building on grid paper.

c. Make an isometric drawing of the building from the corner opposite the one above.

d. How would you describe the building? Write a brief paragraph that explains how the building is different from a ziggurat and how it is similar to a ziggurat. Also describe what you think the building might have been used for.

2. Which of the following is *not* a corner view of the building represented by the base plan?

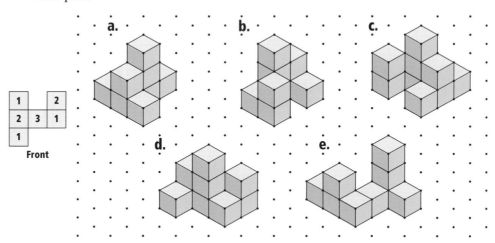

1		2
2	3	1
1		

Front

3. Which drawing below shows the building represented in the base plan viewed from the *front left* corner?

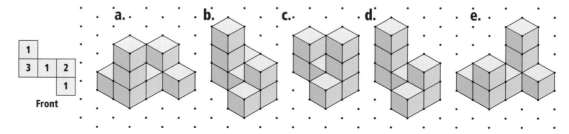

1		
3	1	2
		1

Front

4. The drawing on the left shows one view of a building. Find another view of the building.

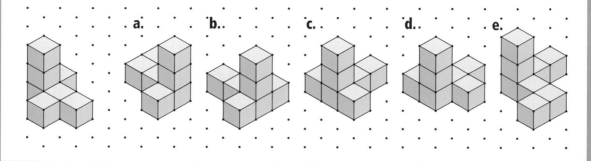

Connections

5. Choose a building in your community. Make a sketch of the building on isometric dot paper. When you are finished with your sketch, answer the following questions:

    a. Is it possible to copy the building exactly on isometric dot paper? Explain how you made your sketch, including any assumptions or simplifications you made.

    b. You will have to guess, but try to build a cube model that looks like a good representation of the building. (If it has a slanted roof, make a model without the roof.) Make a set of building plans for the building.

Houston, Texas

Extensions

6. Emily Hawkins discovered the remains of an interesting building among the ruins of ancient Montarek. Below is a base plan of the building:

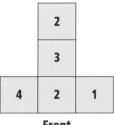

Front

a. Make a cube model of the building. Then, on isometric dot paper, make sketches of the building as it is viewed from each corner—the front right corner, the right back corner, the back left corner, and the left front corner. Label each sketch.

b. On grid paper, make a base plan that is different from the one above, but that represents a building that looks the same as the original when sketched from the front right corner. Explain why the building made from your new base plan would look the same as the original building on dot paper.

The ruins of the Incan city of Machu-Picchu in Peru

7. Using four cubes, make a figure in the shape of a cross. Imagine that the figure can turn in any direction in space, including upside down. Find *every* different way this figure can be drawn on isometric dot paper. Explain why you think you have found all the possible views. Two are shown here as examples:

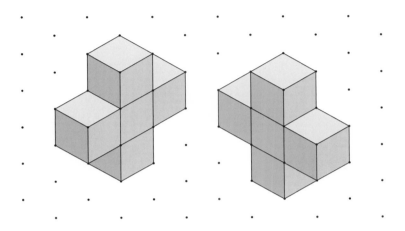

8. Make a T-shaped figure from five cubes. Imagine that the figure can turn in any direction in space. Find *every* different way this figure can be drawn on isometric dot paper. Explain why you think you have found all the possible views.

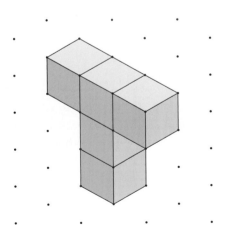

9. Look carefully at each of the following building diagrams:

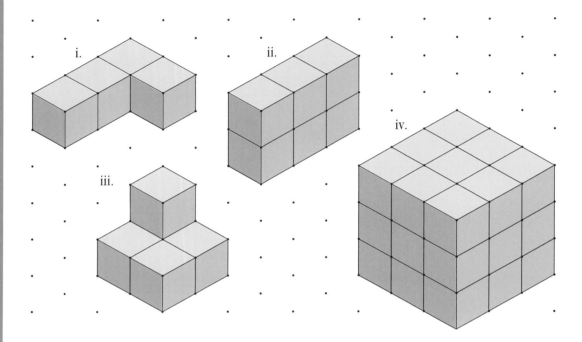

The *volume* of a cube building is a measure of how many *cubic units* it takes to *fill* the building. In other words, the number of cubes needed to make a cube model of a building is the volume of the building.

a. Without making cube models, find the volume of each building above—record how many cubes it would take to construct each of the buildings. If there are different numbers of cubes that could be used to construct a building, list all the possibilities, and explain why the different volumes are possible.

b. Without making cube models, record the perimeter of the base of each of the buildings. As in part a, if there is more than one perimeter possible for a building, list all the possibilities.

Mathematical Reflections

In this investigation you have sketched and examined special kinds of pyramids called ziggurats. These questions will help you summarize what you have learned:

1 Describe a ziggurat.

2 If a cube model of a ziggurat has five layers, each one cube thick, and the top layer is a single cube, how many cubes will it take to make the model? Explain why you think you are correct.

Think about your answers to these questions, discuss your ideas with other students and your teacher, and then write a summary of your findings in your journal. Be sure to include sketches if you think they would help your comments make more sense.

INVESTIGATION 6

Seeing the Isometric View

This investigation will help you improve your ability to read isometric drawings. During this investigation, you will have the opportunity to think about the following:

- How can a drawing help you to visualize the building it describes?
- Can you use your imagination to visualize what a building will look like after some small alteration is made to it?

6.1 Viewing a Building

You have learned to draw isometric representations showing each of the four corners of a building. But can you interpret a drawing that someone else has done? Can you compare the drawing to cube models and identify which model it describes? Can you determine which corner of the building is shown in the picture?

Problem 6.1

In your group, build a cube model of each of these buildings on your building mat. The next page shows views of each building from all four corners. These views also appear on Labsheet 6.1. Match each model to its corner views. On the labsheet, label each view with the building number and the corner from which the building is being viewed: left front, front right, back left, or right back.

Building 1

1	1	2
	3	1
	1	

Front

Building 2

1	1	2
1	3	
	1	

Front

Building 3

1	2	1
	3	1
	2	

Front

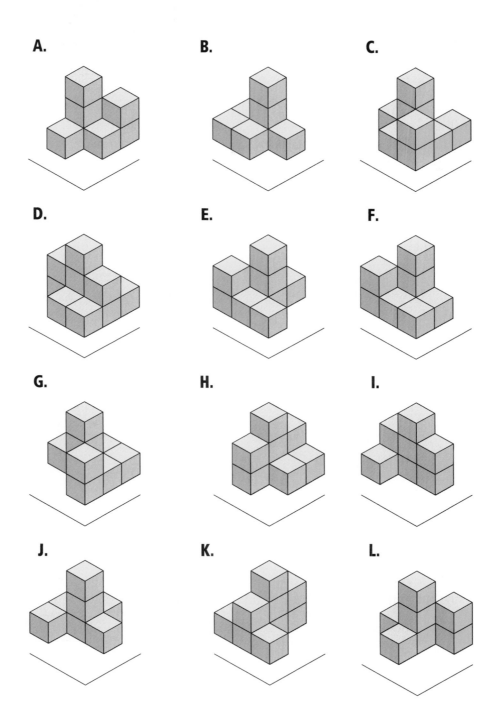

A.

B.

C.

D.

E.

F.

G.

H.

I.

J.

K.

L.

■ Problem 6.1 Follow-Up

Can you remove a cube from building 1 and have the isometric view from any corner still be the same? What about building 2 and building 3?

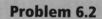

6.2 Removing Cubes

In this problem, you will play with a building in your mind to visualize what it would look like if you removed cubes from it. As you work on this problem, remember that you can always build a cube model to check your imagination—but give your mind a try first. You will be surprised at how much you can improve your visualization skills by thinking hard about the problems and by practicing visualizing things in your mind.

Problem 6.2

In each drawing given, visualize what the figure would look like if the orange cubes were removed. Make an isometric drawing of the result. If you need to, build the model from cubes and look at it.

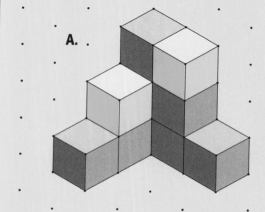

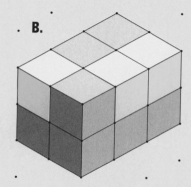

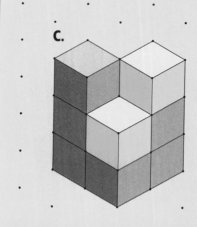

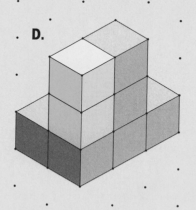

■ Problem 6.2 Follow-Up

Look carefully at A–D. Can you find a different possibility for what the building would look like with orange cubes removed?

6.3 Adding Cubes

In the last problem, you imagined what cube buildings would look like if some cubes were removed. In this problem, you will imagine what buildings will look like if cubes are added. Remember to try to do the problem without cubes first. Then, you can build a model to check your work.

Problem 6.3

In each drawing, one or more cube faces are orange. Picture what the model would look like with a cube added to each orange face. Make an isometric drawing of the result.

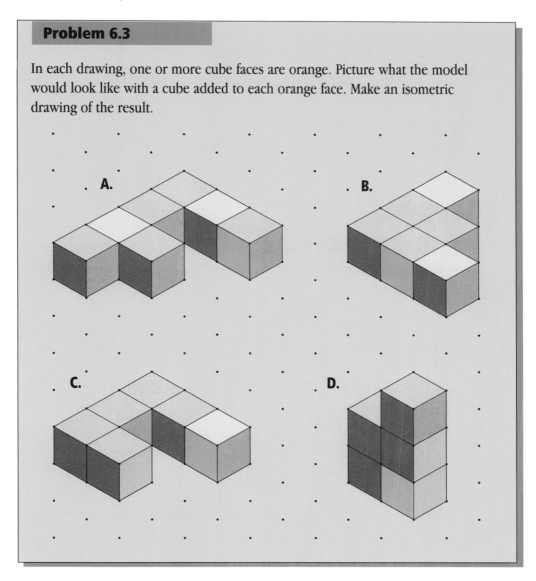

A.

B.

C.

D.

■ Problem 6.3 Follow-Up

Which is harder for you to visualize and draw without building a cube model, adding or removing a cube? Explain why you think this is so.

6.4 Putting the Pieces Together

In this problem, you will look at several buildings made from these two basic shapes:

Your challenge is to figure out how these two shapes were put together to make each building.

  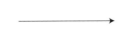 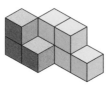

Problem 6.4

In A–F, experiment with the two basic shapes above to make the building shown. Shade the drawings on your labsheet to show how you put the pieces together to make the shape.

A.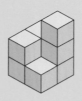

B.

C.

D.

E.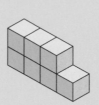

F.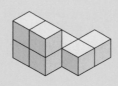

■ Problem 6.4 Follow-Up

Put the two basic shapes together in a way not shown above. Make an isometric drawing of your model.

Applications

1. On a building mat, use cubes to make a model of this building.

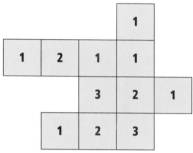

Front

a. For each picture below, indicate from which corner you are viewing the building.

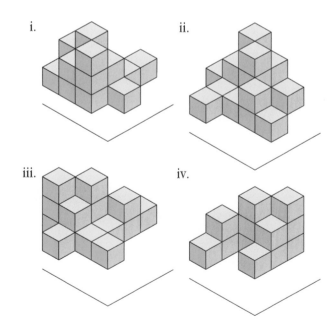

i.

ii.

iii.

iv.

b. Remove a cube from each of the three stacks in the front row of the base plan. Make isometric drawings of all four corners of this new building.

c. Do any of the corner views stay the same as the corresponding corner view on the original building?

2. Visualize what this model would look like with the orange cubes removed. Draw an isometric view of the resulting model from the same corner as the original drawing was made.

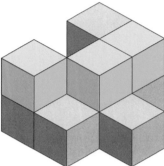

3. Visualize what this model would look like if cubes were added to the orange faces. Draw an isometric view of the resulting model from the same corner as the original model was made.

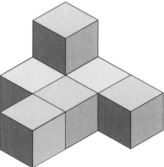

4. Design your own two basic shapes. Use four or five cubes for each shape. Put the shapes together to make a new model. Draw the shapes and the new model on isometric dot paper so that you can challenge a classmate to find how you put the two pieces together.

Connections

5. Talk to your art teacher, a drafting teacher, or an architect about the kind of drawings they make. Report on the similarities and differences between their drawings and the kinds of drawings you have made in this unit.

Extensions

6. Here is a drawing of a simple model made from cubes:

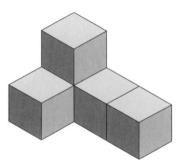

a. How many cubes are in the model?

b. What is the perimeter of the base of the model?

Imagine a model just like the one above but with each of its edge lengths doubled.

c. How many cubes would it take to build the new model?

d. What is the perimeter of the base of the new model?

e. Make an isometric drawing of the new model from the same corner the drawing of the original model was made from.

7. a. The building below is shown from the front right corner. How many cubes would it take to make this building? If there is more than one answer, give the least and the greatest numbers of cubes that could be used.

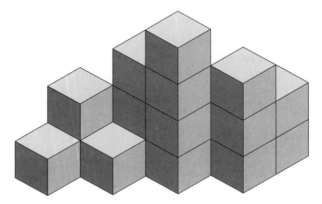

b. Make a base plan for a building made with the minimum number of cubes.

c. Make a base plan for the building made with the maximum number of cubes.

Mathematical Reflections

In this investigation, you have worked on visualizing corner views of buildings, even when the buildings are changed by adding or removing cubes. These questions will help you summarize what you have learned:

1 Summarize how you look at a model built from cubes to see the model in a way that can be drawn on isometric dot paper.

2 If you make an isometric drawing of a model from each of its four corners, will your drawings determine a unique building? Explain why or why not. You may want to use an example in your explanation.

Think about your answers to these questions, discuss your ideas with other students and your teacher, and then write a summary of your findings in your journal.

Design a Building

According to the diary of an architect in ancient Montarek, a building had to be approved by the Council of Montarek before it could be constructed. To have a building approved, an architect had to provide the council with a base plan, a set of building plans, and isometric sketches of the building.

Imagine that you are an architect in ancient Montarek. Design a building that you feel would be useful to the citizens of Montarek. The building does not have to be a ziggurat or any of the other buildings you have studied. This is your opportunity to design a building that *you* think is interesting.

You must follow these steps to have your building approved by the Council of Montarek:

1. Use 25 to 30 cubes to design your building.
2. Make a base plan of your building on grid paper.
3. Make a set of building plans for your building on grid paper.
4. Make four sketches of your building on isometric dot paper—one sketch from each corner.
5. Write a paragraph to the Council of Montarek explaining how your building could be used and why it would benefit the citizens of Montarek.

Looking Back and Looking Ahead

Unit Reflections

Working on problems in this unit helped you to develop your spatial visualization skills. You learned how to read and draw two-dimensional *isometric drawings,* *outline views,* and *base-plans* for three-dimensional buildings and how to build three-dimensional buildings from two-dimensional representations.

Using Your Visualization Skills—Test your spatial reasoning and drawing skills on the following problems.

1 *The following figure is an isometric drawing showing the front-right view of a building made from cubes. Assume that you can see parts of every cube used to build the figure.*

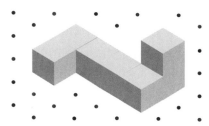

a. Make a base plan for the building.

b. If you were to glue the cubes together, how many cube faces would there be on the outside of the resulting building?

2 *A building made from cubes has the base, front, and right views shown below.*

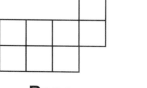

Base

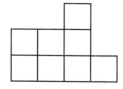

Front

Right

a. How many cubes are needed to construct a minimal building for these plans?

b. How many cubes are needed to construct a maximal building for these plans?

c. Draw base plans for your answers to part a and part b.

3 *The base plan for a building made from cubes is given at the right. On isometric dot paper, draw the view of that building from the left-front corner.*

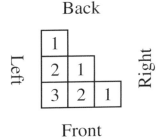

Explaining Your Reasoning—To answer questions about figures made from cubes, you need spatial visualization skills and reasoning.

1. How do you look at a building in order to draw it on isometric dot paper?

2. How do you prepare base, front, and right outline views of a building?

3. How do you analyze a building to make a base plan?

4. How do you build a model from cubes if you are given

    a. an isometric view?

    b. outline views from the base, front, and right of the building?

5. Is there more than one way to make a building of cubes from a given

    a. base plan?

    b. isometric drawing?

    c. set of base, front, and right outline views?

The spatial visualization skills you developed in this unit will be useful in future *Connected Mathematics* units, especially in work on problems about surface area, volume, and symmetry of solid figures. Two-dimensional drawings, photographs, and computer displays are the standard ways of picturing three-dimensional scenes. So, ability to add depth mentally to those images is also useful in many practical and technical tasks.

Glossary

base plan A drawing of the base outline of a building. The number in each square indicates the number of cubes in the stack at that position.

building mat A sheet of paper labeled "front", "back", "left", and "right" used to describe buildings.

isometric dot paper Dot paper in which the distance from a dot to each of the six surrounding dots are all equivalent. The word *isometric* comes from the Greek words *iso*, which means "same," and *metric*, which means "measure." You used isometric dot paper to show different views of your cube models.

line of symmetry A line through a figure so that if the figure were folded on the line, the two parts of the figure would match up exactly.

maximal building The building satisfying a given set of building plans and having the largest possible number of cubes. There is only one possible maximal building for a set of plans, and so this building is called unique.

minimal building A building satisfying a given set of plans and having the smallest possible number of cubes. Because there may be several minimal buildings for a set of plans, the minimal building is not necessarily unique.

set of building plans A set of three diagrams—the front view, the right view, and the base outline.

unique One of a kind. When we say that the building corresponding to a set of plans is unique, we mean that it is the only building that matches the plans.

ziggurat A pyramid-shaped building made up of layers in which each layer is a square smaller than the square beneath it.

Index

Angle of view, 72–76
   ACE, 77–80
Average, building height, 36–37

Base outline, 8–10
Base plan, 8–10
   ACE, 19–21, 33–38, 45–50
   constructing a model from, 15–18, 26–27, 72
   from a model, 63–64
   from multi-view drawings, 31–32, 40–44
   multi-view drawings from, 15–18
Base view, 8–10
Blueprint, 30
Building plan, 15

Cube
   isometric drawing of, 54–55
   puzzles, 22–23
   volume of, 70

Drawing *See* Isometric drawing; Multi-view drawing

Flat Iron building, New York City, 52

Investigation
   Building Plans, 7–25
   Describing Unique Buildings, 40–51
   Isometric Dot Paper Representations, 52–61
   Making Buildings, 26–39

   Seeing the Isometric View, 72–81
   Ziggurats, 62–71
Isometric, 52
Isometric drawing, 52–57
   ACE, 58–60, 65–70
   constructing a model from, 57, 62–64
   reading, 72–76

Journal, 25, 39, 51, 61, 71, 81

Line of symmetry, 6, 10–12
   ACE, 23–24, 48
Looking Back and Looking Ahead: Unit Reflections, 83–84

Machu-Picchu, Peru, 68
Mathematical Highlights, 6
Mathematical Reflections, 25, 39, 51, 61, 71, 81
Maximal model, 41–44
Mayan architecture, 13
Minimal model, 41–44
Mirror image, 6, 10–12
   ACE, 23–24
Model
   ACE, 19–24, 33–38, 45–50, 58–60, 65–70
   constructing from a base plan, 15–18, 26–27
   constructing a base plan from, 63–64
   constructing from isometric drawings, 57, 62–64
   constructing from multi-view drawings, 26–32, 40–44

isometric drawing of, 52–57
matching with an isometric view, 72–76
maximal, 41–44
minimal, 41–44
of a ziggurat, 62–64
Mohenjo-Daro, ruins, 26
Multi-view drawing
 ACE, 33–38, 45–50
 base plan from, 31–32, 40–44
 constructing a model from, 28–30,
 40–44
 views, 8–10, 13–18

Pattern, ziggurat layer, 63
Polygon, 7–18, 48
 ACE, 19–24
Propylaea and the Temple of Athena Nike
 in Athens, Greece, 35

Reflection, 6, 10–12
 ACE, 23–24
Ruins
 Machu-Picchu, Peru, 68
 Mohenjo-Daro, 26
 Propylaea and the Temple of Athena
 Nike in Athens, Greece, 35

Spatial skills, 2–5
 ACE, 19–24, 33–38, 45–50, 58–60,
 65–70, 77–80
 isometric drawing, 52–57, 62–64,
 72–76
 multi-view drawing, 8–18, 26–32,
 40–44
 three-dimensional modeling, 15–18,
 26–32, 40–44, 52–57, 62–64

two-dimensional representation, 7–18,
 26–32, 40–44, 52–57, 72–76
Symmetry, 6, 10–12
 ACE, 23–24, 48

Tchoga Zanbil ziggurat, 63
Three-dimensional model
 ACE, 19–24, 33–38, 45–50, 65–70,
 77–80
 from a base plan, 15–18, 26–27
 base plan from, 63–64
 from isometric drawings, 57, 62–64
 isometric drawings of, 52–57
 matching with an isometric view, 72–76
 from multi-view drawings, 26–32,
 40–44
 multi-view drawings of, 2–5, 7–18
Transformation, reflection, 6, 10–12,
 23–24
Two-dimensional representation
 ACE, 19–24, 33–38, 45–50, 77–80
 constructing a model from, 15–18,
 26–32, 40–44, 62–64
 isometric drawing, 52–57, 62–64,
 72–76
 multi-view drawing, 7–18, 31–32,
 40–44

Unit Project, 82

Volume
 of an irregular figure, 70
 of a cube, 70

Ziggurats, 62–64
 ACE, 65–70